Ivan Ganchev · Nuno M. Garcia
Ciprian Dobre · Constandinos X. Mavromoustakis
Rossitza Goleva (Eds.)

Enhanced Living Environments

Algorithms, Architectures, Platforms, and Systems

Editors
Ivan Ganchev
University of Limerick
Limerick, Ireland

and

University of Plovdiv "Paisii Hilendarski"
Plovdiv, Bulgaria

and

Institute of Mathematics and Informatics
Bulgarian Academy of Sciences
Sofia, Bulgaria

Nuno M. Garcia
Instituto de Telecomunicações
Universidade da Beira Interior
Covilhã, Portugal

and

Universidade Lusófona de Humanidades e Tecnologias
Lisbon, Portugal

Ciprian Dobre
University Politehnica of Bucharest
Bucharest, Romania

and

National Institute for Research
and Development in Informatics
Bucharest, Romania

Constandinos X. Mavromoustakis
University of Nicosia
Nicosia, Cyprus

Rossitza Goleva
New Bulgarian University
Sofia, Bulgaria

https://doi.org/10.1007/978-3-030-10752-9

Acknowledgement and Disclaimer
The work published in this book is supported by the European Union under the EU Horizon 2020 Framework Program and especially the COST Action IC1303 "Algorithms, Architectures and Platforms for Enhanced Living Environments (AAPELE)". The book reflects only the authors' views. Neither the COST Association nor any person acting on its behalf is responsible for the use, which might be made of the information contained in this publication. The COST Association is not responsible for external websites referred to in this publication.

European Cooperation in Science and Technology (COST)

This publication is based upon work from COST Action IC1303 "Algorithms, Architectures and Platforms for Enhanced Living Environments (AAPELE)" supported by COST (European Cooperation in Science and Technology).
COST (European Cooperation in Science and Technology) is a funding agency for research and innovation networks. Our Actions help connect research initiatives across Europe and enable scientists to grow their ideas by sharing them with their peers. This boosts their research, career and innovation.

www.cost.eu

To all colleagues in AAPELE
Ivan Ganchev
Nuno M. Garcia
Ciprian Dobre
Constandinos X. Mavromoustakis
Rossitza Goleva

Foreword

This book is one of the final dissemination activities of the COST Action IC1303 "Algorithms, Architectures and Platforms for Enhanced Living Environments (AAPELE)." The main objective of this COST Action was to promote the synergy between ambient assisted living (AAL) and smart enhanced living environments (ELEs), based on the creation of a research and development (R&D) community of scientists and entrepreneurs. AAPELE has ended with about 160 management committee members and substitutes from 32 countries, 400+ research papers and analytical reports published, three edited books, three special journal issues organized, and 56+ successful projects running (in parallel and/or as continuation) out of 100+ proposals submitted. The aim of this final AAPELE book is to raise even more the awareness of the academic and industrial communities of the AAL/ELE topic by taking into account also the increasing interest of the end-users to be informed and be able to self-manage different living issues of their own. The high interest and multiple running projects in the subject area as well as the large number of pilot platforms developed are a good proof of the importance of this COST Action.

The COST Action AAPELE was supported by partners working in the following areas: (1) analysis of medical data; (2) mesh networking; (3) quality of service (QoS) and quality of experience (QoE) as well as capacity planning analysis; (4) user behavior analysis and network traffic classification; (5) electronic health (eHealh) and mobile health (mHealth); and (6) AAL in specific use-cases.

The main goal of AAPELE was to promote interdisciplinary research on AAL/ELE through the creation of an R&D community of scientists and entrepreneurs, working on different aspects of corresponding algorithms, architectures, and platforms, having in view the advance of the science in this area and the development of new and innovative solutions.

To achieve this goal, the COST Action AAPELE set the following main objectives:

1. To facilitate research on specific AAL/ELE problems related to information and communications technologies (ICT), aiming for the development of new and innovative solutions that are driven by the interest to produce marketable technological solutions that can be easily adopted by the users

2. To synchronize and broaden the scientific activities of all involved partners working in this field in a research-friendly environment, while also allowing more countries and different types of organizations to contribute
3. To create and expand a European R&D community in the AAL/ELE area

The achieved impact of AAPELE can be summarized as follows:

- Creation of an AAL/ELE community of scientists and entrepreneurs acting as a critical mass of researchers with different scientific backgrounds
- Broadening the AAL topic with the ELE concept
- Collection of diverse data from medical, network, and protocol experiments for further analysis
- Application of different statistical tools for big data management in the AAL/ELE area
- End-user profiling for the purposes of AAL/ELE
- Identification of a variety of AAL/ELE testing scenarios
- Development of AAL platforms for conducting advanced experiments and case studies in different ELEs
- Conducting corresponding QoS and QoE analysis
- Designing and testing different ICT infrastructures that are able to integrate different types of devices (sensors, actuators, computers, mobile devices, etc.) from an AAL/ELE service perspective
- Researching on personalized, intelligent algorithms for use in AAL/ELE
- Researching on user interfaces and human–machine interactions (HMI) with special focus on older adults or disabled users
- Studying and applying suitable (mobile) communications protocols for different AAL/ELE applications

This book presents the final output from the AAPELE community and aims to become a cookbook for further activities in the field.

November 2018

Nuno M. Garcia
Rossitza Goleva
Ivan Ganchev

Preface

The increase in medical expenses, due to societal issues such as demographic aging, puts strong pressure on the sustainability of health and social care systems, labor participation, and quality of life (QoL) for the elderly and people with disabilities. In addition, the understanding of the need to have active living and aging, and the corresponding changes in work and family life, has set new challenges to developers and suppliers of new services within personal living environments. In this sense, the enhanced living environments (ELEs) encompass all information and communications technology (ICT) achievements supporting true ambient assisted living (AAL). ELEs promote the provision of infrastructures and services for independent or more autonomous living, via the seamless integration of ICT within homes and residences, thus increasing the QoL for assisted people and autonomously maintaining their preferable living environment as long as possible, without causing disruption in the web of social and family interactions.

Different AAL/ELE technologies are aiming today at creating safe environments around assisted people to help them maintain independent and active living. Most efforts toward the realization of AAL/ELE systems are based on the development of pervasive devices and the use of ambient intelligence to mix these devices together to create a safe environment. There is a missing interaction of multiple stakeholders needing to collaborate for ELEs, supporting a multitude of AAL services. There are also barriers to innovation in the concerned market, the governments, and the health-care sector that still do not take place at an appropriate scale.

Many fundamental issues in ELE remain open. Most of the current efforts still do not fully express the power of human beings and the importance of social connections. Societal activities are less noticed as well. Effective ELE solutions require appropriate ICT algorithms, architectures, platforms, and systems, aiming to advance the science in this area and to develop new and innovative connected solutions. This book provides, in this sense, a platform for the dissemination of research and development efforts and for the presentation of advances in the AAL/ELE area that aim at addressing these challenges.

The book aims to become a state-of-the-art reference, discussing the progress made, as well as prompting future directions on theories, practices, standards, and strategies that are related to AAL/ELE. It was prepared as a Final Publication of the COST Action IC1303 "Algorithms, Architectures and Platforms for Enhanced Living Environments (AAPELE)." The book can serve as a valuable reference for undergraduate students, postgraduate students, educators, faculty members, researchers, engineers, medical doctors, health-care organizations, insurance companies, and research strategists working in this field.

The book chapters were collected through an open, but selective, three-stage submission/review process. Initially, an open call for contributions was distributed among the COST AAPELE community in the summer of 2017. As a result, 24 expressions of interest were made in response to the call and, after some consolidation, a total of 15 extended abstracts were received. These were reviewed by the book editors and their authors were invited to the next stage of full-chapter submission. At the end of this stage, 14 full-chapter proposals were received. All submitted chapters were then peer-reviewed by independent reviewers (including reviewers outside the COST Action AAPELE), appointed by the book editors, and after the first round of reviews 12 chapters remained. These were duly revised according to the reviewers' comments, suggestions, notes, etc., then reviewed again and finally accepted for publication in this book.

The first chapter entitled "Automation in Systematic, Scoping, and Rapid Reviews by an NLP Toolkit: A Case Study in Enhanced Living Environments" analyzes the trends and the state of the art in the AAL/ELE area by utilizing a natural language processing (NLP)-powered tool for automating the surveying process of 70,000+ scientific articles indexed in reputable international digital libraries such as the IEEE Xplore, PubMed, and SpringerLink. The authors demonstrate the applicability of the toolkit in facilitating a robust and comprehensive "eligibility and relevance" analysis of articles, in accordance with the Preferred Reporting Items for Systematic Reviews and Meta-Analyses (PRISMA) surveying methodology. The presented case study demonstrates that, in addition to easing and speeding up the surveying process, the NLP toolkit can show valuable insights and pinpoint the most relevant articles, thus significantly reducing the number of articles that need to be manually assessed by researchers, while also generating informative tables, charts, and graphs. The analysis conducted shows increasing attention from the scientific and research communities toward AAL/ELE over the past 10 years and points to several trends in the specific research topics falling within this scope. In particular, the aggregated results show that there is more interest in ELEs that sense and recognize activities and aid exercising, thus helping the well-being of people. Monitoring and supervision of some more serious health issues, such as accidents and vital signs, have received less attention so far. Regarding the way the data are processed, the edge computing and cloud computing technologies receive a fair amount of attention. Furthermore, sensors and power consumption seem to be of greater interest than communications protocols and machine learning/deep learning.

With respect to ELEs oriented toward activity recognition, the second chapter, "RDF Stores for Enhanced Living Environments: An Overview," considers the handling of large knowledge bases of information from different domains as a complex problem, addressed in the Resource Description Framework (RDF) by adding semantic meaning to the data themselves. The authors explore the RDF store landscape with the aim of finding a specialized database, capable of storing and processing RDF data, which sufficiently meets the ELE storage needs. More specifically, they focus on a Smart Space platform aimed at running on a cluster setup of low-power hardware that can be run locally entirely at home with the purpose of logging data for a reactive assistive system involving activity recognition or domotics. A literature analysis of RDF stores is presented and promising candidates for implementation of consumer Smart Spaces are identified. Based on the insights provided, the authors suggest different relevant aspects of RDF storage systems that need to be considered in AAL/ELE environments and provide a comparison of available solutions.

This is followed by the chapter entitled "Combining Machine Learning and Metaheuristics Algorithms for Classification Method PROAFTN," which brings machine learning and data mining into the picture by showing how the combined metaheuristics with inductive learning techniques can improve the efficiency of the supervised learning classification algorithms for use within AAL/ELE environments for activity recognition and behavior analysis, based on the collected sensor data. The authors' aim is to find a good, suitable, and comprehensive (interpretable) classification procedure that can be applied efficiently in such environments. In order to address the issues faced by the usual supervised learning approaches, especially when dealing with knowledge interpretation and with very large unbalanced labelled data sets, the authors have developed a fuzzy classification method PROAFTN for enabling determination of the fuzzy resemblance measures by generalizing the concordance and discordance indexes used in outranking methods. An improved version of PROAFTN is described in the chapter and compared with other well-known classifiers in terms of the learning methodology and classification accuracy. The authors show the ability of the metaheuristics, when embedded into the PROAFTN, for improving the efficiency of classification.

The next chapter, entitled "Development and Evaluation of Methodology for Personal Recommendations Applicable in Connected Health," proposes a methodology (and corresponding algorithm) for personal recommendations of outdoor physical activities, which is based solely on the user's history data and without relying on collaborative filtering. The proposed recommendation algorithm consists of four phases: data fuzzyfication, activity usefulness calculation, estimation of most useful activities, and activities classification. For the latter, several data mining techniques are compared for use, e.g., decision tree algorithm, decision rule algorithm, Bayes algorithm, and support vector machines. The performance of the proposed recommendation algorithm is evaluated based on a real dataset, collected from a community of 1,000 active users. The results show a high accuracy of 85–95%.

The chapter "Touchscreen Assessment Tool" (TATOO), an Assessment Tool Based on the Expanded Conceptual Model of Frailty provides an overview of the state-of-the-art assessment models of frailty syndrome in the elderly and presents a tool prototype that utilizes mobile technology for assessing the elderly's frailty. The tool is based on a conceptual model, which is expanded to incorporate new aspects related to the usage of technology by elderly, covering the complexity and multidimensionality of modern life. The authors' plan is to further develop the tool as a continuous monitoring instrument of activities performed in daily life, combined with advanced sensor-based measurements and big-data analytics algorithms.

The next chapter "Towards a Deeper Understanding of the Behavioural Implications of Bidirectional Activity-Based Ambient Displays in Ambient Assisted Living Environments" investigates the extent to which the real-time bidirectional exchange of activity information can influence context awareness, social presence, social connectedness, and interpersonal activity synchrony in mediated AAL environments. The chapter contains a background on interpersonal activity synchrony, followed by a description of the design, development, and assessment of a bidirectional ambient display platform. The authors evaluate a conglomerate of activity-based lighting displays in order to determine the effects of real-time bidirectional deployment on behavior and social connectedness. The results presented show tendencies toward an increase in implicit social interactions, more positive social behaviors between the elderly and their caregivers in mediated AAL contexts, and sporadic moments of interpersonal activity synchrony.

The chapter "Towards Truly Affective AAL Systems" considers affective computing as a growing field of artificial intelligence, focused on detecting, obtaining, and expressing various affective states (including emotions, moods, and personality-related attributes), applicable to various affective contexts, including AAL/ELE. The authors discuss the need for integration of affective computing approaches and methods in the context of AAL/ELE systems in order to improve their functionality in terms of rational decision-making and enhancement of social interaction with people requiring the use of these systems. To enrich the emotional capacity of AAL/ELE systems, the authors go beyond simple emotion detection and showing only emotion expressions, and in addition consider the use of emotion generation and emotion mapping on rational thinking and system behavior. The chapter discusses the need and requirements for these processes in the context of various AAL/ELE application domains.

The next chapter, entitled "Maintaining Mental Wellbeing of Elderly at Home," focuses on the problem of providing the most cost-efficient and effective way of supporting mental well-being as well as methods for physical and mental rehabilitation for the elderly at home including recovery from accidents, particularly concentrating on those impacting brain activities. For this, an automated home ICT system, combining progress in applied clinical "know-how" with stimulating engagement through entertainment, rivalry, and "real feeling" of gaming environment in compliance with rehabilitation rules, is envisaged by the authors for utilization by patients, care providers, and family members for the effective use of rehabilitation procedures in familiar home surroundings instead of unfriendly clinical settings. The authors propose a full system solution that integrates a set of state-of-the-art technologies, such as augmented/virtual reality gaming, multi-modal user interfaces, and innovative embedded micro-sensor devices, combined together in a Personal Health Record (PHR) system, supporting the delivery of individual, patient-centered electronic health (eHealth) services both at home, at hospital, or on the move. The formal technical validation tests performed confirm the usability of the developed system.

The chapter "System Development for Monitoring Physiological Parameters in Living Environment" presents a system architecture for physiological parameters monitoring in ELEs. A corresponding laboratory experiment, a field trial, and a case study are described along with a subsequent analysis of the created dataset for finding correlation between monitored physiological parameters. The authors' plan is to enhance the system by utilizing a fuzzy-logic decision algorithm for raising of alerts and to improve the visualization of collected data based on live streaming and cloud support.

The next chapter "Healthcare Sensing and Monitoring" brings attention to the development of cost-effective, real-time, remote sensing and health-status monitoring solutions for elderly and disabled people to help them improve their QoL and create better living conditions in the environment of their choice. The authors provide an overview of relevant sensing technologies, vital signs monitoring techniques, risk and accident detection methods, activity recognition techniques, communications technologies, etc., and conclude that new types of network paradigms, such as the Internet of Things (IoT), will extend traditional sensing and monitoring systems giving an advantage to control the environment.

Staying on the IoT note, the next chapter "Semantic Middleware Architectures for IoT Healthcare Applications" delves into the technical and semantic solutions used to tackle the interoperability issues in IoT-based AAL/ELE heterogeneous environments. By suggesting the use of semantic middleware architectures (consisting of both technical and semantic components) as a complete interoperable solution, the authors present an overview of the existing semantic middleware proposals that address many challenges and requirements regarding the interoperability in IoT systems. The authors then identify research challenges that still remain open, such as scalability, real-time reasoning, provision of a simple application programming interface (API) usable in various application domains, provision of a complete ontology that is able to describe both domains and sensors in IoT, etc. In this regard, the authors envisage the recently proposed Web of Things (WoT) architecture as one of the major candidates for solving the interoperability issues in IoT in general.

The final chapter, entitled "The Role of Drones in Ambient Assisted Living Systems for the Elderly," introduces some of the most recent and interesting applications of drones in creating AAL/ELE environments to help the elderly sustain a better independent lifestyle. A critical analysis and evaluation of drone-related technologies as a disruptive force in many industrial and everyday life applications, and their relationship with AAL/ELE, are presented along with suitable health-care models, different characteristics of relevant AAL/ELE systems and communications protocols, and the main challenges in accepting drones as "flying assistants" to extend the independent living environments of elderly.

The book editors wish to thank all reviewers for their excellent and rigorous reviewing work, and for their responsiveness during the critical stages to consolidate the contributions provided by the authors. We are most grateful to all authors who have entrusted their excellent work, the fruits of many years' research in each case, to us and for their patience and continued demanding revision work in response to reviewers' feedback. We also thank them for adjusting their chapters to the specific book template and style requirements, completing all the bureaucratic but necessary paperwork, and meeting all the publishing deadlines.

November 2018

Ivan Ganchev
Nuno M. Garcia
Ciprian Dobre
Constandinos X. Mavromoustakis
Rossitza Goleva

Organization

Reviewers

Åke Arvidsson	Kristianstad University, Sweden
Serge Autexier	German Research Centre for Artificial Intelligence (DFKI), Germany
Sabina Barakovic	University of Sarajevo/American University in Bosnia and Herzegovina, Bosnia and Herzegovina
Jasmina Barakovic Husic	University of Sarajevo, Bosnia and Herzegovina
An Braeken	Vrije Universiteit, Belgium
Torsten Braun	Universität Bern, Switzerland
Emmanuel Conchon	Université de Limoges, France
Ivan Chorbev	Ss. Cyril and Methodius University in Skopje, FYR Macedonia
Marilia Curado	University of Coimbra, Portugal
Natalia Díaz-Rodríguez	ENSTA ParisTech/Inria Flowers, France
Ciprian Dobre	University Politehnica of Bucharest/National Institute for Research and Development in Informatics, Romania
Ivan Ganchev	University of Limerick, Ireland/University of Plovdiv "Paisii Hilendarski", Bulgaria/Institute of Mathematics and Informatics, Bulgarian Academy of Sciences, Bulgaria
Nuno M. Garcia	Instituto de Telecomunicações, Universidade da Beira Interior/Universidade Lusófona de Humanidades e Tecnologias, Portugal
Rossitza Goleva	New Bulgarian University, Bulgaria
Andrej Grgurić	Ericsson Nikola Tesla d.d., Croatia
Krzysztof Grochla	ITAI PAS, Poland
Petre Lameski	Ss. Cyril and Methodius University in Skopje, FYR Macedonia
Egons Lavendelis	Riga Technical University, Latvia
Constandinos X. Mavromoustakis	University of Nicosia, Cyprus
Rodica Potolea	Technical University of Cluj-Napoca, Romania
Peter Pocta	University of Zilina, Slovakia
Vedran Podobnik	University of Zagreb, Croatia
Susanna Spinsante	Università Politecnica delle Marche, Italy
Vladimir Trajkovik	Ss. Cyril and Methodius University in Skopje, FYR Macedonia
Denis Trcek	University of Ljubljana, Slovenia
Carlos Valderrama	University of Mons, Belgium
Eftim Zdravevski	Ss. Cyril and Methodius University in Skopje, FYR Macedonia

Contents

Automation in Systematic, Scoping and Rapid Reviews by an NLP Toolkit: A Case Study in Enhanced Living Environments 1
Eftim Zdravevski, Petre Lameski, Vladimir Trajkovik, Ivan Chorbev, Rossitza Goleva, Nuno Pombo, and Nuno M. Garcia

RDF Stores for Enhanced Living Environments: An Overview 19
Petteri Karvinen, Natalia Díaz-Rodríguez, Stefan Grönroos, and Johan Lilius

Combining Machine Learning and Metaheuristics Algorithms for Classification Method PROAFTN 53
Feras Al-Obeidat, Nabil Belacel, and Bruce Spencer

Development and Evaluation of Methodology for Personal Recommendations Applicable in Connected Health 80
Cvetanka Smileska, Natasa Koceska, Saso Koceski, and Vladimir Trajkovik

"Touchscreen Assessment Tool" (TATOO), an Assessment Tool Based on the Expanded Conceptual Model of Frailty 96
Alexandra Danial-Saad, Lorenzo Chiari, Yael Benvenisti, Shlomi Laufer, and Michal Elboim-Gabyzon

Towards a Deeper Understanding of the Behavioural Implications of Bidirectional Activity-Based Ambient Displays in Ambient Assisted Living Environments. 108
Kadian Davis-Owusu, Evans Owusu, Lucio Marcenaro, Carlo Regazzoni, Loe Feijs, and Jun Hu

Towards Truly Affective AAL Systems 152
Mara Pudane, Sintija Petrovica, Egons Lavendelis, and Hazım Kemal Ekenel

Maintaining Mental Wellbeing of Elderly at Home 177
Emmanouela Vogiatzaki and Artur Krukowski

System Development for Monitoring Physiological Parameters in Living Environment. 210
Oliver Mladenovski, Jugoslav Achkoski, and Rossitza Goleva

Healthcare Sensing and Monitoring 226
George Vasilev Angelov, Dimitar Petrov Nikolakov, Ivelina Nikolaeva Ruskova, Elitsa Emilova Gieva, and Maria Liubomirova Spasova

Semantic Middleware Architectures for IoT Healthcare Applications 263
Rita Zgheib, Emmanuel Conchon, and Rémi Bastide

The Role of Drones in Ambient Assisted Living Systems for the Elderly 295
Radosveta Sokullu, Abdullah Balcı, and Eren Demir

Author Index 323

Automation in Systematic, Scoping and Rapid Reviews by an NLP Toolkit: A Case Study in Enhanced Living Environments

Eftim Zdravevski[1](✉), Petre Lameski[1], Vladimir Trajkovik[1], Ivan Chorbev[1], Rossitza Goleva[2], Nuno Pombo[3], and Nuno M. Garcia[3]

[1] Faculty of Computer Science and Engineering, University Sts. Cyril and Methodius, Skopje, Macedonia
eftim.zdravevski@finki.ukim.mk

[2] New Bulgarian University, Sofia, Bulgaria

[3] Instituto de Telecomunicaes, Universidade da Beira Interior, Covilh, Portugal

Abstract. With the increasing number of scientific publications, the analysis of the trends and the state-of-the-art in a certain scientific field is becoming very time-consuming and tedious task. In response to urgent needs of information, for which the existing systematic review model does not well, several other review types have emerged, namely the rapid review and scoping reviews. In this paper, we propose an NLP powered tool that automates most of the review process by automatic analysis of articles indexed in the IEEE Xplore, PubMed, and Springer digital libraries. We demonstrate the applicability of the toolkit by analyzing articles related to Enhanced Living Environments and Ambient Assisted Living, in accordance with the PRISMA surveying methodology. The relevant articles were processed by the NLP toolkit to identify articles that contain up to 20 properties clustered into 4 logical groups. The analysis showed increasing attention from the scientific communities towards Enhanced and Assisted living environments over the last 10 years and showed several trends in the specific research topics that fall into this scope. The case study demonstrates that the NLP toolkit can ease and speed up the review process and show valuable insights from the surveyed articles even without manually reading of most of the articles. Moreover, it pinpoints the most relevant articles which contain more properties and therefore, significantly reduces the manual work, while also generating informative tables, charts and graphs.

Keywords: Enhanced living environments · Ambient assisted living NLP toolkit · Automated surveys · Scoping review · Rapid review Systematic review

I. Ganchev et al. (Eds.): Enhanced Living Environments, LNCS 11369, pp. 1–18, 2019.
https://doi.org/10.1007/978-3-030-10752-9_1

1 Introduction

Enhanced and Assisted living environments (ELE/ALE) have been in focus of the researches for more than decade [8]. Adaptation of novel technologies in healthcare has taken a slow but steady pace, from the first wearable sensors for chronic disease conditions and activity detection with offline processing towards implantable or non-invasive sensors supported by advanced data analytics for pervasive and preventive monitoring. The ELE/ALE progress is driven by the rapid advances in key technologies in several complementary scientific areas over the last decade: sensor design and material science; wireless communications and data processing; as well as machine learning, cloud, edge, and fog technologies [18,19,21].

The integration of novel sensors into consumer electronics increases gathering of personal health data. The place and importance of different sensors for healthcare, well-being, and fitness among consumer devices can be tracked by their increasing share on Consumer Electronics Shows promoting self-care and self-regulation. This creates enormous possibility in both healthcare and healthy lifestyle. The availability of data in vast amounts can lead to: cost-effective, personalized, and real-time monitoring, detection and recommendations, both for the end users and healthcare providers [21]. These services (monitoring, detection, recommendation) are significant research topic in ALE/ELE domain. Thus, a large percent of typical ALE/ELE systems aim to monitor daily activities, detect specific events (e.g. falls, or false alarms), automate assistance, and decrease caregiver burden [22]. Continuous vital signs monitoring is an important application area and various sensors have been developed for this purpose. Sensor devices are supported by various algorithms and computational techniques, context modeling, location identification, and anomaly detection [19].

Human activity recognition stands for recognizing human activity patterns from various types of low-level sensor data usually presented as time series data. The activity itself can be represented and recognized at different resolutions, such as a single movement, action, activity, group activity, and crowd activity. Recognizing such activities can be useful in many applications, for example: detecting physical activity level [25], promoting health and fitness [28], and monitoring hazardous events such as falling [2,20].

The current trends in ALE/ELE systems research can be perceived from different perspectives [5]. In this work, we are investigating research topics in the ALE/ELE systems and services domain applied to healthcare and well-being. We identified potentially relevant articles with the following keywords: identification and sensing technologies, activity recognition, risks and accidents detection, tele-monitoring, diet and exercise monitoring, drugs monitoring, vital signs supervision, identification of daily activities, and user concerns like privacy and security.

Systematic reviews, use formal explicit methods, of what exactly was the question to be answered, how evidence was searched for and assessed, and how it was synthesized in order to reach the conclusion. The "Preferred reporting items for systematic reviews and meta-analyses: the PRISMA statement" [13,14] is one of the most widely used methodologies for achieving this. Recently, new forms of reviews have emerged in response to urgent needs for information, for which the existing systematic review model does not fit well [15]. The rapid review is used when time is of the essence. The scoping review is applied when what is needed is not detailed answers to specific questions but rather an overview of a broad field [17]. The evidence map is similar to scoping reviews but is focused on specific visual presentation of the evidence across a broad field. Finally, the realist review is used where the question of interest includes how and why complex social interventions work in certain situations, rather than assume they either do or do not work at all.

Performing any of these reviews types is usually manual and very labor-intensive work. Therefore, we have identified the opportunity to use Natural Language Processing (NLP) and other software engineering methods to automate the analysis, identify relevant articles, generate visualizations of trends and relationships, etc. We have implemented an NLP-based toolkit that performs this, and, in this paper, we show our findings in the AAL/ELE domain.

By exploring the publications over the last decade, we have summarized the state-of-the-art technologies, future research focus and publication statistics related to the following key issues: enabling technology, typical applications and services of ALE/ELE in healthcare and well-being.

The remainder of this article is organized as follows. Section 2 will elaborate the different Natural Language Processing techniques (NLP) we are using, while also describing the processing the collected data. Section 3 presents the results of our analysis in the AAL/ELE use case and discusses them. Finally, in the last section we conclude the paper and point directions for future research.

2 Methodology

This work is an extension of our previous work presented in [3]. Namely, the architecture was reworked for better reusability of intermediate results per the architecture presented in [26], while ensuring compliance with the terms of use of the digital libraries, in regard to the number of requests per unit time. Additionally, the plotting of aggregate results was integrated and streamlined using the Matplotlib library [7] and Networkx [6].

2.1 Search Input Taxonomy

The user input is a collection of keywords that are used to identify potentially relevant articles and a set of properties, which define what are we looking for in the identified articles. In particular, this input is defined with the following parameters, which are further enhanced by proposing synonyms to the search keywords and properties by the NLP toolkit, as described in the following Subsect. 2.4:

Keywords. Search terms or phrases that are used to query a digital library (e.g. ambient assisted living, enhanced living environments, etc.). See example of searched keywords in Figs. 6 and 7. Note that keywords are being searched for independently of each other and duplicates are being removed in a later phase.

Properties. The properties are words or phrases that are being searched in the title, abstract or keywords section of the identified articles. Exemplary properties used in this study can be seen in Figs. 8, 9, 10 and 11.

Property synonyms. In addition to the original form of the properties, also their synonyms or words with similar meaning in the domain terminology, are being searched for in the article's abstract, title and keywords. For each property, only one original form appears in the results for brevity, while the synonyms are omitted. Note that a synonym can be a completely different word, or another form of the same word, such as a verb in another tense or an adjective (e.g. synonyms of Recognition: identification, identify, recognize, recognise (intentionally misspelled), discern, discover, distinguish, etc.). Therefore, instead of showing all those words, only one word per synonym set is being displayed in the results. Synonyms can be provided by the user, or proposed by the toolkit, with a possibility of fine-tuning the proposals. For the considered use case, the list of used properties and property groups is shown in Fig. 1.

Property groups. The property groups are thematically, semantically or otherwise grouped properties for the purpose of more comprehensive presentation of the results. Properties within property groups are being displayed together in charts or tables. The property group has a name (e.g. Topics, Technology, Concerns, etc.), and within a group, there are sets of properties, including their synonyms, such as within the Concerns propriety group: privacy, security and acceptance. Exemplary summary results per property group are presented in 7, while exemplary results per property within groups are shown in Figs. 8, 9, 10 and 11.

Start year. The start year (inclusive) of the articles that we are interested in. Default: current year - 9.

End year. The end year (inclusive) of the articles that we are interested in. Default: current year.

Minimum relevant properties. A number denoting the minimum number of properties that an article has to contain in order to be considered as relevant. Default: 2.

2.2 Enhanced Search Capabilities with WordNet

Before the actual searching starts, the user provided input in the form of keywords and properties is enhanced by proposing synonyms from WordNet [1,12,16], using the NLTK library [4] for Python. In most cases, this increases the robustness of the searched properties by including synonyms that the user might have neglected. However, considering that Word Net is a general-purpose database, some of the proposed synonyms might not be appropriate or relevant.

```
{"Data Management": [["Cloud"], ["Fog"], ["Edge"]],
 "Technology": [["Sensor"], ["Battery", "Energy"], ["Protocol"], ["Machine Learning"], ["Deep Learning", "deep learn"]],
 "Topics": [["Accidents"],
            ["Mobile"],
            ["Diet"],
            ["Exercise", "exercising", "practice", "work out", "workout"],
            ["Vital Signs"],
            ["Activities", "action", "activeness", "activity"]],
 "information delivery and prescriptive insight": [["Recognition",
                                                   "discern",
                                                   "discover",
                                                   "distinguish",
                                                   "identification",
                                                   "identify",
                                                   "recognise",
                                                   "recognize"],
                                                  ["Sensing", "detecting", "detection", "perception", "sense", "spotting"],
                                                  ["Monitoring", "monitor"],
                                                  ["Supervision", "oversight", "supervising", "supervise"]]},
```

LEGEND
Property group
Property (main synonym)
Property (other synonyms)

Fig. 1. List of property groups and properties (main and the synonyms)

In such a case, the user can manually choose which of the proposed synonyms to be included before the actual processing starts.

The toolkit also performs stemming of the properties and the abstract, for a more robust searching. If none of the properties of interest are identified within the abstract, then those articles are removed from the result set, which corresponds to the eligibility step in the PRISMA statement. In addition to this, we can specify the minimum number of properties that need to be identified within an article for it to be considered eligible and potentially relevant.

2.3 Indexed Digital Libraries

As of this moment, the NLP toolkit indexes the following digital libraries (i.e. sources): IEEE Xplore, Springer and PubMed. From PubMed all articles that match the given search criteria (i.e. a keyword) are analyzed. IEEE Xplore results include the top 2000 articles that match given criteria, sorted by relevance determined by IEEE Xplore. For the Springer digital library, the search for each keyword separately is limited to 1000 articles or 50 pages with results, whichever comes first, sorted by relevance determined by Springer.

2.4 Survey Methodology

The methodology used for the selection and processing of the research articles in this section is based on "Preferred reporting items for systematic reviews and meta-analyses: the PRISMA statement" [13,14], as shown in Fig. 2. The goal of PRISMA is to standardize surveys. The first part is gathering articles based on certain criteria, in our case using the search keywords. After the articles are collected, the duplicates are removed and some of the articles are discarded for various reasons, such as relevance, missing meta-data, invalid publication period, etc. Finally, from the selected subset of articles, a qualitative analysis is performed and from those articles, only a certain number is selected for more thorough screening. With this toolkit, we automate most of the steps in the PRISMA approach to significantly reduce the number of articles that need to be manually screened.

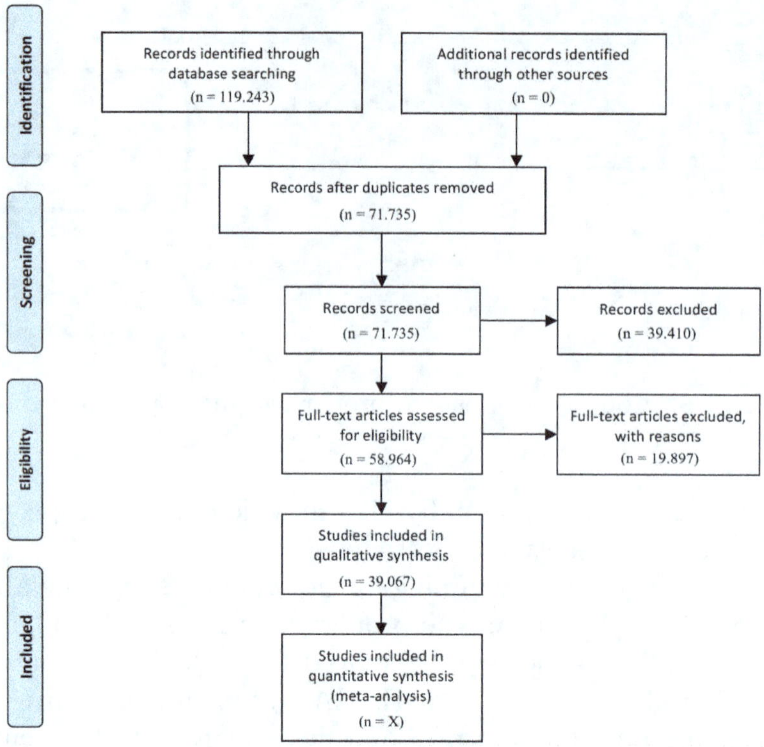

Fig. 2. PRISMA statement workflow with total number of articles for the current survey

Identification and Duplicate Removal. The proposed NLP toolkit performs the identification automatically. First, the possible article candidates are identified by querying the integrated libraries with the same search terms (i.e. keywords). While integrating the results from multiple sources (i.e. digital libraries), duplicate removal is also performed by using the article DOI as their unique identifier. Articles that were already found in another source or because they were identified by another search term, considering that an article can be found by multiple search terms, are not processed again, but still, are counted towards the number of identified articles per source. This means that the same article can be considered to exist in more than one source, therefore the sets of articles per source are not disjoint. After the candidate articles are identified, they are processed, and the properties of the texts are used for selection of the relevant articles. The process of article selection is the same as the one presented in [13,14], except for the last part where articles are manually processed by several researchers.

Augmented Screening and Eligibility Analysis by NLP. After the duplicates were removed, during the screening process discards articles which were not published in the required time period (e.g. last ten years) or for which the title or abstract could not be analyzed due to parsing errors, unavailability or other reasons.

Afterwards, the eligibility analysis is performed, which involves tokenization of sentences [10,23], English stop words removal, stemming and lemmatization [10] using the NLTK library [4] for Python. At the beginning, this is applied to each property, based on which a reverse lookup is created from each stemmed word and phrase to the original property. The same process is also applied to the title, keywords and abstract of each article. As a result of the stemming, for each property, the noun, verb and other forms are also considered. As a result of the lemmatization and the initial synonym proposal, the synonyms of properties are also considered. This results in a more robust analysis. Then, stemmed and lemmatized properties are searched in the cleaned abstract and title and the article is tagged with the properties it contains.

The identified articles are labeled as *relevant* only if they contain at least the minimum relevant properties, defined as an input, in its title or abstract (considering the above NLP-enhanced searching capabilities, thus performing a rough screening. To help in the eligibility analysis, the remaining relevant articles are sorted by number of identified property groups, number of identified properties, number of citations (if available) and year of publication, all in descending order. For the relevant articles the toolkit automatically generates a *Bibtex* file with most important fields that can be included in an article for simplified citations. An *Excel* file is also generated with the following fields: **DOI, link, title, authors, publication date, publication year, number of citations, abstract, keyword, source, publication title, affiliations, number of different affiliations, countries, number of different countries, number of authors, bibtex cite key, number of found property groups, and number of found properties**. The researcher can use this file to drill down and find specific articles by more advanced filtering criteria (e.g. by importing it in Excel). This can facilitate deciding which articles need to be retrieved from their publisher and manually analyzed in more detail in order to determine whether it should be included in the qualitative and quantitative synthesis.

Visualization of Aggregate Results. The results of the processing and retained relevant articles are aggregated by several criteria. The output contains CSV files and charts in vector PDF files for each of the following aggregate metrics:

- By source (digital library) and relevance selection criteria (see Fig. 3).
- By publication year (see Fig. 4a).
- By source and year (see Fig. 4b).
- By search keyword and source (see Fig. 5).
- By search keyword and year (see Fig. 6).
- By property group and year (see Fig. 7).
- By property and year, generating separate charts for each property group (see Figs. 8, 9, 10 and 11).
- By number of countries, number of distinct affiliations and authors, aiming to simplify identification of multidisciplinary articles (e.g. written by multiple authors with different affiliations) (See Fig. 14).

In addition to that, the toolkit also generates graph visualization of the results, where nodes are the properties and the edges are the number of articles that contain the two properties it connects. Articles which do not contain at least two properties and properties that are not present in at least two articles are excluded. An example of this is presented in Figs. 12 and 13. For a clearer visualization, only the top 25% property pairs by number of occurrence are shown (i.e. ones above the 75-th percentile).

A similar graph for the countries of the author affiliations is also generated (see Fig. 14). The top 50 countries by number of collaborations are considered for this graph. Additionally, we show only countries and an edge between them if the number of bilateral or multilateral collaborations between them in the top 5% (above 95-th percentile) within the top 50 countries.

3 Results

In this use case, we used the NLP toolkit with the keywords shown in Fig. 6. We searched for these keywords and automatically identified and screened the articles, as shown in Fig. 2. A more detailed analysis was performed using the properties that were clustered into four groups of properties, each containing at least three property synonyms, as shown in Fig. 1.

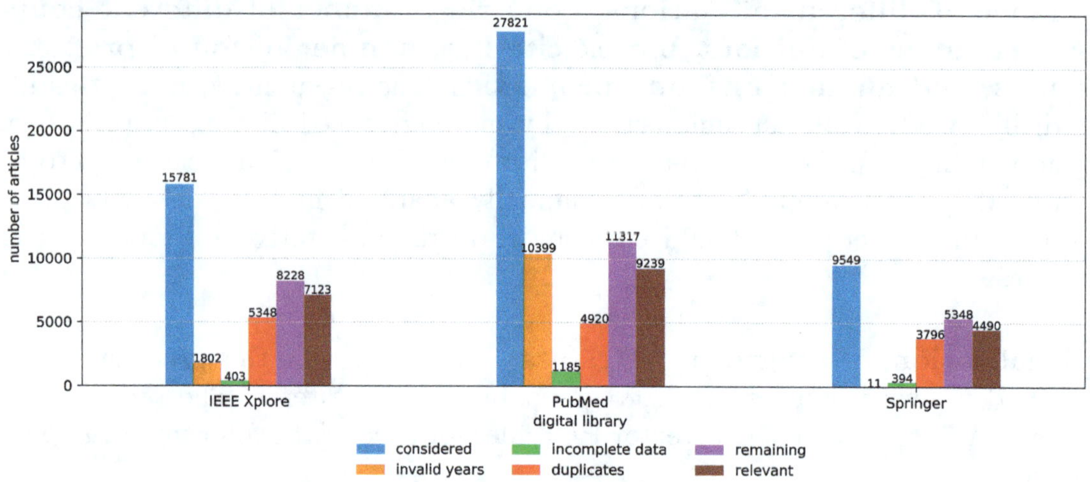

Fig. 3. Number of articles per relevance selection criteria

In Fig. 3, we show the selection process based on the adopted methodology. From all identified articles based on the keywords, first, the system eliminates the ones with incomplete or invalid meta-data. Next, the duplicate entries are eliminated and finally, from the remaining ones, the relevant articles are selected if they contain the minimum number of properties (in this case 1). In Fig. 4a, we present the number of remaining and searched for articles from each year, and in Fig. 4b, the number of relevant articles from each source.

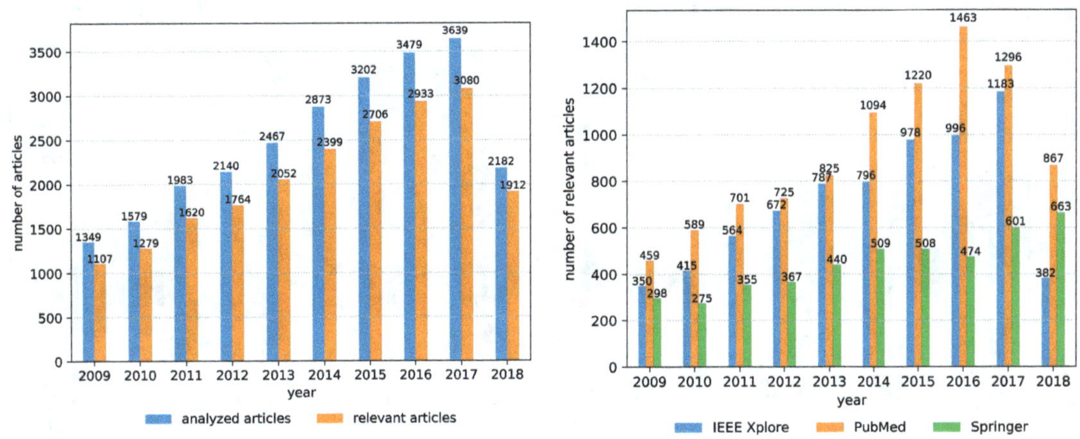

(a) Number of remaining and relevant articles per year

(b) Number of relevant articles from each digital library per year

Fig. 4. Number of articles per year and source

The number of relevant articles grouped by keywords from each source can be seen in Fig. 5. The top 3 keywords by the number of relevant articles are "assistive engineering", "enhanced life environment" and "enhanced support environment". It is interesting to see that they vary in frequency between different sources, which can be expected, considering that for PubMed the number of analyzed articles is unlimited, unlike the other sources.

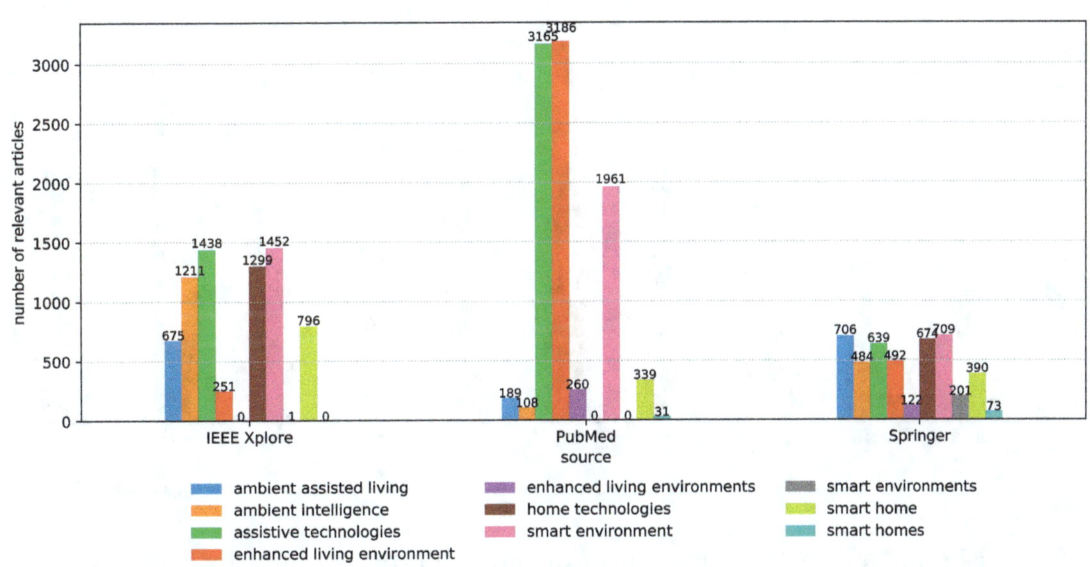

Fig. 5. Number of relevant articles for each keyword from each source

On Fig. 6, the distribution of articles per keyword for each year is shown. Notably, the number of papers for some of the keywords is increasing through the years, while for others it is relatively small.

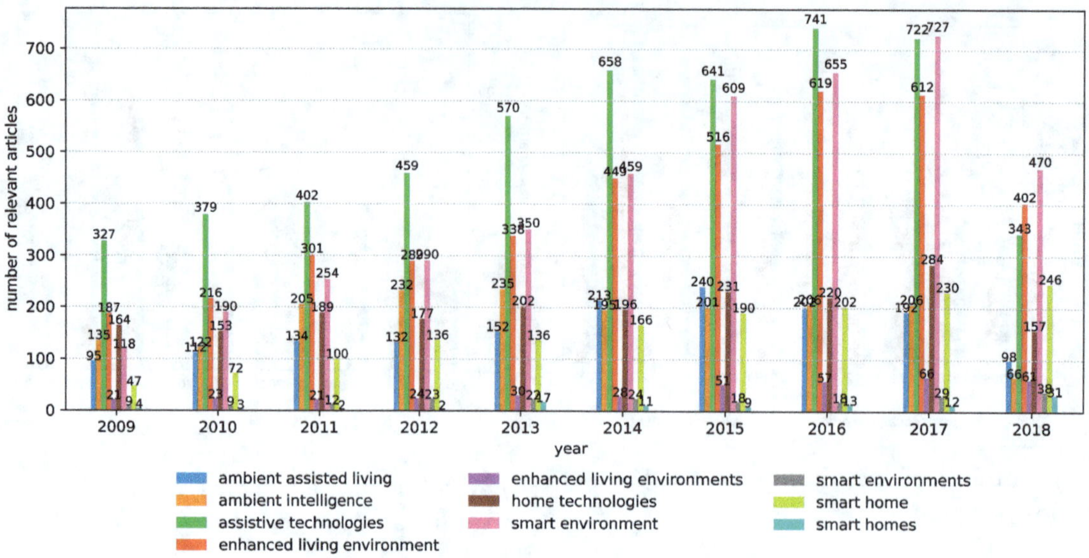

Fig. 6. Number of articles for searched keyword per year

Next, in Fig. 7 we can see the trends of articles mentioning at least one property from each property group, and evidently, all property groups are becoming more relevant. Apparently, the articles are not covering data management as often as the other themes (i.e. technology, topics and information delivery and prescriptive insight).

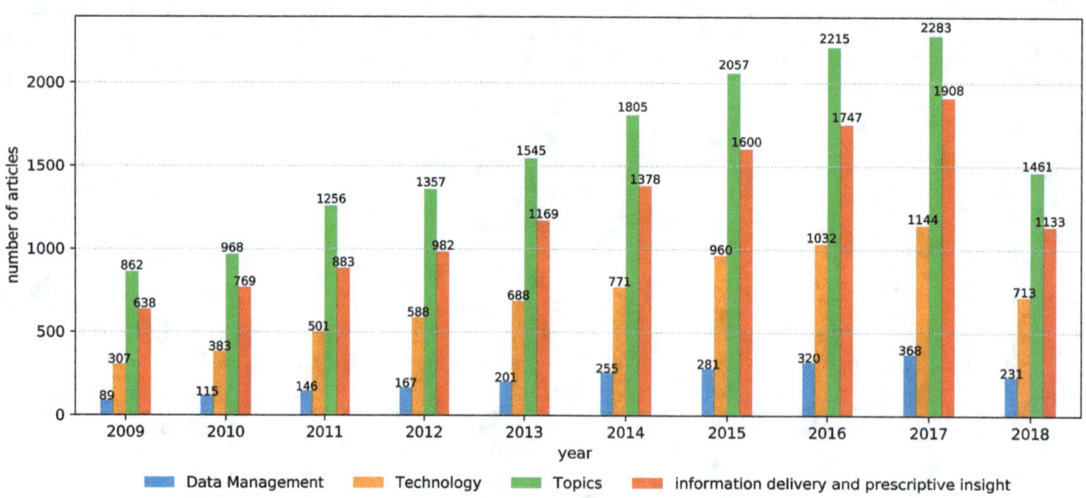

Fig. 7. Number of articles mentioning each property group per year

Properties and keywords follow a similar trend in the number of articles, with most of them reaching the highest number in 2015 and 2016. However, some terms, such as "smart environments", is still on the rise. Note that the numbers from 2018 are inconclusive because, at the time of this analysis, 2018 is not yet finished. Also, the number of articles is increasing in IEEE Xplore and Springer and the in PubMed the number of articles starts decreasing after 2016.

After the initial property analysis, for each property group, we analyze the articles based on each property. In Fig. 8 the results about the Data Management property group is shown. Here, we consider the properties Cloud, Fog and Edge, and their synonyms. The observable trend is that all of the terms are increasing in popularity in the respective research communities. The most popular term in the articles is Edge followed by Cloud and finally Fog computing, which slowly and steadily increases in popularity.

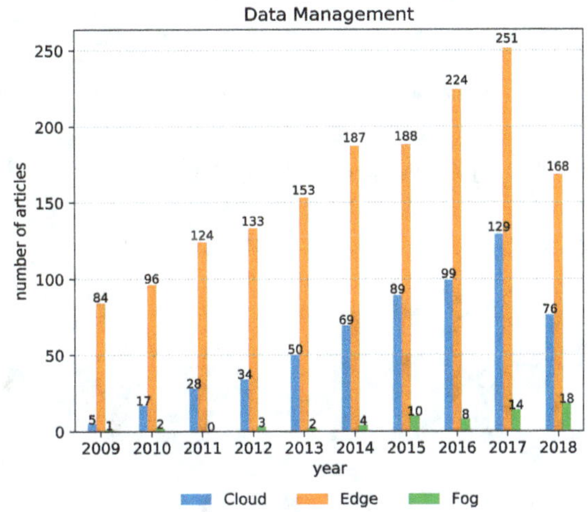

Fig. 8. Article distribution per year and properties in Data Management property group

The second property group is the "Technology", which is consisted of the properties: Battery, Deep Learning, Machine Learning, Protocol and Sensor. These properties cover different technology groups within the surveyed articles. It can be observed that most of the published articles include Sensors and give observation regarding the power consumption, thus include the word battery. Communication is also one of the most popular topics, the word protocol is also often mentioned, while Machine Learning and Deep Learning are encountered sparsely, but are slowly increasing in popularity.

The third property group "Topics" includes the properties: Activities, Accidents, Diet, Exercises, Mobile and Vital Signs. The topics show increasing trends in all of these properties, except for vital signs and accidents. We reason that this is due to the fact that most of the studies that are intended for Enhanced living environments are more interested in prevention and well-being instead of treatment. Accidents and vital signs measurements are also much harder to simulate and need specific hospitals environments to be treated. This does not mean that they are less relevant, rather that it is simply a less attractive research topic.

The final group of properties, "Information delivery and prescriptive insight", contains Sensing, Recognition, Monitoring and Supervision. It can be observed

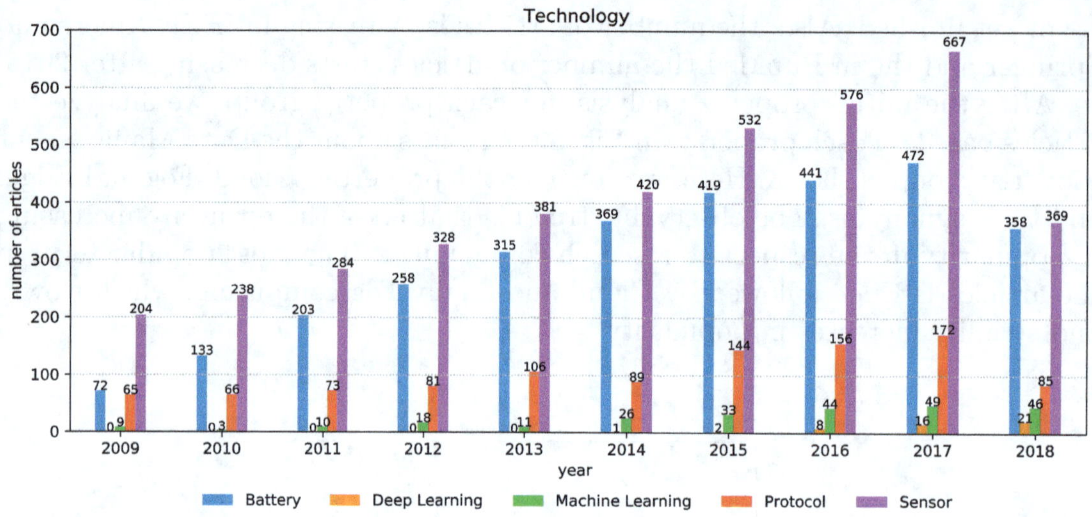

Fig. 9. Article distribution per year and properties in technology property group

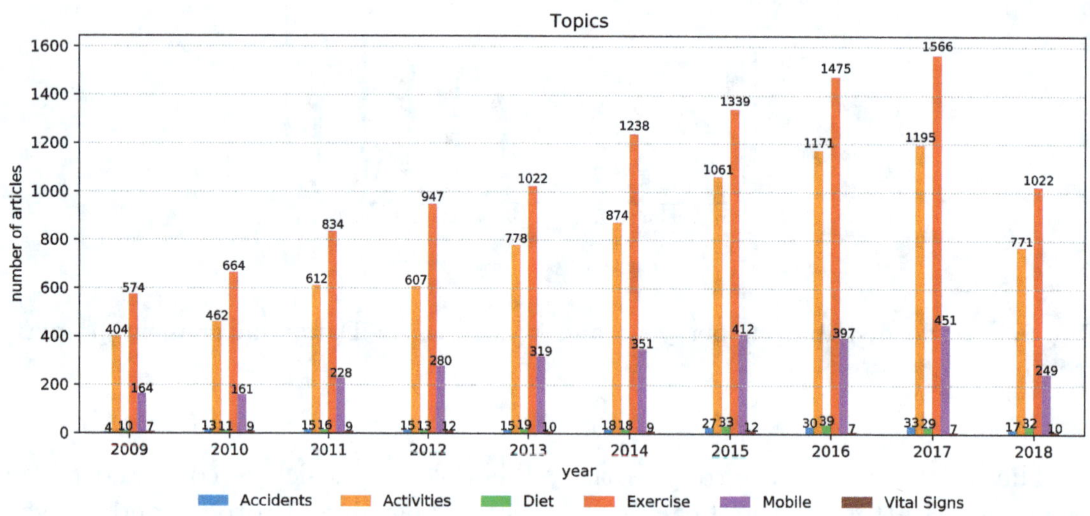

Fig. 10. Article distribution per year and properties in topics property group

that most of the publications are treating Sensing and Recognition and much less Monitoring and Supervision. The latter are much harder to study because of the special regulations related to ethical and processing of human data. The first two, Sensing and Recognition are much easier to simulate and there are many available datasets.

Next, Figs. 12 and 13 show how different properties are related between each other in terms of how often they occur together in the same article. These graphs can be used for guiding the drilling down process and selection of articles that need to be analyzed manually. The darker an edge is, the more articles there are that have the connected keywords. Also it shows that some properties are not often encountered with others (e.g. Cloud and Supervision on Fig. 13).

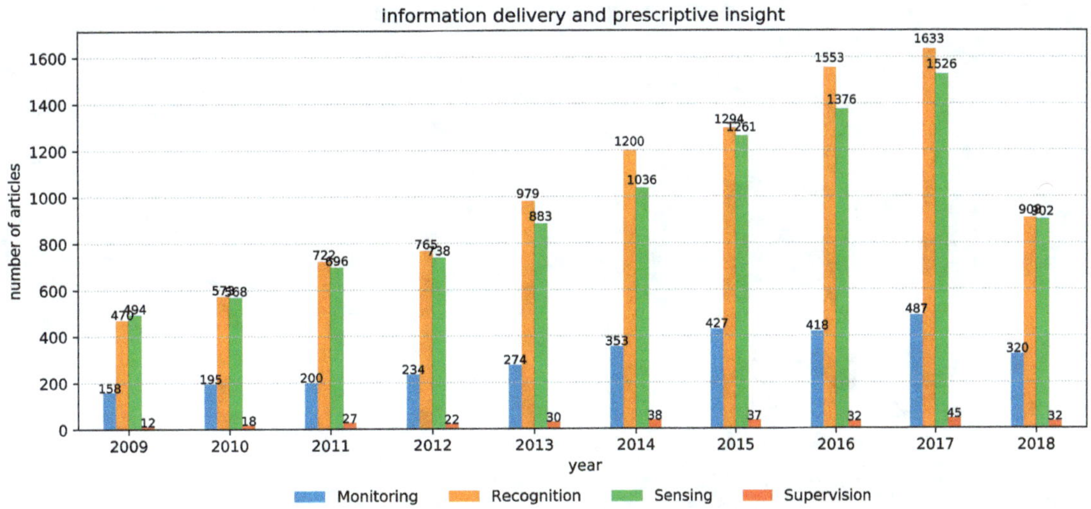

Fig. 11. Article distribution per year and properties in the information delivery and prescriptive insight property group

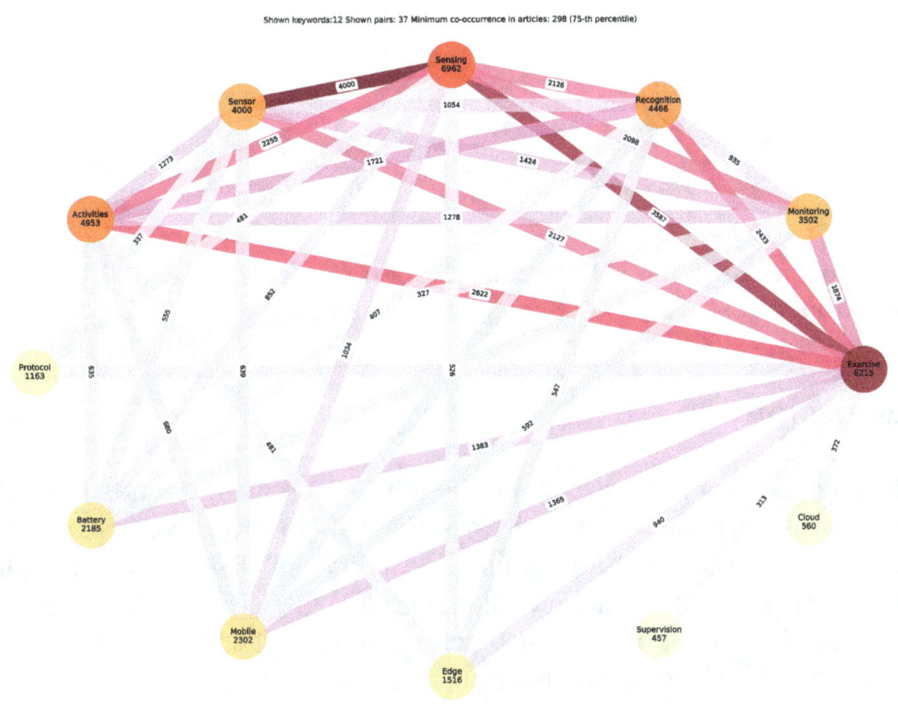

Fig. 12. Graph visualization with circular layout relevant articles by properties. Node labels show the property and number of articles that contain it and edge label shows the number of papers that have the properties it connects.

Finally, Fig. 14 shows how authors from different countries collaborated. This graphs clearly shows that communities exist between some countries. In most cases, we attribute this to geographical location, smaller language barriers, or both.

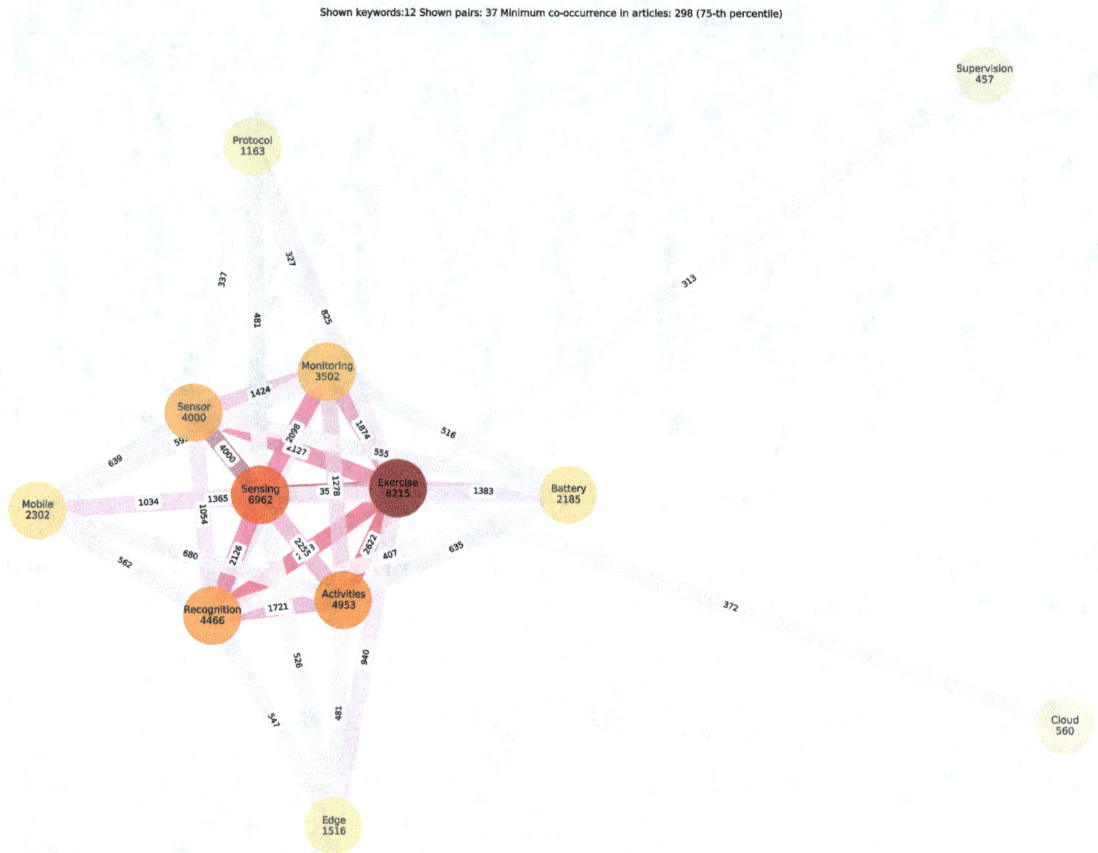

Fig. 13. Graph visualization with circular (i.e. Fruchterman-Reingold) layout relevant articles by properties.

4 Discussion

From this scoping review we can notice some increasing trends over different search keywords over the last decade (see Fig. 6). However, some keywords, such as "ambient assisted living" and "ambient intelligence" this trend is in a declining in the last 5 years. On the contrary, the trend for "assistive technologies" is in an even more rapid increase in the last 5 years, compared to its trend in the last 10 years. Interestingly, the singular form of "enhanced living environment", "smart environment" and "smart home" consistently results in finding more relevant papers than their plural form. From the properties, "deep learning" started to gain attention only in the last few years.

The proposed NLP toolkit was demonstrated through the AAL/ELE use case in this paper. It was also applied to simplify the review process in several previous works [9,11]. Its continued improvement is owed to the constructive feedback obtained from multiple researchers that had tested it. By being able to reuse intermediate results and allowing tweaking and fine-tuning of keywords and properties, the researcher can test different alternatives of keywords and properties very quickly. The toolkit also provides ability to fine-tune the graph plotting thresholds, so the they can show appropriate number of edges. These

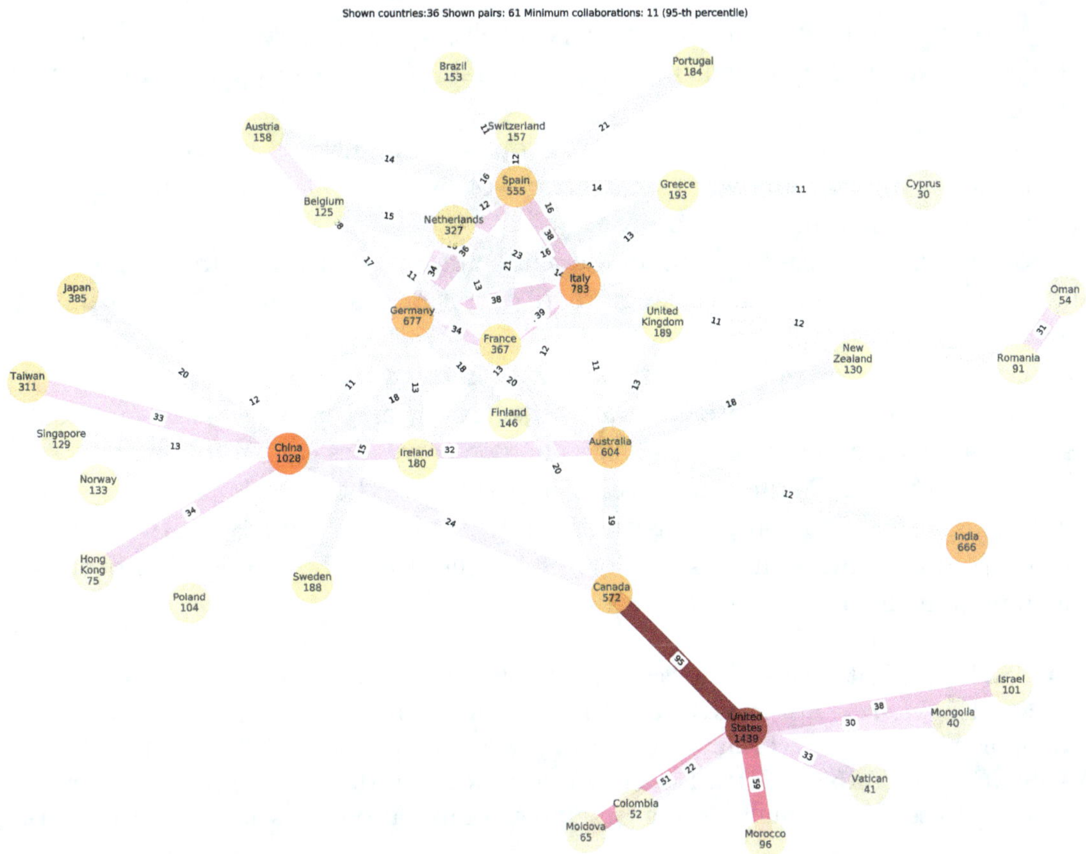

Fig. 14. Graph visualization relevant articles by countries. Node labels show the country and number of publications from it, while edge labels show the number of papers that were published by authors with affiliations from the countries it connects.

default parameters were empirically determined based on extensive analysis with over dozens of different use-cases.

Even though the results of the processing are automatically emailed to the researcher that started the analysis, the toolkit is still lacking a user interface. Right now, we are working on implementing a web-based user interface that will make the toolkit easily available for other researchers. Meanwhile, interested readers are encouraged to contact us for providing the source code or jointly performing a systematic or scoping review.

Another upcoming issue, as the number of users is increasing, is the scalability of the system. Even though we use a Microsoft Azure hosted instance for the toolkit, in order the system to be able to process multiple requests at once we need a more scalable solution, such as one based on Hadoop [24,27].

5 Conclusion

In this paper, we presented an NLP toolkit for speeding up the process of surveying scientific articles and trend analysis meta-studies. By leveraging NLP, it facilitates a robust and comprehensive eligibility and relevance analysis of articles, so the user can focus on reading a small number of potentially relevant articles.

We have presented a use-case of the proposed framework that proves that the framework is able to analyze the abstracts of over 70000 articles automatically and visualize different trends of interest.

For this use case, we can conclude that almost all of the searched keywords and properties have an increasing trend over the years. The aggregate results show that the research community is more interested in Enhanced living environments that sense and recognize activities and aid exercising, thus helping the well-being of people. Monitoring and supervision, and also more serious health issues, such as accidents and vital signs have received less attention from the scientific community. Furthermore, regarding the way the data is processed, Edge computing and Cloud computing receive fairly large attention. Sensors and power consumption are more interesting for researchers than communication protocols and machine/deep learning.

Acknowledgment. This work was partially financed by the Faculty of Computer Science and Engineering at the Ss. Cyril and Methodius University, Skopje, Macedonia and is supported by the networking activities provided by the ICT COST Actions IC1303 AAPELE and CA16226 SHELD-ON. We also acknowledge the support of Microsoft Azure for Research through a grant providing computational resources for this work.

References

1. Agirre, E., Alfonseca, E., Hall, K., Kravalova, J., Paşca, M., Soroa, A.: A study on similarity and relatedness using distributional and wordnet-based approaches. In: Proceedings of Human Language Technologies: The 2009 Annual Conference of the North American Chapter of the Association for Computational Linguistics, pp. 19–27. Association for Computational Linguistics (2009)
2. Alam, M.M., Hamida, E.B.: Surveying wearable human assistive technology for life and safety critical applications: standards, challenges and opportunities. Sensors **14**(5), 9153–9209 (2014)
3. Alla, A., Zdravevski, E., Trajkovik, V.: Framework for aiding surveys by natural language processing. In: Web Proceedings of the ICT Innovations 2017 Conference, IKT-AKT (2017)
4. Bird, S.: NLTK: the natural language toolkit. In: Proceedings of the COLING/ACL on Interactive Presentation Sessions, pp. 69–72. Association for Computational Linguistics (2006)
5. Dimitrievski, A., Zdravevski, E., Lameski, P., Trajkovik, V.: A survey of ambient assisted living systems: challenges and opportunities. In: 2016 IEEE 12th International Conference on Intelligent Computer Communication and Processing (ICCP), pp. 49–53. IEEE (2016)
6. Hagberg, A.A., Schult, D.A., Swart, P.J.: Exploring network structure, dynamics, and function using networkx. In: Varoquaux, G., Vaught, T., Millman, J. (eds.) Proceedings of the 7th Python in Science Conference, Pasadena, CA USA, pp. 11–15 (2008)

7. Hunter, J.D.: Matplotlib: a 2D graphics environment. Comput. Sci. Eng. **9**(3), 90–95 (2007)
8. Kotevska, O., Vlahu-Gjorgievska, E., Trajkovik, V., Koceski, S.: Towards a patient-centered collaborative health care system model. In: 4th IEEE International Conference on Computer Science and Information Technology (IEEE ICCSIT 2011) (2011)
9. Lameski, P., Zdravevski, E., Kulakov, A.: Review of automated weed control approaches: an environmental impact perspective. In: Kalajdziski, S., Ackovska, N. (eds.) ICT 2018. CCIS, vol. 940, pp. 132–147. Springer, Cham (2018). https://doi.org/10.1007/978-3-030-00825-3_12
10. Manning, C., Surdeanu, M., Bauer, J., Finkel, J., Bethard, S., McClosky, D.: The Stanford CoreNLP natural language processing toolkit. In: Proceedings of 52nd Annual Meeting of the Association for Computational Linguistics: System Demonstrations, pp. 55–60 (2014)
11. Maresova, P., et al.: Technological solutions for older people with alzheimer's disease. Current Alzheimer research (2018)
12. Miller, G.A.: WordNet: a lexical database for English. Commun. ACM **38**(11), 39–41 (1995). https://doi.org/10.1145/219717.219748
13. Moher, D., Liberati, A., Tetzlaff, J., Altman, D.G., The PRISMA Group: Preferred reporting items for systematic reviews and meta-analyses: the PRISMA statement. PLOS Med. **6**(7), 1–6 (2009). https://doi.org/10.1371/journal.pmed.1000097
14. Moher, D., et al.: PRISMA-P group: preferred reporting items for systematic review and meta-analysis protocols (PRISMA-P) 2015 statement. Syst. Rev. **4**(1), 1 (2015). https://doi.org/10.1186/2046-4053-4-1
15. Moher, D., Stewart, L., Shekelle, P.: All in the family: systematic reviews, rapid reviews, scoping reviews, realist reviews, and more. Syst. Rev. **4**(1), 183 (2015). https://doi.org/10.1186/s13643-015-0163-7
16. Pedersen, T., Patwardhan, S., Michelizzi, J.: WordNet: similarity: measuring the relatedness of concepts. In: Demonstration papers at HLT-NAACL 2004, pp. 38–41. Association for Computational Linguistics (2004)
17. Peters, M.D., Godfrey, C.M., Khalil, H., McInerney, P., Parker, D., Soares, C.B.: Guidance for conducting systematic scoping reviews. Int. J. Evid.-Based Healthc. **13**(3), 141–146 (2015)
18. Pombo, N., Garcia, N., Bousson, K.: Machine learning approaches to automated medical decision support systems. In: Pandian, V. (ed.) Handbook of Research on Artificial Intelligence Techniques and Algorithms, pp. 183–203. IGI Global, Hershey (2015)
19. Poon, C.C., Lo, B.P., Yuce, M.R., Alomainy, A., Hao, Y.: Body sensor networks: in the era of big data and beyond. IEEE Rev. Biomed. Eng. **8**, 4–16 (2015)
20. Rashidi, P., Mihailidis, A.: A survey on ambient-assisted living tools for older adults. IEEE J. Biomed. Health Inform. **17**(3), 579–590 (2013)
21. Suciu, G., et al.: Big data, internet of things and cloud convergence-an architecture for secure e-health applications. J. Med. Syst. **39**(11), 141 (2015)
22. Trajkovik, V., Vlahu-Gjorgievska, E., Koceski, S., Kulev, I.: General assisted living system architecture model. In: Agüero, R., Zinner, T., Goleva, R., Timm-Giel, A., Tran-Gia, P. (eds.) MONAMI 2014. LNICST, vol. 141, pp. 329–343. Springer, Cham (2015). https://doi.org/10.1007/978-3-319-16292-8_24
23. Webster, J.J., Kit, C.: Tokenization as the initial phase in NLP. In: Proceedings of the 14th Conference on Computational Linguistics, vol. 4, pp. 1106–1110. Association for Computational Linguistics (1992)

24. Zdravevski, E., Lameski, P., Kulakov, A., Jakimovski, B., Filiposka, S., Trajanov, D.: Feature ranking based on information gain for large classification problems with mapreduce. In: Proceedings of the 9th IEEE International Conference on Big Data Science and Engineering, pp. 186–191. IEEE Computer Society Conference Publishing, August 2015. https://doi.org/10.1109/Trustcom-BigDataSe-ISPA.2015.580
25. Zdravevski, E., et al.: Improving activity recognition accuracy in ambient-assisted living systems by automated feature engineering. IEEE Access **5**, 5262–5280 (2017). https://doi.org/10.1109/ACCESS.2017.2684913
26. Zdravevski, E., Kulakov, A.: System for prediction of the winner in a sports game. In: Davcev, D., Gómez, J.M. (eds.) ICT Innovations 2009, pp. 55–63. Springer, Heidelberg (2010). https://doi.org/10.1007/978-3-642-10781-8_7
27. Zdravevski, E., Lameski, P., Kulakov, A., Filiposka, S., Trajanov, D., Jakimovski, B.: Parallel computation of information gain using hadoop and mapreduce. In: Ganzha, M., Maciaszek, L., Paprzycki, M. (eds.) Proceedings of the 2015 Federated Conference on Computer Science and Information Systems. Annals of Computer Science and Information Systems, vol. 5, pp. 181–192. IEEE (2015). https://doi.org/10.15439/2015F89
28. Zdravevski, E., Risteska Stojkoska, B., Standl, M., Schulz, H.: Automatic machine-learning based identification of jogging periods from accelerometer measurements of adolescents under field conditions. PLOS ONE **12**(9), 1–28 (2017). https://doi.org/10.1371/journal.pone.0184216

RDF Stores for Enhanced Living Environments: An Overview

Petteri Karvinen[1], Natalia Díaz-Rodríguez[2(✉)], Stefan Grönroos[1], and Johan Lilius[1]

[1] Information Technologies Department, Åbo Akademi University, Turku, Finland
karvinen.petteri@gmail.com, research@stefang.net, jolilius@abo.fi
[2] ENSTA ParisTech and Inria Flowers, U2IS Department, Palaiseau, France
natalia.diaz@ensta-paristech.fr
http://flowers.inria.fr

Abstract. Handling large knowledge bases of information from different domains such as the World Wide Web is a complex problem addressed in the Resource Description Framework (RDF) by adding semantic meaning to the data itself. The amount of linked data has brought with it a number of specialized databases that are capable of storing and processing RDF data, called RDF stores. We explore the RDF store landscape with the aim of finding an RDF store that sufficiently meets the storage needs of an enhanced living environment, more concretely the requirements of a Smart Space platform aimed at running on a cluster set up of low-power hardware that can be run locally entirely at home with the purpose of logging data for a reactive assistive system involving, e.g., activity recognition or domotics. We present a literature analysis of RDF stores and identify promising candidates for implementation of consumer Smart Spaces. Based on the insights provided with our study, we conclude by suggesting different relevant aspects of RDF storage systems that need to be considered in Ambient Assisted Living environments and a comparison of available solutions.

Keywords: RDF store · RDF frameworks · Benchmark
Smart spaces · Ontologies · Ambient Assisted Living · Semantic Web
Publish/subscribe systems

1 Introduction

With the advent of the open Web and the large amounts of information that it has brought with it, a need for technologies that can handle large quantities of unstructured data in an automated fashion has arisen. Creating intelligent assumptions from the information pools that originate from widely different domains of knowledge is a labour intensive problem when using technologies popular today. A way of semantically representing data with the Resource Description Framework (RDF) and related semantic technologies has emerged

I. Ganchev et al. (Eds.): Enhanced Living Environments, LNCS 11369, pp. 19–52, 2019.
https://doi.org/10.1007/978-3-030-10752-9_2

as a solution in order to mitigate some of the complexities involved when intelligently handling large amounts of knowledge. Storage and retrieval of information in the RDF format is most often performed by using specialised storage systems called RDF stores. The need for these storage systems capable of processing large amount of RDF data is evident by looking at the great effort that has been invested in a whole range of production system ready, RDF stores [24,32,42].

Smart Spaces are information sharing networks that are limited to the scale of rooms and buildings. Because of the cross-domain information sharing between actors, a Smart Space shares some of the same problems as the open Web when it comes to information processing. The information sharing between devices and users in the Smart Space, as well as a seamless device interoperability, and the need for reactive systems, are some of the motivation behind the use of RDF tools [58].

As more knowledge producers are introduced into a Smart Space environment efficient storage is needed in order to handle the growing amount of information constantly added to the Smart Space. The RDF store needs to provide fast data storage operations in order to enable the Smart Space to work smoothly. For Smart Spaces, the task of finding an RDF store is affected by the limited low-power hardware used in Smart Spaces environments. Therefore, a Smart Space needs an efficient RDF data storage that scales well, preferably in a distributed system.

Section 2.2 presents a brief overview of RDF frameworks, Sect. 2.3 presents some fundamental data storage techniques used in RDF stores, and this is followed by a run-trough of RDF store benchmarks suits in Sect. 2.4. Section 3 introduces the Smart-M3 platform with a definition of RDF data storage requirements for the system followed by a short analysis of the suitability of different RDF stores for the platform. In Sect. 4, the integration of a 4store storage option into the Smart-M3 platform and an evaluation of the implementation is outlined. Section 5 concludes the review and identifies future work.

2 Related Work: RDF Stores

RDF provides possibilities in knowledge processing that are not possible in other database models. The new way of thinking about information in these semantic technologies also presents their own challenges and new sets of tools. Even the most fundamental functionality of providing efficient storage and retrieval of information in an RDF data model is an issue that has created a new breed of information storage systems called the RDF stores. Besides providing storage and retrieval of information in the RDF format, RDF stores often consist of software solutions for a number of functionalities related to semantic technologies and information processing.

The RDF data model does not define the physical layout of the data itself, but instead it defines how the information should be presented to the user or the application when it is accessed from the RDF store. This abstraction of information has resulted in large differences in the underlying data structures used for different RDF store. The data structures used for RDF stores range from off-the-shelf relational databases [15,41] to state-of-the-art advanced indexing schemes, which are specifically designed for the RDF data model [51]. As the underlying data structures greatly affect both the performance and the scalability of the storage system, this Section first presents the concepts that have shaped modern RDF stores. This presentation is then followed by a brief run-through of some of the most influential RDF stores. The Section concludes with a discussion of RDF store benchmarking software.

The data storage techniques in RDF stores range from mapping the RDF data model onto existing DBMS to custom DBMS where the data structures used are designed specifically for the RDF data model.

2.1 RDF Store Taxonomy

As the storage techniques have a deterministic effect on the performance of RDF stores, the identification of the core data structures used in RDF stores becomes important for evaluating individual RDF stores. One of the defining features for the real-world performance of RDF stores is how well they can handle the prevalent conjunctive information retrieval requests of the RDF graphs. As a result of this, the performance of RDF stores is tightly bound to how well the index structure can handle the joins that graph pattern matching in queries. In order to grasp the different data structures that are used in RDF stores, this section presents the major data structures and indexing schemes that are an integral part of RDF stores.

A number of papers have been presented on the topic of classifying different types of RDF Stores. The classification is usually based on analyzing the underlying storage methods that are used to implement the RDF data model. The most extensive study on the topic was presented by Faye et al. [34], who surveyed the RDF store landscape and presented a taxonomy of RDF storage techniques and grouped the RDF stores in a tree structure shown in Fig. 1. The main separation is into two groups: *non-native* RDF stores, which are based on existing data storage solutions; and *native* RDF stores, which use data structures designed with the RDF data model in mind. A conscious omission in Faye et al.'s study is that distributed and peer-to-peer RDF stores were not at all considered. A literature survey from SYSTAP [65] includes a moderately extensive discussion on some distributed RDF stores. In the survey, the distributed RDF stores are grouped into *index based systems*, *key-value stores* extended with MapReduce and *main memory systems*. Peer-2-peer RDF stores are discussed in length in [35].

Defining an exact taxonomy of RDF stores, as presented in Fig. 1, and classifying each RDF store can be considered somewhat misleading as RDF stores can incorporate a combination of storage techniques. Some RDF store vendors do not publicize the details for the underlying data structure, and this makes the task even harder. Nevertheless, it is important for the database system administrator to be aware of the different techniques used in the available RDF stores and how they affect both the performance and the scalability of the RDF stores.

Below follows short descriptions of the main techniques used in RDF stores as presented in Fig. 1.

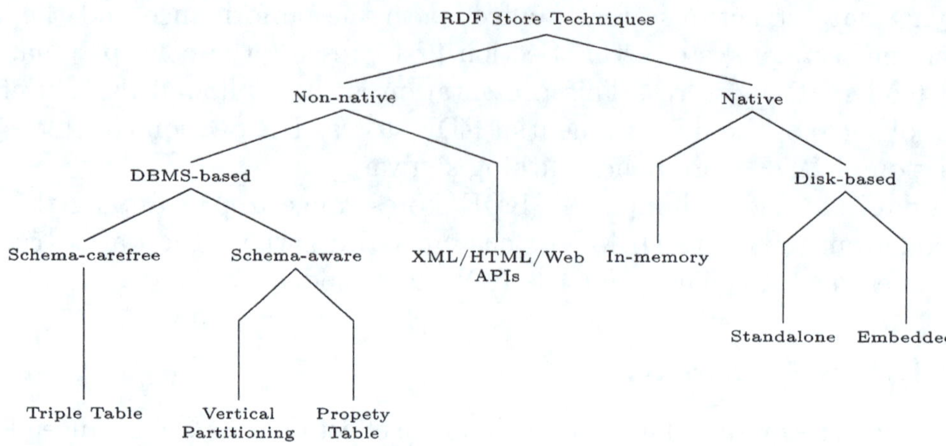

Fig. 1. RDF storage technique classification tree, as presented in [34]

Triple Table. The triple table can be considered the most straight forward way of storing RDF triples. In the triple table approach, the RDF data model is mapped directly onto a three-column wide table, in which each tuple contains the resources for the RDF statement subject, predicate and object. This can easily be implemented in any off-the-shelf RDBMS and it was a popular technique used in early RDF stores such as 3store [41], which maps the RDF graphs into a MySQL RDBMS triple table. A table representation on how the RDF data model could be implemented for a small example RDF graph in a triple table is presented in Table 1.

Table 1. Example of a triple table

Subject	Predicate	Object
place:City#London	rdf:type	place:City#
place:Region#England	rdf:type	place:England#
place:Country#UK	rdf:type	place:Country#
place:City#London	geo:isLocatedIn	place:Place#England
place:Place#England	geo:isPartOf	place:Country#UK
place:City#London	hasPopulation	8174000
place:Place#England	hasPopulation	53010000

A triple table representation as presented above, can be considered a rather naive solution that has some obvious disadvantages. This kind of single table representation will contain large amounts of unnecessary replication of information, as the same resources will appear in several rows. The replication of information is also observable in Table 1 in which several of the subject and predicate fields are repeated. Additionally, this kind of naive triple table implementation will scale poorly since the number of triples in the table grows, as the query time will also grow linearly as the RDF graph grows. This is a limitation that makes the naive triple table infeasible for large datasets, a fact that was also noted in early RDF stores [41].

An improvement to the naive triple table approach is to build meaningful indices that covers the RDF statements. To cover all possible subject, predicate, object combinations, a total of six covering indices is needed. To provide an additional *context* resource for each triple in the RDF graph, the number of covering indices grows to 16. Most modern RDF stores that use a triple table also use some variation of covering indices [31,51].

Property Table. First introduced in the Jena framework in 2006 [66], the *property tables* is a step away from some of the scalability limits that persist in the triple table approach. The basic idea behind the property table is to discover clusters of triple subjects in the knowledge base that share the same properties and to group them into common tables. For each line in the property table one column contains the subject for the triple with one or more columns containing the property values for that subject. A property table grouping for the same example RDF graph as in Table 1 is illustrated in Table 2. As can be observed from Table 2, the triple predicates are not stored in the tables row data, but instead within the table meta data. The aim of this kind of structure is to take advantage of the regularities found in RDF graphs in order to reduce redundant writing of information, and in the process speed up some of the most commonly executed queries.

Table 2. Example of a multi-value property table RDF graph representation

(a) Property table

Subject	Type	geo:hasPopulation	geo:isLocatedIn
place:City#London	place:City#	8174000	place:Region#England
place:Region#England	place:Region#	53010000	NULL
place:Country#UK	place:Country#	63230000	NULL

(b) Left-over triples

Subject	Predicate	Object
place:Region#England	geo:isPartOf	place:Country#UK

One of the major advantages of the property table compared to a triple table is that the number of join operations is reduced for certain types of queries. For example, for queries that needs two or more single-value properties for a subject, all properties can be found on the same tuple row, eliminating the tuple joins that would have otherwise been needed if a triple table had been used. An additional feature which is not possible in a triple table is the possibility to do *attribute typing*, i.e. defining the datatype formats for individual properties in the column schema.

There are numerous ways to group RDF graphs into different property tables. It has been shown that the selected property table scheme dramatically affect the performance of the RDF store [66]. If the property table groupings lead to wide and sparsely populated tables, the tables will be filled by a large amount of NULL values, which in turn can dominate the storage space [18]. The property table approach is also less flexible than the triple table approach as the clustered properties might need rearranging as the data changes to maintain good performance. Furthermore, the query performance is negatively affected when performing queries on RDF graphs for which the property triple match is unknown on a property table since all property tables then must be evaluated.

Vertical Partitioning. The third way to map the RDF data model onto an RDBMS solution is by using *vertical partitioning*. This approach was first introduced in SW-store [18] with the basic principle being that all triples are placed into n two-column tables, for which n is the total number of unique properties in the knowledge base. The first column is used to store the subjects of the triple that have the defined property for the table, and the second column contains the object values for those subjects. The tables are usually sorted by subject, allowing for *self joins* (combination of records in the same table) to be performed faster. A simple example representation of a property table is shown in Table 3.

Table 3. Example of a vertical partitioning (binary table) representation

(a) rdf:type

place:City#London	place:City#
place:Country#UK	place:Country#
place:Place#England	place:Region#

(b) geo:isLocatedIn

place:City#London	place:Place#England

(c) goe:isPartOf

place:Place#England	place:Country#UK

(d) geo:hasPopulation

place:City#London	8174000
place:Place#England	53010000

The use of a vertical partitioning data structure in datasets containing large numbers of predicates will lead to a large number of tables being created. The large number of tables is specifically problematic when executing queries for which several properties for each subject are requested. These types of queries requires self joins each subject that have several of the requested properties. Both relational [18,31] and non-relational column stores have been used in implementations of vertically partitioned RDF stores.

Native RDF Stores. RDF stores that do not rely on existing RDBMS systems, but instead use a custom DBMS system, which use data structures that are tailored to the RDF data model, or store data in main memory, are called *native* RDF stores. Native RDF stores can be divided into *main memory* and *disk* RDF stores depending on the medium where the RDF graphs are stored. *Main memory* RDF stores such as Jena TDB and RYA store the entire RDF graph in the main memory, while disk-based RDF stores, like Virtuoso or 4store, use file systems in combination with custom DBMSs for storing the triple data in secondary or tertiary memories. The main memory approach relies on the fast access times of RAM memory to provide fast query response times, while modern disk-based systems make heavy use of cache techniques to serve frequently occurring queries.

A lot of effort has also gone into the creation RDF storage systems that use peer-to-peer technologies for the storage and retrieval of RDF data. An extensive study of RDF storage systems that take advantage of the peer-to-peer communication model is in [35]. In the study, Filali et al. identify the decentralization, the scalability, and the fault-tolerance provided by peer-to-peer systems as the leading factors that motivated the design of the RDF data stores that were covered.

RDF storage solutions capable of performing queries on large RDF datasets mapped onto distributed file systems and queried using a MapReduce engine have been presented in a number of research papers. SHARD [56], which was one of the earliest peer-to-peer RDF stores presented, uses Hadoop and the HDFS. The RDF graph is grouped into SHARDs that are directly mapped to the HDFS file system. Queries are evaluated by performing triple patterns match MapReduce operations on the SHARDs in a sequential order. Another Hadoop based RDF query system is CliqueSquare [36], which reduces the network traffic by exploiting the built-in replication in the HDFS and a clique-based algorithm to find connected subgraphs to speed up query processing.

RDF storage systems that store the RDF graph in a cluster of individual RDF stores and are queried using a MapReduce system have also been presented. An example of such a system is presented [56], which distributes the RDF graph into overlapping sub-graphs and placing the sub-graphs into individual RDF stores. All SPARQL queries in the system are processed into smaller MapReduce sub-query chunks in a master node that can be processed in parallel by the individual RDF store nodes. This approach can be considered better suited for querying large RDF that do not change since the graph partitioning performed in the master node limits the scalability of the system.

An inherent advantage of peer-to-peer RDF stores is that they offer a direct way to distribute the RDF graphs over hardware nodes. This enables vertical scalability by adding new nodes to the network, and therefore there is no need to redesign of the system in order to achieve scale-out features. Even though the peer-to-peer RDF storage solutions have some advantages, problems relating the overhead caused by the traffic between the nodes, and in that they do not solve the underlying problems caused by splitting up the RDF graphs have been cited as problems are yet to be solved in current peer-to-peer RDF stores [65].

2.2 RDF Frameworks

In addition to individual RDF stores such as BitMat [21], MonetDB [63], TriAD [38], AdPart [40], H2RDF [55], there are a number of RDF-centric frameworks that provide interfaces to third party RDF storage implementations or implement their own internal RDF storage solutions. A listing of the major RDF frameworks with an accompanying description is presented below.

Apache Jena [2] RDF framework originated from the Hewlett Packard Labs and includes a whole range of RDF specific tools from parsers, RDF stores, reasoners and query systems. The libraries support both internal RDF stores and provide libraries to access a number of independent RDF stores. The libraries are Java-based, but bindings for the most common languages are provided.

Developed by Aduna, the OpenRDF Sesame framework [6] is similar to the Apache Jena framework in that it provides a de-facto standard tool set for processing RDF data in Java APIs. Access to most modern RDF stores is provided through the SAIL API part of the framework. The framework has been developed for over ten years and is used by companies in several different industries. The OWLIM platform [24] is a high-performance Java-based semantic repository that is packaged as an implementation of Sesame's SAIL API. Besides serving as an interface to the OWLIM RDF store, the platform also supports reasoning for RDFS, OWL Horst, OWL 2 QL and OWL 2 RL semantics.

Developed by Dave Beckett, the Redland RDF libraries [12], written in C, provide tools for parsing, querying and storage on RDF data. The Redland *storage* library supports a limited number of RDF stores, the default being a custom storage solution based on the Oracles Berkeley DB database. Besides the C API, the libraries have bindings to Ruby, PHP, Python and Perl.

The PerlRDF libraries [11] are a set of Perl libraries similar to the Redland RDF libraries with the aim of providing a Perl interface for RDF tools, in a similar fashion to what OWL API implementaion in Java does, to provide an OWL 2 syntax API.

2.3 Individual RDF Stores

Since the first RDF stores appeared in the early 2000s, a number of surveys and evaluations have been presented that both evaluate the state of RDF stores and discuss the techniques used. An incomplete list of recent studies include: an evaluation of RDF database solutions from 2009 [64], a report over RDF stores done for the European project 2011 [44], a discussion of interesting RDF stores in a literature survey of RDF storage approaches [34]. The RDF stores covered in the studies vary largely based on the aim of the studies. RDF stores briefly covered in this chapter were included on the basis of having either shaped the evolution of RDF stores or being considered a major player in the current state of RDF stores. Below follows a short introduction to these RDF stores.

YARS2. Released in 2004, Yet Another RDF Store (YARS) was one of the first distributed RDF store released to the public. The improved version, YARS2 [43] released in 2006, improved the scalability of the system. YARS2 represents RDF statements as quads, in which the fourth position of the statement is defined as the source of the triple, functioning in a similar fashion as the RDF NAMED GRAPH [4]. The store uses six, alternatively ordered, covering indices: SPOC, POCS, OCSP, CPSO and OSPC. In these indices, S, P and O are the triple *subject*, *predicate* and *object*, and C stands for the *context* of the statement. YARS2 uses an *in memory sparse index* data structure that refers to sorted and blocked data files on disk. In order to save space, only the first two elements of each quad are stored in the sparse index. By doing so, the indexing structure sacrifices insertion speed for better query performance, as all six indices must be calculated in a specific order when inserting new triples. Huffman encoding is used in the data blocks in order to save storage space. The entire lexical value of the triple is indexed in order to speed up the queries that contain FILTER operations.

Virtuoso. Virtuoso is defined as "a general purpose relational/federated database system and application platform" [32] developed by OpenLink Software, and can be considered a full-featured RDF solution with interfaces for the Jena framework, the Sesame and Redland libraries, a limited OWL inference engine, full-text search, relational data analytics and Multi Version Concurrency Control (MVCC) for transaction handling. Virtuoso was originally a relational database that was later extended in order to support RDF data. The software first used a row-wise transaction scheme [33], but the latest version of the software, Virtuoso 7, uses column-wise compressed storage with a vectored execution [31]. The software is provided under both an open-source license for single machines and a commercial license for software that supports federated (distributed) storage and other additional functionality.

Virtuoso uses a quadruplet structure for modelling RDF triples and by doing so extends the subject S, predicate P and object O with a G graph node column representing the graph IRI ID. The earlier versions of Virtuoso used only two covering indices, $<GSPO>$ and $<OGPS>$, for each statement. The index structure was motivated by the assumption that most triples are queried using either the subject or the object. Virtuoso 6 and 7 extended the covering indices to include the optional covering indices $<PSOG>$ and $<POGS>$ as well as the additional indices $<OP>$, $<SP>$ and $<GS>$ for distinct projections. All SPARQL queries in Virtuoso are transformed into SQL statements that are then handled inside Virtuoso's SQL query engine in a similar fashion as Oracle's RDF_Match table function (see Sect. 2.3). The latest version of the software is marketed as scaling up to datasets over a trillion triples.

4store. 4store [42] is an open-source RDF store that was originally developed by Garlik in order to be used in the company's personal data protection products. As Garlik moved on to their new clustered RDF-store, 5store, 4store has been maintained by the 4store user community.

Even if 4store is labelled as the logical successor of 3store [41], it shares very little code with its predecessor. The main feature that has remained is the mapping of RDF resources as integers. The data structure used in 4store resembles the property table used in Jena SDB rather than the triple table used in 3store. RDF statements are defined as quadruplets or *quads* consisting of a *subject*, a *predicate*, an *object* and a *model* that is used analogously with the RDF NAMED GRAPH. The indexing and distribution of the RDF graph to nodes in 4store is based on hashing algorithms.

For the query optimization, 4store executes *bind* operations in a descending order based on a selectivity factor evaluated on the basis of statistical predicate frequency tables. The resulting bindings are combined in the master node, and as such produce the final query results. The evaluation of FILTER operations is delayed towards the end of the query execution in order to limit the cost of transforming the lexical values of RDF resources. The indexing structure gives good performance for most queries, but queries with unknown predicates on a knowledge base with many unique predicates will be at a disadvantage due to the large number of tables required by the property table-like structure used in 4store.

4store does possess some clear deficiencies compared to other leading RDF stores. The major deficiencies are an incomplete SPARQL 1.1 support, and a lack of both transaction handling and built-in inference engines. However, a separate version of 4store that supports backward inferencing on a *minimal RDFS* set [60] has been developed, but is yet to be included in the official 4store release.

SYSTAP, BigData. BigData is a RDF platform targeting the Semantic Web and it has been developed by Systap LLC since 2006. BigData was initially released in a single node version that is currently named *journal*. BigData has later been extended to a clustered version of the software called *federation*. The *journal* version is in principal a main memory RDF store, while the federation version uses a "dynamic horizontal partitioning architecture" that is inspired by BigTable [27]. The *journal* version is aimed for smaller knowledge bases that can fit into the main memory of a single node, whereas the federation is aimed at handling large knowledge bases that do not fit onto a single node. Like Virtuoso, the BigData software is published under both an open-source and a commercial license [13]. At the time of writing, the open-sourced version of the software can be used without a commercial license for knowledge bases less than 50 million triples. Transaction support using an MVCC system is available for both the *journal* and the *federation* versions of the software.

Jena TDB. The original Jena RDF store [66] (now called Jena SDB) was developed by the Hewlett Packard labs. The software system was initially an RDBMS mapped onto a property table indexing scheme. The current RDF storage provided by the Jena framework, the Jena TDB, has diverged from the original version of Jena and can now be considered as a single node main memory RDF store. The change is motivated by the significantly better performance offered by keeping the RDF graph in the main memory compared to the initial disk based system, for which further development has been discontinued. Another of the selling points for the Jena TDB RDF storage solution is the extensive tools provided with the Jena framework.

Allegrograph. Developed by Franz Inc, Allegrograph [1] is a commercial grade graph database for RDF data, containing a range of RDF tools. Allegrograph represents triples in *assertions* and each triple is mapped into a *subject*, a *predicate*, an *object*, a *graph* and a *triple-id* assertion. The triple-id is mainly used for graph extension when performing direct graph reification for RDF graphs. The system uses a combination of dictionaries, seven different indices and a cache handling system in order to provide the storage and retrieval of the RDF data.

Knowledge bases in Allegrograph can be queried using both the SPARQL language and a specialized Prolog instruction set. The system supports full RDFS and partial OWL reasoning through its RacerPro [39] software, which is built on *tableau* calculus. Rather unique features found in Allegrograph are the possibilities for doing *geospatial inferencing* as well as *temporal reasoning*. Federation and ACID compliant transactions are also supported[1]. The system can be accessed by the number of programming languages or through the Jena platform.

OWLIM. OWLIM [24] is a family of semantic repositories that provides storage, inference and novel data-access features for RDF data. The software comes in three different versions: a main memory RDF store for datasets up to 100 million statements called OWLIM-Lite (previously SwiftOWLIM), a file system based RDF store for larger data volumes called OWLIM-SE (previously BigOWLIM) and a replication cluster RDF store called OWLIM-Enterprise.

All the OWLIM versions are accessible through the package interface layer in the Sesame SAIL platform. The query engine for OWLIM-Lite relies on the Sesame framework, while the other versions use their own built-in query engines. In addition to the SPARQL 1.1 language support, OWLIM-SE and OWLIM-Enterprise also support *full text search* through the Lucene [3] text search engine. OWLIM uses an embedded reasoning engine developed at Ontotext, which performs reasoning based on forward-chaining of the entailment rules over the RDF triple patterns with variables. A relatively unique feature for OWLIM-SE is the possibility for the user to receive notifications on changes in triples by using a publish/subscribe mechanism.

[1] The ACID properties of a DBMS that allow safe sharing of data are Atomicity, Consistency, Isolation, and Durability.

Oracle Spatial and Graph 10g-12c, and Oracle NoSQL. RDF and semantic inference support were initially introduced to the Oracle RD-BMS in 2005 [50]. Version 11g of the Oracle RDBMS that was released in 2007 provided native RDF storage that scales up to billions of triples. Also included in the release of version 11g was OWL inference and the integration to prominent RDF technologies such as Jena, Sesame and Protégé [22]. The RDF graphs in Oracle 11g are modelled using relational tables and views that are optimized for semantic data. RDF graphs can be accessed in the system by using mixed SQL and SPARQL queries. Nevertheless, all SPARQL queries are translated in runtime into table/join structures that are executed by the underlying DBMS[2].

A separate software product provided by the Oracle Corporation that has RDF support is the Oracle NoSQL database [9]. The underlying storage is based on the key-value store, Oracle Java Berkeley DB (previously SleepyCat DB). Oracle NoSQL supports SPARQL queries as well as inferencing, and it can be accessed through the Jena interface.

RDF-3X. Introduced in 2010 by the Plank Institute, RDF-3X [51] is an academic effort intended to improve the RDF storage architecture. The RDF-3X RDF store uses a RISC-style [7] architecture with a streamlined indexing structure combined with a streamlined query optimisation approach.

In RDF-3X, all triples are stored in a single triple table, and each triple is sorted lexicographically into one compressed B+ tree. In order to compress the storage of triples and to simplify the processing of queries, triple literals are replaced with identifiers using a mapping dictionary. When querying the knowledge base, the triple patterns are translated into string identifiers and the resulting literals get translated back to strings using a direct mapping index.

All six possible permutations of the covering indices are built for each triple and inserted into clustered B+ trees. This index structure ensures that single index lookups are possible for every triple pattern. For each tuple in the B+ tree leaf nodes value, byte-level compression is performed based on the delta difference of the preceding tuples. Similarities between neighbouring tuples in the B+ tree are exploited in order to gain a high level of compression. Additional aggregate indices (*SP*, *PS*, *SO*, *OS*, *PO*, *OP*, *S*, *P*, *O*) are also built in order to speed up the SPARQL queries that include partial triple patterns.

SPARQL queries are transformed and performed using tuple calculus. This is motivated by the fact that it eliminates a large part of the merge joins that are prevalent in property table approaches. The query optimization within RDF-3X is based on identifying the lowest-cost execution plan based either on the selectivity of the calculations for executing frequent join paths or alternatively on a through and specialized histogram of data when the join path data is not available.

The first version of the RDF-3X software was mainly optimized for retrieving information from RDF graphs. Later versions of the software include a compact

[2] http://download.oracle.com/otndocs/tech/semantic_web/pdf/oradb_semantic_overview.pdf.

differential indices and an integrated versioning, which enables the deferral of changes to the RDF graph that can be merged with the main RDF graph in batch operations. The additions enabled online updates to the knowledge base and provided time travel queries that offer both flexibility and consistency through a transaction concurrency control system [52]. The index structure in combination with the query optimisations used give RDF-3X a good performance in many types of queries, although it has been noted that the performance of RDF-3X degrades for unbound queries and queries where the selectivity factor is low [52].

Trinity.RDF. Trinity.RDF [67] is a main-memory RDF graph database based on the Trinity [62] distributed graph system. The system was designed to handle large Web scale data. Trinity.RDF introduces graph database specific features that are not available in other RDF stores like random walks and reachability that can be used for data analytics and data mining purposes.

The defining feature for Trinity.RDF is that queries are performed using graph exploration instead of relational joins common in many other RDF stores. This graph exploration is claimed to provide especially good performance compared to current solutions for graph walking queries, which, at the time of writing, shows superior performance compared to state-of-the-art systems in a number queries.

2.4 RDF Store Benchmarks

Since the introduction of RDF stores, a number of benchmark suites ([19,25,37], Waterloo SPARQL Diversity Test Suite (WatDiv) [20], Bio2RDF [26], Yago2 and 3 [46]) have been presented in order to measure RDF stores. The methods used in the benchmark differ somewhat from each other, but most of the benchmarks include at least the measurements *load time* for inserting datasets to the RDF store and the measurements on *query performance* using either synthetic or real world datasets. The accuracy of how well the benchmark measures real world performance has been questioned [30], and therefore, the benchmarks are included in this chapter as they provide a general impression of both the scalability and performance of RDF stores.

One of the earliest RDF benchmarks was the Leigh University Benchmark (LUBM) [37] released in 2005. The benchmark aimed to evaluate the reasoning capabilities and the query performance of RDF storage solutions by using OWL knowledge bases. The datasets used in the benchmarks are generated using an ontology dataset generator, which replicates university setting with triple data relating to professors, students and courses. The test suite provides 14 evaluation queries that can be used in order to evaluate the semantic inference and the reasoning capabilities of RDF stores while at the same time providing execution times for the aforementioned queries. The LUBM group does not provide updated experimental results for RDF stores, but the benchmarking suite has been used by several RDF store developers to compare the performance of their RDF stores against other RDF stores.

Another benchmark suite using synthetic data is the Berlin SPARQL Benchmark (BSBM) [25] that was first presented in 2009. Like LUBM, BSBM measures RDF store query speed using a number of SPARQL queries, but the evaluation is focused on explore and update scenarios in a business intelligence use case. The test suite includes multi-client benchmarks that are performed through a HTTP SPARQL front end in the RDF store.

The SPARQL Performance Benchmark (SP^2Bench) [61] introduced in 2009 uses SPARQL construct operator constellations and broader data access patterns in order to evaluate RDF stores in non-application specific use cases. The SP^2Bench suit uses artificially generated datasets related to publications, with a benchmark end goal to cover a large range of use cases. The SP^2Bench suite uses a total of 17 SPARQL queries in order to benchmark RDF store performance.

DBpedia SPARQL Benchmark [49] is a project that aims to provide a generic SPARQL benchmark creation methodology by using real world datasets. In 2011 [49], Morandi et al. present methods for how they extracted sample data subsets from the DBpedia dataset, and how they from the resulting dataset derive 25 unique SPARQL queries that can be used in order to benchmark the performance of RDF stores.

A table of the different RDF benchmark suites experiments is presented below. From the table, one can note that there are several orders of magnitude differences between the dataset sizes in the different benchmark experiments. The BSBM testing suite experiments are the largest in scale and can therefore be considered the most extensive. In addition to the experiment done by the benchmark creators mentioned above, both individual RDF store developers and independent sources have performed experiments using the different benchmarking suites. As the results of these other experiments are hard to compare in the scope of this chapter, they are not included (Table 4).

Table 4. Comparison of different RDF benchmarks, modified from [49].

	LUBM	SP^2Bench	BSBM v3.0	BSBM v3.1	DBPSD
RDF stores tested	DLDB-OWL, Sesame OWL-JessKB	ARQ, Redland, SDB, Sesame, Virtuoso	Virtuoso, 4store, Jena-TDB, Jena-SDB	BigData, BigOWLIM, Jena-TDB, Virtuoso 6 & 7	Virtuoso, Jena-TDB, BigOWLIM, Sesame
Test data	Syntetic	Syntetic	Syntetic	Syntetic	Real
Dataset size (millions of triples)	0.1–6.9	0.01–1	100, 200	10–150000	14–300
Use case	Universities	DBLP	E-commerce	E-commerce	DBpedia
Classes	43	8	8	8	239 + 300K
Properties	32	22	51	51	1200

In the BSBM v3.0 experiment run in 2010, Virtuoso 6 and 4store were shown to have the best performance of the tested RDF stores with a nearly equal performance in most queries performed. Virtuoso 7 showed the best results in the BSBM v3.1 benchmarks experiment, with Virtuoso 7 showing an order of magnitude better performance compared to the other RDF stores regarding both scalability and query execution time.

One obvious conclusion that can be drawn from the benchmark experiments is that there is a large difference in query execution times and scalability between RDF stores. The performance improvement shown in the Virtuoso 7 compared to other RDF stores and previous versions of Virtuoso can be interpreted as a sign that there is yet much optimization to be done for RDF stores in the future.

3 RDF Stores in the Context of Smart Spaces

The concept of smart spaces was introduced to enable an intelligent interaction of information between entities in both the physical and the virtual environment of an enclosed space. The vision was to build smart spaces that can be seen as a small version of the broader "Internet of things" concept. Considering that a smart space can contain a plethora of different actors producing information in varying domains, the choice of using semantic technologies has become a logical for the implementation of the smart space concept.

Even if the use of semantic technologies can be considered a rather novel feature for the Smart-M3 platform we will use, it also raises a need for efficient RDF data storage and retrieval in order to enable the information sharing inside the smart space environment. The insufficiency of the currently available RDF stores in the Smart-M3 is one of the motivation behind the task of the work done in this chapter; to improve on the storage solution currently used in the Smart-M3 software. The end goal being that the platform can become a viable alternative for use in real world applications. To evaluate the suitability of RDF stores for the smart spaces, we start with an introduction to the Smart-M3 platform followed by the defining of the storage requirement for smart spaces. Lastly, an analysis of how well different RDF stores suit the defined requirements is given.

3.1 RDF Storage in Smart-M3

Smart-M3[3] is an implementation of the smart space concept that originated from a collaboration between the Nokia Corporation and the VTT technical Research Centre of Finland starting in 2006.

The motivation behind the Smart-M3 is to create a **M**ulti-device, **M**ulti-domain and **M**ulti-vendor platform for information sharing between devices and people in smart spaces. Even if the concepts of intelligent rooms or buildings is not in itself a novel concept, most implementation of intelligent spaces on the market are bound to vendor specific devices or are limited to specific types of devices. The idea behind the Smart-M3 platform is to let any device or user

[3] https://github.com/smart-m3, https://sourceforge.net/projects/smart-m3.

belonging to the smart space, regardless of the vendor of the device, to join the smart space and to add to the common information pool. The devices and people, or *knowledge processor* (KP) as they are called in Smart-M3, can share information through a central service in the smart space called a *semantic information broker* (SIB). A depiction of the logical layout of a Smart-M3 environment is presented in Fig. 2 below.

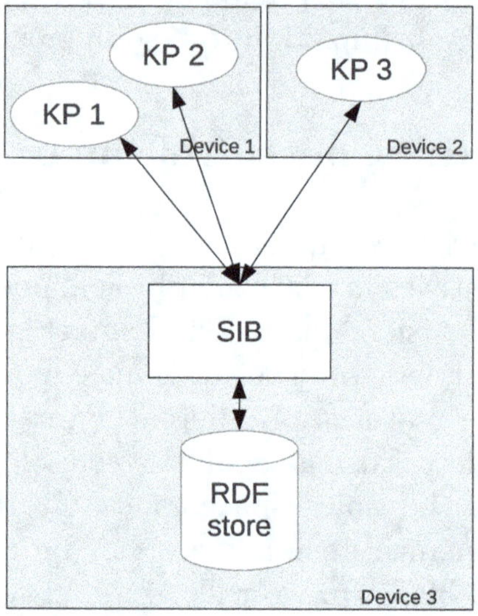

Fig. 2. Smart-M3 overview

The SIBs act as mediators of communication between KPs through the rules and syntax specified in the Smart Space Access Control (SSAP) [8] protocol. The SSAP protocol defines the following operations that a KP can perform on a SIB: *join* the SIB, *leave* the SIB, *subscribe* to changes to certain pieces of information, *unsubscribe* from an active subscription, *add* triple/triples to the SIB, *remove* triple/triples, *update* a triple and *query* the SIB. The most novel of the operations mentioned above are subscribe and unsubscribe[4], which provide the smart space with a publish/subscribe paradigm. This paradigm works through users defining persistent triple matching subscription queries that are triggered whenever a change has occurred in the corresponding triples for the query in the knowledge base. When a subscription is triggered, the SIB notifies the KP that produced the subscription about the changes that has happened related to the subscription since the last notification. In a sense, one can look at it as the SIB notifying the KP that an event has happened in the smart space.

The early use cases for the Smart-M3 were related to intelligent homes [29, 58,59], in which interaction between the devices and the users in the home were made easier by automating events and centralizing how functions of devices were accessible. Since then, other use cases ranging from home entertainment

[4] The OWLIM-SE software suite offers a somewhat similar notification system.

systems [57] to person health monitoring security [45] or bioimaging [28] purposes have been proposed.

As was briefly mentioned earlier, one of the major factors affecting the performance of the Smart-M3 platform is the underlying RDF store that is used in the SIB. Most of the activity in smart space environments involves either adding pieces of information to the knowledge base or accessing the information in the knowledge base. When considering how prevalent these operations are in combination with the large difference in performance of the different RDF stores that were discussed in Sect. 2.3, the choice of storage solution for the Smart-M3 does have impact the performance of the system as a whole.

The earliest versions of the Smart-M3 platform used a RDF store that relied on an embedded MySQL database that was accessed using a specialized domain modeling language. The most recent version of the Smart-M3 SIB, RedSIB, uses the libraries found in the Redland framework [12] for all its data storage needs. Consequently, the Redland storage library gives Smart-M3 access to storage modules that use embedded RDF stores, in-memory RDF stores or native RDF stores. All the RDF storage modules are listed in Table 5 alongside some of the functional and non-functional features for each module.

The default storage module in Redland is the embedded Berkeley DB (BDB) with an enabled hash indexing option. This module is also the default storage option used in the RedSIB software. In the BDB storage module, the triples are mapped to the BDB key-value store with the help of three indices: *SP2O*, *SO2P* and *PO2S*, for which the (S, P, O) resources to the left of the *2* build the *key* and the resource on the right side represents the *value*. The BDB storage solution performs well when small RDF graphs are used, but the scalability of this storage solution is limited by the indexing scheme used. The indexing scheme leads to vast amounts of storage space needed to store large RDF graphs, rendering the module unusable in Smart-M3 environments that contain large knowledge bases. Of the other modules listed in Table 5, Virtuoso is the only full-featured RDF store capable of handling datasets over tens of millions of triples. The Virtuoso storage module includes the option to use an internal query engine for handling SPARQL queries.

3.2 Problems Related to the Existing RDF Stores in RedSIB

In the latest version of RedSIB, the publish/subscribe functionality was implemented with the help of two separate RDF store instances that keep track of triples that have been added and removed. As triples are added to the storage instances, they get matched with the active subscriptions in the SIB in order to evaluate if the subscription should trigger. Caching features are used to limit the overhead that the publish/subscribe functionality causes. Nevertheless, the insertion and the removal of triples become linearly slower with every subscription that is added to the RedSIB [48].

One feature missing in all of the alternatives for the Redland libraries is the lack of scale-out capabilities. As one of the aims has been to create a scalable

Table 5. A feature run down on RDF storage modules provided by the Redland storage library

Module	Storage type	Persistent storage	Scalability	Transaction support	Named graphs	Additional notes
Berkeley DB	Key-value store	Yes	Tested up to 10MT	Yes	Yes	Large disk usage when the indexed option is used
MySQL 3 an 4	RDBMS	Yes	Larger data models	Yes	No	-
PostgreSQL	RDBMS	Yes	Larger data models	Yes	No	Indexed but not optimized
SQLite	RDBMS	Unknown	Unknown	No	Unknown	-
Virtuoso 6	Row-wise RDBMS	Yes	1B+ triples	No	Yes	-
Memory	In-memory	No	Poor	No	Optional	Fast with small models
File	In-memory/file storage	Yes	Poor	No	No	Uses the memory module on a file
URI	In-memory	No	Poor	No	No	Uses the memory module on a file
3store	Triple table	Yes	A few million triples	No	No	Alpha quality support

solution that can be extended when the need for more storage space and processing power is needed, this was concluded to be a desirable function for the RDF store used in RedSIB.

3.3 Previous RDF Store Evaluations for Smart Spaces

The use of RDF stores for smart spaces was explored during the DIEM project in 2011 [53]. In the study, Allegrograph, OWLIM-SE, Virtuoso, 4store and Bigdata were chosen for the evaluation based on the fact that they were identified as capable of handling up to 10 billion triples knowledge bases. The study includes a feature run-through for each of the possible stores with some commentary on the suitability of each store as a part of the smart space environment. At the time of the evaluation, none of the RDF stores provided full SPARQL 1.1 coverage as it was still in draft status. In the evaluation, no conclusive recommendation of what RDF store would fit the Smart-M3 best was made. The major observations made in this direction were that OWLIM-SE was identified as having favourable usability aspects and Virtuoso was noted to show a good query performance. What can be considered an omission in the DIEM study is that the hardware constraints of typical Smart-M3 platforms was not properly taken into account. Even though it is often favourable to run the SIB using low-power commodity hardware that are running all the time, the study only considered RDF store benchmark experiments run on server grade hardware. Furthermore, a great deal of progress has happened in the field of RDF stores since the study was made, warranting a new evaluation of the possible RDF stores.

3.4 Defining Requirements in Smart Spaces

The major factor that has affected the outlining of the requirement definition for the storage solution for the Smart-M3 platform is how well it fits into the vision of a scalable in-house smart space system. The envisioned system implies that the RDF store used in RedSIB should be able to store a large amount of RDF triples, while at the same time it should continue to serve the information sharing needs of the smart space environment. With these assumptions in mind, a conscious decision was made to aid the decision process of choosing an RDF store in a cluster structure that consists of several low-energy hardware nodes. It was therefore concluded that a preference should be made for selecting RDF stores for which the triples in the RDF store could be distributed between the low-energy nodes.

For the evaluation, the feasibility of a centralized clustered in-home SIB box, a hardware prototype (hereafter referenced as prototype) that consists of two ODROID U2 [5] development boards. The boards are based on the Samsung Exynos 5 32-bit ARM architecture chipsets with each board equipped with 2 GB of DDR2 SDRAM and an 8 GB SDCARD memory modules. To be considered in the evaluation, the proposed RDF stores should be able to run on the prototype hardware.

Defining requirements for the RDF stores for the Smart-M3 in this evaluation relies on rough estimates, as no Smart-M3 environment has been created that could give an accurate representation of the storage needs of a large scale smart space environment. As discussed in Sect. 2.3, the properties of the RDF dataset that are used and the type of queries that are normally performed in a smart space setting will affect the performance of the RDF-store. Additionally, the size of the datasets that the underlying RDF store can handle will limit the scalability of the system. To know how the above mentioned factors affect the functionality of the Smart-M3 system, it would be preferable to know in advance what kind of data is to be used in the Smart-M3[5].

The defining factor of many of the use case scenarios is that the system will need to handle frequent small inserts and deletions of triples. For updates of

[5] Unfortunately, for the evaluation in this chapter, no figures for either the performance or the scalability of the future needs of the envisioned large scale smart space environment were available at the outline and the only option was to use estimates.

the knowledge base, this works well in RDF stores that do not need to perform expensive index updates every time the knowledge base has been updated. The frequent updates were identified as a possible concern for the index-based RDF solution for which batched triple inserts and removes are preferred.

For evaluation purposes, it was decided that the RDF stores should at a bare minimum be able to handle an arbitrarily chosen number of ten millions of triples, based on what can be considered to be a reasonable number of triples that a smart space should be able to serve. The criteria for the RDF stores in this evaluation are that they should be able to keep loading this number of triples, while at the same time they should be able to perform simple queries within the millisecond range.

At the outlook the evaluation, there were no hard criteria on how fast queries should be handled in a smart space. As is observable from RDF store benchmarks, it is not unreasonable to expect a modern RDF store to be able to execute simple SPARQL queries in milliseconds. This order of magnitude of query execution times should reasonably be assumed not to incur noticeable delays in the RedSIB software. More complex queries require more execution time and this can potentially slow down the Smart-M3 system due to only one query being processed at a time, effectively leaving the whole system waiting for the query to finish before a new query is performed.

RDF store transaction support was not considered to be an obligatory feature as the Smart-M3 software does not, at the time of writing, have support for transactions. Nevertheless, it is not unreasonable to expect that transactions will become part of future releases of the RedSIB software in order to support transactions, as it is a proven method for handling the reliability and security aspects of sensitive information. For this reason, transaction database operation support was considered as a desirable feature for future use. However, the introduction of transactions in the RedSIB software is out of the scope for the work performed in this chapter.

Even though data persistence and data integrity might not be a hard requirement in all smart space environments, there are certain use cases, such as those involving medical data, for which the integrity of the data in the smart space is of high importance. When considering main memory RDF stores, the recoverability of data in case of machine failure or sudden power loss is an issue that cannot be ignored. However, since the RedSIB software does not currently support reversible transactions, transactional data recoverability was considered a preferable feature of the RDF stores, but not a strict requirement. A reasonable system for making regular back-ups of the data would suffice for the RDF stores.

To ensure that the ethos of openness as pertained for the Smart-M3 project, it was considered mandatory that the RDF store should be provided under both an open-source license, and preferably a free-to-use license. This requirement limits the number of possible RDF stores as many of the more mature RDF stores discussed in Sect. 2.3 that support distributed storage are released under a commercial license.

A non-functional requirement worth mentioning is that due to the limited time frame available for the integration of a new RDF store into the Smart-M3 in combination with the extensive use of the Redland storage library in RedSIB, it is mandatory that the chosen RDF store should be interfacable with the RedSIB software through the Redland storage library. A summary of the requirements and desired features for RDF stores are listed in Table 6 below.

Table 6. Features identified as pertinent when considering an RDF store for smart spaces

Criteria	Requirement
Ease of implementation	Should be implementable in 2 months as part of the RedSIB platform
Hardware criterion	Should run on the prototype hardware
Query language	Should support at least the most essential parts of the SPARQL 1.1 standard
Scalability	Should scale to at least ten million triples. Scale-out feature is preferable
Security	Transaction support is preferable for future needs
Data provenance	Named graphs like feature should be supported for future needs
Data persistence	The storage should as bare minimum offer backups

3.5 RDF Stores Short-List

As was presented in the previous section, there are numerous RDF stores available with both free and commercial licensing options. Considering the requirements listed in Table 6, the list of suitable RDF stores for smart space becomes significantly shorter. Based on these criteria, short-listed promising RDF stores were identified: 4store, Virtuoso, OWLIM, Bigdata and RDF-3X. A discussion on the identified alternatives will follow.

3.6 4store in Smart-M3

4store is one of the few distributed RDF stores that is released under both an open-source and a free-to-use license. 4store has performed favourably in the BSBM version 3.1 experiment, performing on par with Virtuoso 6 for a large number of evaluated queries. An advantage to 4store is that the set up process for 4store back ends is not complicated compared to other RDF stores. Additionally, 4store uses a triple representation that is very close to that used in the Redland libraries, and it uses the Raptor and Rasqal Redland libraries, meaning that the integration of 4store into the Redland storage library can reasonably be assumed to be performed within the allotted time frame.

A concern that was raised for the 4store systems was how well the prototype hardware would handle the heavy use of UMAC 64-bit hashing functions in

4store. The developers of 4store offer no guarantees for the performance and stability of 4store on 32-bit hardware, as 4store has only been tested using 64-bit based systems. Additional concerns were that the 4store software in its current form has some other lack in transaction support and that a large part of the SPARQL 1.1 language is yet to be implemented in 4store.

3.7 Virtuoso in Smart-M3

Virtuoso has shown some of the best query performances in RDF benchmarks of all complete RDF stores, especially version 7 of the software. Virtuoso has also been shown to be able to scale up to datasets over trillions of triples [14]. The compliance with the latest version of SPARQL is also good in Virtuoso, and it can be considered a well-documented system with a sizeable number of active developers working on improving the system. The fact that a storage module for Virtuoso 6 has already been created for the Redland storage library means that adding a Virtuoso option to the RedSIB software is a trivial task. The biggest downside for Virtuoso is, that compared to 4store and Bigdata, that the open source version of the software does not support federation.

3.8 Bigdata in Smart-M3

A third alternative considered was the Bigdata software, which is provided under both open-source and free-to-use license. The software is well-documented, and it showed a comparable performance with both 4store and Virtuoso 6 in the BSBM 3.1 experiment.

A major unfavourable factor when considering Bigdata as RDF store in Smart-M3 is that there is a large difference in the data structures used by Bigdata and the triple representation used in the Redland storage library. Due to the limited time to complete the project, creating the necessary interface between Bigdata and *librdf* was concluded infeasible, and therefore Bigdata had to be discarded as a possible candidate for the project.

3.9 RDF-3X in Smart-M3

The forth storage solution considered was to use a state-of-the-art RDF store in Smart-M3. The most promising alternative was identified as RDF-3X, with the motivation being that it performed well in independent benchmarks and that it had a simple interface. Additionally, it was written in C and it uses a simple triple structure, which would make the implementation of the interface to the Redland libraries considerably easier. The official release of the RDF-3X does not support distributed storage out of the box, but it has been shown that RDF-3X can be used in a cluster setting if it is motivated.

3.10 Choice of RDF Store

The requirements discussed in Sect. 3.4 severely limited the possible alternatives for the selection of an RDF store. Most of the distributed RDF stores that were mature and had good scalability were only available under commercial licenses. The only open-sourced distributed mature RDF stores that are released under a free-to-use license are 4store and Bigdata, which show comparable performance results in internal BSBM tests run on the prototype hardware. Based on the observations presented in this section, a choice was made to integrate 4store as a storage option in the RedSIB software.

4 Implementation and Evaluation

As motivated from previous sections, 4store was identified as the only viable addition to the array of RDF storage options for the Smart-M3 platform and the RDF store was subsequently integrated as a storage option in the RedSIB software during a two month time period. This section presents a rough overview of the integration of 4store into the RedSIB software. This presentation is followed by an evaluation of the implementation in comparison to the default RDF storage option in RedSIB.

4store Integration into Smart-M3. As the RedSIB software almost exclusively uses the Redland libraries for handling all its storage needs, it was a natural choice to integrate 4store to the RedSIB software through the Redland storage library. An overview of the logical structure on how the integration of 4store into Smart-M3 was accomplished is outlined in Fig. 3. The additions that were created are: the 4store C front end, which serves as an interface to the functions in the 4store front end; the 4store Model/Storage inside the Redland storage library, which is used to perform database operations on the 4store back end; and the 4store Query module inside the Redland storage library, which is used to evaluate SPARQL queries on the 4store back ends.

4store C Front End. At the start of the implementation, the only interfaces available for accessing the 4store back ends was either through a HTTPS front end [10] or through a command line front end. As these interfaces are not suitable to be used in the Redland storage library, the first point of action was to create a separate 4store front end with C bindings. The aim with the new front end was to support the functionality of both the 4store Model/Storage module and the 4store Query module. A list of the functionality that the 4store C front end should support is presented below:

- creation of connections to 4store back ends
- addition of individual triples
- bulk insertion of triples
- removal of individual triples

- removal of entire named graphs
- evaluation of SPARQL queries

The front end was implemented as a Linux shared library. The shared library was based on, unrelated to the work done towards this chapter, work done by the Perl Community during a Perl Hackathon event in London 2012. The original library had the functionality of supporting basic triple matching operations and was aimed to be an addition to the Trine framework [11]. As the syntax for RDF::Trine is very similar to that of the Redland storage API, most of the work performed in the original library could be used directly with only minor modifications. The additions made especially for the librdf integration consisted of functionality for adding and removing triples and performing SPARQL queries on 4store back ends. Transactional support was not included as it is not yet supported in 4store, but it could be added to the 4store C front end if the support for it was added to the 4store software in the future.

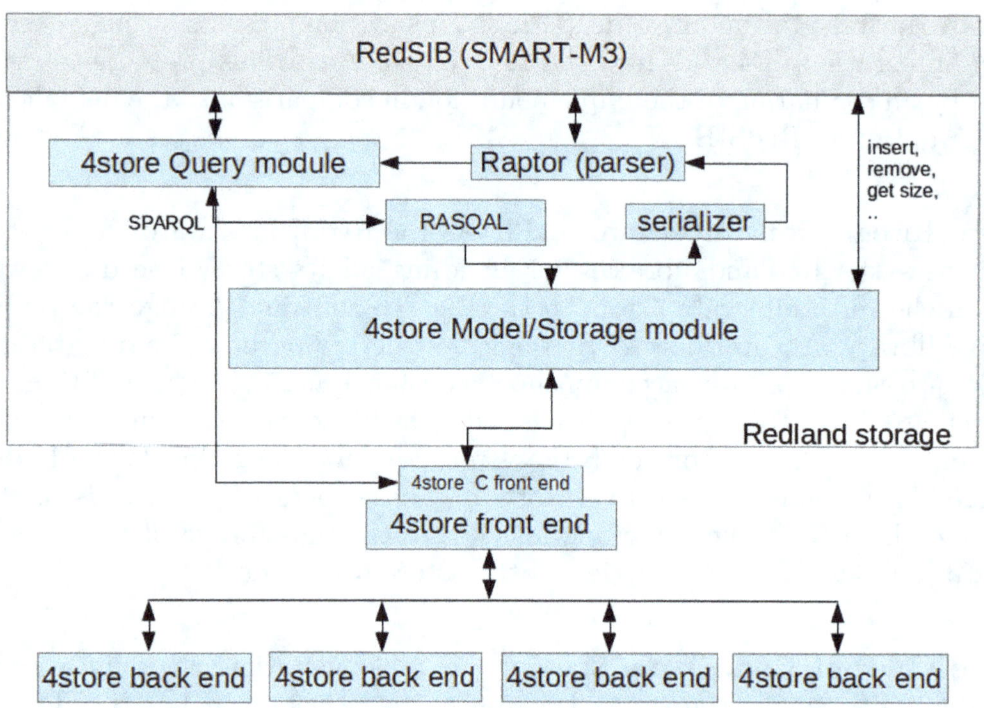

Fig. 3. Logical overview of the integration of 4store into Redland *librdf* and Smart-M3

Integration of 4store into the Redland Libraries. After the appropriate functionality had been added to the 4store C front end, the integration of 4store into the librdf library was started. First the 4store Model/Storage module was integrated and when it was completed, the integration of the 4store Query module followed.

4store uses the Raptor [16] library to parse and serialize RDF data and the RASQAL [17] library to parse SPARQL queries that both are part of the Redland library collection. Additionally, the triple representation structure in the Redland libraries is similar to the ones used in 4store. The similarities alleviated the implementation of a large part of the functions for the 4store Model/Storage and the Query modules as the need for triple representation transform was minimal.

4store Model/Storage Module. The librdf library makes a distinction between Model and Storage. For the access of the underlying storage solution, the librdf library uses two separate modules: a *model* module that works as an interface that the user can call to access the triples and a *storage* module that the model module can call upon to perform operations in the underlying storage solution. Applications create instances of the storage module that can later be bound to an instance of a model module. A more in-depth description of the modules and their functionality can be found in an article by Dave Beckett released in 2001 [23]. For simplicity purposes, the Model and the Storage modules are treated as a single module in this work.

Model/Storage modules inside librdf give a limited number of functions that can be called from applications to perform actions on the underlying storage. The functions can be grouped based on their functionality into actions that are related to the creation, initialization and closing of connections to the underlying storage module, the addition and removal of statements to and from the storage module, fetching of triples from the storage using triple matching patterns and the optional transactional and statement context-related functionality.

The 4store Model/Storage module was implemented in a similar fashion to the respective Virtuoso Model/Storage module. The functions provided in the Model/Storage module are transformed into the appropriate 4store C front end operations that ensure that the relevant actions are performed in the 4store knowledge base.

4store Query Module. The librdf has an internal query handler module in librdf for query processing and an external query module for using the RDF stores own query engine. The librdf internal query processing in librdf is performed by translating the SPARQL query into corresponding RASQAL statements that can be evaluated on the storage module. The functionality of the internal query processing only encompassed a limited set of the SPARQL language with most of the SPARQL 1.1 features yet to be implemented at the moment.

For native RDF stores that implement their own query engine, the internal query processing in librdf can be considerer to be rather inefficient as a result of fact that the query optimization of the query engine in librdf is done based on the in-data structures of the embedded storage modules. In addition to that, the query capabilities of the librdf are limited in functionality compared to query engines in native RDF stores. It was therefore a conscious decision to let the query engine process all the queries for 4store.

When using the 4stores own query engine, the queries are passed directly onto the 4store C front end, in which the 4stores' own query engine evaluates the query. The query bindings that are produced in the 4store query engine are passed back to the Redland query interface where they are processed and serialized. Queries can also be performed through the librdf's internal query engine, but without any guarantees of accuracy and performance of receiving the correct results.

Changes in RedSIB. No major structural changes had to be made inside the RedSIB software. An option to use the 4store module was included in the same fashion as the other storage option, with the exception that the 4store storage instance was set to use the 4stores' own query engine for evaluating SPARQL queries and importing multiple triples to 4store is performed as an bulk operation.

4.1 Experiments

Almost all the functionality that was set out in the planning phase of the work was completed during the allotted time. All the functionality for the 4store storage module in librdf thought of in the planning phase was also indeed implemented. The bulk insert was implemented using the same procedure as in 4store itself. The similarities on how triples handles in both 4store and librdf made the work easier. The major difference was that 4store stores triples as quads, while librdf stores triples as triple statements extended with the context field. This difference was resolved by setting the context resource to the name of the Smart-M3 smart space instance name. In RedSIB, this implies that all triples will be inserted in 4stores with the smart space instance name as the model for all triples.

The evaluation of the implementation non-functional aspects is more difficult, mostly due to the vagueness of the criteria set out in Sect. 3.4. An attempt to measure the query performance and scalability was nonetheless performed using the LUBM data generator [37] and the provided test queries.

LUBM Experiment Setup. The test queries ware performed on the Smart-M3 system using data generated with the LUBM data generator using options for 1 and 10 universities. The LUBM dataset size for one university option consists of approximately 100K triples and the dataset for the ten universities option consists of approximately 1,2 million triples. The 14 text queries from the LUMB test suite was then performed on the Smart-M3 system with the BDB and 4store storage options through the Smart-M3 Python KPI interface.

LUBM Experiment Results. The results from the benchmark are displayed in Figs. 4 and 5 below. Missing from the figure are the results from the BDB option as they could not be produced with that storage option. Even with the smaller dataset, none of the queries could successfully be performed when the BDB storage was used.

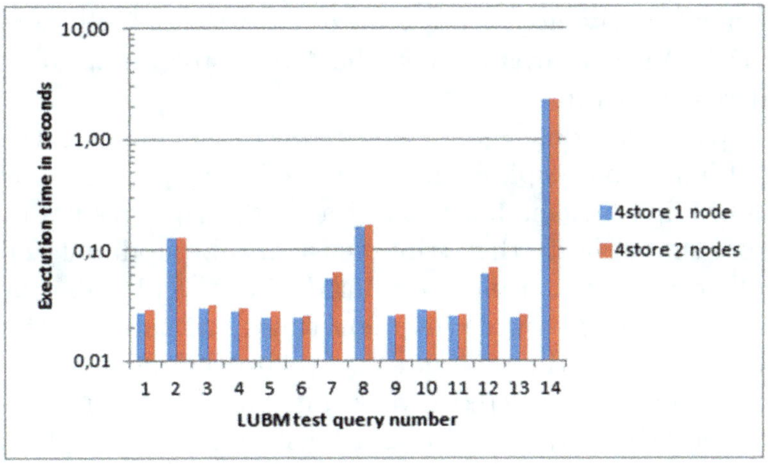

Fig. 4. Experimental run of LUBM test queries for the dataset with one university

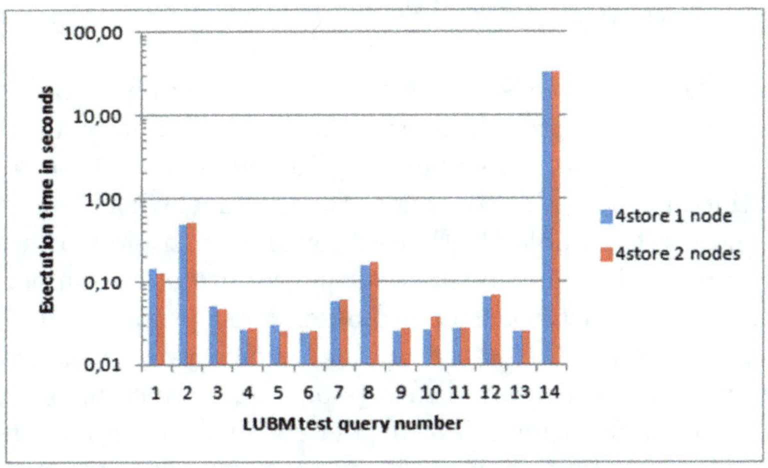

Fig. 5. Experimental run of LUBM test queries for the dataset with ten universities

As can be noted in Figs. 4 and 5 above, the query execution times are not that affected by the number of 4store back end nodes that are used in small to moderately sized datasets. The main advantage of the distributed 4store knowledge base is that it makes the system as a whole capable of storing larger datasets. The inability of the Smart-M3 system with the BDB storage option to produce results even with the smallest dataset clearly points out the limitations of the query capabilities for the default storage option in the Smart-M3.

The implementation of the Smart-M3 query modules can take SPARQL queries and execute them without any major overhead compared to running the queries directly through the other 4store front end. SPARQL UPDATE operations were not implemented in the 4store query module in librdf as the knowledge base modification operations that are already present in the librdf storage module were considered sufficient to serve the needs of the smart space. As can be noted from the experiment results, the 4store storage option in Smart-

M3 can serve significantly larger dataset sizes than the default storage option of the Berkeley DB. With regards to this, the 4store storage option in Smart-M3 can be considered successful.

An unanticipated flaw detected in 4store during the implementation was that the inserting of individual triples is a highly inefficient process compared to the bulk insertion of triples. A modification of a single triple results in that all the indices in 4store that contain that triple must also be updated. This feature of 4store was not properly taken into account during the planning phase, leading to significantly slower single triple insertion times compared to the BDB based storage module. The long time it takes to update the indices of a large 4store knowledge bases can be considered a very unfavourably feature in smart space use cases for which the majority of operations are related to the addition and removal of individual triples.

5 Discussion and Future Work

In this chapter, the RDF store's landscape was outlined based on publicly available literature in Sect. 2.3 and summarized in Table 7. The Smart-M3 platform was introduced and the problems related to the current RDF store in the RedSIB were identified in Sect. 3. According to the findings, when exploring available RDF stores, the most suitable RDF store for the Smart-M3 project was identified as the 4store. The implementation and results of the integration of the chosen system into a Smart Space environment were presented in Sect. 4.

Even if the integration of 4store on the whole system was successful, the 4store had drawbacks that resulted in a poor performance in Smart Space use cases consisting of single triple addition and removal. Therefore, further scalability storage solutions to run efficiently on low-power devices must be studied.

The Smart-M3 system was not able to scale to the lengths envisioned for an off-line ambient intelligence setting. This inability is due to factors outside the scope of the underlying RDF store. The most obvious fault of Smart-M3 is the incapacity to import knowledge bases larger than 60K triples at a time, the limits of the restricted SSAP protocol and the overall instability of the system.

Furthermore, the best suiting RDF store choice is highly dependent on the intended use case. The type of low-energy profile hardware used in Smart Space environments needs a different type of RDF store than for example large scale Web data mining systems. Finding the right RDF store for the use case and the hardware implies knowledge about the system needs before it is built, a task that can be very challenging to predict. Luckily, the RDF framework is very lenient when it comes to migrating from an RDF store to another. This means that several RDF stores need to be evaluated in order to find the right one by using a minimal amount of effort. Future work should evaluate newer RDF stores such as BitMat, MonetDB, TriAD, AdPart, H2RDF, etc. Other benchmark tests may include WatDiv, Bio2RDF, Yago2. While we focused on reasoning capabilities, other RDF store functionality should be further assessed depending on the use case; for instance, evaluating OWL reasoning, filter capabilities, nested queries,

Table 7. List of features for a selection of RDF stores

Name, creator	Storage technique	Programming language	State	Licence	Supported query languages	Distributed storage	Semantics support	Documentation quality	Discussed in this chapter
4store, Garlik	Custom DBMS	C	Open-source development	GPL v3	SPARQL	Yes	None/separate RDFS version	Poor	Yes
5store, Garlik	Custom DBMS	C	Active	Commercial	SPARQL	Yes	Unknown	Not available	No
AllegroGraph, Franz Inc	Graph store	Lisp	Active	Closed source free/ commercial	SPARQL	Free/ commercial	Unknown	Good	No
BigData, SYSTAP LLC		Java	Active	GPL2/ commercial	SPARQL	Yes	RDFS	Decent	Yes
OWLIM-SE, Ontotext		Java	Active	Commercial	SPARQL	Yes	RDFS, OLW Horst and Max, OWL2 QL	Good	Yes
Mulgara	Unknown	Java	Active	OSL-3.0 and Apache v2	SPARQL	Yes	Unknown	Decent	No
Ontobroker, Semafora	3d-party	Java	unknown	Commercial	subset of SPARQL	Yes	RDFS OWL, OWL2	Decent	No
Oracle Spatial and Graph 11g/12c	Oracle DB	Java	active	Commercial	SPARQL	Yes	RDFS OWL2 SKOS	Decent	No
OWLIM-Lite, Ontotext		Java	Active	LGPLv2	SPARQL	No	RDFS, OLW Horst and Max, OWL2 QL and RL	Good	Yes
RDF-3X, Planc institute	Vertex partitioning	C	Academic research	Free for non-commercial use	Limited SPARQL 1.1	Yes	None	Poor	Yes
Virtuoso 6/7, Openlink	Relational table/column graph	C/C++	Active	GPL v2 and commercial	SPARQL	Yes	Limited OWL2	Good	Yes
YARS2	Unknown	Java	Discontinued	Find out	SPARQL	I guess not but could be	None	Poor	To some extent
Trinity.RDF, Microsoft research	Graph database	Java	Research	Unknown	SPARQL 1.1	Yes	Find out	Not available	Yes
Jena TDB	Main memory	Java	Active	Apache 2.0	SPARQL 1.1	Find out	Yes	Good	No
Jena SDB	RDBMS	Java	Active	Commercial	SPARQL 1.1	Find out	Yes	Good	No
RYA	Main memory	Same as Accumulo	Java	Academic research	SPARQL	Yes	No	Poor	No

property paths, etc. For less low-power and less domain specific review on RDF storage and solutions we refer the reader to [34,47,54].

Distributing the knowledge base over several RDF store nodes is not a choice that should be taken lightly. Even though, in theory, the distribution seems to provide a good way in order to achieve scalability in a system, in many cases, the distribution often means adding complexity to the system that cannot be motivated by the upsides of the distributed storage. When dealing with Smart Spaces, one can speculate that in most cases it is best to store the knowledge base on one node and to delay the distribution of RDF stores until the system cannot possibly scale vertically any more. Again, the standardized RDF data format makes the migration to a scalable RDF store easy.

A lot of interesting research is being conducted within both RDF stores and energy-efficient devices. Future work within the context of RDF stores in Smart Spaces would be to further explore a wider array of RDF stores and to investigate how well they perform on a range of low-power hardware suitable for Smart Spaces.

Acknowledgments. The authors acknowledge EU COST Action IC1303 Algorithms, Architectures and Platforms for Enhanced Living Environments (AAPELE www.aapele.eu) within the WG4 - Medical Data Acquisition and Algorithms.

References

1. Allegrograph. http://franz.com/agraph/support/documentation/current/agraph-introduction.html
2. Apache Jena website. https://jena.apache.org/
3. Apache Lucene, a high-performance, full-featured text search library. http://lucene.apache.org/
4. Named graph wikipedia page. http://en.wikipedia.org/wiki/Named_graph
5. Odroid XU development board. http://www.hardkernel.com/main/products/prdt_info.php?g_code=G137510300620
6. OpenRDF Semame website. http://www.openrdf.org/
7. Reduced instruction set computing Wikipedia page. http://en.wikipedia.org/wiki/Reduced_instruction_set_computing
8. Architecture for Sofia Interoperability Platform - Deliverable 5.22: Logical Service Architecture. ARTEMIS JU SP3 D5.22-v1.0, ARTEMIS JUs SP3/100017: Smart Objects For Intelligent Applications (SOFIA), March 2009. http://www.sofia-community.org/files/SOFIA_D5-22-LogicalServiceArchitecture-v1-2011-01-02_0.pdf
9. Oracle NoSQL Database. White Paper, September 2011. http://www.oracle.com/technetwork/database/nosqldb/learnmore/nosql-database-498041.pdf
10. 4store SPARQL HTTP server wiki (2012). http://4store.org/trac/wiki/SparqlServer
11. RDF: Trine - An RDF Framework for Perl. Webpage (2012). http://search.cpan.org/gwilliams/RDF-Trine-1.007/lib/RDF/Trine.pm
12. Redland librdf RDF API: library (2012)
13. Database, bigdata: architecture, May 2013

14. BSBM V3.1 Results, April 2013. http://wifo5-03.informatik.uni-mannheim.de/bizer/berlinsparqlbenchmark/results/V7/index.html
15. Oracle Spatial and Graph: 12c RDF. Semantic graph (2013)
16. Raptor RDF syntax: library (2013)
17. Rasqal RDF query: library (2013)
18. Abadi, D.J., Marcus, A., Madden, S., Hollenbach, K.: SW-store: a vertically partitioned DBMS for Semantic Web data management. VLDB J. **18**(2), 385–406 (2009)
19. Abadi, D.J., Marcus, A., Madden, S.R., Hollenbach, K.: Using the Barton libraries dataset as an RDF benchmark. Technical report, MIT-CSAIL-TR-2007-036, MIT (2007)
20. Aluç, G., Hartig, O., Özsu, M.T., Daudjee, K.: Diversified stress testing of RDF data management systems. In: Mika, P., et al. (eds.) ISWC 2014. LNCS, vol. 8796, pp. 197–212. Springer, Cham (2014). https://doi.org/10.1007/978-3-319-11964-9_13
21. Atre, M., Chaoji, V., Zaki, M.J., Hendler, J.A.: Matrix bit loaded: a scalable lightweight join query processor for RDF data, pp. 41–50(2010)
22. Beauregard, B.: Oracle database 11g semantic technologies. Technical report (2011)
23. Beckett, D.: The design and implementation of the Redland RDF application framework. In: Proceedings of the 10th International Conference on World Wide Web, WWW 2001, pp. 449–456. ACM, New York (2001)
24. Bishop, B., Kiryakov, A., Ognyanoff, D., Peikov, I., Tashev, Z., Velkov, R.: OWLIM: a family of scalable semantic repositories. Technical report (2010)
25. Bizer, C., Schultz, A.: The Berlin SPARQL benchmark. Int. J. Semant. Web Inf. Syst. **5**(2), 1–24 (2009)
26. Callahan, A., Cruz-Toledo, J., Ansell, P., Dumontier, M.: Bio2RDF release 2: improved coverage, interoperability and provenance of life science linked data. In: Cimiano, P., Corcho, O., Presutti, V., Hollink, L., Rudolph, S. (eds.) ESWC 2013. LNCS, vol. 7882, pp. 200–212. Springer, Heidelberg (2013). https://doi.org/10.1007/978-3-642-38288-8_14
27. Chang, F., et al.: Bigtable: a distributed storage system for structured data. ACM Trans. Comput. Syst. **26**(2), 4:1–4:26 (2008)
28. Díaz-Rodríguez, N., Kankaanpää, P., Saleemi, M.M., Lilius, J., Porres, I.: Programming biomedical smart space applications with bioimagexd and pythonrules, pp. 10–11(2011)
29. Rodríguez, N.D., Lilius, J., Cuéllar, M.P., Calvo-Flores, M.D.: Extending semantic web tools for improving smart spaces interoperability and usability. In: Omatu, S., Neves, J., Rodriguez, J.M.C., Paz Santana, J.F., Gonzalez, S.R. (eds.) Distributed Computing and Artificial Intelligence. AISC, vol. 217, pp. 45–52. Springer, Cham (2013). https://doi.org/10.1007/978-3-319-00551-5_6
30. Duan, S., Kementsietsidis, A., Srinivas, K., Udrea, O.: Apples and oranges: a comparison of RDF benchmarks and real RDF datasets. In: Proceedings of the 2011 ACM SIGMOD International Conference on Management of Data, SIGMOD 2011, pp. 145–156. ACM, New York (2011)
31. Erling, O.: Virtuoso, a hybrid RDBMS/graph column store. IEEE Data Eng. Bull. **35**(1), 3–8 (2012)
32. Erling, O., Mikhailov, I.: RDF support in the virtuoso DBMS. In: Pellegrini, T., Auer, S., Tochtermann, S., Schaffert, S. (eds.) Networked Knowledge - Networked Media. SCI, vol. 221, pp. 7–24. Springer, Heidelberg (2009). https://doi.org/10.1007/978-3-642-02184-8_2

33. Erling, O., Mikhailov, I.: Virtuoso: RDF support in a native RDBMS. In: de Virgilio, R., Giunchiglia, F., Tanca, L. (eds.) Semantic Web Information Management, pp. 501–519. Springer, Berlin (2009). https://doi.org/10.1007/978-3-642-04329-1_21
34. Faye, D.C., Curé, O., Blin, G.: A survey of RDF storage approaches. ARIMA J. **15**, 11–35 (2012)
35. Filali, I., Bongiovanni, F., Huet, F., Baude, F.: A survey of structured P2P systems for RDF data storage and retrieval. In: Hameurlain, A., Küng, J., Wagner, R. (eds.) Transactions on Large-Scale Data- and Knowledge-Centered Systems III. LNCS, vol. 6790, pp. 20–55. Springer, Heidelberg (2011). https://doi.org/10.1007/978-3-642-23074-5_2
36. Goasdoué, F., Kaoudi, Z., Manolescu, I., Quiané-Ruiz, J., Zampetakis, S.: CliqueSquare: efficient Hadoop-based RDF query processing. In: Journées de Bases de Données Avancées, BDA 2013, Nantes, France, October 2013
37. Guo, Y., Pan, Z., Heflin, J.: LUBM: a benchmark for OWL knowledge base systems. Web Semant. Sci. Serv. Agents World Wide Web **3**(2–3), 158–182 (2005)
38. Gurajada, S., Seufert, S., Miliaraki, I., Theobald, M.: TriAD: a distributed shared-nothing RDF engine based on asynchronous message passing, pp. 289–300 (2014)
39. Haarslev, V., Hidde, K., Möller, R., Wessel, M.: The RacerPro knowledge representation and reasoning system. Semant. Web **3**(3), 267–277 (2012)
40. Harbi, R., Abdelaziz, I., Kalnis, P., Mamoulis, N., Ebrahim, Y., Sahli, M.: Accelerating SPARQL queries by exploiting hash-based locality and adaptive partitioning. VLDB J. Int. J. Very Large Data Bases **25**(3), 355–380 (2016)
41. Harris, S., Gibbins, N.: 3store: efficient bulk RDF storage, June 2003
42. Harris, S., Lamb, N., Shadbolt, N.: 4store: the design and implementation of a clustered RDF store. In: Scalable Semantic Web Knowledge Base Systems, SSWS 2009, pp. 94–109 (2009)
43. Harth, A., Decker, S.: Optimized index structures for querying RDF from the web. In: Proceedings of the Third Latin American Web Congress, LA-WEB 2005, Washington, DC, USA, p. 71. IEEE Computer Society (2005)
44. Haslhofer, B., Roochi, E.M., Schandl, B., Zander, S.: Europeana RDF store report. Technical report. University of Vienna, Vienna, March 2011
45. Hosseinzadeh, S., Virtanen, S., Díaz-Rodríguez, N., Lilius, J.: A semantic security framework and context-aware role-based access control ontology for smart spaces, p. 8 (2016)
46. Mahdisoltani, F., Biega, J., Suchanek, F.M.: YAGO3: a knowledge base from multilingual Wikipedias. In: CIDR (2013)
47. Modoni, G.E., Sacco, M., Terkaj, W.: A survey of RDF store solutions. In: 2014 International Conference on Engineering, Technology and Innovation (ICE), pp. 1–7, June 2014
48. Morandi, F., Roffia, L., D'Elia, A., Vergari, F., Cinotti, S.T.: RedSib: a smart-M3 semantic information broker implementation. In: Balandin, S., Ovchinnikov, A. (eds.) Proceedings of the 12th Conference of Open Innovations Association FRUCT, Oulu, Finland, pp. 86–98. State University of Aerospace Instrumentation (SUAI), November 2012
49. Morsey, M., Lehmann, J., Auer, S., Ngomo, A.-C.N.: DBpedia SPARQL benchmark - performance assessment with real queries on real data. In: ISWC 2011 (2011)
50. Murray, C.: Oracle® spatial resource description framework (RDF). Technical report, July 2005. http://download.oracle.com/otndocs/tech/semantic_web/pdf/rdfrm.pdf

51. Neumann, T., Weikum, G.: The RDF-3X engine for scalable management of RDF data. VLDB J. **19**(1), 91–113 (2010)
52. Neumann, T., Weikum, G.: x-RDF-3X: fast querying, high update rates, and consistency for RDF databases. Proc. VLDB Endow. **3**(1–2), 256–263 (2010)
53. Oraskari, J., Törmä, S.: Smart–M3 storage solutions. Aalto University, Department of Computer Science and Engineering, July 2011
54. Özsu, M.T.: A survey of rdf data management systems. Front. Comput. Sci. **10**(3), 418–432 (2016)
55. Papailiou, N., Konstantinou, I., Tsoumakos, D., Karras, P., Koziris, N.: H_2 RDF+: high-performance distributed joins over large-scale RDF graphs, pp. 255–263. IEEE (2013)
56. Rohloff, K., Schantz, R.E.: High-performance, massively scalable distributed systems using the MapReduce software framework: the SHARD triple-store. In: PSI EtA, p. 4 (2010)
57. Saleemi, M.M., Díaz-Rodríguez, N., Lilius, J.: Erratum to: exploiting smart spaces for interactive TV applications development. J. Supercomput. **70**(3), 1617 (2014)
58. Mohsin Saleemi, M., Díaz Rodríguez, N., Lilius, J., Porres, I.: A framework for context-aware applications for smart spaces. In: Balandin, S., Koucheryavy, Y., Hu, H. (eds.) NEW2AN/ruSMART -2011. LNCS, vol. 6869, pp. 14–25. Springer, Heidelberg (2011). https://doi.org/10.1007/978-3-642-22875-9_2
59. Saleemi, M.M., Suenson, E., Lilius, J., Porres, I.: Ontology driven smart space application development. In: Semantic Interoperability: Issues, Solutions, and Challenges, pp. 101–125 (2012)
60. Salvadores, M., Correndo, G., Harris, S., Gibbins, N., Shadbolt, N.: The design and implementation of minimal RDFS backward reasoning in 4store. In: Antoniou, G., et al. (eds.) ESWC 2011. LNCS, vol. 6644, pp. 139–153. Springer, Heidelberg (2011). https://doi.org/10.1007/978-3-642-21064-8_10
61. Schmidt, M., Hornung, T., Lausen, G., Pinkel, C.: SP2Bench: a SPARQL performance benchmark. CoRR, abs/0806.4627 (2008)
62. Shao, B., Wang, H., Li, Y.: Trinity: a distributed graph engine on a memory cloud. In: Proceedings of the 2013 ACM SIGMOD International Conference on Management of Data, SIGMOD 2013, pp. 505–516. ACM, New York (2013)
63. Sidirourgos, L., Goncalves, R., Kersten, M., Nes, N., Manegold, S.: Column-store support for RDF data management: not all swans are white. Proc. VLDB Endow. **1**(2), 1553–1563 (2008)
64. Stegmaier, F., Gröbner, U., Döller, M., Kosch, H., Baese, G.: Evaluation of current RDF database solutions. In: Proceedings of the 10th International Workshop on Semantic Multimedia Database Technologies (SeMuDaTe), 4th International Conference on Semantics and Digital Media Technologies (SAMT) (2009)
65. Thompson, B.: Literature Survey of Graph Databases, January 2013. http://www.systap.com/pubs/graph_databases.pdf
66. Wilkinson, K.: Jena property table implementation. In: SSWS, Athens, Georgia, USA, pp. 35–46 (2006)
67. Zeng, K., Yang, J., Wang, H., Shao, B., Wang, Z.: A distributed graph engine for web scale RDF data. Proc. VLDB Endow. **6**(4), 265–276 (2013)

Combining Machine Learning and Metaheuristics Algorithms for Classification Method PROAFTN

Feras Al-Obeidat[1], Nabil Belacel[2(✉)], and Bruce Spencer[3]

[1] Zayed University, Abu-Dhabi, UAE
[2] Digital Technology Research Center, National Research Council, Ottawa, Canada
nabil.belacel@nrc-cnrc.gc.ca
[3] University of New Brunswick, Fredericton, Canada

Abstract. The supervised learning classification algorithms are one of the most well known successful techniques for ambient assisted living environments. However the usual supervised learning classification approaches face issues that limit their application especially in dealing with the knowledge interpretation and with very large unbalanced labeled data set. To address these issues fuzzy classification method PROAFTN was proposed. PROAFTN is part of learning algorithms and enables to determine the fuzzy resemblance measures by generalizing the concordance and discordance indexes used in outranking methods. The main goal of this chapter is to show how the combined meta-heuristics with inductive learning techniques can improve performances of the PROAFTN classifier. The improved PROAFTN classifier is described and compared to well known classifiers, in terms of their learning methodology and classification accuracy. Through this chapter we have shown the ability of the metaheuristics when embedded to PROAFTN method to solve efficiency the classification problems.

Keywords: Machine learning · Supervised learning · PROAFTN Metaheuristics

1 Introduction

In this chapter we introduce and compare various algorithms which have been used to enhance the performance of the classification method PROAFTN. It is a supervised learning that learns from a training set and builds set of prototypes to classify new objects [10,11]. The supervised learning classification methods have been applied extensively in Ambient Assisted Living (AAL) from sensors' generated data [36]. The enhanced algorithm can be used for instance to activity recognition and behavior analysis in AAL on sensors data [43]. It can be applied for the classification of daily living activities in a smart home using the generated sensors data [36]. Hence, the enhanced PROAFTN classifier can be integrated to active and assisted living systems as well as for smart homes

I. Ganchev et al. (Eds.): Enhanced Living Environments, LNCS 11369, pp. 53–79, 2019.
https://doi.org/10.1007/978-3-030-10752-9_3

health care monitoring frameworks as any classifiers used in the comparative study presented in this chapter [47]. This chapter is concerned with the supervised learning methods where the given samples or objects have known class labels called also training set, and the target is to build a model from these data to classify unlabeled instances called testing data. We focus on the classification problems in which classes are identified with discrete, or nominal, values indicating for each instance to which class it belongs, among the classes residing in the data set [21,60]. Supervised classification problems require a classification model that identifies the behaviors and characteristics of the available objects or samples called training set. This model is then used to assign a predefined class to each new object [31]. A variety of research disciplines such as statistics [60], Multiple Criteria Decision Aid (MCDA) [11,22] and artificial intelligence have addressed the classification problem [39]. The field of MCDA [10,63] includes a wide variety of tools and methodologies developed for the purpose of helping a decision model (DM) to select from finite sets of alternatives according to two or more criteria [62]. In MCDA, the classification problems can be distinguished from other classification problems within the machine learning framework from two perspectives [2]. The first includes the characteristics describing the objects, which are assumed to have the form of decision criteria, providing not only a description of the objects but also some additional preferential information associated with each attribute [22,51]. The second includes the nature of the classification pattern, which is defined in both ordinal, known as sorting [35], and nominal, known as multicriteria classification [10,11,63]. Classification based machine learning models usually fail to tackle these issues, focusing basically on the accuracy of the results obtained from the classification algorithms [62].

This chapter is devoted to the classification method based on the preference relational models known as outranking relational models as described by Roy [52] and Vincke [59]. The method presented in this paper employs a partial comparison between the objects to be classified and prototypes of the classes on each attribute. Then, it applies a global aggregation using the concordance and non-discordance principle [45]. Therefore it avoids resorting to conventional distance that aggregates the score of all attributes in the same value unit. Hence, it helps to overcome some difficulties encountered when data is expressed in different units and to find the correct preprocessing and normalization data methods. The PROAFTN method uses concordance and non-discordance principle that belongs to MCDA field developed by Roy [52,54]. Moreover, Zopounidis and Doumpos [63] dividing the classification problems based on MCDA into two categories: sorting problems for methods that utilize preferential ordering of classes and multicriteria classification for nominal sorting there is no preferential ordering of classes. In MCDA field the PROAFTN method is considered as nominal sorting or multicriteria classification [10,63]. The main characteristic of multicriteria classification is that the classification models do not automatically result only from the training set but depend also on the judgment of an expert. In this chapter we will show how techniques from machine learning and optimization can determine the accurate parameters for fuzzy the classification method

PROAFTN [11]. When applying PROAFTN method, we need to learn the value of some parameters, in case of our proposed method we have boundaries of intervals that define the prototype profiles of the classes, the attributes' weights, *etc.* To determine the attributes' intervals, PROAFTN applies the discretization technique as described by Ching *et al.* [20] from a set of pre-classified objects presenting a training set [13]. Even-though these approaches offer good quality solutions, they still need considerable computational time. The focus of this chapter concerns the application of different optimization techniques based on meta-heuristics for learning PROAFTN method. To apply PROAFTN method over very large data, there are many parameters to be set. If one were to use the exact optimization methods to infer these parameters, the computational effort that would be required is an exponential function of the problem size. Therefore, it is sometimes necessary to abandon the search for the optimal solution, using deterministic algorithms, and simply seek a good solution in a reasonable computational time, using meta-heuristics algorithms. In this paper, we will show how inductive learning method based on meta-heuristic techniques can lead to the efficient multicriteria classification data analysis.

The major characteristics of the multicriteria classification method compared with other well known classifiers can be summarized as follows:

- The PROAFTN method can apply two learning approaches: deductive or knowledge based and inductive learning. In the deductive approach, the expert has the role of establishing the required parameters for the studied problem for example the experts' knowledge or rules can be expressed as intervals, which can be implemented easily to build the prototype of the classes. In the inductive approach, the parameters and the classification models are obtained and learned automatically from the training dataset.
- PROAFTN uses the outranking and preference modeling as proposed by Roy [52] and it hence can be used to gain understanding about the problem domain.
- PROAFTN uses fuzzy sets for deciding whether an object belongs to a class or not. The fuzzy membership degree gives an idea about its weak and strong membership to the corresponding classes.

The overriding goal of this study is to present a generalized framework to learn the classification method PROAFTN. And then compare the performance and the efficiency of the learned method against well-known machine learning classifiers.

We shall conclude that the integration of machine learning techniques and meta-heuristic optimization to PROAFTN method will lead to significantly more robust and efficient data classification tool.

The rest of the chapter is organized as follows: Sect. 2 overviews the PROAFTN methodology and its notations. Section 3 explains the generalized learning framework for PROAFTN. In Sect. 4 the results of our experiments are reported. Finally, conclusions and future work are drawn in Sect. 5.

2 PROAFTN Method

This section describes the PROAFTN procedure, which belongs to the class of supervised learning to solve classification problems. Based on fuzzy relations between the objects being classified and the prototype of the classes, it seeks to define a membership degree between the objects and the classes of the problem [11]. The PROAFTN method is based on outranking relation as an alternative to the Euclidean distance through the calculation of an indifference index between the object to be assigned and the prototype of the classes obtained through the training phase. Hence, to assign an object to the class PROAFTN follow the rule known as concordance and no discordance principle as used by the outranking relations: if the object a is judged indifferent or similar to prototype of the class according to the majority of attributes "concordance principle" and there is no attribute uses its veto against the affirmation "a is an indifferent to this prototype" "no-discordance principal", the object a is considered indifferent to this prototype and it should be assigned to the class of this prototype [11,52].

PROAFTN has been applied to the resolution of many real-world practical problems such as acute leukemia diagnosis [14], asthma treatment [56], cervical tumor segmentation [50], Alzheimer diagnosis [18], e-Health [15] and in optical fiber design [53], asrtocytic and bladder tumors grading by means of computer-aided diagnosis image analysis system [12] and it was also applied to image processing and classification [1]. PROAFTN also has been applied for intrusion detection and analyzing Cyber-attacks [24,25]. Singh and Arora [55] present an interesting application of fuzzy classification PROAFTN to network intrusion detection. In this paper authors find that PROAFTN outperforms the well known classifier Support Vector Machine [55]. The following subsections describe the notations, the classification methodology, and the inductive approach used by PROAFTN.

2.1 PROAFTN Notations

The PROAFTN notations used in this paper are presented in Table 1.

2.2 Fuzzy Intervals

Let A represents a set of objects known as a training set. Consider a new object a to be classified. Let a be described by a set of m attributes $\{g_1, g_2, ..., g_m\}$. Let the k classes be $\{C^1, C^2, ..., C^k\}$. The different steps of the procedure are as follows:

For each class C^h, a set L_h of prototypes is determined. For each prototype b_i^h and each attribute g_j, an interval $[S_j^1(b_i^h),\ S_j^2(b_i^h)]$ is defined where $S_j^2(b_i^h) \geq S_j^1(b_i^h)$. Two thresholds $d_j^1(b_i^h)$ and $d_j^2(b_i^h)$ are introduced to define the fuzzy intervals: the pessimistic interval $[S_j^1(b_i^h), S_j^2(b_i^h)]$ and the optimistic interval $[S_j^1(b_i^h)-d_j^1(b_i^h), S_j^2(b_i^h)+d_j^2(b_i^h)]$. The pessimistic intervals are determined by applying discretization techniques from the training set as described in [26,28].

Table 1. Notations and parameters used by the PROAFTN method

A	Set of objects with known labels $\{a_1, a_2, ..., a_n\}$ the preassigned objects (training set)
$\{g_1, g_2, ..., g_m\}$	Set of m attributes:
Ω	set of k classes such as: $\Omega = \{C^1, C^2, ..., C^k\}$, $k \geq 2$
B^h	Prototype set of hth category, where $B^h = \{b_i^h \mid h = 1, ..., k, i = 1, ..., L_h\}$
B	Set of all prototypes, such as $B = \bigcup_{h=1}^{k} B^h$
$[S_j^1(b_i^h),\ S_j^2(b_i^h)]$	The interval of the prototype b_i^h for each attribute g_j in class C^h with $j = 1, 2, ..., m$
$d_j^1(b_i^h)$ and $d_j^2(b_i^h)$	The preference thresholds belong to b_i^h for each attribute g_j in class C^h
w_{jh}	The weight of attribute g_j for the class C^h

The classical data mining techniques, such as decision tree, numerical domains "continuous numeric values" into intervals and the discretized intervals are treated as ordinal "discretized" values during induction. Ramírez-Gallego *et al.* [29] present more details on different approaches used for data discretization in machine learning. In our case the discretized intervals are treated as intervals and they are not treated as discrete value. As a result, PROAFTN avoids losing information in the induction process and also can use both inductive and deductive learning without transforming the continue values to discrete data. In deductive learning, the rules in our case can also be given by interacting with the expert in the form of ranges or intervals, and then can be optimized during the learning process. Figure 2 depicts the representation of PROAFTN's intervals. To apply PROAFTN, the pessimistic interval $[S_{jh}^1, S_{jh}^2]$ and the optimistic interval $[q_{jh}^1, q_{jh}^2]$ [13] of each attribute in each class need to be determined. Figure 2 depicts the representation of PROAFTN's intervals. When evaluating a certain quantity or a measure with a regular or crisp interval, there are two extreme cases, which we should try to avoid. It is possible to make a pessimistic evaluation, but then the interval will appear wider. It is also possible to make an optimistic evaluation, but then there will be a risk of the output measure to get out of limits of the resulting narrow interval, so that the reliability of obtained results will be doubtful. To overcome this problem we have introduced fuzzy approach to features' or criteria evaluation as presented in Fig. 1 [16]. They permit to have simultaneously both pessimistic and optimistic representations of the studied measure [23]. This is why we introduce the thresholds $d1$ and $d2$ for each attribute to define in the same time the both pessimistic interval $[S_j^1(b_i^h), S_j^2(b_i^h)]$ and the optimistic interval $[S_j^1(b_i^h) - d_j^1(b_i^h), S_j^2(b_i^h) + d_j^2(b_i^h)]$ [13]. The carrier of a fuzzy interval (from S1 minus d1 to S2 plus d2) will be chosen so that it guarantees not to override the considered quantity over necessary limits, and the kernel (S1 to S2) will contain the most true-like values [61]. To apply PROAFTN, the

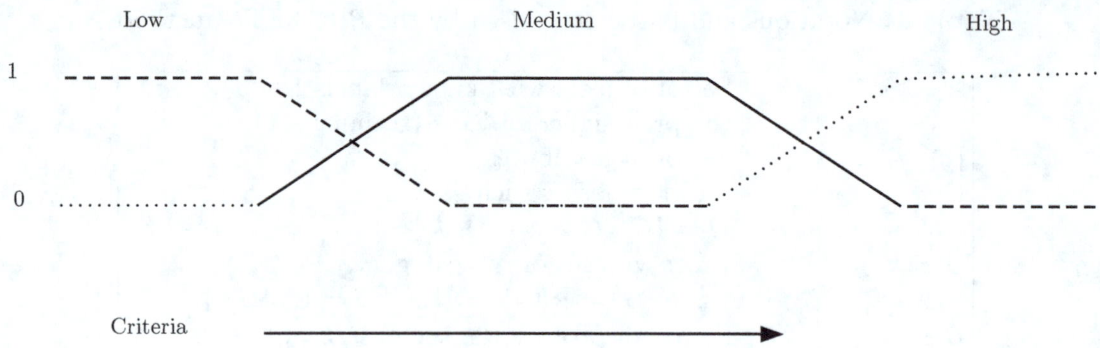

Fig. 1. Fuzzy approach for features evaluation

pessimistic interval $[S_{jh}^1, S_{jh}^2]$ and the optimistic interval $[q_{jh}^1, q_{jh}^2]$ [13] for each attribute in each class need to be determined, where:

$$q_{jh}^1 = S_{jh}^1 - d_{jh}^1 \qquad q_{jh}^2 = S_{jh}^2 + d_{jh}^2 \tag{1}$$

applied to:

$$q_{jh}^1 \leq S_{jh}^1 \qquad q_{jh}^2 \geq S_{jh}^2 \tag{2}$$

Hence, $S_{jh}^1 = S_j^1(b_i^h)$, $S_{jh}^2 = S_j^2(b_i^h)$, $q_{jh}^1 = q_j^1(b_i^h)$, $q_{jh}^2 = q_j^2(b_i^h)$, $d_{jh}^1 = d_j^1(b_i^h)$, and $d_{jh}^2 = d_j^2(b_i^h)$. The following subsections explain the stages required to classify the testing object a to the class C^h using PROAFTN.

2.3 Computing the Fuzzy Indifference Relation

The initial stage of classification procedure is performed by calculating the fuzzy indifference relation $I(a, b_i^h)$ or also called the fuzzy resemblance measure. The fuzzy indifference relation is based on the concordance and non-discordance principle which represents the relationship (membership degree) between the object to be assigned and the prototype [10,11]; it is formulated as:

$$I(a, b_i^h) = \left(\sum_{j=1}^{m} w_{jh} C_{jh}^i(a, b_i^h) \right) \prod_{j=1}^{m} \left(1 - D_{jh}^i(a, b_i^h)^{w_{jh}}\right) \tag{3}$$

where w_{jh} is the weight that measures the importance of a relevant attribute g_j of a specific class C^h:

$$w_{jh} \in [0, 1], \quad \text{and} \quad \sum_{j=1}^{m} w_{jh} = 1$$

$C_{jh}^i(a, b_i^h)$ is the degree that measures the closeness of the object a to the prototype b_i^h according to the attribute g_j.

$$C_{jh}^i(a, b_i^h) = \min\{C_{jh}^1(a, b_{i1}^h), C_{jh}^{i2}(a, b_i^h)\}, \tag{4}$$

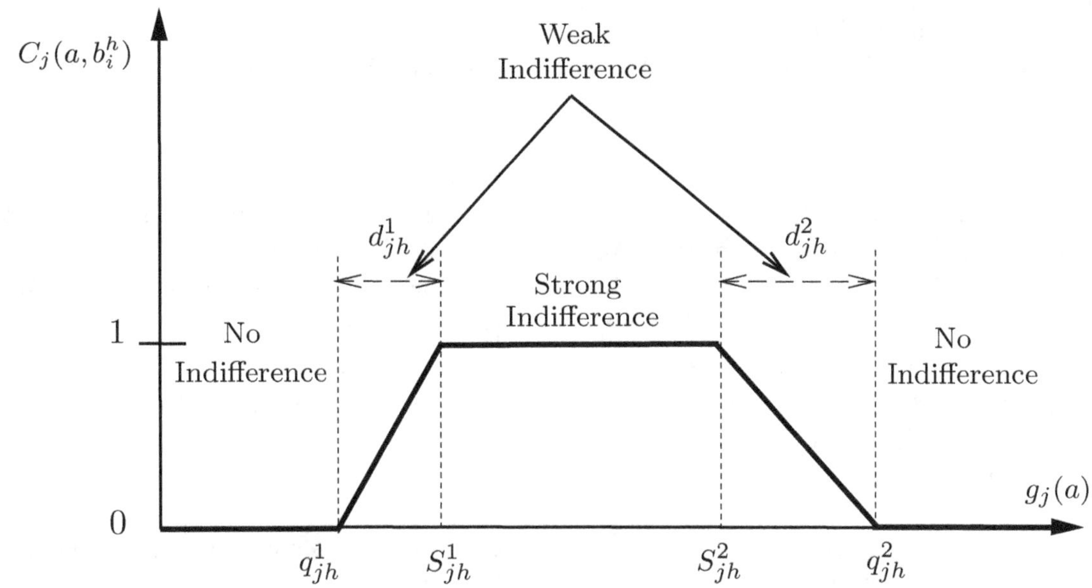

Fig. 2. Graphical representation of the partial indifference concordance index between the object a and the prototype b_i^h represented by intervals.

where

$$C_{jh}^{i1}(a, b_i^h) = \frac{d_j^1(b_i^h) - \min\{S_j^1(b_i^h) - g_j(a), d_j^1(b_i^h)\}}{d_j^1(b_i^h) - \min\{S_j^1(b_i^h) - g_j(a), 0\}}$$

and

$$C_{jh}^{i2}(a, b_i^h) = \frac{d_j^2(b_i^h) - \min\{g_j(a) - S_j^2(b_i^h), d_j^2(b_i^h)\}}{d_j^2(b_i^h) - \min\{g_j(a) - S_j^2(b_i^h), 0\}}$$

$D_{jh}^i(a, b_i^h)$, is the discordance index that measures how far the object a is from the prototype b_i^h according to the attribute g_j. Two veto thresholds $v_j^1(b_i^h)$ and $v_j^2(b_i^h)$ [11], are used to define this value, where the object a is considered perfectly different from the prototype b_i^h based on the value of attribute g_j. In general, the value of veto thresholds are determined by an expert familiar with problem. In this study the effect of the veto thresholds is not considered and only the concordance principle is used, so Eq. (3) is summarized by:

$$I(a, b_i^h) = \sum_{j=1}^{m} w_{jh} C_{jh}^i(a, b_i^h) \tag{5}$$

For more illustrations, the three comparative cases between the object a and prototype b_i^h according to the attribute g_j are obtained (Fig. 2):

- case 1 (strong indifference):
  $C_{jh}^i(a, b_i^h) = 1 \Leftrightarrow g_j(a) \in [S_{jh}^1, S_{jh}^2]$; (*i.e.*, $S_{jh}^1 \leq g_j(a) \leq S_{jh}^2$)
- case 2 (no indifference):
  $C_{jh}^i(a, b_i^h) = 0 \Leftrightarrow g_j(a) \leq q_{jh}^1$, or $g_j(a) \geq q_{jh}^2$

- case 3 (weak indifference):
  The value of $C^i_{jh}(a, b^h_i) \in (0, 1)$ is calculated based on Eq. (4). (*i.e.*, $g_j(a) \in [q^1_{jh}, S^1_{jh}]$ or $g_j(a) \in [S^2_{jh}, q^2_{jh}]$)

The partial fuzzy indifference relation is represented by the trapezoidal membership function. This type of functions are well studied in the references [42] and [9]. Table 2 presents the performance matrix which is used to evaluate the prototype of classes on a set of attributes. The rows of the matrix represent the prototypes of the classes and the columns represent the attributes. The intersection between the row i and the column j corresponds to the partial indifference relation $C^i_{jh}(a, b^h_i)$ between the prototype b^h_i and the object a to be assigned according to the attribute g_j.

Table 2. Performance matrix of prototypes of the class C^h according to their partial fuzzy indifference relation with an object a to be classified.

	g_1	g_2	...	g_j	...	g_m
b^1_1	$C^1_{11}(a, b^1_1)$	$C^1_{21}(a, b^1_1)$	...	$C^1_{j1}(a, b^1_1)$	...	$C^1_{m1}(a, b^1_1)$
b^1_2	$C^2_{11}(a, b^1_2)$	$C^2_{21}(a, b^1_2)$	...	$C^2_{j1}(a, b^1_2)$	...	$C^2_{m1}(a, b^1_2)$
$\vdots$	$\vdots$	$\vdots$	...	$\vdots$	...	$\vdots$
b^h_i	$C^i_{1h}(a, b^h_i)$	$C^i_{2h}(a, b^h_i)$	...	$C^i_{jh}(a, b^h_i)$	...	$C^i_{mh}(a, b^h_i)$
$\vdots$	$\vdots$	$\vdots$	...	$\vdots$	...	$\vdots$
$b^k_{L_k}$	$C^{L_k}_{1k}(a, b^k_{L_k})$	$C^{L_k}_{2k}(a, b^k_{L_k})$	...	$C^{L_k}_{jk}(a, b^k_{L_k})$	...	$C^{L_k}_{mk}(a, b^k_{L_k})$

2.4 Evaluation of the Membership Degree

The membership degree $\delta(a, C^h)$ between the object a and the class C^h is calculated based on the indifference degree between a and its closest neighbor in the set of prototype B^h of the class C^h. To calculate the degree of membership of the object a to the class C^h, PROAFTN apply the formulae given by the Eq. 6.

$$\delta(a, C^h) = \max\{I(a, b^h_1), I(a, b^h_2), ..., I(a, b^h_{L_h})\} \tag{6}$$

2.5 Assignment of an Object to the Class

Once the membership degree of the testing "unlabeled" object a is calculated, the PROAFTN classifier will assign this object to the right class C^h by following the decision rule given by Eq. 7.

$$a \in C^h \Leftrightarrow \delta(a, C^h) = \max\{\delta(a, C^i)/i \in \{1, ..., k\}\} \tag{7}$$

3 Introduced Meta-heuristic Algorithms for Learning PROAFTN

The classification procedure used by PROAFTN to assign objects to the preferred classes is summarized in Algorithm 1.

Algorithm 1. PROAFTN classification procedure.

Input:A: set of objects; K: the number of classes; w_j^h the weight of the attribute j of the class h. A is divided into training and testing sets.
Output:$\delta(a, C^h)$: the membership degree of object a to class C^h
Step 1: Building the classification model for PROAFTN:
Assign a relative importance weights $w_j^h, j = 1, .., m; h = 1, ..., k$ to the attributes;
From the training set : Apply the discretization and inductive algorithm to build the prototype of the classes as in [7,16]. Each prototype b_h^i is defined by m attributes $g_j, j = 1, .., m$ with its score in each attribute is defined by two intervals: - pessimistic:$[S_j^1(b_i^h), S_j^2(b_i^h)]$; and - optimistic $[d_j^1(b_i^h), d_j^2(b_i^h)]$ as presented in Fig. 2.
Step 2: Compute the indifference relation between the object a and the prototype b_i^h of the class h:

$$I(a, b_i^h) = \sum_{j=1}^{m} w_j^h C_j(a, b_i^h) \tag{8}$$

$$C_j(a, b_i^h) = \min\{C_j^1(a, b_i^h), C_j^2(a, b_i^h)\}, \tag{9}$$

where

$$C_j^1(a, b_h^i) = \frac{d_j^1(b_i^h) - \min\{S_j^1(b_h^i) - g_j(a), d_j^1(b_i^h)\}}{d_j^1(b_i^h) - \min\{S_j^1(b_h^i) - g_j(a), 0\}},$$

$$C_j^2(a, b_h^i) = \frac{d_j^2(b_i^h) - \min\{g_j(a) - S_j^2(b_h^i), d_j^2(b_i^h)\}}{d_j^2(b_i^h) - \min\{g_j(a) - S_j^2(b_h^i), 0\}}$$

Step 3: Evaluation of the membership degree:

$$\delta(a, C^h) = \max\{I(a, b_1^h), I(a, b_2^h), ..., I(a, b_{L_h}^h)\} \tag{10}$$

Step 3: Assign the object a to the class:

$$a \in C^h \Leftrightarrow \delta(a, C^h) = \max\{\delta(a, C^i)/i \in \{1, ..., k\}\} \tag{11}$$

The rest of the chapter is to present the different methodologies based on machine learning and metaheuristic techniques for learning the classification method PROAFTN from data. The goal of the development of such methodologies is to obtain, from the training data set, the PROAFTN parameters that achieve the highest classification accuracy by applying the Algorithm 1. For this purpose, different learning methodologies are summarized in the following subsections.

3.1 Learn and Improve PROAFTN Based on Machine Learning Techniques

In [7,13], new methods were proposed to learn and improve PROAFTN based on machine learning techniques. The proposed learning methods consist of two stages: the first stage involves using a novel discretization technique to obtain the required parameters for PROAFTN, and the second stage is the development of a new inductive approach to construct PROAFTN prototypes for classification. Three unsupervised discretization methods – Equal Width Binning (EWB), Equal Frequency Binning (EFB) and k-Means – were used to establish PROAFTN parameters as described in algorithm. Algorithm 2 explains the utilization of discretization techniques and Chebyshev's theorem to obtain the parameters $\{S^1, S^2, d^1, d^2\}$ for PROAFTN. Firstly, the discretization technique is used to initially obtain the intervals $\{S^1_{jh}, S^2_{jh}\}$ for each attribute in each class. Secondly, Chebyshev's theorem is utilized to tune the generated intervals by discretization technique to obtain $\{d^1_{jh}, d^2_{jh}\}$ [16].

Algorithm 2. Developed techniques to obtain $\{S^1, S^2, d^1, d^2\}$

$z \leftarrow$ Number of classes
$m \leftarrow$ Number of attributes
$k \leftarrow$ Number of intervals (*i.e.,* number of clusters or bins)
for $h \leftarrow 1, z$ **do**
  for $j \leftarrow 1, m$ **do**
    Apply the discretization algorithm (k-Means, or EFB)
    The generated k clusters/bins represents the intervals' boundaries (*i.e.,* $\{S^1_{jh}, S^2_{jh}\}$:)
    Apply Chebyshev's on each interval to get $\{d^1_{jh}, d^2_{jh}\}$:
    for $r \leftarrow 1, k$ **do**
      calculate the mean (μ) and the standard deviations (σ)
      for $t \leftarrow 2, 5$ **do**
        Calculate the ratio of values, which are between $\mu \pm t\sigma$
        if ratio $\geqslant (1 - 1/t^2)100$ **then**
          select $(\mu - t\sigma, \mu + t\sigma)$ as first interval i.e. Where:
          $S^{1r}_{jh} = \mu - t\sigma$, $S^{2r}_{jh} = \mu + t\sigma$
          $q^{1r}_{jh} = \mu - (t+1)\sigma$, $q^{2r}_{jh} = \mu + (t+1)\sigma$
          $d^{1r}_{jh} = S^{1r}_{jh}$ - q^{1r}_{jh} and $d^{2r}_{jh} = q^{2r}_{jh}$ - S^{2r}_{jh}
        end if
      end for
    end for
  end for
end for

Thereafter, an induction approach was introduced to compose PROAFTN prototypes to be used for classification. To evaluate the performance of the proposed approaches, a general comparative study was carried out between DT algorithms (C4.5 and ID3) and PROAFTN based on the proposed learning techniques. That portion of the study concluded that PROAFTN and DT algorithms

(C4.5 and ID3) share a very important property: they are both interpretable. In terms of classification accuracy, PROAFTN was able to outperform DT [16].

A superior technique for learning PROAFTN was introduced using Genetic algorithms (GA). More particularly, the developed technique, called GAPRO, integrates k-Means and a genetic algorithm to establish PROAFTN prototypes automatically from data in near optimal form. The purpose of using GA was to automate and optimize the selection of number of clusters and the thresholds to refining the prototypes. Based on the results generated by 12 typical classification problems, it was noticed that the newly proposed approach enabled PROAFTN to outperform widely used classification methods. The general description of using k-Means with GA to learn the PROAFTN classifier is documented in [7,13]. A GA is an adaptive metaheuristic search algorithm based on the concepts of natural selection and biological evolution. GA principles are inspired by Charles Darwin's theory of "survival of the fittest"; that is, the strong tend to adapt and survive while the weak tend to vanish. GA was first introduced by John H. Holland in the 1970s and further developed in 1975 to allow computers to evolve solutions to difficult search and combinatorial systems, such as function optimization and machine learning. As reported in the literature, GA represents an intelligent exploitation of a random search used to solve optimization problems. In spite of its stochastic behavior, GA is generally quite effective for rapid global searches for large, non-linear and poorly understood spaces; it exploits historical information to direct the search into the region of better performance within the search space [32,49].

In this work, GA is utilized to approximately obtain the best values for the threshold β and the number of clusters κ. The threshold β represents the ratio of the total number of objects from training set within each interval of each attribute in each class. As discussed earlier, to apply the discretization k-Means, the best κ value is required to obtain the intervals: $[S_j^1(b_i^h),\ S_j^2(b_i^h)]$, $[d_j^1(b_i^h),\ d_j^2(b_i^h)]$ and thresholds β as illustrated in Algorithm 4. In addition, the best value of β is also required to build the classification model that contains the best prototypes as described in Algorithm 4. Furthermore, since each dataset may have different values for κ and β, finding the best values for β and κ to compose PROAFTN prototypes is considered a difficult optimization task. As a result, GA is utilized to obtain these values. Within this framework, the value for β varies between 0 and 1 (*i.e.*, $\beta \in [0, 1]$), and the value for κ changes from 2 to 9 ($\kappa \in 2, ..., 9$). The formulation of the optimization problem, which is based on maximizing classification accuracy to provide the optimal parameters (κ and β), is defined as:

$$\begin{aligned} P\colon \text{Maximize} \quad & \frac{100}{n}\sum_{r=1}^{n} f_r(\kappa,\beta) \qquad (12) \\ \text{Subject to:} \quad & \kappa \in \{2, ..., 9\}; \\ & \beta \in [0, 1] \end{aligned}$$

where the objective or fitness function f depends on the classification accuracy and n represents the set of training objects/samples to be assigned to different classes. The procedure for calculating the fitness function f is described in Algorithm 3. In this regard, the result of the optimization problem defined in Eq. (12) can vary within the interval [0, 100].

Algorithm 3. Procedure to calculate objective function f.

Step 1: Apply k-Means (based on generated κ) to discretize the attributes
Step 2: Build the prototypes based on generated β, according to Algorithm 4
Step 3: Perform the classification procedure according to Algorithm 1
Step 4: Compare the value of the new class with the true class C as follows:
    Return the value 1 if object a_r belongs to the class C of a_r, or 0 otherwise

---

Algorithm 4. Building the classification model for PROAFTN.

Determine a ***threshold*** β as reference for interval selection
$k \leftarrow$ Number of classes
$i \leftarrow$ Prototype's index
$m \leftarrow$ Number of attributes
$\kappa \leftarrow$ Number of intervals/(clusters) for each attribute
$I^r_{jh} \leftarrow$ Intervals $\{S^{1r}_{jh}, S^{2r}_{jh}\}$ for each attribute g_j in each class C^h
$\Re \leftarrow$ Percentage of values within the interval I^r_{jh} per class
Generate PROAFTN intervals according to algorithm 2
$p \leftarrow 0$
for $h \leftarrow 1, k$ **do**
    $i \leftarrow 0$
    for $g \leftarrow 1, m$ **do**
        for $r \leftarrow 1, \kappa$ **do**
            if $\Re$ of $I^r_{jh} \geq \beta$ **then**
                Choose this interval to be part of the prototype b^h_i
                Go to next attribute g_{m+1}
            else
                Discard this interval and find another one ($i.e.$, I^{r+1}_{jh})
            end if
        end for
    end for
    if $(b^h_i \neq \emptyset \; \forall g_{jh})$ **then** $i \leftarrow i + 1$
    end if
    (Prototypes' composition):
    The selected branches from attribute g_1 to attribute g_m represent the induced prototypes for the class C^h
end for

3.2 Learning PROAFTN Using Particle Swarm Optimization

A new methodology based on the particle swarm optimization (PSO) algorithm was introduced to learn PROAFTN. First, an optimization model was formulated, and thereafter a PSO was used to solve it. PSO was proposed to induce the classification model for PROAFTN in so-called PSOPRO by inferring the best parameters from data with high classification accuracy. It was found that PSOPRO is an efficient approach for data classification. The performance of PSOPRO applied to different classification datasets demonstrates that PSOPRO outperforms the well-known classification methods.

PSO is an efficient evolutionary optimization algorithm using the social behavior of living organisms to explore the search space. Furthermore, PSO is easy to code and requires few control parameters [17]. The proposed approach employs PSO for training and improving the efficiency of the PROAFTN classifier. In this perspective, the optimization model is first formulated, and thereafter a PSO algorithm is used for solving it. During the learning stage, PSO uses training samples to induce the best PROAFTN parameters in the form of prototypes. Then, these prototypes, which represent the classification model, are used for assigning unknown samples. The target is to obtain the set of prototypes that maximizes the classification accuracy on each dataset.

The general description of the PSO methodology and its application is described in [6]. As discussed earlier, to apply PROAFTN, the pessimistic interval $[S^1_{jh}, S^2_{jh}]$ and the optimistic interval $[q^1_{jh}, q^2_{jh}]$ for each attribute in each class need to be determined, where:

$$q^1_{jh} = S^1_{jh} - d^1_{jh} \qquad\qquad q^2_{jh} = S^2_{jh} + d^2_{jh} \tag{13}$$

applied to:

$$q^1_{jh} \leq S^1_{jh} \qquad\qquad q^2_{jh} \geq S^2_{jh} \tag{14}$$

Hence, $S^1_{jh} = S^1_j(b^h_i)$, $S^2_{jh} = S^2_j(b^h_i)$, $q^1_{jh} = q^1_j(b^h_i)$, $q^2_{jh} = q^2_j(b^h_i)$, $d^1_{jh} = d^1_j(b^h_i)$, and $d^2_{jh} = d^2_j(b^h_i)$.

As mentioned above, to apply PROAFTN, the intervals $[S^1_{jh}, S^2_{jh}]$ and $[q^1_{jh}, q^2_{jh}]$ satisfy the constraints in Eq. (14) and the weights w_{jh} must be obtained for each attribute g_j in class C^h. To simplify the constraints in Eq. (14), the variable substitution based on Eq. (13) is used. As a result, the parameters d^1_{jh} and d^2_{jh} are used instead of q^1_{jh} and q^2_{jh}, respectively. Therefore, the optimization problem, which is based on maximizing classification accuracy providing the optimal parameters $S^1_{jh}, S^2_{jh}, d^1_{jh}, d^2_{jh}$ and w_{jh}, is defined here,

$$\begin{aligned} P\text{: Maximize} \quad & f(S^1_{jh}, S^2_{jh}, d^1_{jh}, d^2_{jh}, w_{jh}) \\ \text{Subject to:} \quad & S^1_{jh} \leq S^2_{jh}; d^1_{jh}, d^2_{jh} \geq 0 \\ & \sum_{j=1}^{m} w_{jh} = 1 \\ & 0 \leq w_{jh} \leq 1 \end{aligned} \tag{15}$$

where f is the function that calculates the classification accuracy, and n represents the number of training samples used during the optimization. The procedure for calculating the fitness function $f(S^1_{jh}, S^2_{jh}, d^1_{jh}, d^2_{jh}, w_{jh})$ is described in Table 3.

Table 3. The steps for calculating the objective function f.

For all $a \in A$:
Step 1: - Apply the classification procedure according to Algorithm 1
Step 2: - Compare the value of the new class with the true class C^h
- Identify the number of misclassified and unrecognized objects
- Calculate the classification accuracy (*i.e.* the fitness value):
$f = \dfrac{\text{number of correctly classified objects}}{n}$

To solve the optimization problem presented in Eq. (15), PSO is adopted here. The problem dimension D (*i.e.,* the number of parameters in the optimization problem) is described as follows: Each particle $\mathbf{x}$ is composed of the parameters $S^1_{jh}, S^2_{jh}, d^1_{jh}, d^2_{jh}$ and w_{jh}, for all $j = 1, 2, ..., m$ and $h = 1, 2, ..., k$. Therefore, each particle in the population is composed of $D = 5 \times m \times k$ real values (*i.e.,* $D = dim(\mathbf{x})$).

3.3 Differential Evolution for Learning PROAFTN

A new learning strategy based on the Differential Evolution (DE) algorithm was proposed for obtaining the best PROAFTN parameters. The proposed strategy is called DEPRO. DE is an efficient metaheuristics optimisation algorithm based on a simple mathematical structure that mimics a complex process of evolution. Based on results generated from a variety of public datasets, DEPRO provides excellent results, outperforming the most common classification algorithms.

In this direction, a new learning approach based on DE is proposed for learning the PROAFTN method. More particularly, DE is introduced here to solve the optimization problem introduced in Eq. (15). The new proposed learning technique, called DEPRO, utilizes DE to train and improve the PROAFTN classifier. In this context, DE is utilized as an inductive learning approach to infer the best PROAFTN parameters from the training samples. The generated parameters are then used to compose the prototypes, which represent the classification model that will be used for assigning unknown samples. The target is to find the prototypes that maximize the classification accuracy on each dataset. The full description of the DE methodology and its application to learn PROAFTN is described in [4]. The general procedure of the DE algorithm is presented in Algorithm 5.

The procedure for calculating the fitness function $f(S^1_{jh}, S^2_{jh}, d^1_{jh}, d^2_{jh}, w_{jh})$ is described in Table 3. The mutation and crossover steps to update the elements (genes) of the trial individual $\mathbf{v}_i$ based DEPRO are performed as follows:

Algorithm 5. Differential Evolution Steps.

Initialization
Evolution
repeat
  Mutation
  Recombination
  Evaluation
  Selection
until (termination criteria are met)

$$v_{ihj\tau} = \begin{cases} x_{r_1hj\tau} + F(x_{r_2hj\tau} - x_{r_3hj\tau}), & \text{if } (rand_\tau < \kappa) \text{ or } (\rho = \tau) \\ x_{ihj\tau}, & \text{otherwise.} \end{cases} \tag{16}$$

$$i, r_1, r_2, r_3 \in \{1, ..., N_{pop}\}, \quad i \neq r_1 \neq r_2 \neq r_3;$$
$$h = 1, ..., k; \quad j = 1, ..., m; \quad \tau = 1, ..., D$$

where F is the mutation factor $\in [0, 2]$, and κ is the crossover factor. This modified operation (*i.e.,* Eq. (16)) forces the mutation and crossover process to be applied on each gene τ selected randomly for each set of 5 parameters $S^1_{jh}, S^2_{jh}, d^1_{jh}, d^2_{jh}$ and w_{jh} in $\mathbf{v}_i$ for all $j = 1, 2, ..., m$ and $h = 1, 2, ..., k$.

3.4 A Hybrid Metaheuristic Framework for Establishing PROAFTN Parameters

As discussed earlier, there are different ways to classify the behavior of metaheuristic algorithms based on their characteristics. One of these major characteristics is to identify whether the evolution strategy is based on population-based search or single point search. Population-based methods deal in every iteration with a set of solutions rather than with a single solution. As a result, population-based algorithms have the capability to efficiently explore the search space, whereas the strength of single-point solution methods is that they provide a structured way to explore a promising region in the search space. Therefore, a promising area in the search space is searched in a more intensive way by using single-point solution methods than by using population-based methods [58]. Population-based methods can be augmented with single-point solution methods to improve the search mechanism. While the use of population-based methods ensures an exploration of the search space, the use of single-point techniques helps to identify good areas in the search space. One of the most popular ways of hybridization concerns the use of single-point search methods in population-based methods. Thus, hybridization that in some way manages to combine the advantages of population-based methods with the strengths of single-point methods is often very successful, which is the motivation and the case for this work. In many applications, hybrids metaheuristics have proved to be quite beneficial in improving the fitness of individuals [37,38,57]. In this methodology, a new hybrid of metaheuristics approaches were introduced to obtain the best PROAFTN parameters configuration for a given problem. The two proposed hybrid approaches are: (1) Particle Swarm optimization (PSO) and Reduced Variable Neighborhood Search (RVNS), called PSOPRO-RVNS; and (2) Differential Evolution (DE) and RVNS, called DEPRO-RVNS. Based on the generated results on both training and testing data, it was shown that the performance of PROAFTN is significantly improved compared with the previous study presented in the previous sections (Sects. 3.2 and 3.3). Furthermore, the experimental study demonstrated that PSOPRO-RVNS and DEPRO-RVNS strongly outperform well-known machine learning classifiers in a variety of problems. RVNS is a variation of the metaheuristic Variable Neighborhood Search (VNS) [33,34]. The basic idea of the VNS algorithm is to find a solution in the search space with a systematic change of neighborhood. The basic VNS is very useful for approximate solutions for many combinatorial and global optimization problems; however, the major limitation is that it is very time consuming because of the utilization of ingredient-based approaches as it is used as a local search routine. RVNS uses a different approach; the solutions are drawn randomly from their neighborhood. The incumbent solution is replaced if a better solution is found. RVNS is simple, efficient and provides good results with low computational cost [30,34]. In RVNS, two procedures are used: shake and move. Starting from the initial solution (the position of prematurely converged individuals) $\mathbf{x}$, the algorithm selects a random solution $\mathbf{x}'$ from the initial solution's neighborhood. If the generated $\mathbf{x}'$ is better than $\mathbf{x}$, it replaces $\mathbf{x}$ and the algorithm starts all over again with the same neighborhood. Otherwise, the algorithm continues with the next neighborhood structure. The pseudo-code of RVNS is given in Algorithm 6.

Algorithm 6. Random Variable Neighborhood Search steps.

```
Require:
  Define neighborhood structures N_k for k = 1, 2, ..., k_max, that will be used in the
  search
  Get the initial solution x and choose stopping condition
  k ← 1
  while k < k_kmax do
     Shaking:
       Generate a point x' at random from the k-th neighborhood of x (x' ∈ N_k(x))
     Move or not:
     if x' is better than the incumbent x then
        x ← x'
        k ← 1
     else
        set k ← k + 1
     end if
  end while
```

In [13] the RVNS heuristics is used to learn the PROAFTN classifier by optimizing its parameters that are presented as intervals namely the pessimistic and optimistic intervals. In this light, a hybrid of metaheuristics is proposed here for training the PROAFTN method. In this regard, the two different hybrid approaches PSO augmented with RVNS (called PSOPRO-RVNS) and DE augmented with RVNS (called DEPRO-RVNS) are proposed for solving this optimization problem. The two proposed training techniques presented in (Sects. 3.2 and 3.3) are integrated with the single point search RVNS, to improve the performance of PROAFTN. The details on how DE and RVNS have been used together to learn the PROAFTN classifier is described in [5]. And in the same context, the details of the application of PSO and RVNS to learn PROAFTN is described in [3]. To use RVNS to find a better solution provided by PSO or DE in each iteration, the following equations are considered to update the boundary for the previous solution $\mathbf{x}$ containing $(S^1_{jh}, S^2_{jh}, d^1_{jh}, d^2_{jh})$ parameters:

$$l_{\lambda jbh} = x_{\lambda jbh} - (k/k_{max})x_{\lambda jbh} \tag{17}$$

$$use\, x instead\, of\, s u_{\lambda jbh} = x_{\lambda jbh} + (k/k_{max})x_{\lambda jbh} \tag{18}$$

where $l_{\lambda jbh}$ and $u_{\lambda jbh}$ are the lower and upper bounds for each element $\lambda \in [1, \ldots, D]$. Factor k/k_{max} is used to define the boundary for each element and $x_{\lambda jbh}$ is the previous solution for each element $\lambda \in [1, \ldots, D]$ provided by PSO.

The use of the hybrid PSO/DE augmented with RVNS for learning PROAFTN is explained here and for more details please see [5]. Using PSO, the elements for each particle position $\mathbf{x}_i$ consisting of the parameters $S^1_{jh}, S^2_{jh}, d^1_{jh}$ and d^2_{jh} are updated using:

$$x_{i\lambda jbh}(t+1) = x_{i\lambda jbh}(t) + v_{i\lambda jbh}(t+1) \tag{19}$$

where the velocity update $\mathbf{v}_i$ for each element based on $\mathbf{P}^{Best}_i$ and $\mathbf{G}^{Best}$ is formulated as:

$$\begin{aligned} v_{i\lambda jbh}(t+1) = \varpi(t)v_{i\lambda jbh}(t)+ \\ \tau_1\rho_1(P^{Best}_{i\lambda jbh} - x_{i\lambda jbh}(t))+ \\ \tau_2\rho_2(G^{Best}_{\lambda jbh} - x_{i\lambda jbh}(t)) \end{aligned} \tag{20}$$

$$i = 1, ..., N_{pop}; \quad \lambda = 1, ..., D$$

$$j = 1, ..., m; \quad b = 1, ..., L_h; \quad h = 1, ..., k$$

where $\varpi(t)$ is the inertia weight that controls the exploration of the search space. τ_1 and τ_2 are the individual and social components/weights, respectively. ρ_1 and ρ_2 are random numbers between 0 and 1. $\mathbf{P}^{Best}_i(t)$ is the personal best position of the particle i, and $\mathbf{G}^{Best}(t)$ is the neighborhood best position of particle i. Algorithm 6 demonstrates the required steps to evolve the velocity $\mathbf{v}_i$ and particle position $\mathbf{x}_i$ for each particle containing PROAFTN parameters. The *shaking* phase to randomly generate the elements of $\mathbf{x}'$ is given by:

$$x'_{\lambda jbh} = l_{\lambda jbh} + (u_{\lambda jbh} - l_{\lambda jbh}).rand[0, 1] \tag{21}$$

Accordingly, the *moving* is applied as:

$$\text{If } f'(x'_{\lambda jbh}) > f(x_{\lambda jbh}) \text{ then } x_{\lambda jbh} = x'_{\lambda jbh} \tag{22}$$

The steps that explain the employment of RVNS to improve PROAFTN parameters are listed in Algorithm 7.

Algorithm 7. The RVNS heuristic for learning the classification method PROAFTN

Require:
Get PSO or DE premature-solution as initial solution **x** which contains $S^1_{jh}, S^2_{jh}, d^1_{jh}$ and d^2_{jh}
Calculate the objective function $f(\mathbf{x})$ of the optimization problem in Eq. (15).
Stopping condition k is set to 4
repeat
  $k \leftarrow 1$
  Shaking:
  while $k < k_{kmax}$ **do**
    for each parameter of parameters $(S^1_{jh}, S^2_{jh}, d^1_{jh}, d^2_{jh}) \in \mathbf{x}$ **do**
      Update the boundary for each parameter according to Eqs. (17 and 18)
      Randomly generate new position $\mathbf{x}'$ from k-th neighborhood for $\lambda^{th} \in N_k(\tau)$ (Eq. (21))
    end for
    Submit $\mathbf{x}'$ to calculate the new fitness value (f') according to Eq. (15)
    Move or not (Eq. (22)):
    if $f'(x')$ is better than the incumbent $f(\mathbf{x})$ **then**
      $\mathbf{x} \leftarrow \mathbf{x}'$
      $k \leftarrow 1$
    else
      set $k \leftarrow k + 1$
    end if
  end while
until stopping condition is met
return the best generated point $\mathbf{x}'$ to PSO or DE to continue the search

---

4 Comparative Study with PROAFTN and Well Known Classifiers

The proposed methodologies were implemented in Java and applied to 12 popular datasets: Breast Cancer Wisconsin Original (BCancer), Transfusion Service Center (Blood), Heart Disease (Heart), Hepatitis, Haberman's Survival (HM), Iris, Liver Disorders (Liver), Mammographic Mass (MM), Pima Indians Diabetes (Pima), Statlog Australian Credit Approval (STAust), Teaching Assistant Evaluation (TA), and Wine. The details of the datasets' description and their dimensionality are presented in Table 4. The datasets are in the public domain and are available at the University of California at Irvine (UCI) Machine Learning Repository database [8].

Table 4. Description of datasets used in our experiments.

	Dataset	Instances	Attributes	Classes
1	BCancer	699	9	2
2	Blood	748	4	2
3	Heart	270	13	2
4	Hepatitis	155	19	2
5	HM	306	3	2
6	Iris	150	4	3
7	Liver	345	6	2
8	MM	961	5	2
9	Pima	768	8	2
10	STAust	690	14	2
11	TA	151	5	3
12	Wine	178	13	3

To summarize, a comparison of the various approaches introduced throughout this research for learning PROAFTN – GAPRO, PSOPRO, DEPRO, PSOPRO-RVNS and DEPRO-RVNS – is presented in Table 5. One can see that DEPRO-RVNS and PSOPRO-RVNS perform the best.

Table 5. The performance of all approaches for learning PROAFTN introduced in this research study based on classification accuracy (in %). The average accuracy and average ranking is also included.

Dataset	GA-PRO	PSOPRO	DEPRO	PSOPRO-RVNS	DEPRO-RVNS
BCancer	96.76	97.14	96.97	97.33	97.05
Blood	75.43	79.25	79.59	79.46	79.61
HM	83.85	84.27	83.74	84.36	83.81
Heart	71.95	86.04	84.17	87.05	85.37
Hepatitis	73.84	75.73	80.36	76.27	76.10
Iris	96.57	96.21	96.47	96.30	96.66
Liver	71.83	69.31	71.01	70.97	70.99
MM	84.92	82.31	84.33	84.07	84.77
Pima	72.19	77.47	75.37	77.42	77.23
STAust	81.78	86.09	85.62	86.10	86.04
TA	52.44	60.55	61.80	60.62	62.72
Wine	97.33	96.79	96.87	96.72	97.10
Average accuracy	79.91	82.60	83.03	83.06	**83.12**
Average rank	3.58	3.33	3.08	2.58	**2.42**

Table 7 summarizes and gives robust analysis on a comparison that includes the developed approaches of learning PROAFTN classifier against other classifiers. As observed, both approaches DEPRO-RVNS and PSOPRO-RVNS strongly outperform other classifiers. Therefore, the developed approaches can be classified into three groups, based on their performances:

- Best approaches: DEPRO-RVNS and PSOPRO-RVNS.
- Middle approaches: DEPRO and PSOPRO.
- Weakest approach: GA-PRO.

It should be noted also that DEPRO-RVNS and PSOPRO-RVNS are efficient in terms of computation speed. One of the advantages of DE and PSO over other global optimization methods is that they often converge faster and with more certainty than other methods. Furthermore, utilizing RVNS inside DE and PSO improved the search for good solutions in a shorter time (Table 5).

Table 6. Experimental results based on classification accuracy (in %) to measure the performance of the well-known classifiers on the same datasets

Dataset	C4.5 J48	NB	SVM SMO	NN MLP	*k*-NN Ibk, k = 3	PART	RForest n = 500	GLM	Deep learning
BCancer	94.56	95.99	96.70	95.56	97.00	97.05	97.4	97.9	97.9
Blood	77.81	75.40	76.20	78.74	74.60	79.61	76.1	74.9	78.7
Heart	76.60	83.70	84.10	78.10	78.89	73.33	57.6	60.4	54.9
Hepatitis	80.00	85.81	83.87	81.94	84.52	82.58	90.1	92.6	94.8
HM	71.90	74.83	73.52	72.87	70.26	72.55	73.1	69.2	67.2
Iris	96.00	96.00	96.00	97.33	95.33	94.00	95.3	96.7	90.7
Liver	68.70	56.52	58.26	71.59	61.74	63.77	71.8	73.0	74.1
MM	82.10	78.35	79.24	82.10	77.21	82.21	80.8	84.9	84.7
Pima	71.48	75.78	77.08	75.39	73.44	73.05	77.4	78.3	75.4
STAust	85.22	77.25	85.51	84.93	83.62	83.62	86.7	88.9	86.8
TA	59.60	52.98	54.30	54.30	50.33	58.28	66.1	52.3	39.6
Wine	91.55	97.40	99.35	97.40	95.45	92.86	97.8	98.9	97.7

Comparison with was done against implementations provided in WEKA [27] for neural network multi-level perceptron (NN MLD), naive Bayes (NB), decision trees (PART), C4.5 and k nearest neighbour (knn). We used H2O for deep learning (h2o DL) [19] and generalized linear models (h2o GLM) [44]. We used R's implementation of random forest (RFOREST) [41] with n = 500 trees. PROAFTN and decision trees share a very important property: both of them use the white box model. Decision trees and PROAFTN can generate classification models which can be easily explained and interpreted. However, when evaluating any classification method there is another important factor to be considered:

Table 7. Mean accuracy rankings. The algorithms developed in this paper are marked in bold.

Algorithm	Mean rank
DEPRO-RVNS	4.75
PSOPRO-RVNS	4.75
h2o GLM	5.29
PSOPRO	5.50
DEPRO	6.08
RForest 500	6.25
h2o DL	7.04
GA-PRO	8.08
SVM SMO	8.12
NN MLP	8.12
NB	9.54
PART	9.62
C4.5	10.62
k-NN	11.21

classification accuracy. Based on the experimental study presented in Sect. 4, the PROAFTN method has proven to generate a higher classification accuracy than decision tree such as C4.5 [46] and other well-known classifiers learning algorithms including Naive Bayes, Support Vector Machines (SVM), Neural Network (NN), K- Nearest Neighbor K-NN, and Rule Learner (see Table 6). That can be explain by the fact that PROAFTN using fuzzy intervals. A general comparison between PROAFTN based on the proposed learning approaches adopted in this paper (PRO-BPLA) and other machine learning classifiers is summarized in Table 8. The observations made in this table are based on evidence of existing empirical and theoretical studies as presented in [40]. We have also added some evidence based on the results obtained using the developed learning methodology introduced in this research study. As a summary, Table 8 compares the properties of some well known machine learning classifiers against the properties of the classification method PROAFTN.

In this chapter, we have presented the implementation of machine learning and metaheuristics algorithms for parameters training of multicriteria classification method. We have shown that learning techniques based on metaheuristics proved to be a successful approach for optimizing the learning of PROAFTN classification method and thus greatly improving its performances. As has been demonstrated, every classification algorithm has its strengths and limitations. More particularly, the characteristics of the method and whether it is strong or weak depend on the situation or on the problem. For instance, assume the problem at hand is a medical dataset and the interest is to look for a classification method for medical diagnostics. Suppose the executives and experts are looking

Table 8. Summary of the of well-known classifiers versus PRO-BPLA properties (the best rating is **** and the worst is *)

	DT	NB	SVM	NN	k-NN	PART	PRO-BPLA	RForest	GLM	Deep Learning
Accuracy in general	**	*	***	***	**	**	****	****	****	****
Dealing with discrete/-continuous attributes	***not directly	** not continuous	** not discrete	** not discrete	** not directly discrete	** not directly continuous	**** continuous & discrete	** not directly continuous	** not directly discrete	** not directly discrete
Tolerance to noise	**	**	**	*	*	*	***	**	**	***
Training time	**	***	*	*	****	**	*	**	*	*
Testing time	****	***	****	****	*	****	***	***	****	****
Dealing with danger of overfitting	**	***	**	*	***	**	**	***	*	*
Model parameter handling	***	***	*	*	***	***	****	****	**	*
Interpretability	****	****	*	*	**	****	****	***	*	*

for a high level of classification accuracy and at the same time they are very keen to know more details about the classification process (*e.g.,* why the patient is classified to this category of disease). In such circumstances, classifiers such as Deep Learning networks, k-NN, or SVM may not be an appropriate choice, because of the limited interpret-ability of their classification models. Although deep learning networks have been successfully applied to some health-care application and in particularly into medical imaging, they suffered from some limitations such as the limited interpret-ability of their classification results; they require a very large balanced labeled data set; the preprocessing or change of input domain is often required to bring all the input data to the same scale [48]. Thus, there is a need to look for other classifiers that reason about their outputs and can generate good classification accuracy, such as DTs (C4.5, ID3), NB, or PROAFTN.

Based on the experimental and the comparative study presented in Table 8, the PROAFTN method based on our proposed learning approaches has good accuracy in most instances and can deal with all types of data without sensitivity to noise. PROAFTN uses the pairwise comparison and therefore, there is no need for looking for suitable normalization technique of data like the case of other classifiers. Furthermore, PROAFTN is a transparent and interpretable classifier where it's easy to generalize the classification rules from the obtained prototypes. It can use both approaches deductive and inductive learning, which allow us to use in the same time historical data with expert judgment to compose the classification model. To sum up, there is no complete or comprehensive classification algorithm that can handle or fit all classification problems. In response to this deficiency, the major task of this work is to review an integration of methodologies from three major fields, MCDA, machine learning, and optimization based metaheuristics, through the aforementioned classification method PROAFTN. The target of this study was to exploit the machine learning techniques and the optimization approaches to improve the performance of PROAFTN. The aim is to find a good suitable and comprehensive (interpretable) classification procedure that can be applied efficiently in many applications including the ambient assisted living environments.

5 Conclusions and Future Work

The target of this chapter is to exploit the machine learning techniques and the optimization approaches to improve the performance of PROAFTN. The aim is to find a good suitable and comprehensive (interpretable) classification procedure that can be applied efficiently in health applications including the ambient assisted living environments. This chapter describes the ability of the metaheuristics when embedded to the classification method PROAFTN in order to classify new objects. To do this we compared the improved PROAFTN methodology with those reported previously on the same data and same validation technique (10-cross validation). In addition to reviewing several approaches to modeling and learning classification method PROAFTN, this chapter also presents new ideas to further research in the areas of data mining and machine learning. Below are some possible directions for future research.

1. The fact that PROAFTN has several parameters to be obtained for each attribute and for each class, which provides more information to assign objects to the closest class. However, in some cases this may cause some limitation on the speed of learning, particularly when using metaheuristics, as we presented in this paper. Possible future solutions could be summarized as follows:
   - Utilizing different approaches for obtaining the weights. One possible direction is to use a features ranking approach by using some strong algorithms that perform well in the aspect of dimensionality reduction.
   - Determining intervals bounds for more than one prototype before performing optimization. This would involve establishing the intervals' bounds *a priori* by using some clustering techniques, hence improving and speeding up the search and improving the likelihood of finding the best solutions.
2. As we know the performance of approaches based on the choice of control parameters varies from one application to another. However, in this work the control parameters are fixed for all applications. A better control of parameter choice for the metaheuristics based PROAFTN algorithms will be investigated.

3. To speed up the PROAFTN learning process, possible improvement could be made by using parallel computation. The different processors can deal with the fold independently in the cross validation folds process. The parallelism can be also applied in the composition of prototypes of each class.
4. In this chapter, an inductive learning is presented to build the classification models for the PROAFTN method. PROAFTN also can apply the deductive learning that allows the introduction of the given knowledge in setting PROAFTN parameters such intervals and/or weights to build the prototype of classes.

References

1. Al-Obeidat, F., Al-Taani, A.T., Belacel, N., Feltrin, L., Banerjee, N.: A fuzzy decision tree for processing satellite images and landsat data. Procedia Comput. Sci. **52**, 1192–1197 (2015)
2. Al-Obeidat, F., Belacel, N.: Alternative approach for learning and improving the MCDA method PROAFTN. Int. J. Intell. Syst. **26**(5), 444–463 (2011)
3. Al-Obeidat, F., Belacel, N., Carretero, J.A., Mahanti, P.: Automatic parameter settings for the PROAFTN classifier using hybrid particle swarm optimization. In: Farzindar, A., Kešelj, V. (eds.) AI 2010. LNCS (LNAI), vol. 6085, pp. 184–195. Springer, Heidelberg (2010). https://doi.org/10.1007/978-3-642-13059-5_19
4. Al-Obeidat, F., Belacel, N., Carretero, J.A., Mahanti, P.: Differential evolution for learning the classification method PROAFTN. Knowl.-Based Syst. **23**(5), 418–426 (2010)
5. Al-Obeidat, F., Belacel, N., Carretero, J.A., Mahanti, P.: A hybrid metaheuristic framework for evolving the PROAFTN classifier. Spec. J. Issues World Acad. Sci. Eng. Technol. **64**, 217–225 (2010)
6. Al-Obeidat, F., Belacel, N., Carretero, J.A., Mahanti, P.: An evolutionary framework using particle swarm optimization for classification method PROAFTN. Appl. Soft Comput. **11**(8), 4971–4980 (2011)
7. Al-Obeidat, F., Belacel, N., Mahanti, P., Carretero, J., et al.: Discretization techniques and genetic algorithm for learning the classification method PROAFTN. In: International Conference on Machine Learning and Applications, ICMLA 2009, pp. 685–688. IEEE (2009)
8. Asuncion, A., Newman, D.: UCI machine learning repository (2007)
9. Ban, A., Coroianu, L.: Simplifying the search for effective ranking of fuzzy numbers. IEEE Trans. Fuzzy Syst. **23**(2), 327–339 (2015). https://doi.org/10.1109/TFUZZ.2014.2312204
10. Belacel, N.: Multicriteria classification methods: methodology and medical applications. Ph.D. thesis, Free University of Brussels, Belgium (1999)
11. Belacel, N.: Multicriteria assignment method PROAFTN: methodology and medical application. Eur. J. Oper. Res. **125**(1), 175–183 (2000)
12. Belacel, N., Boulassel, M.: Multicriteria fuzzy assignment method: a useful tool to assist medical diagnosis. Artif. Intell. Med. **21**(1–3), 201–207 (2001)
13. Belacel, N., Raval, H., Punnen, A.: Learning multicriteria fuzzy classification method PROAFTN from data. Comput. Oper. Res. **34**(7), 1885–1898 (2007)
14. Belacel, N., Vincke, P., Scheiff, J., Boulassel, M.: Acute leukemia diagnosis aid using multicriteria fuzzy assignment methodology. Comput. Methods Programs Biomed. **64**(2), 145–151 (2001). https://doi.org/10.1016/S0169-2607(00)00100-0

15. Belacel, N., Wang, Q., Richard, R.: Web-integration of PROAFTN methodology for acute leukemia diagnosis. Telemed. J. e-Health **11**(6), 652–659 (2005)
16. Belacel, N., Al-Obeidat, F.: A learning method for developing PROAFTN classifiers and a comparative study with decision trees. In: Butz, C., Lingras, P. (eds.) AI 2011. LNCS (LNAI), vol. 6657, pp. 56–61. Springer, Heidelberg (2011). https://doi.org/10.1007/978-3-642-21043-3_7
17. van den Bergh, F., Engelbrecht, A.: A study of particle swarm optimization particle trajectories. Inf. Sci. **176**(8), 937–971 (2006). https://doi.org/10.1016/j.ins.2005.02.003
18. Brasil Filho, A.T., Pinheiro, P.R., Coelho, A.L.V., Costa, N.C.: Comparison of two MCDA classification methods over the diagnosis of Alzheimer's disease. In: Wen, P., Li, Y., Polkowski, L., Yao, Y., Tsumoto, S., Wang, G. (eds.) RSKT 2009. LNCS (LNAI), vol. 5589, pp. 334–341. Springer, Heidelberg (2009). https://doi.org/10.1007/978-3-642-02962-2_42
19. Candel, A., Parmar, V., LeDell, E., Arora, A., Lanford, J.: Deep Learning with H2O, September 2016. http://h2o.ai/resources
20. Ching, J., Wong, A.K., Chan, K.: Class-dependent discretization for inductive learning from continuous and mixed-mode data. IEEE Trans. Pattern Anal. Mach. Intell. **17**(7), 641–651 (1995)
21. Crammer, K., Singer, Y.: On the learnability and design of output codes for multiclass problems. Mach. Learn. **47**(2–3), 201–233 (2002)
22. Doumpos, M., Zopounidis, C.: A multicriteria classification approach based on pairwise comparisons. Eur. J. Oper. Res. **158**(2), 378–389 (2004)
23. Dubois, D., Prade, H., Sabbadin, R.: Decision theoritic foundations of qualitative possibility theory. Eur. J. Oper. Res. **128**, 459–478 (2015)
24. El-Alfy, E.S.M., Al-Obeidat, F.N.: A multicriterion fuzzy classification method with greedy attribute selection for anomaly-based intrusion detection. Procedia Comput. Sci. **34**, 55–62 (2014)
25. El-Alfy, E.S.M., Al-Obeidat, F.N.: Detecting cyber-attacks on wireless mobile networks using multicriterion fuzzy classifier with genetic attribute selection. Mob. Inf. Syst. **501**, 585432 (2015)
26. Fayyad, U., Irani, K.: Multi-interval discretization of continuous-valued attributes for classification learning. In: XIII International Joint Conference on Artificial Intelligence (IJCAI 1993), pp. 1022–1029 (1993)
27. Frank, E., Hall, M.A., Witten, I.H.: The WEKA Workbench. Online Appendix for "Data Mining: Practical Machine Learning Tools and Techniques", Fourth edn. Morgan Kaufmann, Burlington (2016)
28. Garcia, S., Luengo, J., Saez, V., Herrera, F.: A survey of discretization techniques: taxonomy and empirical analysis in supervised learning. IEEE Trans. Knowl. Data Eng. **25**(4), 734–750 (2013). https://doi.org/10.1109/TKDE.2012.35
29. García, S., Ramírez-Gallego, S., Luengo, J., Benítez, J.M., Herrera, F.: Data discretization: taxonomy and big data challenge. WIREs Data Mining Knowl. Discov. **6**, 5–21 (2016). https://doi.org/10.1002/widm.1173
30. Glover, F.W., Kochenberger, G.A.: Handbook of Metaheuristics. Kluwer Academic Publishers, Norwell (2003)
31. Goebel, M., Gruenwald, L.: A survey of data mining and knowledge discovery software tools. ACM SIGKDD Explor. Newslett. **1**(1), 20–33 (1999)
32. Goldberg, D.: Genetic Algorithms in Search, Optimization, and Machine Learning. Addison-Wesley Professional, Boston (1989)
33. Hansen, P., Mladenovic, N.: Variable neighborhood search for the p-median. Location Sci. **5**(4), 207–226 (1997)

34. Hansen, P., Mladenovic, N.: Variable neighborhood search: principles and applications. Eur. J. Oper. Res. **130**(3), 449–467 (2001)
35. Ishizaka, A., Nemery, P.: Assigning machines to incomparable maintenance strategies with electre-sort. Omega **47**, 45–59 (2014). https://doi.org/10.1016/j.omega.2014.03.006
36. Ivascu, T., Cincar, K., Dinis, A., Negru, V.: Activities of daily living and falls recognition and classification from the wearable sensors data. In: E-Health and Bioengineering Conference (EHB), pp. 627–630. IEEE (2017)
37. Jung, S., Moon, B.: A hybrid genetic algorithm for the vehicle routing problem with time windows. In: GECCO, pp. 1309–1316 (2002)
38. Kim, J.P., Moon, B.R.: A hybrid genetic search for circuit bipartitioning. In: GECCO, p. 685 (2002)
39. Kotsiantis, S.: Supervised machine learning: a review of classification techniques. Informatica **31**, 249–268 (2007)
40. Kotsiantis, S.B., Zaharakis, I.D., Pintelas, P.E.: Machine learning: a review of classification and combining techniques. Artif. Intell. Rev. **26**(3), 159–190 (2006)
41. Law, A.: Breiman and Cutler's Random Forests for Classification and Regression, October 2015. https://cran.r-project.org/web/packages/randomForest/randomForest.pdf
42. Marchant, T.: A measurement-theoretic axiomatization of trapezoidal membership functions. IEEE Trans. Fuzzy Syst. **15**(2), 238–242 (2007). https://doi.org/10.1109/TFUZZ.2006.880000
43. Monekosso, D., Florez-Revuelta, F., Remagnino, P.: Ambient assisted living [guest editors' introduction]. IEEE Intell. Syst. **30**(4), 2–6 (2015). https://doi.org/10.1109/MIS.2015.63
44. Nykodym, T., Kraljevic, T., Hussami, N., Rao, A., Wang, A.: Generalized Linear Models with H2O, September 2016. http://h2o.ai/resources
45. Perny, P., Roy, B.: The use of fuzzy outranking relations in preference modelling. Fuzzy Sets Syst. **49**, 33–53 (1992)
46. Quinlan, J.R.: Improved use of continuous attributes in C4.5. J. Artif. Intell. Res. **4**, 77–90 (1996)
47. Ranasinghe, S., Machot, F.A., Mayr, H.C.: A review on applications of activity recognition systems with regard to performance and evaluation. Int. J. Distrib. Sens. Netw. **12**(8) (2016). https://doi.org/10.1177/1550147716665520
48. Rav, D., et al.: Deep learning for health informatics. IEEE J. Biomed. Health Inform. **21**(1), 4–21 (2017). https://doi.org/10.1109/JBHI.2016.2636665
49. Reeves, C.R., Rowe, J.E.: Genetic Algorithms: Principles and Perspectives. A Guide to GA Theory. Kluwer Academic Publishers, Norwell (2002)
50. Resende Monteiro, A.L., Manso Correa Machado, A., Lewer, M., Henrique, M.: A multicriteria method for cervical tumor segmentation in positron emission tomography. In: 2014 IEEE 27th International Symposium on Computer-Based Medical Systems (CBMS), pp. 205–208. IEEE (2014)
51. Roy, B.: Multicriteria Methodology for Decision Aiding. Kluwer Academic, Norwell (1996)
52. Roy, B.: Multicriteria Methodology for Decision Aiding. Nonconvex Optimization and Its Applications. Springer, Heidelberg (2013). https://doi.org/10.1007/978-1-4757-2500-1
53. Sassi, I., Belacel, N., Bouslimani, Y.: Photonic-crystal fibre modeling using fuzzy classification approach. Int. J. Recent Trends Eng. Technol. **6**(2), 100–104 (2011)
54. Sharlig, A.: Décider sur plusieurs critères, panorama de laide à la décision multicritère. Press polytechniques Romandes, Lausanne (1985)

55. Singh, N., Arora, H.: Network intrusion detection using feature selection and PROAFTN classification. Int. J. Sci. Eng. Res. **6**(4), 466–472 (2015)
56. Sobrado, F., Pikatza, J., Larburu, I., Garcia, J., de Ipiña, D.: Towards a clinical practice guideline implementation for asthma treatment. In: Conejo, R., Urretavizcaya, M., Pérez-de-la Cruz, J. (eds.) CAEPIA-TTIA 2003. LNCS, pp. 587–596. Springer, Heidelberg (2004). https://doi.org/10.1007/978-3-540-25945-9_58
57. Talbi, E.-G., Rahoual, M., Mabed, M.H., Dhaenens, C.: A hybrid evolutionary approach for multicriteria optimization problems: application to the flow shop. In: Zitzler, E., Thiele, L., Deb, K., Coello Coello, C.A., Corne, D. (eds.) EMO 2001. LNCS, vol. 1993, pp. 416–428. Springer, Heidelberg (2001). https://doi.org/10.1007/3-540-44719-9_29
58. Talbi, E.G.: A taxonomy of hybrid metaheuristics. J. Heuristics **8**(5), 541–564 (2002). https://doi.org/10.1023/A:1016540724870
59. Vincke, P.: Multicriteria Decision-Aid. Wiley, Hoboken (1992). https://books.google.ca/books?id=H2NRAAAAMAAJ
60. Witten, H.: Data Mining: Practical Machine Learning Tools and Techniques. Morgan Kaufmann Series in Data Management Systems. Morgan Kaufmann Publishers, San Francisco (2005)
61. Wu, X.: Fuzzy interpretation of discretized intervals. IEEE Trans. Fuzzy Syst. **7**(6), 753–759 (1999)
62. Zopounidis, C., Doumpos, M.: Multicriteria preference disaggregation for classification problems with an application to global investing risk. Decis. Sci. **32**(2), 333–385 (2001)
63. Zopounidis, C., Doumpos, M.: Multicriteria classification and sorting methods: a literature review. Eur. J. Oper. Res. **138**(2), 229–246 (2002)

Development and Evaluation of Methodology for Personal Recommendations Applicable in Connected Health

Cvetanka Smileska[1], Natasa Koceska[2](✉), Saso Koceski[2], and Vladimir Trajkovik[3]

[1] Netcetera, 1000 Skopje, Macedonia
[2] Faculty of Computer Science, University "Goce Delchev" - Stip, Stip, Macedonia
natasa.koceska@ugd.edu.mk
[3] Faculty of Computer Science and Engineering, University "Ss Cyril and Methodius" - Skopje, Skopje, Macedonia

Abstract. In this paper, a personal recommendation system of outdoor physical activities using solely user's history data and without application of collaborative filtering algorithms is proposed and evaluated. The methodology proposed contains four phases: data fuzzification, activity usefulness calculation, estimation of most useful activities, activities classification. In the process of classification several data mining techniques were compared such as: decision trees algorithms, decision rules algorithm, Bayes algorithm and support vector machines. The proposed algorithm has been experimentally validated using real dataset collected in a certain period of time from a community of 1000 active users. Recommendations generated by the system were related to weight loss. The results show that our generated recommendations have high accuracy, up to 95%.

Keywords: Recommendation algorithm · Classification algorithm Connected health · Personal healthcare · Data processing

1 Introduction

Globally, the burden of non-communicable diseases (NCDs) is growing. They are the leading cause of morbidity and mortality and place a great financial strain on the economy [1]. Sadly, this 'invisible' epidemic which is attributable to common, modifiable risk factors, including physical inactivity, tobacco use, the harmful use of alcohol, and unhealthy diet, imposes a great strain on health systems, resulting in a healthcare work force crisis in many nations [1]. An important factor in prevention and treatment of chronic diseases, as well as supporting healthy aging, is the maintenance of a healthy lifestyle in terms of daily physical activity. Physical inactivity is stated to be one of the leading cause of global mortality, and the World Health Organization (WHO), the United Nations and numerous national governments now view the promotion of physical activity as a public health priority [2, 3]. According to a study,

I. Ganchev et al. (Eds.): Enhanced Living Environments, LNCS 11369, pp. 80–95, 2019.
https://doi.org/10.1007/978-3-030-10752-9_4

incorporating walking or cycling into longer journeys, provides over half the weekly recommended activity, which can be an efficient way of achieving physical activity guidelines and improving population health [4, 5].

Recent research has focused on integrating physical activity into prevention, treatment and rehabilitation of NCDs [6, 7]. Study has shown that the quality of patients' life with the chronic deceases as cardiovascular diseases, diabetes, chronic obstructive pulmonary disease and some types of cancer, can be significantly improved by giving the patients personalized recommendations for physical activities. This can be done using a recommender system (RS) that collects data from various sources and provides/recommends the content that user needs in the moment [8–10].

Building recommender systems requires a multi-disciplinary approach that takes advantage of various computer science fields like machine learning, data mining and information retrieval, and even human-computer interaction [11, 12]. The recommender systems are using collaborative filtering, content based or hybrid approach for generating recommendations. Collaborative filtering is one of the most used and successfully applied methods for personalized RS, for which a large and continuously active literature exists [13–16].

It is an algorithm for matching people with similar interests for the purpose of making recommendations [17]. Since the patients' records contain highly sensitive data, some argue that collaborative filtering is not appropriate approach to be used in systems that are working with high degree of confidentiality [18, 19], and are choosing content-based techniques for generating prediction and recommendation models in healthcare.

In this paper, a personal recommendation system for outdoor physical activities is presented. The system does not use collaborative filtering technique, so the recommendations are generated using the user's history activities. In order to find the best classification technique for generating personalized recommendations with high accuracy, we investigated the techniques used in other research studies, and adopted those that were proven to give most accurate results in the healthcare field. The system was tested using the same dataset as in the previous work for COHESY recommender algorithm [20]. The results showed that our system can generate recommendations with high accuracy (up to 95%), without using collaborative filtering methods.

2 Related Work

In the last decade, many prediction and recommendation models, using various approaches and techniques, have been presented in the field of healthcare. Most of them are used for diagnosing or identifying patients with high risk of particular diseases. Only few of them are focusing on personalized recommendations for improving patients' health. Different classification techniques were compared and analyzed in many studies on healthcare in order to find the one that will give highest accuracy. A research on 12 years Kuwait patient data have used different classification techniques: logistic regression, k-nearest neighbors (k-NN), multifactor dimensionality reduction and support vector machines to identify patients with high risk for diabetes type 2, hypertension and comorbidity. Their results have shown that the support vector machine classifier gives slightly better results, with 81% accuracy [21]. Another research on heart disease prediction has compared the accuracy of Naïve Bayes, K-NN and decision list classifiers on patient data, taking into account different parameters as sex, smoking, weight, alcohol intake, high salt diet, exercise, blood sugar, heart rate, bad cholesterol, blood pressure, etc. The decision tree classifier outperformed the other classifiers with accuracy of 99.2% [22]. Similar work has been presented in cerebrovascular disease prediction model on a 493 patients from Taiwan where decision tree classifier C4.5 have given best results, compared with Bayesian classifier and back propagation neural network classifier [23]. Multiple decision tree algorithms have been adopted on diabetes patients from hospitals in Oman for achieving high accuracy disease risk predictive model. The evaluation of the prediction performance of J48, Decision Stump, REP Tree and Random Forest (RF) have been presented. The model built using RF had less MAE (mean absolute error) and high precision and recall results, compared with the other model results [24].

Algorithm that generates recommendations and suggestions for preventive intervention has been presented in a COHESY system [20]. The presented algorithm analyzes the user's activities and then recommends the most useful activity to the user. Grouping of users with similar characteristics has been done with classification and filtering algorithms. In order to compare the results with this algorithm presented in [20] we used the same dataset of 1000 active users from a mobile sport activity service, SportyPal. The SportyPal system is capable of reading parameters for a particular activity, such as path length, speed, time interval, consumed calories. We applied classification models on the user's activities to investigate the accuracy of the model. In our paper we used the classification methods that have proven to give accurate predictions in other research works in the field of connected health.

3 Description of the Recommendation Algorithm

The main purpose of the activity recommender system is to discover and recommend the most useful activities to the user. The impact of each activity over the user's health state should be determined first and only those activities that have positive influence should be recommended. Since the user does not provide feedback after execution of various activities the system will rely upon the provided measurements variations.

3.1 Data Representation

The system is collecting and storing information regarding activities and measurements defined as vectors with several attributes:

(1) Activity (user, type, time, duration, calories, distance)
(2) Measurement (user, parameter, time, value)

Each activity performed by a user is described with several parameters used for generating recommendations, such as: activity type, activity duration, distance passed and calories burned. The users performed twenty different types of activities: Cycling, Running, Driving, Walking, Hiking, Road-cycling, Blading, Sailing, Skiing, Horse riding, Paragliding, Rowing, Free style, Cross-skiing, Swimming, Snowboarding, Flying, Surfing and Golfing.

As for measurements body weight was recorded. This parameter has been chosen because it is strongly correlated with physical health. So, maintaining a healthy weight is important for health. In addition to lowering the risk of heart disease, stroke, diabetes, and high blood pressure, it can also lower the risk of many different cancers [25, 26].

Examples of activity and measurements vectors:

- Measurement (Ana, weight, 3rd Jan 2016 17:00, 74 kg)
- Activity (Ana, skiing, 5th Jan 2016 14:00, 90 min, 20 km).

3.2 Data Processing

The raw weight data obtained from the users should be filtered and transformed into appropriate format for further processing. Only measurements that have significant changes in the value have been taken into consideration. Three different thresholds were tested.

Namely, it was assumed that the measurement is valid if the value change is bigger or equal to 0.5 kg, 1 kg or 1.5 kg. The other values are treated as noise. Example:

$$\left|Value_{a-tx} - Value_{a+ty}\right| \geq D, \;\; where \;\; D \in \{0.5,\; 1,\; 1.5\} \tag{1}$$

Where $Value_{a-tx}$ is the value measured before the start of activity a, and $Value_{a+ty}$ is the value measured after activity a, is finished.

3.3 Recommendation Algorithm

The recommendation algorithm is composed of four phases (Fig. 1).

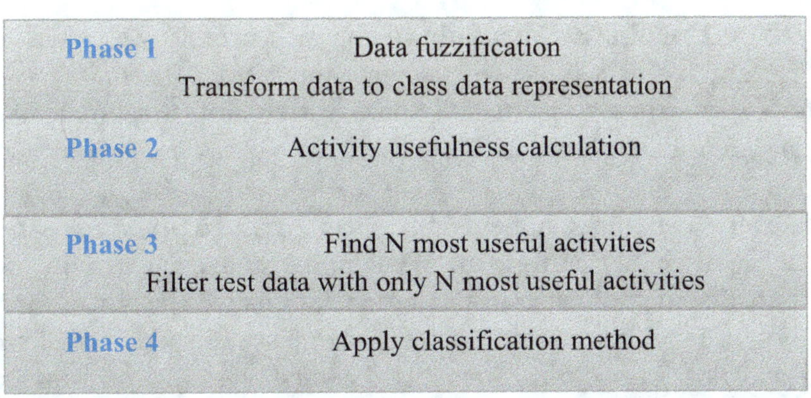

Fig. 1. Phases of recommendation algorithm

Phase 1: Data Fuzzification. After initial separation of dataset into training and test data (we used 60% of the data as train data and 40% of the data as test data), data fuzzification method has been applied on both subsets. For better semantic meaning several different classes are calculated for each kind of activity (Running, Cycling, Walking, etc.), for each user. This is done because of the difference of the duration, calories and distance for each kind of physical activity (for example: the distance of activity "cycling" is bigger than walking and running, assuming it is done for the same time period).

In this process all user's activities are taken into consideration and for every activity parameter (total time, distance and calories) proper class is assigned. Equal size ranges are used. Class calculation is done according to the following formula:

$$V_{class} = ceiling\left(\frac{v - v_{\min}}{v_{\max} - v_{\min}} N\right) \tag{2}$$

Where:

- N: is the number of classes that we want to use,
- v_{max}, v_{min}: are the max and min value of the parameter value for that kind of activity (running, cycling, walking, etc.),
- v: is the raw value that we want to transform into a class value,
- $ceiling(x) = \lceil x \rceil$: is the smallest integer not less than x.

Example: for a walking activities, where minimum time is 10 min and maximum time is 180 min, we want to find the class for an activity x, with time 50 min, and we want to have 5 class representation.

We will have: $ceiling\ (\frac{50-10}{180-10} 5) = 2$.

In our experiment we tested with several number of classes, and we got the best results for three class data representation. The data set is not very large, with average of 35 valid activities per valid users, and using more classes will give many different type of activities and smaller number of done recommendations (valid activities are the activities that have not zero usefulness, and a valid user is a user that had at least one recommended activity).

Phase 2: Activity Usefulness Calculation. For each activity we calculate its usefulness, and for each kind of activity we calculate the factor of importance. Finding the usefulness for every activity is the most important step in this recommendation model. An activity is said to be useful (positively useful in our case) if it contributed towards weight loss.

Between every two measurements there can be zero to n $(n > 0)$ number of activities that the user has performed. We assume that each activity between two measurements had some influence in the parameter change (weight).

Each activity can contribute to more than one measurement parameter change. For each activity, we look for two measurements. The first one is the measurement that was taken before the activity had started and has the biggest validity according to the model in Fig. 2, and the other measurement is the one taken after the activity had finished and had biggest validity according to the model in Fig. 3. We used the same models that were used in the COHESY recommender algorithm [20]. The measurements that were taken right before the activity was performed had the biggest validity. In this case we used the cumulative normal distribution (Fig. 2).

The validity of the measurements that were given after the activity has finished should slowly increase, then they should reach a maximum and afterwards they should slowly decrease. We used the same Gamma distribution model as in [20] (Fig. 3). The moment of the reached maximum is set to be 7 days.

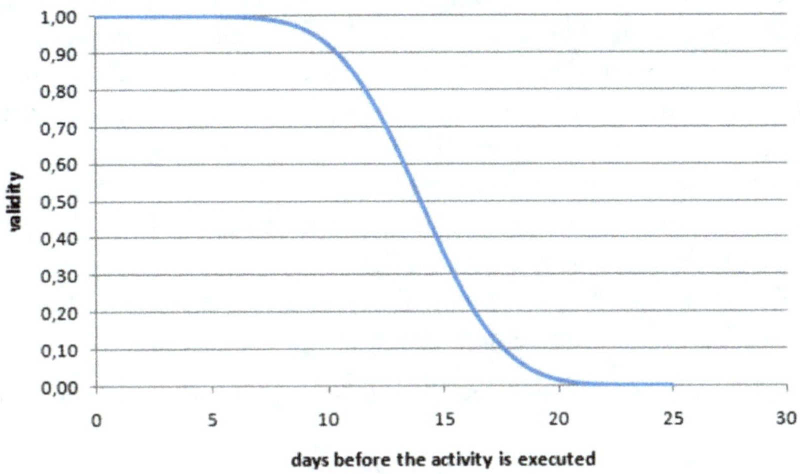

Fig. 2. Validity of a measurement before the activity is executed [20]

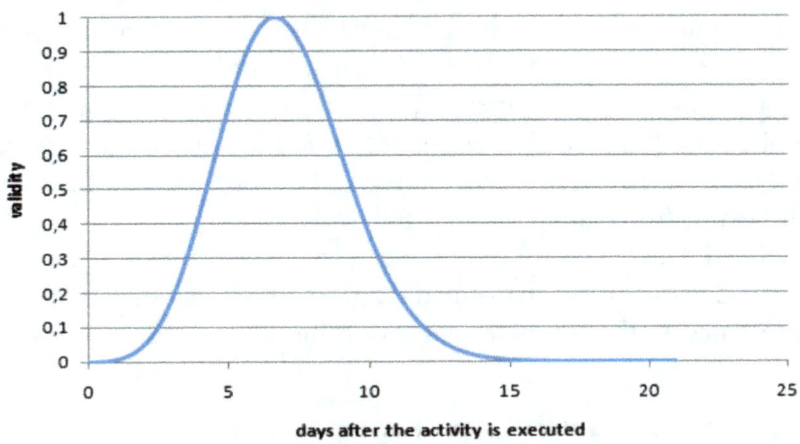

Fig. 3. Validity of a measurement after the activity is executed [20]

The usefulness value of an activity depends on the measurement value change. If the difference of the values (weight difference) between two measurements that are in a valid range (according to Fig. 3) has greater value, than the usefulness of the activities performed in the time range between these two measurement has greater value, too. The usefulness of each activity is calculated as follows:

$$U_A = \left(value_{Mp} - value_{Mn}\right) validity_{Mp}\ validity_{Mn}\ F_A \tag{3}$$

Where:

- U_A is the usefulness of activity A;
- $value_{Mp}$ is the parameter value (weight) of the measurement with biggest validity, taken before the activity has started, according the model presented in Fig. 2;
- $value_{Mn}$ is the parameter value (weight) of the measurement, taken after the activity has finished and had biggest validity, according the model presented in Fig. 3;
- $validity_{Mp}$ is the validity of the measurement taken before the activity has started and has the biggest validity, according to the cumulative normal distribution model;
- $validity_{Mn}$ is the validity of the measurement taken after the activity has finished, calculated with Gamma distribution model;
- F_A is the factor of importance for an activity, and it is an indicator of how much an activity contributed to measurement change.

The factor of importance for every activity is calculated as follows:

$$F_A = \frac{X_A}{N} \tag{4}$$

Where, X_A is the number of occurrences of activity A between two measurements and N is the total number of activities performed between two measurements.

The factor value is in the range [0, 1]. If there was only one activity that influences a parameter change in the measurement data, then its factor of importance will be one.

For example, if we have n activities between two measurements, of which x of them are 'walking', y are 'running' and z are 'cycling', then the factor for the walking type of activities will be x/n, for running y/n and for cycling z/n.

Having defined the factor of importance data class transformation can be performed. The raw data and the transformed data, to which classification method can be applied are presented in the following tables (Tables 1 and 2).

Table 1. Raw data representation

Type of activity	Total time (min)	Distance (m)	Calories
Running	25	4200	320
Walking	40	3700	250
Running	60	9350	580
Cycling	125	25530	1205
Swimming	25	970	410

Table 2. Class data representation

Type of activity	Time class	Distance class	Calories class	Factor of importance	Usefulness
Running	1	2	3	1	0.3
Walking	2	3	1	0.7	−0.1
Running	2	4	3	0.2	0.7
Cycling	3	3	2	0.5	−0.4
Swimming	1	2	1	0.6	0.9

Phase 3: Find N Most Useful Activities and Filter Test Data with Only N Most Useful Activities. In this step top N most useful activities for a given user are calculated and recommended. In our approach we recommend only the activities that will help the user to lose weight. Tests have been made using N = 10 (we recommend maximum ten most useful activities), and N = 1 (we recommend only the most useful activity). Test data are filtered against these recommendations. This way the test data will consists only of the activities that the user performed as recommendations. In Table 3 the results are shown based on the different test parameters.

Table 3. Results table

Accuracy	Weight difference	Number of max different given recommendations	Number of recommendations performed by the user
85%	0.5 kg	1	245
89%	0.5 kg	10	812
93%	1 kg	10	679
95%	1 kg	1	162

Phase 4: Apply Classification Methods on Test Data. In the final phase of the proposed methodology different classification algorithms are applied on test data. Tests with different parameters have been performed for each classification algorithm and accuracy, precision, recall and the mean absolute error are analyzed. Following classification methods are considered: Decision trees algorithms (Decision stump, J48 and Random Forest), Decision rules algorithm (Decision table), Bayes algorithm (Naïve Bayes) and Support vector machines (LibSVM).

4 Evaluation

4.1 Methodological Approach

For evaluation of the proposed algorithm, a specific methodology that consists of six steps has been defined:

(1) User u and moment m are chosen (using percentage split);
(2) All activities and measurements performed by u before m as a local training set are considered for generating recommendations. The other activities after moment m are used for testing the recommendations;
(3) Recommendation algorithm is used to generate recommendations for weight loss. For each activity a_u we calculate their usefulness for weight loss (if the user gained weight the usefulness is negative);
(4) The activities are grouped by their type (kind of activity, total time class, distance class and calories class), and sorted by their usefulness;
(5) The most useful activities for weight loss are considered for recommendation. The recommended activities are compared with the activities from the test data (after moment m). If they have the same usefulness (positive), then we consider to have a positive recommendation. If we don't find that type of activity in the test set, we assume that the user didn't implement the recommendation;
(6) Classification methods are applied on the test data (which is consisted only of the recommended activities), to analyze the accuracy of the algorithm.

Few more constraints are added to filter the observations generated according to the above method in order to get more relevant results. For the purpose of the experiment at least 2 measurements in the local training sets of all observations should be present, the period between consecutive measurements $next(a_u)$ and $prevp(a_u)$ should be at least 5 days and at most 20 days. Additionally, *au* should not be performed in the last 2 days of the interval because we want to increase the chances that the activity influenced $next(a_u)$.

4.2 Experimental Evaluation

The dataset used for this experiment is outdoor activity data set collected from the SportyPal service. The collected dataset is generated by 1000 users. Six different attributes are used for classification purpose: activity type, total time, calories burned, distance passed, the calculated factor of importance and usefulness (positive or negative) (Table 2).

Three types of activities (representing 90% of all activities performed) are analyzed: Walking, Running and Cycling (Figs. 4, 5 and 6). The cycling activities represented 10% of the analyzed activities (from running, walking and cycling), walking represented 30% of the activities, and running represented 60% of the activities.

- The recommendations of activities with longer distances had biggest accuracies.
- The walking recommendations had highest accuracy when the duration time was in the range of 90 min to 120 min and the calories spent were between 500 and 1000.
- The running recommendations had highest accuracy when the total time was in the range of 60 min to 90 min, for distances from 15 to 20 km.
- The cycling recommendations had highest accuracies for short durations and calories expenditure to 1000.

As we are using class data representation for better manipulation of the data and for classification purposes, we analyzed the accuracy of the given recommendations for different number of classes.

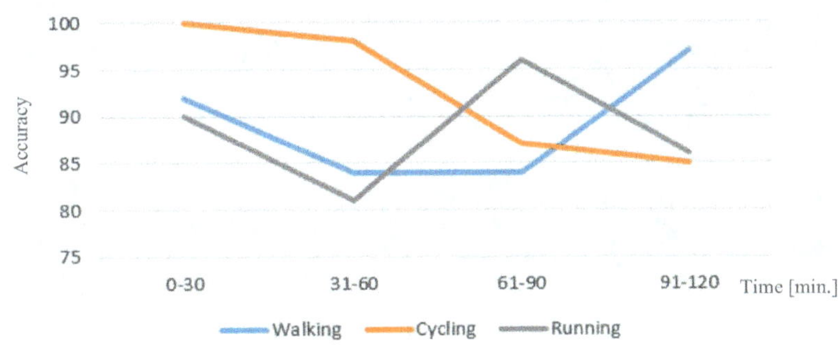

Fig. 4. Accuracy of recommendations by time range (in minutes)

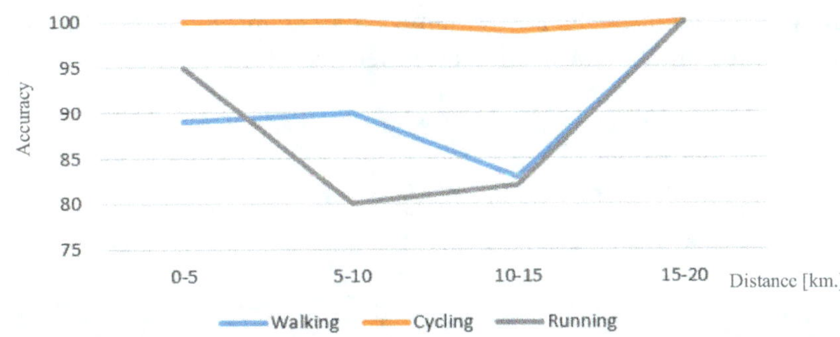

Fig. 5. Accuracy of recommendations by distance range (in kilometers)

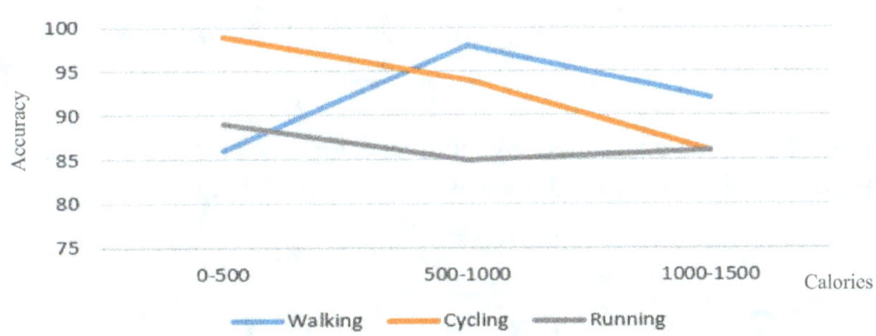

Fig. 6. Accuracy of recommendations by calories range

We can see from Figs. 7, 8 and 9, that as we increase the number of classes, we get less recommendations. The accuracy reaches some peak in a three class representation and that is why we used this number of classes. The accuracy of the recommendations increases as we have bigger weight difference for generating valid recommendations. Because there are fluctuations of the weight during the day, when we are considering only 0.5 kg difference in measurement change, we are not sure if that difference was influenced by some other factors as food/liquid intake, time of the measurement (in the morning or later during the day), or is it just as a result of the performed activities. That is why the accuracy of the recommendations gives better performance when considering measurement difference of 1 kg and even 1.5 kg.

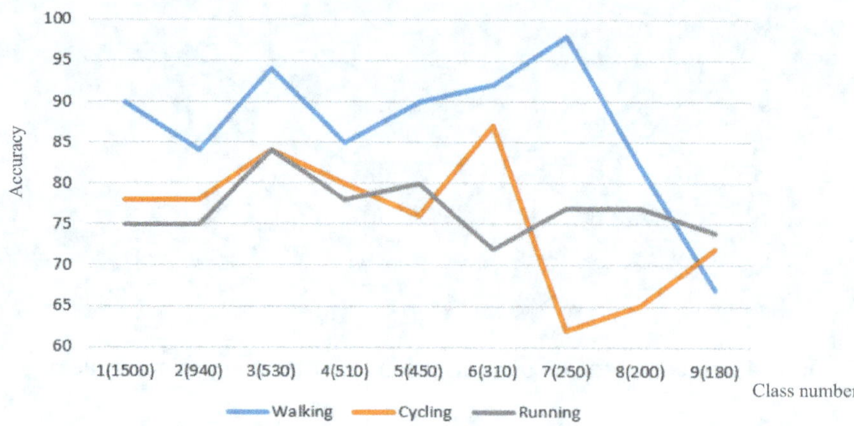

Fig. 7. Accuracy of recommendations, by number of parameter classes for activities: class number (number of recommendations), for least difference of 0.5 kg

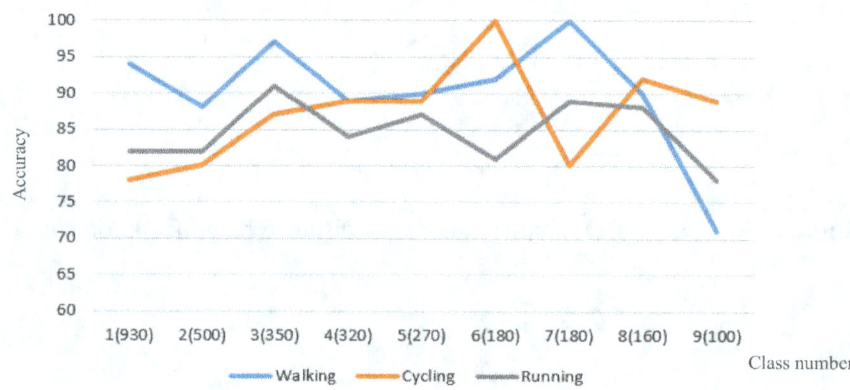

Fig. 8. Accuracy of recommendations, by number of parameter classes for activities: class number (number of recommendations), for least difference of 1 kg

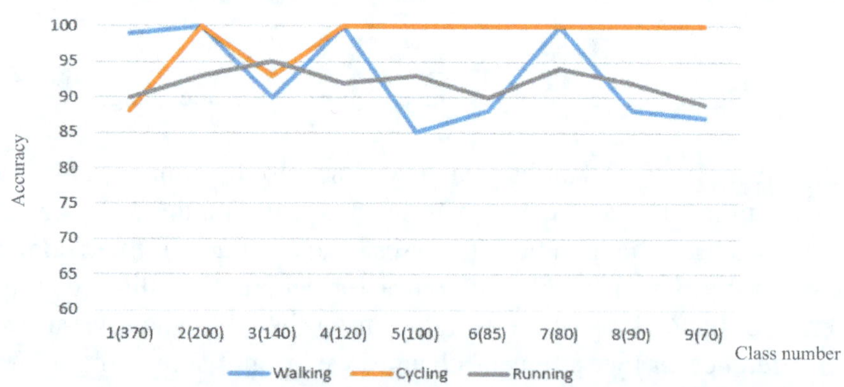

Fig. 9. Accuracy of recommendations, by number of parameter classes for activities: class number (number of recommendations), for least difference of 1.5 kg

Metrics Used

Although the accuracy is very important factor to analyze the performance of recommendation algorithms, used alone as a metric it is not enough [27].

Therefore, in our work additional metrics are used: accuracy, mean absolute error (MAE), precision and recall to evaluate and compare the recommendation performance of the used algorithms. The accuracy of the system is high as the MAE of the prediction system is low. A well-performed prediction system should maximize the precisions and recalls. Precision can be thought of as a measure of a classifiers exactness. Recall can be thought of as a measure of a classifiers completeness [28]. The mean absolute error is used to measure how close forecasts or predictions are to the eventual outcome, without considering their direction. It measures accuracy for continuous variables.

$$Precision = \frac{tp}{tp + fp} \tag{5}$$

$$Recall = \frac{tp}{tp + fn} \tag{6}$$

$$Accuracy = \frac{tp + tn}{tp + tn + fp + fn} \tag{7}$$

$$F_1 = 2 * \frac{Precision * Recall}{Precision + Recall} \tag{8}$$

Where:

- *tp*: true positives (number of examples predicted positive that are actually positive)
- *fp*: false positives (number of examples predicted positive that are actually negative)
- *tn*: true negatives (number of examples predicted negative that are actually negative)
- *fn*: false negatives (number of examples predicted negative that are actually positive)
- F_1 score is the harmonic average of the precision and recall (F1 score reaches its best value at 1 and worst at 0).

The different metrics for several classifiers: LibSVM, Decision Stump (DS), J48, Naïve Bayes (NB), Decision Table (DT) and Random Forest (RF), are shown on Fig. 10, where the top N (N = 1 and N = 10) most useful activities are recommended.

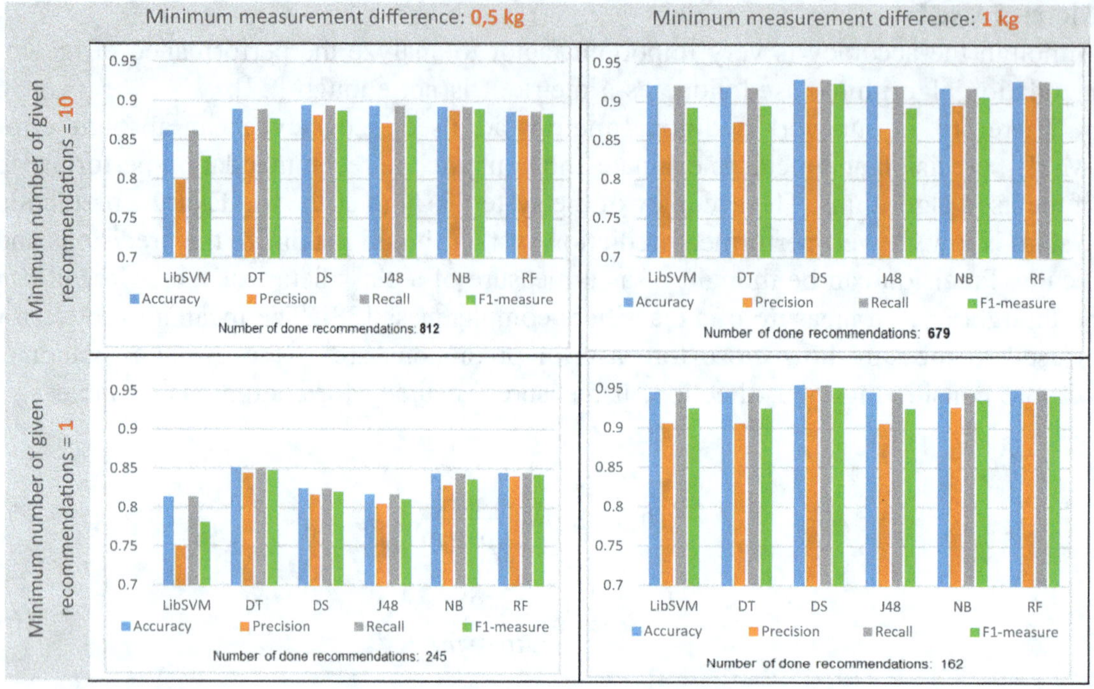

Fig. 10. Metrics results of evaluating the performance of classifiers

Experimental Results

This activity recommender system model incorporates several classification algorithms:

- We used a 10-fold cross validation with: J48, Decision Stump, Decision Table, LibSVM and Naïve Bayes, because the data set (consisted of 1000 users) is not very large.
- RF has been built on 10 trees.
- The classifiers showed results with accuracy from 85% to 95% depending of the parameters value.
- The classifiers performed with higher accuracy when taking into account only measurement difference of more than 1 kg.
- Classifiers: Decision Stump (DS), Decision Table (DT) and Random Forest (RF) showed a better general performance over LibSVM, Naïve Bayes (NB) and J48.
- The best performance of the recommender algorithm is with accuracy of 95% (Decision Stump), when recommending only one best activity to the user and the measurement difference is more than 1 kg, but unfortunately this was performed on a small scale data (due to the parameter restrictions), consisted of only 162 valid activities.
- The analysis of the data showed that the most important parameter when recommending physical activities is the distance of the activity. With longer distance activity recommendations, the accuracy of the model increased.

- Even though the users performed overall 20 different activities, only Walking, Running and Cycling were taken into consideration when analyzing the data since they were consisting 90% of all activities.
- The cycling activities represented around 10% of the analyzed activities (only running, walking and cycling), walking represented around 30% of the activities, and running represented almost 60% of the activities.

Overall, the performance of the classifiers for generating recommendations without using collaborative filtering technique has been very effective with accuracy of 85% to 95% when using measurement difference bigger than 0.5 kg and 1 kg, and even bigger accuracy when using measurement difference bigger than 1.5 kg.

5 Conclusion and Future Work

In this paper, we presented and compared the results of several data mining techniques for activity recommender system. For the generation of the recommendations, only the user's history data of activities and measurements were used. Even without using any collaborative filtering techniques in the process of generating recommendations, the accuracy of the given recommendations showed great results with accuracy of (85% to 95%). We used the same data set from a sport activity service, SportyPal [29], as in the COHESY algorithm implemented in the previous work. The analyzed results also showed that the accuracy rises when the difference change in the parameter (weight) is bigger. Further study on testing different algorithms and recommendation methodologies can be considered to achieve better accuracy. Also new real medical data set, of patients with chronic diseases can be considered to be used to test the proposed recommender algorithm, and continue with its improvement.

Acknowledgement. The authors acknowledge EU COST Action IC1303 Algorithms, Architectures and Platforms for Enhanced Living Environments (AAPELE www.aapele.eu).

References

1. World Health Organization (WHO), World Health Statistics 2012, pp. 34–41. WHO Press, Geneva, Switzerland (2012)
2. Nelson, M.E., et al.: Physical activity and public health in older adults: recommendation from the American College of Sports Medicine and the American Heart Association. Circulation **116**(9), 1094 (2007)
3. Start active, stay active: a report on physical activity for health from the four home countries, Chief Medical Officers, Department of Health, United Kingdom (2011)
4. Costa, S., Ogilvie, D., Dalton, A., Westgate, K., Brage, S., Panter, J.: Quantifying the physical activity energy expenditure of commuters using a combination of global positioning system and combined heart rate and movement sensors. Prev. Med. **81**, 339–344 (2015)
5. Kotevska, O., Vlahu-Gjorgievska, E., Trajkovic, V., Koceski, S.: Towards a patient-centered collaborative health care system model. Int. J. Comput. Theory Eng. IJCTE **4**(6), 1025–1029 (2012)

6. Physical activity strategy for the WHO European Region 2016–2025. World Health Organization, Vilnius, Lithuania (2015)
7. Koceski, S., Koceska, N.: Evaluation of an assistive telepresence robot for elderly healthcare. J. Med. Syst. **40**(5), 121 (2016)
8. Falk, K.: Practical Recommender Systems. Manning Publications Co., Shelter Island (2016)
9. Trajkovik, V., Vlahu-Gjorgievska, E., Koceski, S., Kulev, I.: General assisted living system architecture model. In: Agüero, R., Zinner, T., Goleva, R., Timm-Giel, A., Tran-Gia, P. (eds.) MONAMI 2014. LNICST, vol. 141, pp. 329–343. Springer, Cham (2015). https://doi.org/10.1007/978-3-319-16292-8_24
10. Kulev, I., Vlahu-Gjorgievska, E., Trajkovik, V., Koceski, S.: Development of a novel recommendation algorithm for collaborative health - care system model. Comput. Sci. Inf. Syst. **10**(3), 1455–1471 (2013)
11. Burke, R.: Hybrid web recommender systems. In: Brusilovsky, P., Kobsa, A., Nejdl, W. (eds.) The Adaptive Web. LNCS, vol. 4321, pp. 377–408. Springer, Heidelberg (2007). https://doi.org/10.1007/978-3-540-72079-9_12
12. Koceski, S., Petrevska, B.: Empirical evidence of contribution to e-tourism by application of personalized tourism recommendation system. Ann. Alexandru Ioan Cuza Univ. -Econ. **59** (1), 363–374 (2012)
13. Marinho, L.B., et al.: Social tagging recommender systems. In: Ricci, F., Rokach, L., Shapira, B., Kantor, P.B. (eds.) Recommender Systems Handbook, pp. 615–644. Springer, Boston, MA (2011). https://doi.org/10.1007/978-0-387-85820-3_19
14. Eirinaki, M., Vazirgiannis, M.: Web mining for web personalization. ACM Trans. Internet Technol. (TOIT) **3**(1), 1–27 (2003)
15. Ramakrishnan, N.: PIPE: Web personalization by partial evaluation. IEEE Internet Comput. **4**(6), 21–31 (2000)
16. Karimi, R.: Active learning for recommender systems. KI-Künstliche Intelligenz **28**(4), 329–332 (2014)
17. Jannach, D., Zanker, M., Felfernig, A., Friedrich, G.: Recommender Systems: an Introduction. Cambridge University Press, Cambridge (2010)
18. Wiesner, M., Pfeifer, D.: Health recommender systems: concepts, requirements, technical basics and challenges. Int. J. Environ. Res. Public Health **11**(3), 2580–2607 (2014)
19. Ramakrishnan, N., Benjamin, J.K., Batul, J.M., Ananth, Y.G., George, K.: When being weak is brave: privacy in recommender systems. IEEE Internet Comput. **6**, 54–62 (2001)
20. Trajkovik, V., Koceski, S., Vlahu-Gjorgievska, E., Kulev, I.: Evaluation of health care system model based on collaborative algorithms. In: Adibi, S. (ed.) Mobile Health. SSB, vol. 5, pp. 429–451. Springer, Cham (2015). https://doi.org/10.1007/978-3-319-12817-7_19
21. Bassam, F., Channanath, A.M., Behbehani, K., Thanaraj, T.A.: Predictive models to assess risk of type 2 diabetes, hypertension and comorbidity: machine-learning algorithms and validation using national health data from Kuwait—a cohort study (2013)
22. Soni, J., Ansari, U., Sharma, D., Soni, S.: Predictive data mining for medical diagnosis: an overview of heart disease prediction. Int. J. Comput. Appl. **17**(8), 43–48 (2011)
23. Duen-Yian, Y., Ching-Hsue, C., Yen-Wen, C.: A predictive model for cerebrovascular disease using data mining. Expert Syst. Appl. **38**(7), 8970–8977 (2011)
24. Hussein, A.S., Omar, W.M., Li, X., Ati, M.: Efficient chronic disease diagnosis prediction and recommendation system. In: IEEE EMBS Conference on Biomedical Engineering and Sciences (IECBES), pp. 209–214. IEEE (2012)
25. Van der Burg, J.M., Gardiner, S.L., Ludolph, A.C., Landwehrmeyer, G.B., Roos, R.A., Aziz, N.A.: Body weight is a robust predictor of clinical progression in Huntington disease. Ann. Neurol. **82**, 479–483 (2017)

26. Bangalore, S., Fayyad, R., Laskey, R., DeMicco, D.A., Messerli, F.H., Waters, D.D.: Body-weight fluctuations and outcomes in coronary disease. N. Engl. J. Med. **376**(14), 1332–1340 (2017)
27. Brownlee, J.: Machine learning mastery. http://machinelearningmastery.com/classification-accuracy-is-not-enough-more-performance-measures-you-can-use/. Accessed 01 Aug 2018
28. Op den Akker, H., Cabrita, M., Op den Akker, R., Jones, V.M., Hermens, H.J.: Tailored motivational message generation: a model and practical framework for real-time physical activity coaching. J. Biomed. Inform. **55**, 104–115 (2015)
29. SportyPal service. http://sportypal.com/. Accessed 01 Aug 2018

"Touchscreen Assessment Tool" (TATOO), an Assessment Tool Based on the Expanded Conceptual Model of Frailty

Alexandra Danial-Saad[1,2], Lorenzo Chiari[3], Yael Benvenisti[4(✉)], Shlomi Laufer[5], and Michal Elboim-Gabyzon[6]

[1] Occupational Therapy Department, Faculty of Social Welfare and Health Sciences, University of Haifa, Haifa, Israel
[2] The Arab Academic College for Education in Israel, Haifa, Israel
[3] Department of Electrical, Electronic, and Information Engineering, University of Bologna, Bologna, Italy
[4] Mediterranean Towers Ventures, Ganei Tikva, Israel
yaelbenvenisti@gmail.com
[5] Faculty of Industrial Engineering and Management, The Technion, Haifa, Israel
[6] Physical Therapy Department, Faculty of Social Welfare and Health Sciences, University of Haifa, Haifa, Israel

Abstract. Frailty is a common clinical syndrome in older adults; it carries an increased risk of negative health events and outcomes including falls, incident disability, hospitalization, and mortality. Therefore, it is critical to identify high-risk subsets of the elderly population and explore new arenas for frailty prevention and treatment. This chapter will provide an overview of the current state of assessment models for frailty syndrome in the elderly and will describe a new assessment tool based on mobile technology, which takes account and advantage of the ways in which elderly people interact with a touchscreen. While healthcare providers and researchers in the field of aging have long been aware of the changing characteristics and needs of older people living in the community, there has not been any marked change in frailty syndrome assessment models until now. In the twenty-first century world with its technological advancements, the elderly require new, special physical skills combining perceptual, motor, and cognitive abilities for their functional daily activities and for maintaining their independence and quality of life.

We believe a conceptual model of frailty can be expanded to incorporate new aspects related to the usage of technology by the elderly, better covering the complexity and multidimensionality of modern life. In addition, in our vision, that the expanded conceptual model can be operationalized and translated into an assessment tool.

In the last part of this chapter, we will present the "Touchscreen Assessment Tool" (TATOO), an assessment tool based on this expanded conceptual model. This novel tool assesses elderly people's frailty and functioning using a touchscreen, a representative technology required for several activities involved

I. Ganchev et al. (Eds.): Enhanced Living Environments, LNCS 11369, pp. 96–107, 2019.
https://doi.org/10.1007/978-3-030-10752-9_5

in daily functioning in the modern world. Most importantly, we present the TATOO prototype, which we plan to develop in the future as a continuous monitoring instrument for activities performed in daily life, combined with advanced sensor-based measuring and big data analytics algorithms.

Keywords: Frailty syndrome · Elderly · Touchscreen Assessment Tool

1 Background

Frailty syndrome is a common syndrome in the elderly, with a multi-factor etiology [1]. Frailty syndrome consists of the basic characteristic of increased susceptibility to biological, physiological, and mental stressors. Impairments in multiple organ systems (such as the musculoskeletal system, the cardiovascular system, and the hematological system) cause depletion in physiological and mental reserves and decrease resistance, thereby impeding the recovery ability of the elderly as well as their ability to maintain physiological and psychosocial homeostasis [2]. Accordingly, as previous studies have pointed out, frailty is related to a higher prevalence of disability, falls, hospitalization, and mortality in community-dwelling older people. It is a major predictor of clinical outcomes and prognosis following any extrinsic stress, such as medical procedure, acute illness, proximal hip fracture, or hospitalization [3–5].

The understanding of frailty has evolved over the years from a basic description of dependence on others to a more dynamic model that encompasses biomedical and psychosocial aspects. It depicts a complex interplay among a person's characteristics, such as age, gender, lifestyle, socioeconomic background, morbidities, and affective, cognitive, or sensory impairments. Currently, as there is no firm agreement among experts on the definition of frailty, it can be considered an amorphous concept, a situation that impedes our ability to identify it in the elderly and assess their condition.

Frailty, comorbidity, and disability are all common in the elderly, with overlaps and reciprocal interactions making it sometimes difficult to distinguish among them [6, 7]. Disability, defined as "difficulty or dependency in performing activities that are essential to independent living" [6], often worsens a person's frailty, but not all elderly with disabilities are frail and not all the frail elderly have disabilities [8].

A major requirement at present is to move from theoretical discussion on definitions of frailty to outlining practical and operational definitions that enable actual screening, assessment, and treatment of frailty, as well as differentiating frailty-related and unrelated conditions. For example, one major manifestation of frailty is functional decline, but functional decline in the elderly is part of the normal aging process and is not always an indicator of frailty.

Frailty is dynamic in nature and can be viewed as a process parallel to the process of aging; and age increases the risk of frailty [9]. The elderly population is heterogeneous in terms of chronological age and biological, psychological, and social factors, and hence, they cannot be considered a single entity. Thus, researchers often group older adults by chronological age, for example, considering adults ranging in the age group 60–75 years as a younger-old group, and individuals over 75 as an older-old group [10]. The challenge is then to find a point in time when a given elderly patient moves from only aging to becoming frail as well.

Despite being progressive and chronic, frailty syndrome is also reversible in the pre-frailty stage and in the early stages of frailty; accordingly, screening of the elderly population is required for early detection of elderly who are frail or at risk of becoming frail. Continuous monitoring, preventive interventions, and treatment programs should be made routine in healthcare for the ever-growing elderly population all over the world [11, 12]. In contrast to the early stages, advanced frailty syndrome is irreversible, but its rate of progression can still be reduced to some extent, with the possibility of reducing and preventing complications and improving quality of life [13].

A crucial need in this regard is to operationalize the concept of frailty by developing validated, reliable, feasible assessment tools to capture all the clinical aspects of geriatric frailty. It should be emphasized that diagnosing an older person as frail has implications at several levels, ranging from the individual to health policy and systems.

The complexity of frailty and the difficulty in distinguishing between natural aging and pathological conditions have led to the development of models and instruments that attempt to comprehensively cover all the aspects of the condition [5, 14–16]. Numerous diagnostic tools for frailty have been developed in recent years. A systematic review by Buta et al. [17] identified 67 frailty instruments, of which only 9 were highly cited. The instruments most used are the physical frailty phenotype, followed by the frailty index (also called the "deficit accumulation index") [17].

The physical frailty phenotype is the single most widely used instrument for assessing frailty [17], and is based on the frailty phenotype model developed by Fried et al. [5]. It stipulates a cluster of consensus elements of clinical presentation of frailty: age-related changes in body mass, muscle strength, endurance, pattern of walking, and level of physical activity [5, 14, 18]. The crucial points involved in frailty versus normal age-related change in this model are the existence of multiple impaired elements and the degree of change. The physical phenotype of frailty was operationalized by Fried et al. and validated by the Cardiovascular Health Study [5]. As per the study, frailty is characterized by the presence of three or more of the following five components: (1) unintentional weight loss (more than 4.55 kg in a year), (2) muscle weakness (grip strength in the lowest 20% at baseline, adjusted for gender and body mass index), (3) poor endurance and energy (evaluated by self-report of exhaustion), (4) slow walking speed (time to walk 15 ft, adjusting for gender and standing height), and (5) low physical activity level (measured by kilocalories expended per week). Scores on these parameters are categorized into three levels of frailty: (1) robustness (none of the criteria), (2) pre-frailty (one or two criteria), and (3) frailty (three or more criteria) [5].

Another common tool is the frailty index, developed by Rockwood et al. [19], which comprises 70 items on the presence and severity of diseases, ability to perform activities of daily living (ADLs; e.g., getting dressed, bathing, mobility), and physical and neurological signs from clinical examinations. The frailty index focuses on objective measures of the amount of accumulated deficits/functional losses, reflecting the degree of exhaustion of reserves [16].

Cesari et al. [16] compare the physical phenotype of frailty and the frailty index and find that the two tools provide "distinct and complementary clinical information about the risk profile of an older person" [16]. The authors suggest that the purposes of the tools are different and that their respective usage should be determined by the timing of the assessment, with physical frailty phenotype tool used as a screening tool for quick identification of frailty as a gross category and the frailty index as part of a comprehensive geriatric assessment to serve as reference data for following the elderly over time, making subsequent assessments, and examining the efficiency of targeted interventions [16].

The existence of numerous measurement tools indicates a lack of agreement on the conceptual framework and components of frailty, appropriate assessment items, purpose of use (risk assessment, etiology, research methodologies design), clinical practicality, and differentiating between disability and frailty [17, 20]. However, efforts to establish consensus are ongoing and the seeds of agreement can be seen [17, 21, 22].

2 Operational Definitions of Frailty

It is recognized that operational definitions of frailty should be: (1) multi-dimensional, based on the connections between physical, psychological, and social domains, and not constrained to physical function; (2) clearly distinct from disability; (3) cognizant of comorbidity (presence of ≥ 2 diseases); (4) proven valid for predicting negative outcomes; (5) feasible; and (6) continuous and not categorical in terms of scoring.

Measurement of frailty should be based on continuous scores due to the nature of frailty, which is a progressive process. Raphael et al. [23] claimed that the degree of frailty on that continuum is a result of the interaction between **personal factors** and **environmental factors**. They described both types of factors in detail: "'personal factors' include the immediate cognitive (e.g., memory loss), physical (e.g., reduced mobility), psychological (e.g., depression, lack of self-efficacy), and spiritual factors (e.g., loss of hope or meaning), while 'environmental factors' include financial, social (e.g., availability of friends or family), living situation (e.g., many steps, danger in one's neighborhood), and legal (e.g., not being able to drive because of legislation) factors."

We believe that using technology can be crucial in integrating personal and environmental factors. The novel assessment tool described here is based on "**person–environment interactions**," and it tries to overcome the insufficient emphasis on the environmental aspect reflected in previous tools by leveraging the common use of technology in ADLs in the modern world. Technologies such as touchscreens, voice recognition systems, artificial intelligence, etc., are becoming increasingly prevalent in daily life among the general population and considerably more among older adults [24].

The traditional methods for assessing frailty syndrome in the elderly, however, do not use these emerging technologies, which facilitate continuous, passive, objective assessments. A tool reflecting their technological affordances can considerably improve accuracy, including by reflecting the context (a person's natural environment).

Evidence for this approach has been shown in recent years in healthcare in general, with medical tests that no longer rely solely on subjective evaluations but also employ objective evaluations using advanced algorithms [25, 26].

Moreover, since the percentage of elderly people in the world is increasing along with their life expectancy, clinicians cannot rely on individual face-to-face meetings to evaluate and monitor each person over time because of both the economic costs involved in these tests and the lack of manpower [27]. Hence, to diagnose and monitor over time the frailty of an older person and allow him/her to receive treatment/intervention to improve his/her condition, or prevent deterioration, we as a society must develop new, effective, inexpensive technology-based assessment tools. Figure 1 below illustrates the components that should be included in the modern assessment of frailty.

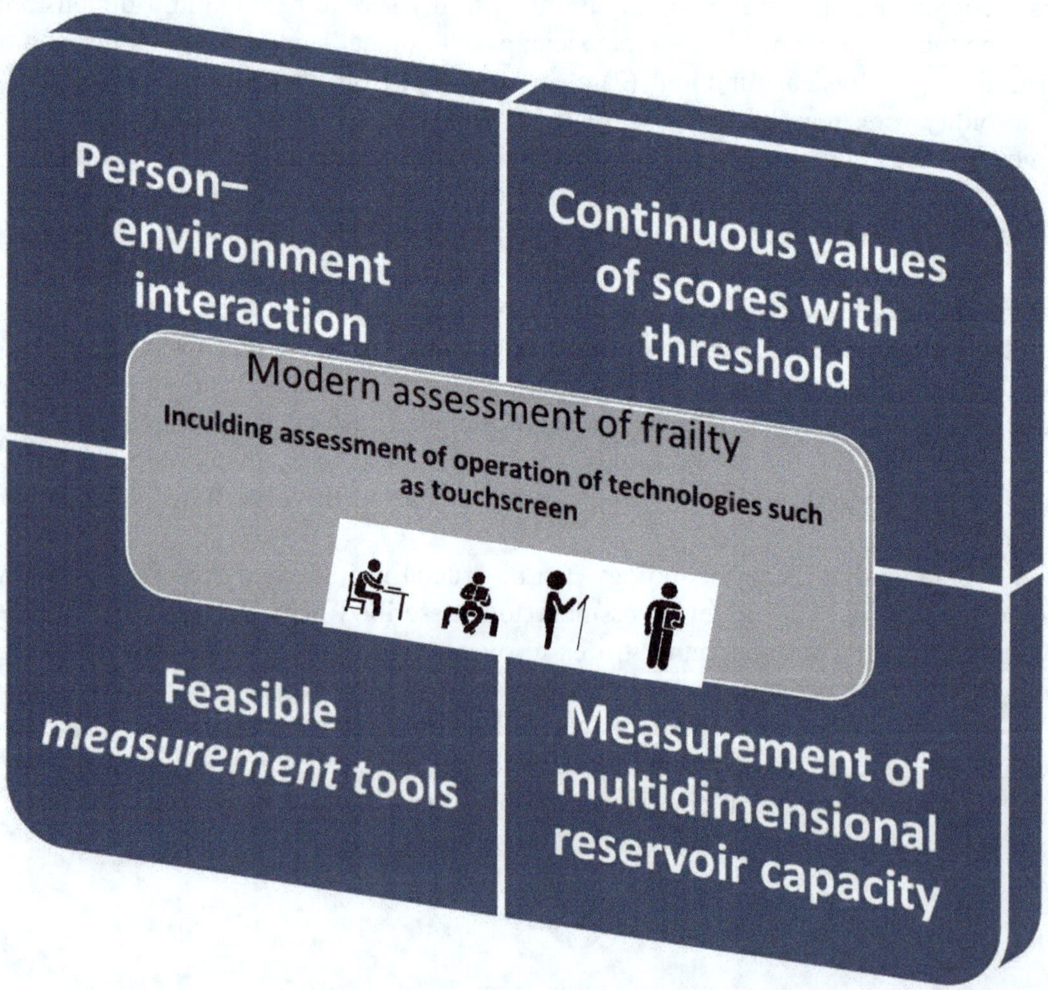

Fig. 1. Mandatory components of frailty assessment

3 A Touchscreen Tool for Assessment Based on the Expanded Conceptual Model of Frailty

We believe that the conceptual framework of frailty is incomplete and does not cover all the aspects of the real life of individuals in the modern world. The model should be extended to reflect the performance of the elderly engaged in daily activities in an environment in which technology is embedded in each one of the three components of the human function (physical, psychological, and social). In today's highly technology-oriented world, elderly individuals are obliged to interact safely and proficiently not only with technological applications designed for their benefit, but also with multiple technological devices developed for the general (and often young) population.

The use of a touchscreen is an excellent example of a technological application that has become prevalent in all aspects of modern life. Due to the convenience, design flexibility, and ease involved in manipulating touch interfaces [28], this technology is frequently used in public settings and is one of the most dominant ways by which the elderly interact with modern computing devices [28]. Touchscreens are now used by the elderly to perform multiple daily functional activities in pursuing their social, personal and occupational activities, ranging from buying a ticket for public transportation, ordering food in a restaurant, withdrawing money from an ATM, or accessing health services and health information. Using a touchscreen is also related to the social and leisure domains of human functions as it is used for communicating via smartphone and for personal interactions via social media (such as Facebook); hence, it may reflect the degree of social inclusion and social support the elderly have in coping with loneliness issues.

Our idea is consistent with Nourhashémi et al. [22] who asserted that frailty in elderly persons should be assessed in the context of a combination of not only biological, physiological, and social changes, but also **environmental changes**. The modern world is characterized by such rapid changes in the several aspects of daily life, with a growing pervasiveness of technological components. These technologies should enhance the elderly's independence in life's roles, make their leisure activities more meaningful, and enhance their self-esteem.

Following the modification of the frailty model, an operational definition and an assessment tool are required to measure the ability of the elderly to operate technology, in this case, the touchscreen (see Fig. 1).

The transfer from normal aging into dynamic frailty status is a continuous process that can be investigated through changes in how operating a touchscreen, as an example of a pervasive technology of daily use, changes over time. We assume that operating the touchscreen may be a sensitive way of detecting early signs of frailty and, accordingly, that it can be used as a screening tool for quick identification of pre-frailty as a gross category with the potential of further development once integrated into a comprehensive geriatric assessment to serve as reference data for following the elderly over time and for examining the efficacy of the targeted interventions.

4 The TATOO and Its Importance

In recent years, research and clinical studies have focused on finding ways and criteria to assess the status of the elderly people, in order to identify situations in which support is needed to enable their continued independent active aging in the community. An increasing part of daily functioning involves the use of touchscreens to perform tasks in various areas of life, such as communication, administrative tasks, healthcare, etc. The specific physical, perceptual, and cognitive skills required to use touchscreens may be affected by a multisystem decline in body functions and capabilities that occur during aging, such as decreased reaction speed, worsening eye–hand coordination, decreased muscle strength, and sensory decline [1]. Thus, differences in the ability to successfully operate a touchscreen are expected between young and old adults. These differences may be intensified in frail older adults and in older adults with age-related pathological conditions, such as arthritis, stroke, or Parkinson's disease. While most age-related physiological changes (e.g., cardiovascular changes) affect human performance, the body systems most relevant to the operation of a touchscreen are the sensory-perceptual system, the psychomotor system, and cognition.

Therefore, it is essential to identify evaluation tools that can measure the actual interaction between an elderly person and a touchscreen, as a representation of many technological interfaces that require similar skills. Furthermore, a well-fitted technology may contribute to the elderly by engage them in basic and instrumental activities of daily living, enhance their independence, provide meaningful leisure activities, and help them acquire more self-esteem and become productive members of mainstream society. The process of achieving an optimal match between technology and the elderly should involve an assessment of their needs, emotional state, preferences, and acceptance.

Among technology professionals who play a central role in prescription, provision, and adaptation of devices to meet the elderly's needs, there is a lack of dependable assessment tools to determine elderly behavior and needs while using touchscreen devices. Daniel-Saad and Chiari [24] developed a software application called TATOO to evaluate performance components of the use of touchscreens in a comprehensive and objective manner. The tool was developed by gaining a consensus regarding the user skills required to operate various touchscreen devices. A six-step procedure was used to collect and validate the required skills by a multidisciplinary team of 52 experts. TATOO consists of six tasks, each of which provides information on a functional component required when using a touchscreen, such as tap, swipe, pinch, drag, and so on. Performance of each task is summarized by a numeric and graphic report of the following parameters:

1. **Timing:** includes Start Time, Reaction Time, Test Duration, Total Touch Time (the time the finger is on the screen while tapping and dragging), and Total Flight Time (the time the finger is up in the air between drags).
2. **Movement range and pressure measurement:** the report shows a graphical "taps map and path drawing" representing the location of the taps, the path the client has used to drag, and the pressure applied while executing each drag.
3. **Mode of operation:** the number of fingers used to operate for each skill.

4. **Accuracy:** the report shows numerical and graphical information that presents trials that were completed successfully or not completed. The information includes the location of the first tap on the screen, Total Touch Outside the Target, Total Drag Attempts, and Drag Completed Successfully or Not Completed.

The TATOO was used primarily to assess touchscreen performance by children. Currently, we are in the process of adjusting the system to assess the performance of the elderly population, particularly focusing on the detection of early stages of frailty. The system can be used for routine and periodic evaluation of the elderly by healthcare personnel. Health professionals such as physicians, occupational therapists, physical therapists, or nurses can use TATOO because of its easy method of operation, which is not time consuming to learn or implement. Information supplied by TATOO provides objective data that enable clinical decisions (such as prescribing treatment) by multi-disciplinary healthcare professionals. Integrating the system to the healthcare services will enable early assessment of change or regression in the visual–perceptual motor function of the elderly to enable early intervention and prevention of reversible deterioration or complication.

The current study was approved by the Helsinki Committee of the University of Haifa. The sample will be composed of 300 elderly people divided into three age groups as follows: 1. Younger adults (40–65 years); 2. Young-old adults (65 to 75 years) and 3. Older-old adults (over 75 years). The inclusion criteria are: ability to understand simple commands; living independently in the community or in independent living facilities; and ability to walk independently with or without walking aid. Exclusion criteria are: neurological diseases and severe orthopedic and cardiopulmonary conditions that may affect performance of daily activities; pain, impairments, or medical conditions that may prohibit performance of required activities; and serious uncorrected vision or hearing impairment. Younger adults will be recruited from the institutes' campus; young-old and older-old adults will be recruited from community centers for the elderly. All participants will provide written consent following a detailed explanation of the study.

The study will include three stages: 1. performance in a battery of clinical assessments to characterize the participants' physical and cognitive status and level of frailty; 2. capturing of data by the TATOO; 3. Data analysis.

Stage 1: Characterization of the participants. The following information will be collected from all the eligible and consenting participants: (a) socio-demographic data (such as age, gender, marital status, years of education, use of the Internet, frequency of use of touch screens, level of income); (b) medical history. For participants from the two elderly groups, additional evaluation will be done to characterize them in term of (a) level of functioning in performing basic daily activities, measured by Index of Independence in Activities of Daily Living—Katz index; (b) fear of falling, using the Activities-specific Balance Confidence (ABC) Scale, (c) cognitive status, by the Montreal Cognitive Assessment (MoCA) questionnaire; (d) fine motor performance; and (e) level of frailty (measured by frailty phenotype instrument). It should be mentioned that the frailty phenotype instrument includes assessment of bilateral handgrip strength using a calibrated JAMAR hand dynamometer (Sammons Preston Rolyan, IL, USA) and walking speed measured by stopwatch. In addition, balance ability is measured by the "timed Up & Go" (TUG) test (an index for dynamic balance function). Fine motor performance is measured by calibrated hydraulic pinch gauge (Ernest Bontage) and by the Functional Dexterity Test (FDT).

Stage 2: Capture of data by the TATOO system. Following the performing of the six TATOO tasks, which will last for approximately 10 min, each participant will evaluate TATOO usability and user satisfaction by completing the System Usability Scale (SUS).

Stage 3: Data Analysis. We will determine the correlations between TATOO and performance measures as well as frailty level, and create a composite score which will include traditional measures and TATOO performance.

In a preliminary pilot study with nine older-old adults (mean age 80.4, SD 4.5) the TATOO's usability was rated as "very good" (average score of SUS 77.5) in terms of: effectiveness, efficiency and user satisfaction. The two healthcare professionals who conducted the trials reported that TATOO, from their point of view, was very user friendly in terms of short time assessment. Moreover, the interface was easy to learn and use, and the tool motivated the elderly to cooperate with the healthcare professionals.

Preliminary analysis demonstrates that young age, previous experience with a touch screen device, and high frequency of usage of touch screen positively correlate with better performance ability of the TATOO in term of timing and accuracy. Additionally, the amount of pressure on the screen is related to the accuracy requirements for task completion.

Conclusions regarding the correlation between TATOO scores and the degree of frailty of the elderly will be possible only after completing the current study with a large sample of participants ranging between younger and older-old adults.

Following is a presentation of the TATOO performance of a single female subject (initials HV), age 79 years. This subject is categorized as robust as defined by physical frailty phenotype, is independent in all activities of daily living, and presents with grip strength within the normal range per age. In contrast, however, HV presents with a low score (22/30) in the MOCA, indicating mild cognitive impairment. In addition, the fine dexterity measurement scores of both hands were very low, indicating low neuromotor function of the hand. TATOO performance was characterized by the use of one finger to tap the screen when the time duration of the task was short and the task was easy; when the time duration was longer, or the task was more complex, the pattern of tapping changed to using more than one finger.

HV's TATOO accuracy parameters were low. For example, she made 17 attempts to drag the five items of clothing, and in 14 of these attempts she was unable to place the item correctly. (see Fig. 2 for screen display). This finding was consistent with her low score on the Fine Dexterity Test (FDT; 61.3 seconds) performed by the dominant hand.

Start Time:	16:02
Reaction Time [sec]:	2.81
Test Duration [sec]:	55
Total Flight Time [sec]:	22
Total Touch Time [sec]:	17.5
Total Drag Attempts:	14
Drag Completed Successfully:	5
Drag Not Completed:	0
Total Touch Outside the Target:	17
Touch with Multi-Fingers:	7

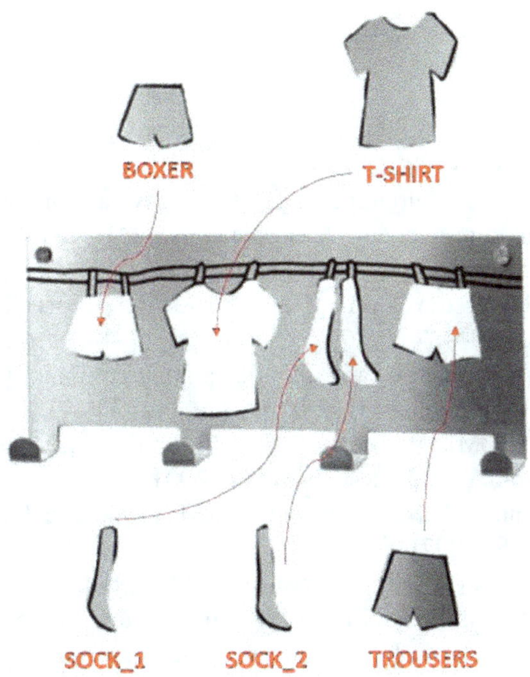

Fig. 2. Example of a screen display during a TATOO test, which includes the task and performance data of variables such as total touch time and touch time outside the target. (Color figure online)

5 Practical Implications

Frailty among the elderly leads to an increase in the use of health and welfare services and an increase in morbidity and mortality. Developing modern screening tools that are sensitive to early identification of frailty in the elderly and continuous monitoring is essential at the personal, national, and international levels. Knowledge of the course of development of frailty will enable identification of at-risk elderly and contribute to planning interventions and treatments to monitor and assist in situations of decreased physical and cognitive functioning. This will inevitably lead to better health outcomes, more disability-adjusted life years, and improved quality of life, as well as bringing economic savings [3].

The TATOO is a novel operational translation of an extended concept model of frailty of the elderly. It may become an important supplement to the toolbox available to clinical professionals treating the elderly. The current prototype provides quick, integrated information regarding the actual status of the elderly in relation to three crucial elements (fine motor, cognitive, and perceptual skills) reflecting performance and independence in basic and instrumental activities of daily living. Important point that should be emphasized is that TATOO has the potential to provide unique information that can be added to existing frailty indicators such as muscle weakness and slow walking speed. However, further studies should be performed to analyze the relative contribution and level of sensitivity and specificity of TATOO as a frailty screening and monitoring tool, comparing it to other frailty indicators.

References

1. Markle-Reid, M., Browne, G.: Conceptualizations of frailty in relation to older adults. J. Adv. Nurs. **44**(1), 58–68 (2003)
2. Bergman, H., Ferrucci, L., Guralnik, J., et al.: Frailty: an emerging research and clinical paradigm—issues and controversies. J. Gerontol. A **62**(7), 731–737 (2007)
3. Kim, D.H., Schneeweiss, S., Glynn, R.J., Lipsitz, L.A., Rockwood, K., Avorn, J.: Measuring frailty in medicare data: development and validation of a claims-based frailty index. J. Gerontol. A **73**(7), 980–987 (2017)
4. Kojima, G.: Frailty as a predictor of disabilities among community-dwelling older people: a systematic review and meta-analysis. Disabil. Rehabil. **39**(19), 1897–1908 (2017)
5. Fried, L.P., Tangen, C.M., Walston, J., et al.: Frailty in older adults: evidence for a phenotype. J. Gerontol. A **56**(3), M146–M157 (2001)
6. Campbell, A.J., Buchner, D.M.: Unstable disability and the fluctuations of frailty. Age Ageing **26**(4), 315–318 (1997)
7. Gobbens, R.J., Luijkx, K.G., Wijnen-Sponselee, M.T., Schols, J.M.: Toward a conceptual definition of frail community dwelling older people. Nurs. Outlook **58**(2), 76–86 (2010)
8. Fried, L.P., Ferrucci, L., Darer, J., Williamson, J.D., Anderson, G.: Untangling the concepts of disability, frailty, and comorbidity: implications for improved targeting and care. J. Gerontol. A **59**(3), M255–M263 (2004)
9. Robinson, T.N., Eiseman, B., Wallace, J.I., et al.: Redefining geriatric preoperative assessment using frailty, disability and co-morbidity. Ann. Surg. **250**(3), 449–455 (2009)
10. Czaja, S.J., Rogers, W.A., Fisk, A.D., Charness, N., Sharit, J.: Designing for Older Adults: Principles and Creative Human Factors Approaches. CRC Press, London (2009)
11. Fried, L.P., Hadley, E.C., Walston, J.D., et al.: From bedside to bench: research agenda for frailty. Sci. Aging Knowl. Environ. **2005**(31), 24 (2005)
12. Sacha, J., Sacha, M., Soboń, J., Borysiuk, Z., Feusette, P.: Is it time to begin a public campaign concerning frailty and pre-frailty? A review article. Front. Physiol. **8**, 484 (2017)
13. Chen, X., Mao, G., Leng, S.: Frailty syndrome: an overview. Clin. Interven. Aging **9**, 433 (2014)
14. Chin, A., Paw, M.J., Dekker, J.M., Feskens, E.J., Schouten, E.G., Kromhout, D.: How to select a frail elderly population? A comparison of three working definitions. J. Clin. Epidemiol. **52**(11), 1015–1021 (1999)
15. Rockwood, K., Fox, R.A., Stolee, P., Robertson, D., Beattie, B.: Frailty in elderly people: an evolving concept. CMAJ **150**(4), 489 (1994)
16. Cesari, M., Gambassi, G., Abellan van Kan, G., Vellas, B.: The frailty phenotype and the frailty index: different instruments for different purposes. Age Ageing **43**(1), 10–12 (2013)

17. Buta, B.J., Walston, J.D., Godino, J.G., et al.: Frailty assessment instruments: systematic characterization of the uses and contexts of highly-cited instruments. Ageing Res. Rev. **26**, 53–61 (2016)
18. Winograd, C.H., Gerety, M.B., Chung, M., Goldstein, M.K., Dominguez Jr., F., Vallone, R.: Screening for frailty: criteria and predictors of outcomes. J. Am. Geriatr. Soc. **39**(8), 778–784 (1991)
19. Rockwood, K., Song, X., MacKnight, C., et al.: A global clinical measure of fitness and frailty in elderly people. CMAJ **173**(5), 489–495 (2005)
20. Cesari, M., Prince, M., Thiyagarajan, J.A., et al.: Frailty: an emerging public health priority. J. Am. Med. Dir. Assoc. **17**(3), 188–192 (2016)
21. Rodriguez-Mañas, L., Fried, L.P.: Frailty in the clinical scenario. Lancet **385**(9968), e7–e9 (2015)
22. Nourhashémi, F., Andrieu, S., Gillette-Guyonnet, S., Vellas, B., Albarède, J.L., Grandjean, H.: Instrumental activities of daily living as a potential marker of frailty: a study of 7364 community-dwelling elderly women (the EPIDOS study). J. Gerontol. A **56**(7), M448–M453 (2001)
23. Raphael, D., Cava, M., Brown, I., et al.: Frailty: a public health perspective. Can. J. Publ. Health **86**(4), 224–227 (1995)
24. Danial-Saad, A., Chiari, L.: A multidisciplinary approach for developing an assessment tool for touch screen devices. Disabil. Rehabil. Assist. Technol. **13**, 1–9 (2017)
25. Erickson, B.J., Korfiatis, P., Akkus, Z., Kline, T.L.: Machine learning for medical imaging. Radiographics **37**(2), 505–515 (2017)
26. Lee, J.G., et al.: Deep learning in medical imaging: general overview. Korean J. Radiol. **18** (4), 570–584 (2017)
27. Sirven, N., Rapp, T.: The cost of frailty in France. Eur. J. Health Econ. **18**(2), 243–253 (2017)
28. Caprani, N., O'Connor, N.E., Gurrin, C.: Touch screens for the older user. In: Auat Cheein, F. (ed.) Assistive Technologies. IntechOpen, London (2012)

Towards a Deeper Understanding of the Behavioural Implications of Bidirectional Activity-Based Ambient Displays in Ambient Assisted Living Environments

Kadian Davis-Owusu[1(✉)], Evans Owusu[2], Lucio Marcenaro[3], Carlo Regazzoni[3], Loe Feijs[4], and Jun Hu[4]

[1] Faculty of Industrial Design Engineering, Delft University of Technology, Landbergstraat 15, 2628CE Delft, The Netherlands
k.a.davis-owusu@tudelft.nl

[2] Eindhoven, The Netherlands
owboateng@gmail.com

[3] DITEN, Università degli Studi di Genova, 16145 Genoa, Italy
{lucio.marcenaro,carlo.regazzoni}@unige.it

[4] Department of Industrial Design, Eindhoven University of Technology, 5612AZ Eindhoven, The Netherlands
{l.m.g.feijs,j.hu}@tue.nl

Abstract. In this chapter, we investigate the extent to which the real-time bidirectional exchange of activity information can influence context-awareness, social presence, social connectedness, and importantly interpersonal activity synchrony in mediated ambient assisted living (AAL) environments. Additionally, we describe the design, development, and assessment of a bidirectional ambient display platform to support real-time activity awareness and social connectedness in mediated AAL contexts. In a semi-controlled study, we evaluate a conglomerate of activity-based lighting displays, to determine the effects of real-time bidirectional deployment on behaviour and social connectedness. Exploiting everyday objects, human activity levels are projected with a Philips Hue lamp, LED wallet, and LED walking cane, which render this information based on predefined patterns of light. Results from the current study show tendencies toward (1) an increase in implicit social interactions (*e.g.,* the sense of experienced social presence and connectedness), (2) more positive social behaviours between the elderly and their caregivers in mediated AAL contexts, and (3) sporadic moments of interpersonal activity synchrony however, further investigation is necessary to determine the extent of this variable in mediated AAL contexts.

The work conducted in this chapter was carried out while the first author was a candidate in the Joint Doctorate on Interactive and Cognitive Environments (ICE) at the Eindhoven University of Technology and the University of Genova, which resulted in the following dissertation [22].

I. Ganchev et al. (Eds.): Enhanced Living Environments, LNCS 11369, pp. 108–151, 2019.
https://doi.org/10.1007/978-3-030-10752-9_6

Keywords: Human activity recognition
Ubiquitous and mobile interfaces · Interpersonal activity synchrony
Context-aware frameworks and sensing
Affective and social interfaces · Ambient Intelligence for AAL
Smart devices and intelligent products

1 Introduction

In the 21st century, ageing populations around the world are increasing dramatically. Nowadays, most persons can expect to live until they are 60 and beyond, which according to the World Health Organization[1], is a 'first time occurrence' in mankind's history. Population ageing presents critical challenges, which include but are not limited to the following (i) frailty, (ii) physical disabilities, (iii) cognitive and cardiovascular diseases as well as (iv) vulnerabilities to social isolation and loneliness. Despite these difficulties, many older adults are insistent on striving to maintain their autonomy and quality of life [27]. Therefore, social engagement and enhancing the quality of life of older adults are of a high priority on the political agendas of many ageing societies including Europe and Asia. Notably, this problem space presents challenges and opportunities for designing and developing technology-rich environments capable of supporting healthy and active ageing as demonstrated by the researchers in [10,35,61].

Ambient Assisted Living (AAL)[2] encompasses a broad range of Information and Communications Technologies (ICT) for enhancing functional independence, social interaction, and the overall quality of life among older adults. Currently, most AAL interventions are geared toward safety and ambulatory monitoring for emergency detection. Such systems are mostly driven by Ambient Intelligence (AmI) and can be seamlessly interwoven into the existing life patterns of older adults. In fact, ambient Intelligence (AmI), aspires to detect people's state and adaptively respond to their needs and behaviours through the integration of ubiquitous technologies in their environment [82]. Drawing from disciplines such as artificial intelligence, human computer interaction, pervasive/ubiquitous computing, and computer networks, AmI systems can sense, reason, and adapt to offer personalized services based on the user's context, intentions, and emotions [1,16]. In this way, such systems, also known as context-aware systems [66], can be integrated into AAL environments to provide better care and support for the elderly living independently.

Weiser's vision for ubiquitous computing is described in his seminal work entitled *The Computer for the 21st Century* [86]. In his narrative, Weiser envisaged a world where technology would silently reside in the background or periphery of the user's attention and is available at a glance when needed. Consequently, the allocation of minimum attentional resources would enable peripheral interaction with a system as suggested in the following statement. "The most profound technologies are those that disappear. They weave themselves into the fabric of

[1] http://www.who.int/news-room/fact-sheets/detail/ageing-and-health.
[2] http://www.aal-europe.eu/.

everyday life until they are indistinguishable from it" [86, p. 1]. To this end, ubiquitous computing aims to enable calm technology [87], whereby information is transported easily between the center and periphery of attention. To achieve this, ambient displays, a sub-discipline of AmI, generally refer to systems intended for portraying various types of context information, *e.g.*, weather, stock prices, or the presence or activities of others in the periphery of the users' attention [62].

Within the AAL domain, some studies [11,15,18,19,55,58,65,69,84] have demonstrated benefits associated with aesthetically pleasing and informative ambient displays to raise context awareness and strengthen social interaction. Also, previous works including our very own [21,25,27] have demonstrated that physical activity information equally shared between two remote users can provide a sense of peripheral presence and interpersonal awareness; thus stimulating positive social behaviours in AAL contexts. However, these behavioural implications following the receipt of real-time activity cues through bidirectional activity-based ambient displays in remote AAL contexts have not been dealt with in depth. Therefore, this chapter further investigates the behavioural implications of real-time bidirectional activity-based ambient displays in mediated AAL contexts and is foreseen to provide further insights into the potential benefits and usage possibilities of bidirectional activity-based ambient displays. Consequently, this can inform the design decisions regarding the functionality, adoption, and acceptance within mediated AAL environments.

In the remaining sections of this chapter, we will discuss the following. First, we will review the literature on social well-being and its related measures. Then, we describe our design rationale and provide an overview of our system. After that, we present a user study describing our evaluation process, and later we expound upon our findings on the effect of the system on social connectedness, social presence, and interpersonal activity synchrony. Ultimately, we make our conclusions and discuss our plans for future work.

2 Social Well-Being and Related Measures

To begin with, it is necessary to understand the notion of social well-being as a critical aspect of 'ageing in place'. Social well-being has become a central topic in gerontological research [44,74] and is defined by the authors in [47] as "the appraisal of one's circumstance and functioning in society" (p. 122). According to Abraham Maslow's hierarchy of needs, love and a sense of belonging are vital for human functioning, which transcends to the primal need for intimacy, family, and friendship [53].

In Maslow's hierarchy, once physiological and safety needs are met then a person can strive to satisfy the need for love and belonging, which is essential to fulfil esteem needs and if possible attain a state of self-actualization. Therefore, sociality is crucial for well-being, as human beings are naturally driven by an inherent desire to belong and maintain strong and lasting bonds [5]. Accordingly, this need is satisfied through regular and positive interactions with long-term social contacts [5].

Throughout the past decades, several researchers in psychology and social sciences have documented substantial empirical evidence on the impact of social relationships on promoting health, longevity, and optimal physical functioning in older adults [50,89]. In particular, socially active senior citizens are often physically and mentally healthier when compared to those who are socially isolated [17,88]. However, the absence of close family ties and fulfilling social relationships may cause undesirable implications such as loneliness and depression in older adults [72].

With the onset of better employment or educational opportunities, geographical distance between family members has become a primary barrier for effective communication and the provision of care for older adults [7]. Essentially, while living apart, it is crucial to stay connected and keep abreast of each others' activities. Although the proliferation of computer-mediated technologies such as instant messaging, free or relatively cheap Voice over IP calls, and email can augment communication, such technologies are sometimes intrusive and require more attentional resources for communication. As such, this chapter explores the concept of social connectedness through peripheral technology designed to facilitate real-time activity awareness and improve interaction between the elderly and their caregivers in mediated environments. To reduce disturbances in daily life activities, we believe that an indirect means of awareness of each other's context and activities can sustain close connections and reduce the risks of social isolation and loneliness among older adults.

2.1 Social Connectedness

The generally accepted use of the term *social connectedness* usually refers to a sense of "belongingness and relatedness between people" [81, p. 1]. Also, Van Bel *et al.* discuss the importance of understanding the temporal aspects of belongingness, which can be experienced on two levels, *i.e.*, the (i) 'momentary' or (ii) 'continuous' feeling of connectedness. However, the authors in [80] gave precedence to the long-term experience, which is more distinctive in relatively stable interpersonal relationships; whereas the short-term experience of connectedness can be influenced by a person's current emotion, their present assessment of their sense of belongingness or their interactions with another individual. Other factors such as age, context, gender, personality traits, culture, individual preferences, and previous relationship experience can also affect how people experience social connectedness [34].

Altogether, a sense of belonging appears to be embodied in the concept of social connectedness, such that an increase in social connectedness can lead to the positive feeling of having enough social contacts and also, support the personal assessment of being a valued member of a group. To determine a person's social connectedness with others, Van Bel *et al.* suggest the following five dimensions [81].

1. Relationship Salience – The continued sensation of presence and togetherness with another despite being in different locations.

2. Contact quality – The subjective assessment of the quality of interaction with others in a person's social network.
3. Shared understanding – having common interests, ideologies, and perspectives with people in one's social network.
4. Knowing each others' experiences – becoming emotionally aware of each other's subjective feelings along with recognizing and understanding the counterpart's experience and how they think.
5. Feelings of closeness – examines the intensity of the attachment with one person against all other relationships. Also, assesses the quality of communication and emphasizes confidentiality and openness in relationships.

Awareness systems build on the construct of connectedness oriented communication, which is closely aligned with the exchange of affective and relational information aimed at maintaining relationships and promoting a strong sense of connectedness [52]. Basically, social connectedness assesses the emotional experience of belongingness and can be measured qualitatively by determining heightened feelings of closeness, commonalities between relational partners, and the mutual expression of feelings and thoughts [81]. The construct can be approached quantitatively by assessing how one perceives their social situation (*i.e.*, social appraisal) and their personal evaluation of relationship salience (*i.e.*, the presence of another) [81].

While the notion of social connectedness is difficult to measure, the design community has noticed its relevance to tailor novel socially aware technologies to facilitate a sense of belonging in mediated environments [84]. However, there are other applicable measurements (*e.g.*, social presence) related to this phenomenon that will now be addressed.

2.2 Social Presence

Despite many attempts to define social presence, the scientific community has not yet reached a consensus on its definition. A more concrete view is formulated by Biocca *et al.* in [8], where they define social presence as a "sense of being with another in a mediated environment" (p. 10), not only replicating face-to-face interactions but also considering the mediated experience of human and non-human intelligence (*e.g.*, artificial intelligence). This shorthand definition further elaborates on the "moment-to-moment awareness of co-presence of a mediated body and the sense of accessibility of the other being's psychological, emotional, and intentional states" [8, p. 10]. Therefore, social presence is categorized into three distinct levels as explicated by Biocca *et al.* below [8].

1. *Level one (the perceptual level)* – one becomes aware of the co-presence of the mediated other.
2. *Level two (the subjective level)* – is comprised of four dimensions describing the perceived accessibility of the mediated other's:
   - attentional engagement
   - emotional state

  - comprehension
  - behavioural interaction

3. *Level three (the intersubjective level)* – assesses the degree of symmetry or correlation between one's own feeling of social presence and their impressions of the mediated other's psychological sense of social presence. It goes further to examine concepts such as interdependent actions *e.g.,* reciprocity/motor mimicry in mediated environments, which is closely related to the notion of interpersonal activity synchrony [14], a concept generally known to foster socially cohesive behaviours in relationships, a focal point to be investigated in this chapter.

2.3 Coordinated Actions – Interpersonal Activity Synchrony

For many years, coordinated actions have been considered to enhance relationships and are deemed as an essential component of social behaviour and interactions [4,6,12–14]. In addition, scholars such as [4,12] suggest a possible link between perception and behaviour such that automatic mimicry can be evoked by the mere perception of an interaction partner's behaviour. In this chapter, interpersonal activity synchrony is investigated through a set of analogous and sometimes overlapping terms namely (i) behavioural coordination, (ii) coordinated action, (iii) motor coordination/synchrony, and (iv) emotion contagion.

Coordinated behaviour has been shown in a variety of contexts such as parent-infant bonding [14], teacher-student interactions [6], and intimate relationships [45], such that coordinated action, *i.e.,* interpersonal activity synchrony is regarded as an indicator of social interaction. In particular, previous studies have examined this construct with reference to the synchronization of bodily actions such as oscillations of rhythmic limb [68] and lower leg [67] movements. Likewise, some scholars have found evidence of interpersonal motor coordination while two people either (i) walked side-by-side [79,90] or (ii) swayed side-by-side in rocking chairs [64]. Added to motor synchrony, other studies have investigated coordinated behavioural markers in terms of the mimicry of conversations, collective musical behaviour, dancing, laughter, facial expression, and emotions [13,33]. Altogether, these indicators can be combined under one umbrella term, emotion contagion, which is defined as follows. *"The tendency to automatically mimic and synchronize facial expressions, vocalizations, postures, and movements with those of another person's and, consequently, to converge emotionally"* [40, p. 5].

A key problem with much of the literature examining behavioural coordination is that they tend to focus on face-to-face interactions with very little studies conducted in mediated environments. While we wholeheartedly agree that face-to-face interaction is perhaps one of the most active forms of interpersonal interaction [59,70], given its offerings of immediate feedback, engagement, and interpretation of non-verbal communication cues among others, we also believe that there is a need to explore other types of interaction, especially for enabling peripheral interaction in AAL. As mentioned earlier, Biocca *et al.* highlighted interdependent actions as a critical determinant of social presence in mediated environments [8]. Thus, in an attempt to facilitate coordinated behaviour in mediated AAL environments, this chapter evaluates the extent to which the system can trigger or influence interpersonal activity synchrony.

2.4 Interpersonal Synchrony – Computational Methods in the Field

Very few studies [30,33,43] address the issue of interpersonal synchrony in mediated environments. Thus, to gain a deeper understanding of this social phenomenon we had to review studies demonstrating synchrony in both real life and mediated contexts. From the literature reviewed, *e.g.*, [30,43,64,79] we can infer the following indicators of synchrony.

- co-action
- coordination
- mimicry
- emotion contagion

So, how do we compute interpersonal activity synchrony in mediated AAL environments? Findings from different studies suggest that activity synchrony is determined by calculating the autocorrelation [76] or Pearson correlation [78] of the linear coupling of activity patterns. Also, researchers such as Haken *et al.* have considered an in-phase approach to synchrony such that motor signals are homologous and in synchrony [37]. Concerning mediated environments, scholars such as those in [30,43] suggest cross-correlation measures for computing physiological linkage – a related measure of emotion contagion. Moreover, Biocca *et al.* conferred in their model of social presence that the degree of symmetry or correlation is a measure of social presence [8].

Although correlation measures are critical for calculating interpersonal synchrony, there are other mathematical constructs to consider. For example, Hove and Risen discussed the necessity of imposing a temporal lag (lasting a couple of seconds) following the reference behaviour in the cross-correlation calculation so that mimicry and by extension synchrony can be determined [42].

Considering the previously explored computational methods for evaluating interpersonal activity synchrony, we will employ cross-correlation measures for assessing this phenomenon in this chapter. Furthermore, we will impose a lag to compute this cross-correlation. More details on our evaluation and data analytical methods will be described later in this chapter. We will now provide an brief overview of our bidirectional activity-based system and subsequently discuss our methodology.

3 System Overview

3.1 Design Rationale

As mentioned earlier, our bidirectional activity-based implementation is an ambient lighting system that detects human activities and provides visual feedback through a LED cane, LED wallet, and Philips hue light orbs to create a sense of awareness and social connectedness between older adults and their caregivers. We were guided by the following design heuristics obtained through a thorough review of the literature [51,54,83], interviews with design experts, and our own findings from previous research [23,26,28] using ambient displays.

- The system should be practical, not distracting, portable, perceptible, comfortable, meaningful, reliable, subtle, discrete, aesthetically pleasing, accessible and safe.
- The system should accommodate the vision and motor impairments of the elderly population and should appeal to the intrinsic motivation to share knowledge.
- The system should support ease of use, affordance and learnability bearing in mind that the elderly are susceptible to cognitive impairments, which affects their attention and memory.
- The system should support the elderly's autonomy and should seamlessly fit into their existing lifestyle patterns.

Motivated by the central goal of designing usable, acceptable, and accessible products for the elderly and their caregiver counterparts we sought to determine appropriate everyday objects for conveying activity information that would meet our design criteria. This was done over the course of several brainstorming sessions with experts in the field, designers, and prospective users. Notably, to provide an "always connected" service, we were interested in complementing our already existing Hue lighting system with portable ambient lighting devices. After much deliberation and reference to the Smart Cane System designed by [49], we decided that the LED cane and wallet were most suited for conveying activity information while simultaneously adhering to the design heuristics.

3.2 System Components

The entire system is composed of 5 major subsystems as illustrated in Fig. 1. A remote server subsystem resides in the central part of the system and is responsible for classifying human activities and relaying detected activities to other subsystems. A LED and Hue subsystem are located on each side of the remote server subsystem, respectively. Each LED subsystem consists of a waist-mounted smartphone, an Espressif (ESP) microcontroller with Wi-Fi capability, and an LED ring or strip. The waist-mounted phone is equipped with an accelerometer and a gyroscope for measuring the proper acceleration and orientation of the body, respectively (*cf.* [25]). A custom built Android application *i.e.,* the LED controller application (app.), collects the accelerometer and gyroscope readings (sensor data) at a frequency of 50 Hz (cf. [20]) and sends it to the remote server subsystem for classification. The Android application maintains two socket connections to the central remote server, one for sending sensor data to the server for classification and the other for receiving the classified activities of the counterpart. Subsequently, the classified activities received are mapped to activity levels and then transformed to lighting property encodings, which is later broadcasted to the led strip/ring via the ESP microcontroller Wi-Fi module. To achieve this, the waist mounted phone requires a 3G/4G internet connection by which data is streamed to the remote server and a portable Wi-Fi hotspot to provide an internet connection to the ESP Wi-Fi module.

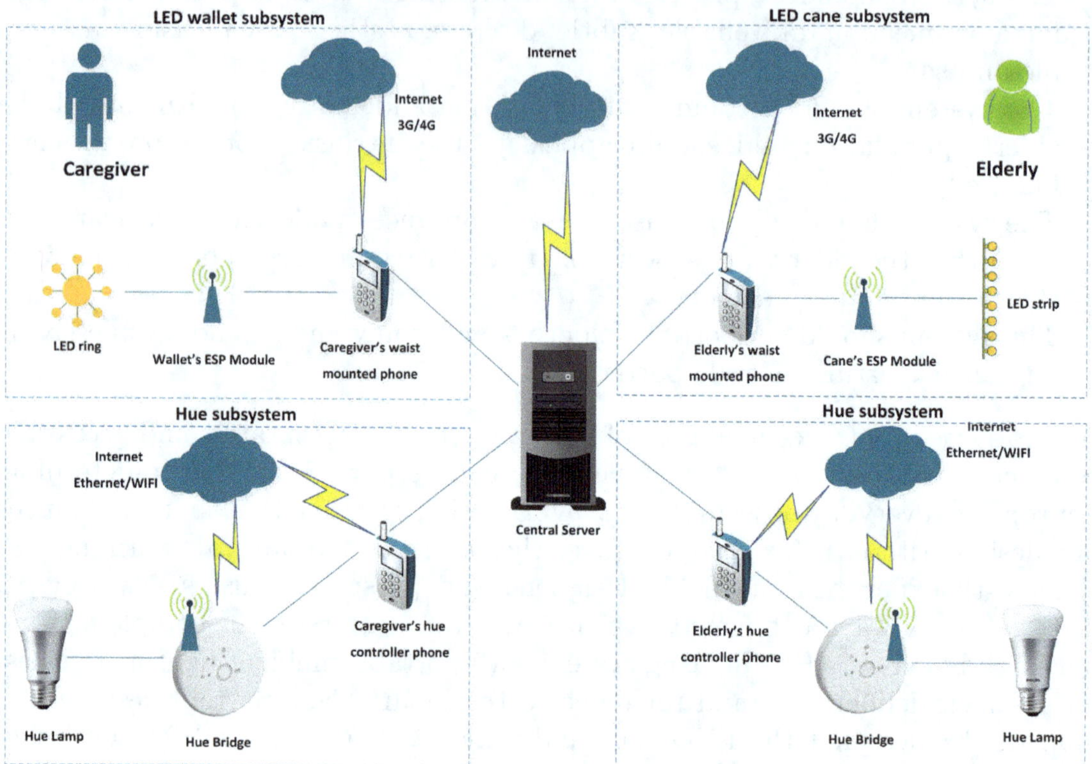

Fig. 1. An overview of the bidirectional activity-based system adapted from [24].

Besides, the Hue subsystem consists of a mobile phone with Wi-Fi internet connection and a Philips Hue bridge and bulb. Another custom-built Android application (*i.e.*, the Hue controller), maintains a single socket connection to the central server subsystem for receiving the classified activities of the partner. The Hue controller then relays this information to the hue bulbs as light property encodings via the hue bridge. The Hue subsystems are deployed indoors to convey bidirectional activity information while users are situated in the comfort of their homes while the LED devices are carried when users are outdoors. This enables an "always connected" system to users. Please refer to [24] for more details on our real-time activity-based bidirectional framework.

4 Methodology

In a semi-controlled study, we evaluated a conglomerate of activity-based lighting displays designed in [21,24,26], to determine the effects of bidirectional deployment on behaviour and social connectedness. Our experimental approach can be described in three main stages, which are listed below.

1. *The Pre-trial* – Following the design and development of our real-time bidirectional activity-based implementation in [24], we conducted two practice sessions with a prospective caregiver and the elderly stakeholders to identify system glitches and obtain technical insights and practical recommendations for system deployment and improvement.
2. *The Real Deployment* – Following system adjustments, our bidirectional activity-based system was deployed in semi-controlled mediated environments to evaluate the effects on synchronized activities, context-awareness, social connectedness and social presence, information clarity, attentional engagement, and the users' willingness to adopt the system.
3. *Post Deployment Interview* – We conducted a series of in-depth interviews to determine the participants' experiences and acceptance of our activity-based system and how it affected their behaviour.

Ekman *et al.* maintain that synchrony is inherently activated by the degree to which people are exposed to the same stimulus [30]. The authors further highlight a study by Hasson *et al.* [39] whereby participants were exposed to an identical visual stimulus (*i.e.,* a movie scene) to incite synchronized cortical activity. Accordingly, influencing our study design decision to expose half of our participants to the same stimulus (*i.e.,* scripted activities of an actor) to induce interpersonal activity synchrony. Inspired by the previous studies on interpersonal synchrony [14,57] and physiological linkage [30,43] to enhance interpersonal connectedness we assume the relevance of these constructs to provide social support in AAL environments. As such, we defined the following research questions.

- To what extent does activity awareness through a bidirectional activity-based system impact the synchronization of the counterpart's activity level with that of the caregiver?
- How does the activity level of an actor (caregiver) modulate the activity levels of their counterpart?
- What are the implications of the bidirectional activity-based system on
    - social connectedness,
    - social presence,
    - context-awareness,
    - information clarity,
    - attentional engagement and,
    - the users' willingness to adopt the system?

4.1 Participants

Participants were recruited through personal networks and referrals from a retired professor, and engineer in the Netherlands. Notably, both the retired professor and the engineer acted as proxies to represent prospective elderly recruits.

Thus, before experimentation all system requirements, designs, prototypes, and the study design were repeatedly cross-validated with these proxies. This was done as a measure to guarantee system functionality, user comfort, and privacy so that they could proceed with the recruitment. Overall, twenty-four persons (twelve pairs) participated in the study.

Table 1. Demographic characteristics of participants

Role	Name	Age	Gender	Marital status	Education level
Caregiver	A	31	M	Married	MSc
	B	26	F	Single	MSc
	C	26	F	Married	MSc
	D	75	M	Married	PhD
	E	31	F	Married	MSc
	F	27	F	Single	MSc
	G	21	F	Single	WO
	H	65	F	Married	HBO
	I	35	F	Married	MSc
	J	67	F	Married	HBO
	K	73	M	Married	PhD
	L	61	F	Married	MBO
Counterpart	M	32	M	Married	MSc
	N	28	F	Single	MSc
	O	31	F	Single	MSc
	P	69	M	Married	PhD
	Q	33	M	Married	MSc
	R	40	M	Married	PDEng
	S	24	M	Single	WO
	T	71	F	Married	MBO
	U	67	M	Married	MBO
	V	68	M	Married	WO
	W	74	M	Married	HBO
	X	73	M	Married	MBO

The following are criteria for the inclusion and exclusion of participants in this study.

- Equal numbers of younger adults and elderly participations are essential for this study.
- Prospective younger adults should be over 18 years while prospective older adults had to be over 65 years of age.

- All prospective older adults should be relatively healthy with no history of chronic, motor, or mental diseases.
- All prospective older adults should live independently and demonstrate the ability to execute their ADLs on their own.
- Equal numbers of male and female participations are valuable for this study.

Each participant was assigned to one of two distinct user groups: (i) caregiver – who is expected to execute a series of scripted activities while simultaneously maintaining awareness of their counterpart through the proposed bidirectional activity-based system and (ii) the counterpart – who upon receiving the caregivers' activities via the ambient display is expected to carry out their activities at their own free will. In this study, an elderly participant could serve as a caregiver, which was determined by the preliminary results in [25], showing evidence of elderly persons caring for their fellow elderly loved ones. The participant demographics are presented in Table 1. To preserve anonymity, caregivers are indicated by letters A–L and their respective counterparts are disguised using letters M–X, and not names.

Participants ranged in age from 21–75 (mean age = 47.8 and standard deviation = 20.8). In addition, we noticed that our sample size was comprised of the relatively 'young elderly'. Participants were from different cultural backgrounds. In particular, the sample was dominated by the Dutch (58%), followed by the Chinese (17%), the Malaysians 13%, and a few (4% each) Ghanaian, Iranian, and Tanzanian participants. All participants except one pair were somewhat familiar with each other. For example, most elderly participants were members of clubs and societies for retired professionals in the Netherlands, while others were neighbours, friends, colleagues, or relatives. In addition, all participants were educated having attained either secondary diplomas, bachelor, master, or doctoral degrees. No participant reported ill health. The experiment was conducted in English and Dutch to facilitate the Dutch speaking participants. Participants received information of the protocol and provided their written, informed consent according to the Central Committee on Research Involving Human Subject[3].

4.2 Experiment Set-Up

The experiment was conducted in two separate living labs at the Eindhoven University of Technology (Tu/e). These rooms were each equipped with the following items: a sofa, dining table and chairs, books, map of the building, notebook and pen, music for relaxing, coffee table, computers with WiFi connection, dumbbells and exercise videos, refreshments, newspapers, games (puzzles, bowling, and diabolo), Philips Hue light Orbs, which formed part of the room design, Philips Hue bridge, smartphone (with the custom-built Hue controller app *cf.* Fig. 1), and a portable LED ambient display (cane for the counterpart and wallet for the caregiver). Figure 2 demonstrates the set-up of the rooms before and after the ambient displays were deployed while Fig. 3 depicts sample game and exercise items in the rooms.

[3] http://www.ccmo.nl/en/.

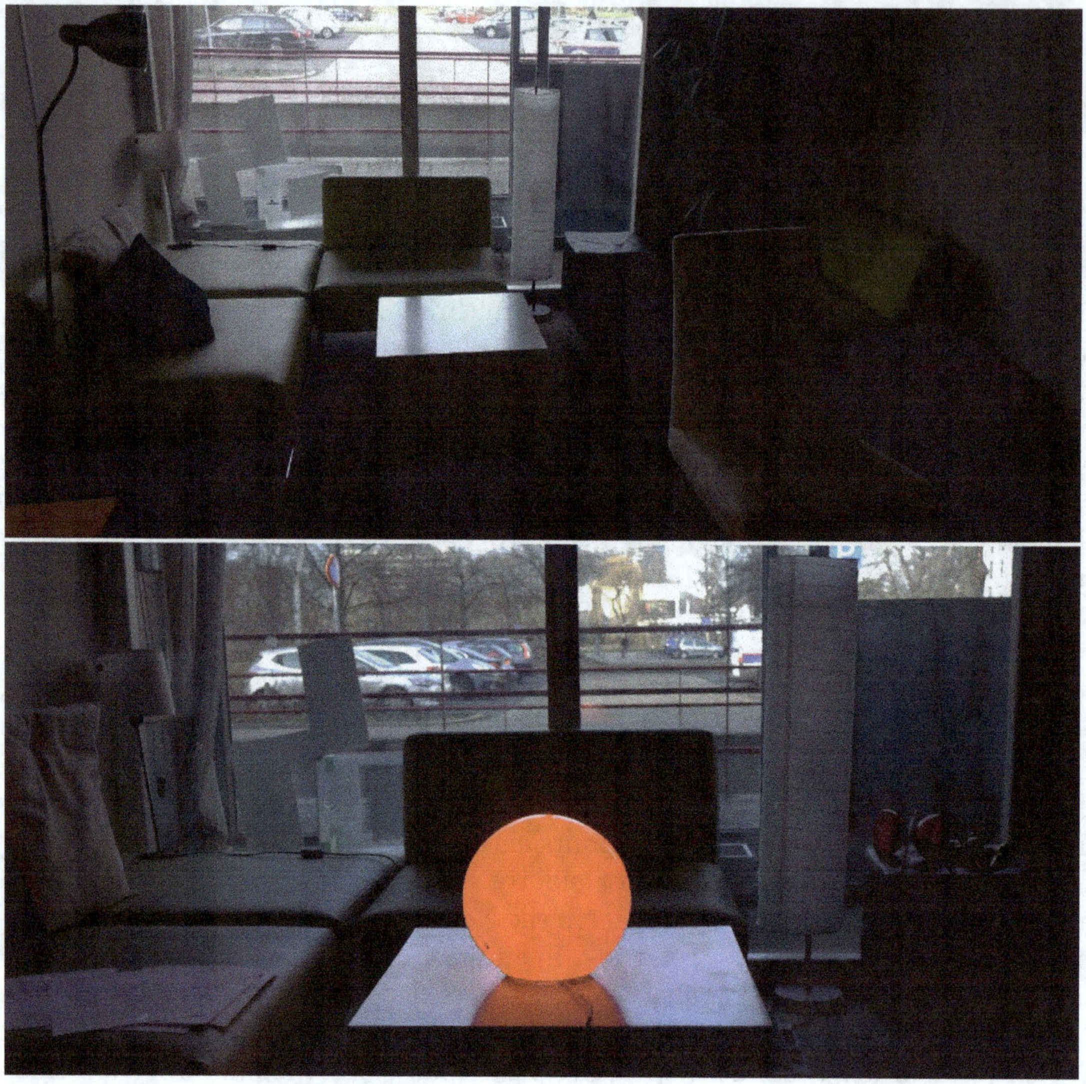

Fig. 2. Snapshots of the experiment set-up pre- and post deployment of the ambient displays.

Adhering to the protocol for activity detection described in [20,24,25], our hybrid SVM-HMM HAR model deployed in a central server subsystem, was used to detect six basic activities (standing, sitting, walking, walking upstairs and downstairs, and laying) from data received via a waist-mounted smartphone equipped with accelerometer and gyroscope sensors and an internet connection. Activities classified are saved on the server before they are sent to the Hue and LED controller subsystems. These controller subsystems are responsible for abstracting the detected activities into activity levels and mapping them to coloured lighting encodings and finally transmitting them to the ambient display components of the bidirectional system. The ambient display components of the system are the Hue light orbs, NeoPixel LEDs fitted on a wallet and a cane as illustrated in Fig. 4.

Fig. 3. An illustration of the sample games and exercises available in the rooms.

The displays render red coloured lighting for high activity levels (walking, walking upstairs and downstairs), green for passive activity levels (standing and walking), and blue coloured lighting for resting activity level (laying).

4.3 Evaluation Measures

- *Social Connectedness* – Participants rated their perceptions of their feelings of relational closeness toward their counterpart using the IOS scale [3].
- *Social Presence* – Participants evaluated their sense of co-presence, perceived attentional engagement, and their perception of behavioural interdependence using an adapted version of the Networked Minds Social Presence Inventory developed by [38].

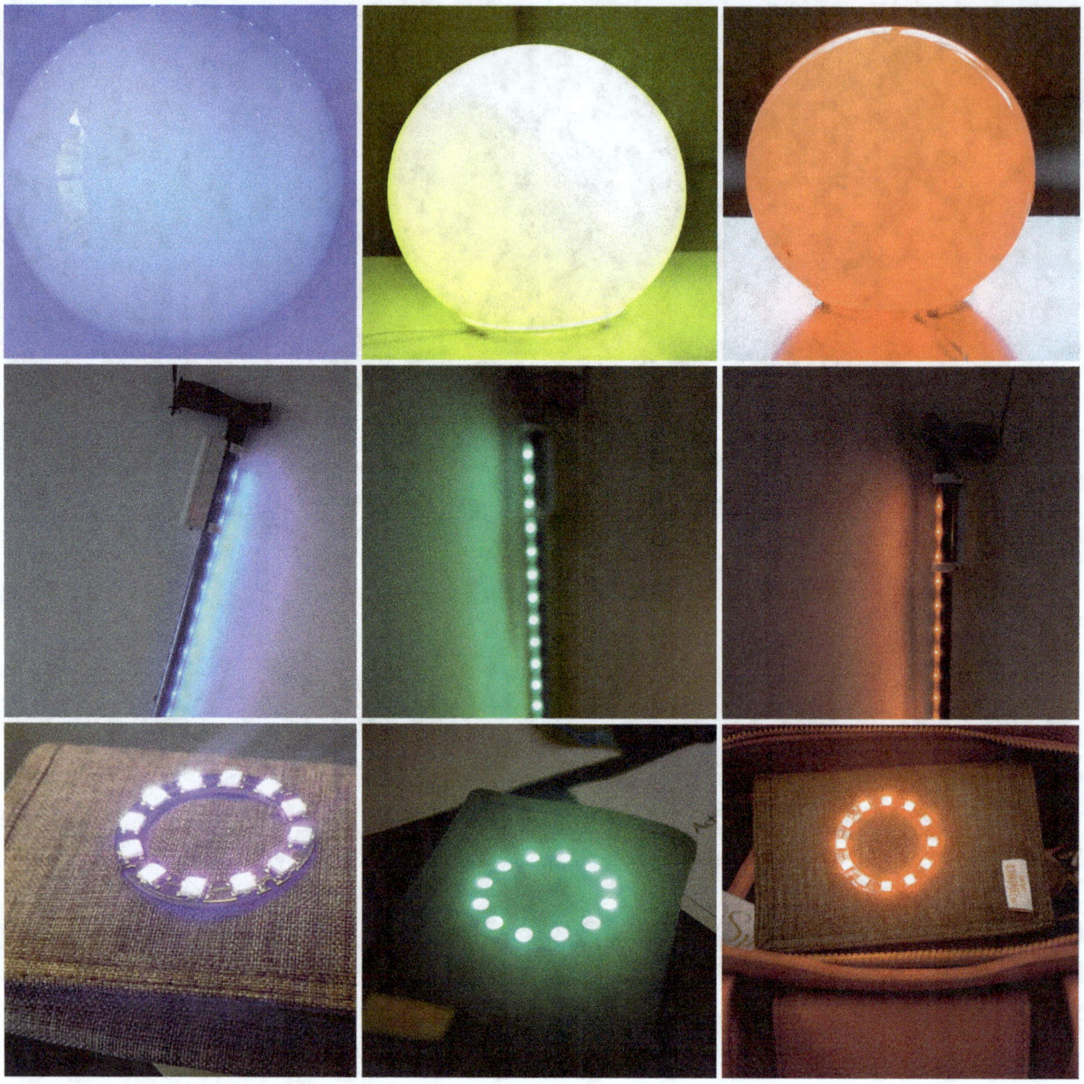

Fig. 4. A pictographic representation of the activity-based ambient display components captured during experimentation. (Color figure online)

- *Interpersonal Activity Synchrony* – Using cross-correlation measures we calculated the extent of coordinated actions between the caregiver and their counterpart in mediated AAL contexts.
- *Willingness to Adopt* – Using a scale of 1–10 with 10 being the most willing, participants were asked to describe their willingness to adopt bidirectional activity-based ambient displays in their own homes.
- *Post-test Interview Questions* – Participants gave their qualitative input on context-awareness, system relevance and usability, aesthetics, adoption, and evaluated their experience with and without the ambient displays.

4.4 Experiment Protocol

We employed a repeated measures design [32], with one independent variable namely the interaction style (with activity-based ambient light and with white light). There were two experimental conditions having two interaction styles each lasting for 30 min each.

- *With activity-based ambient light* – such that there is a bidirectional exchange of activity level information between the caregiver–counterpart pair using smart objects such as the Philips Hue, a LED cane, and wallet. This is the intervention condition.
- *With white light* – such that there is no exchange of activity information between caregiver and their counterpart. This is the control condition.

In both conditions, the caregiver followed a script and performed a similar sequence of activities. To minimize carry-over and order effects, we counter-balanced interaction styles using an AB-BA format [32]. There were two experimenters to facilitate this study. The dependent variables examined include (i) the synchrony of activity levels – interpersonal activity synchrony (on the part of the counterpart), (ii) context-awareness, (iii) social connectedness, (iv) social presence (behavioural interdependence *i.e.*, the counterpart's synchronized actions with the caregiver), (v) information clarity, (vi) attentional engagement, and (vii) system adoption.

Prior to the experiment, the experimenters ensured that the server was properly communicating with all subsystems. Thereafter, a meet and greet session was held with each caregiver–counterpart pair. The experimenters elaborated on the experimental details such as the significance of the light encodings, experimental conditions, measurement instruments, ambient displays, and moderated the signing of the informed consent forms. Each caregiver–counterpart pair was then fitted with the waist-mounted smartphone.

Subsequently, both the caregiver and their counterpart were placed in two separated living labs. Note that upon arrival, participants were orientated with their environment and told that they were not limited to remain indoors during each condition. In particular, caregivers were encouraged to follow a script comprising of five activities each lasting six minutes. Caregivers were also advised to execute the activities in sequential order. An example of the scripted sequence of activities is given below.

1. Read book or the newspaper or browse the internet
2. Do some physical exercise
3. Do some mental activity *e.g.*, puzzle
4. Take a stroll
5. Lie on the couch

In contrast, the counterparts were not expected to follow a script. Instead, they were given a deck of activity cards (see Fig. 5 indicating the types of activities they could perform within the experiment), bearing in mind that there were no restrictions in the order or time spent in a particular activity. Additionally, counterparts were instructed to record the sequence of activities performed and the time spent in each activity in the notebook provided. This was done to establish the ground truth in a minimally invasive way.

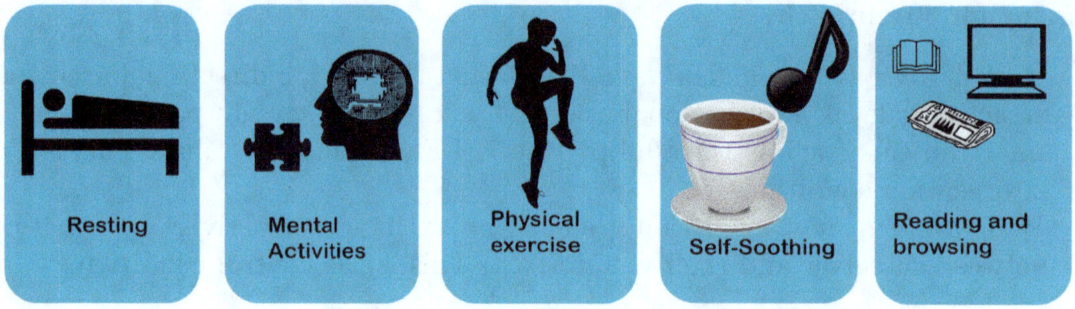

Fig. 5. A snapshot describing the possible activities, which could be performed in the experiment.

After the experiment preliminaries were completed, in a pre-test participants ranked their assessment of relationship closeness with their counterpart. Each experimental condition lasted for 30 min. Also, at the end of each experimental condition all participants completed a post-test ranking their interpersonal closeness with the IOS scale. Following the completion of both experimental conditions, participants ranked their experience of social presence using an adapted version of the social presence questionnaire [38] and thereafter participated in a post-evaluation interview, which was audio-taped. Interviews conducted in Dutch were facilitated and translated with the assistance a native Dutch speaker.

5 Quantitative Results

The results from both interactions styles, *i.e.,* (i) with activity-based ambient light and (ii) with white light were analysed using the R Project for Statistical Computing. The analytical methods and research outcomes are presented and discussed below.

5.1 Clarity of Perceived Bidirectional Activity Levels

From the shorthand definition of social presence [8], it can be inferred that an understanding of a mediated body's intentional states is an important prerequisite for promulgating social presence in mediated environments. Figure 6 shows a scatter plot of the clarity of the information perceived in both interaction styles.

Noteworthy differences were found in the reports of information clarity with respect to the perception of activity levels in the activity-based ambient light interaction and that of white light. Statistically, a one-way ANOVA with repeated measures gave $F(1,23) = 70$ and $p = 1.97e{-}08$. Furthermore,

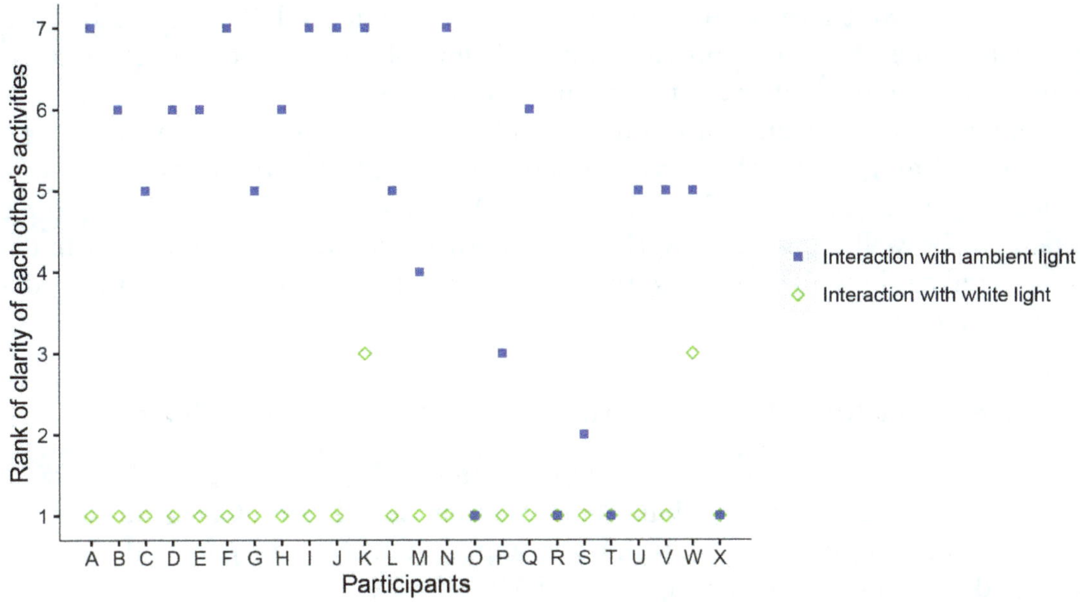

Fig. 6. Scatter plot portraying the clarity of perceived bidirectional activity levels.

by computing the η_p^2 (partial eta squared) measure, we obtained an effect size of 0.75, which is substantial according to the recommendations for the magnitude of effect sizes by [56]. From the results, we can infer that the information portrayed in the "activity-based ambient light" interaction was clear and meaningful. However, this will be confirmed later by the qualitative results.

5.2 Perceived Attentional Engagement

From our study findings in [21,25,26] that the overuse of attentional resources was a marked limitation in both studies. A remarkable result to emerge from

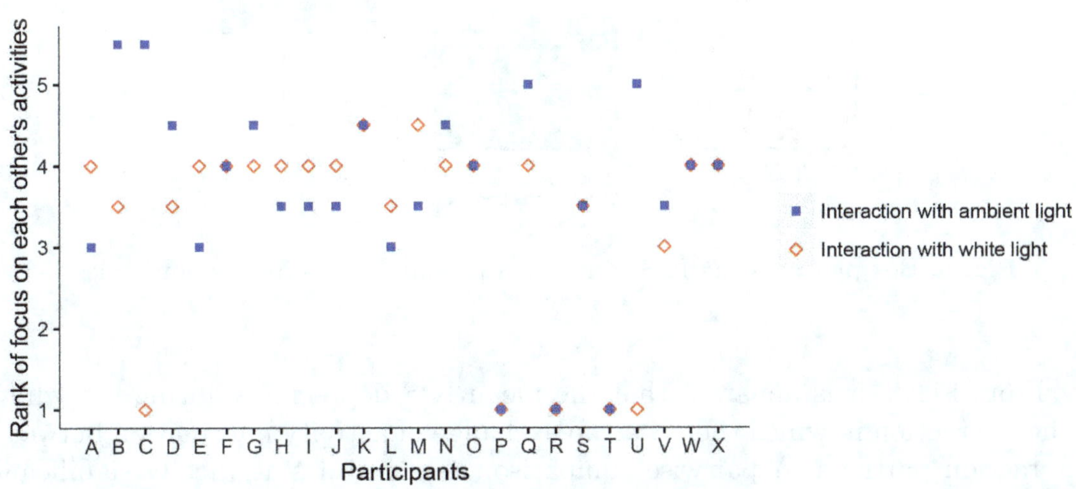

Fig. 7. Scatter plot of the estimated attentional resources utilized per interaction style.

the data is that there were fewer accounts of attentional burden during system deployment. Figure 7 provides an overview of the subjective estimates of attentional resources utilized in both interaction styles.

The scatter plots illustrate almost similar distributions between the "with white light" and the "with activity-based ambient light" interaction styles with no statistically significant difference ($p = 0.195$) between them. Our findings appear to be well supported by the participants' qualitative accounts of multitasking only taking occasional glances at their partner's activities to avoid distraction and concentrate on their primary tasks.

5.3 Relationship Closeness Pre- and Post Interaction Styles

As discussed in our review of social connectedness, Van Bel *et al.* highlighted the feeling of closeness as a dimension of social connectedness [81]. Consequently, this measure was computed to determine the implications on interpersonal closeness with and without the activity-based ambient display.

A one-way analysis of variance (ANOVA) with repeated measures was calculated, which revealed a statistically significant difference between the self-reported IOS pre- and post- experiments with $F(2, 46) = 16.25$ and $p = 4.58\text{e}{-06}$. In addition, by computing the η_p^2 measure yielded an effect size of 0.41, which is reasonably large according to the recommendations for the magnitude of effect sizes by [56]. Figure 8 portrays a box plot of the perceived relationship closeness pre- and post- interaction styles.

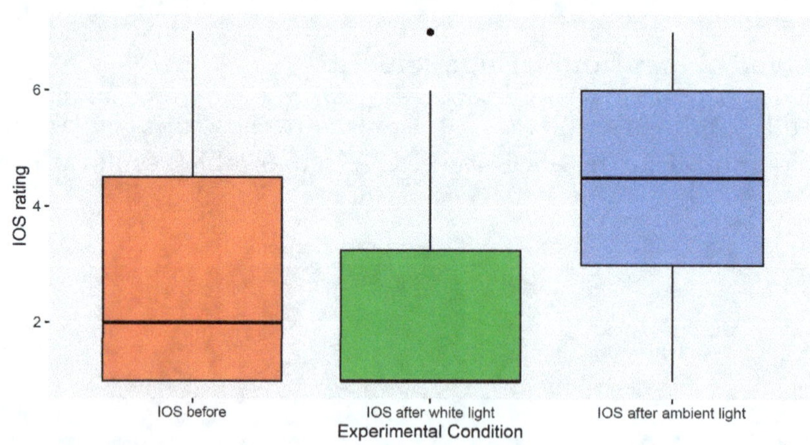

Fig. 8. Box plot showing IOS estimation pre- and post- interaction styles.

From Fig. 8, it is apparent that the mean IOS depreciates during the white light interaction in which there was no exchange of activity information between interaction partners. A pairwise comparison revealed a statistically significant difference in relationship closeness before stimulus exposure and following the interaction with activity-based ambient light resulting in a p-value of 0.00251.

Comparing the IOS ratings before exposure and post the interaction with white light did not reveal a statistical difference ($p = 0.0568$).

5.4 Estimation of Co-presence

The findings from the study in [25], point to the likelihood of experienced social presence – the feeling of being with mediated the other [8]. As we sought to validate this finding, participants gave their estimations of perceived co-presence in each interaction style. By deploying a one-way ANOVA with repeated measures we obtained a statistically significant result with $F(1, 23) = 26.74$ and $p = 3.05\text{e}{-}05$.

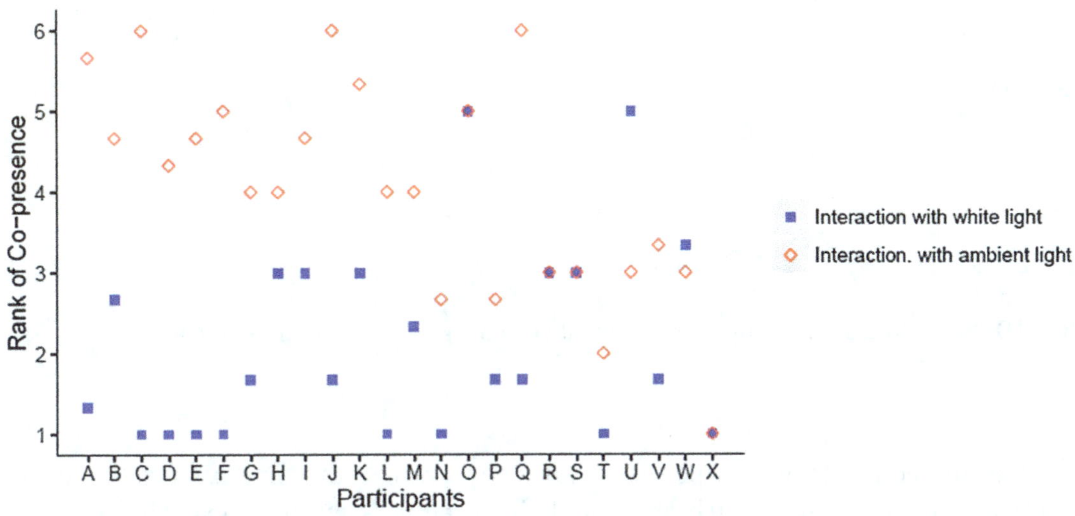

Fig. 9. Scatter plot illustrating the extent of co-presence between participant pairs.

Moreover, using η_p^2 we obtained an effect size of 0.54, which is relatively large according to the rules of thumb on the magnitude of effect sizes by [56]. From Fig. 9, it is apparent that there were more reports of experienced co-presence in the "activity-based ambient light" interaction when compared to the interaction "with white light". This finding reinforces the usefulness of bidirectional activity-based displays for stimulating social presence.

5.5 The Extent of the Caregivers' Influence on the Counterparts' Activity Levels

Behavioural interdependence is underlined as an important dimension of social presence [8]. Thus, self-reports of interdependent actions could complement the cross-correlation analysis on sensed activity data. Recall that this measure was only ranked by the counterparts as caregivers were expected to strictly follow the activity script. A one-way ANOVA with repeated measures revealed a statistically significant difference between the reported influence with $F(1, 11) = 10.24$

and $p = 0.00845$. Also, by calculating η_p^2 the results show an effect size of 0.48, which is large enough according to the rules of thumb on the magnitude of effect sizes by [56]. Figure 10 demonstrates the degree of symmetry of the counterparts' activity levels with that of the caregiver.

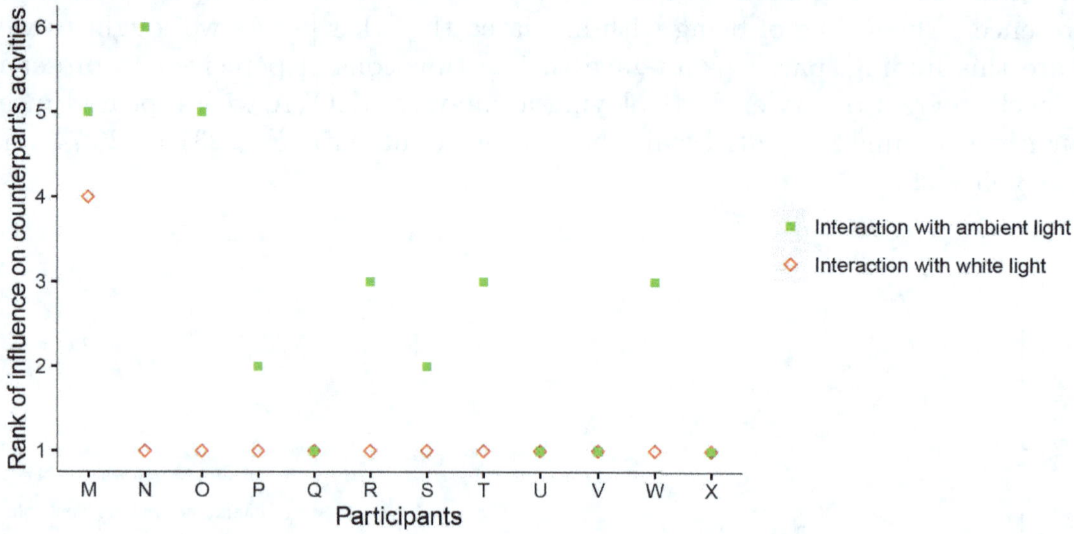

Fig. 10. Scatter plot showing the extent of the caregivers' influence on the counterparts' activity levels.

Overall, counterparts reported that they were more motivated to coordinate their activity levels with that of their caregivers while interacting with the activity-based ambient light in comparison to their interaction with white light. This confirms our assumption that a stimulus is necessary to create awareness and prompt a behavioural change to act upon the information received in mediated environments. In the case of the "with white light" interaction, the activity information was unknown, and hence there was no interaction.

5.6 System Adoption

Following system deployment, we wanted to determine the number of participants who were interested in adopting the system in the long-term. Logically, system adoption was only computed for the "with activity-based ambient light" interaction style. In this case, both the caregivers and their counterparts stated their perceptions on future system adoption. Their subjective attitudes toward adoption are depicted in Fig. 11. The findings suggest that participants were moderately inclined toward system adoption in the long-run. Additional insights are further implied in the qualitative analysis.

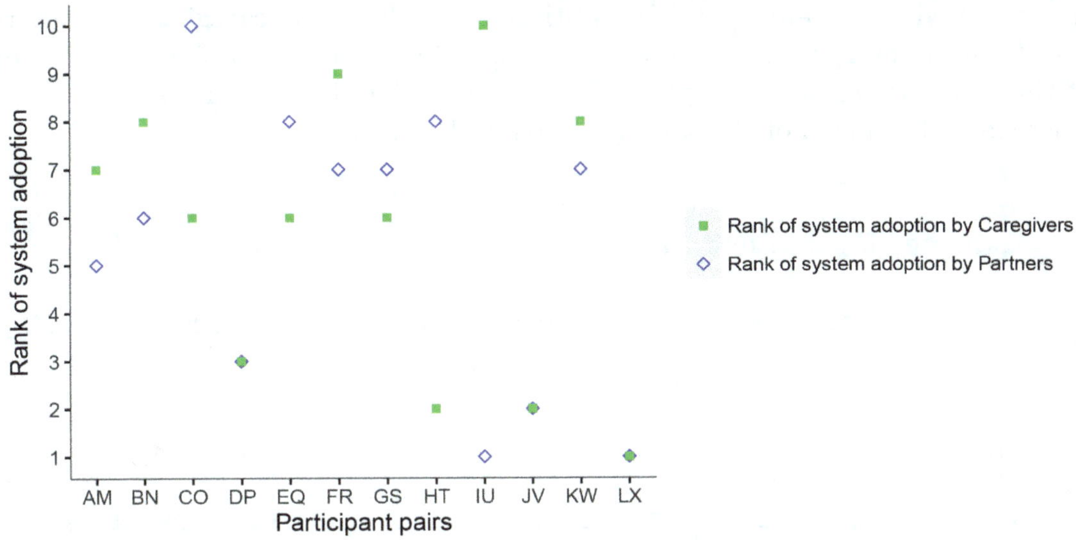

Fig. 11. Scatter plot representing the subjective ratings on system adoption.

5.7 Towards Interpersonal Activity Synchrony – The Caregiver's Influence on Their Counterpart's Activity Levels

To analyse interpersonal activity synchrony, we calculated the sample cross-correlation coefficient (CCF) [71] between activity levels of caregivers and their counterparts for every 6-min interval that the caregivers remained in an activity level specified by the script. Due to time constraints, the script specified 5 activities to be performed within a 30-min interval. Therefore, activity levels were distributed equally in 6-min intervals. Note that resting, passive, and active activity levels were assigned the following values 0, 1, and 2, respectively.

As described in the system architecture of the bidirectional ambient display platform (*cf.* [24]), the server detected a maximum of two activities for every 5 s worth of data from the waist-mounted smartphone. This implies that a minimum of 2.5 s of sensor data was required in order to detect an activity. This introduced a minimum lag of 2.5 s (1 *lag unit*) and a maximum lag between 5 s (2 *lag units*) and 7.5 s (3 *lag units*) for an activity to be collected, detected, and transmitted to a participant. The sample CCF of time-series variables x and y, representing both the caregiver's and their counterpart's activity levels respectively, at time t, given a lag τ was calculated as follows: Given a sample cross-covariance,

$$\sigma_{xy}(\tau) = \frac{\sum_{t=1}^{n-\tau}(x_{t+\tau} - \bar{x})(y_t - \bar{y})}{n}$$

the sample cross-correlation (CCF) is given by:

$$\rho_{xy}(\tau) = \frac{\sigma_{xy}(\tau)}{\sqrt{\sigma_x(0)\sigma_y(0)}}$$

where n is number of activity levels detected within a 6-min interval and $\bar{x}$ and $\bar{y}$ are the means of the activity levels of a participant pair (*i.e.*, elderly –

caregiver) within a 6-min interval. With negative lags, the caregiver is made to lead their counterpart to serve as a reference for analysing activity synchrony of the counterpart. The sample (CCF) was calculated for each 6-min interval. Thereafter, the mean of the sample CCFs with lags

$$-1 \leq \tau \leq -3$$

were estimated for each interval.

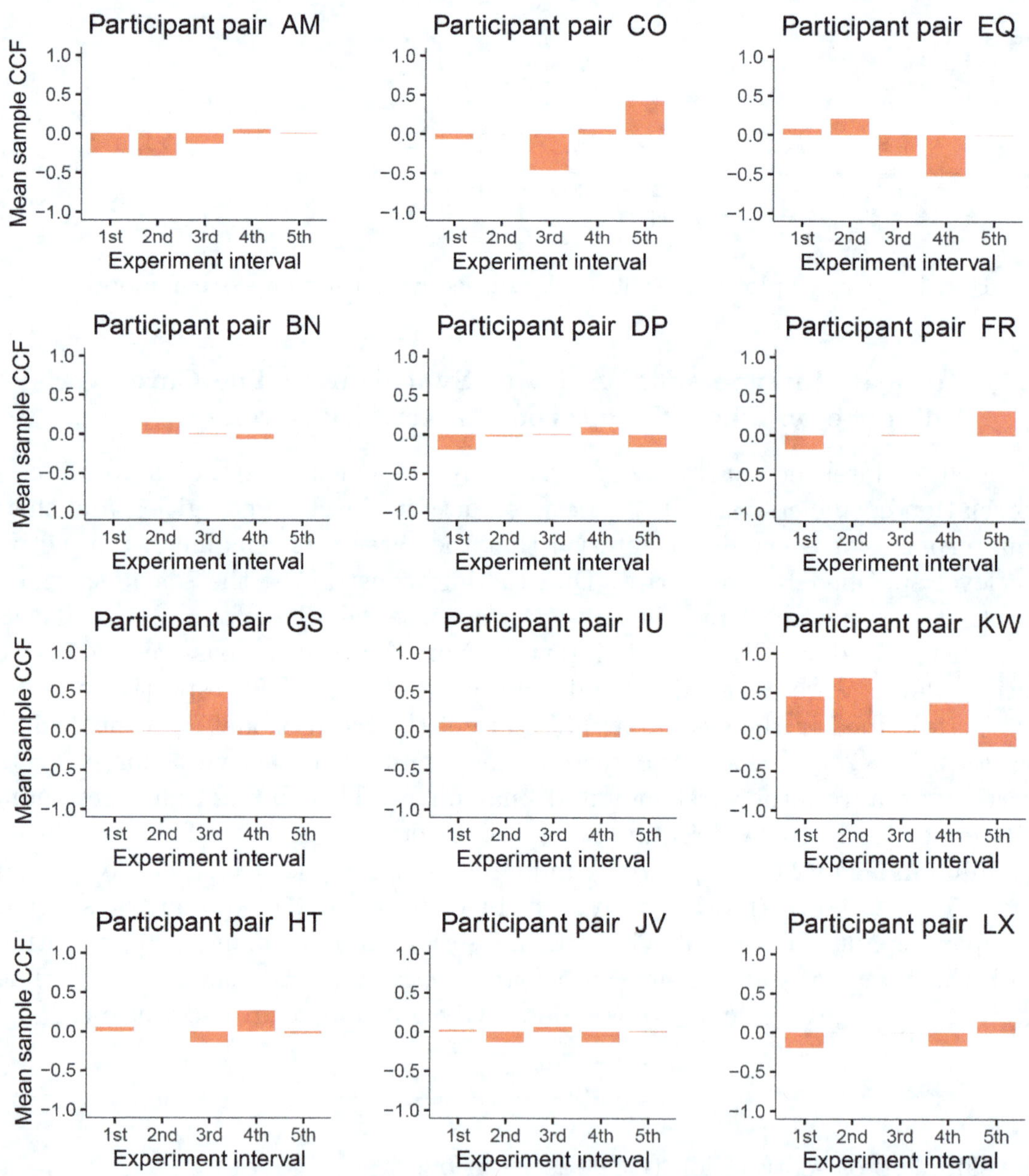

Fig. 12. Mean sample CCF for the activity-based interaction.

From the analysis shown in Fig. 12, we found no statistically significant pattern of activity synchrony between caregiver and their counterparts in the "with activity-based ambient light" interaction style. In some instances, we observed a significant positive correlation (indicating interpersonal activity synchrony) as in the case of the participant pair KW, but there was no other significant positive or negative correlations among the remaining cases. Consequently, these findings need to be interpreted with caution as we are unable to make any significant assertions regarding interpersonal activity synchrony on the basis that there was also no consistent sample CCFs within and between interaction styles.

Table 2. Percentage of time spent in activity levels

	Resting (%)	Passive (%)	Active (%)
Ambient light	17.06	68.1	14.8
White light	26.4	60.9	12.8

Notwithstanding the lack of synchrony, we observed that in the activity-based ambient light interaction, counterparts were in most cases as equally or more active than their caregivers whilst counterparts were frequently observed to be less active than their caregivers during the interaction with white light. Table 2 portrays the percentages of time partners spent in each activity level per interaction style. While Figs. 13 and 14 demonstrate the mean activity levels with white light and with activity-based ambient light.

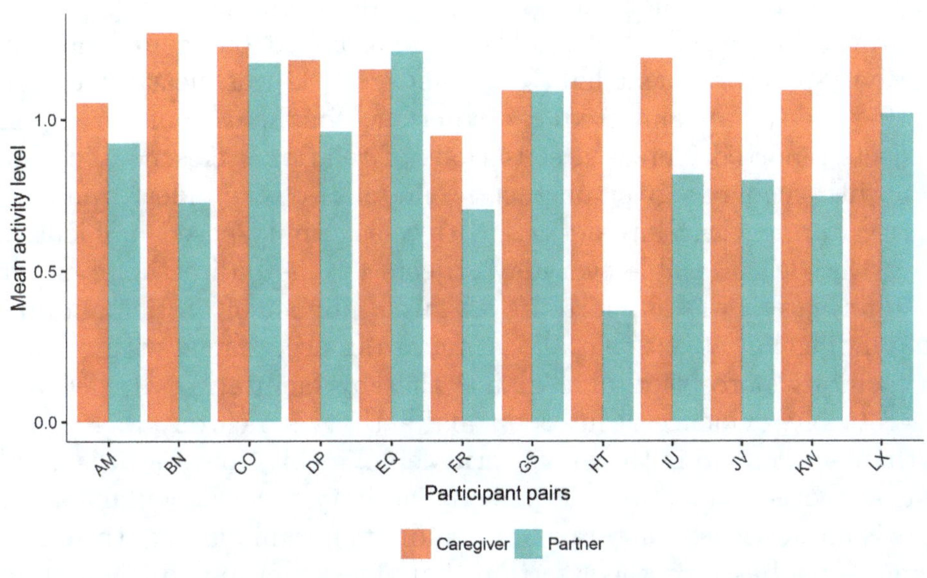

Fig. 13. Mean activity levels in the interaction with white light.

This finding together with estimations of the influence of the receipt of caregivers' activity information on their counterparts points to the possibility of interpersonal activity synchrony in long-term deployments of the system.

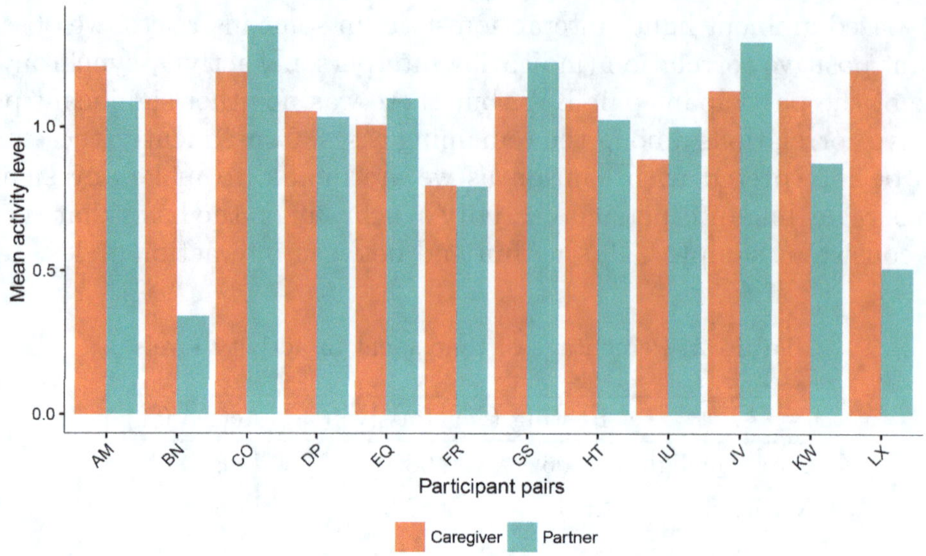

Fig. 14. Mean activity levels in the interaction with activity-based ambient light.

5.8 Discussion

In this experiment, we aspired to investigate how the exchange of activity information between two user groups (caregivers and their counterparts) would affect the following: interpersonal synchrony on the part of the counterpart, interpersonal relationship closeness, co-presence, behavioural interdependence, information clarity, attentional engagement, system adoption, and interpersonal activity synchrony. The results have further strengthened our confidence that the "with activity-based ambient light" interaction style was clearly more effective for affecting the social connectedness experience in the case of our experiment. The subjects reported increased sensations of relational closeness, co-presence, co-action with their caregiver partner in the case of the elderly, and information clarity during their interactions with the activity-based ambient display. Moreover, the idea of usable everyday objects for the bidirectional exchange of activity information was supported by a large number of participants. In addition, the findings on attentional allocation are in accordance with our intended goal to facilitate perception at a glance thereby facilitating divided attention [46]. Regrettably, evidence of interpersonal activity synchrony was significantly weaker than anticipated in this short-term deployment. However, it is worthwhile to note that the assessment of interpersonal activity synchrony in mediated environments is not trivial. In fact, in [63] Rashidi *et al.* reminds us of the difficulty in measuring ADLs based on the assertion that the sequence and the way in which activities are performed may vary across individuals. From this claim, it is clear that this assumption not only holds true for the recognition of ADLs in general, but also for computing interpersonal activity synchrony using peripheral displays in AAL environments. Likewise, [30] also articulated their uncertainties regarding the extent to which synchrony can occur in mediated environments. Although there were spontaneous instances of interpersonal activity synchrony as clarified in our qualitative analysis, we believe that 30 min was not enough to significantly affect interpersonal activity synchrony in mediated domains. Further work will focus on longer deployments to estimate the effects on interpersonal activity synchrony in mediated AAL environments. We will now present the qualitative findings, which was done to ascertain a subjective viewpoint and corroborate our findings on the aforementioned dependent variables ((i) interpersonal activity synchrony (on the part of the counterpart), (ii) context-awareness, (iii) social connectedness, (iv) social presence (behavioural interdependence *i.e.*, the counterpart's synchronized actions with the caregiver), (v) information clarity, (vi) attentional engagement, and (vii) system adoption) examined in the quantitative research.

6 Qualitative Results

Our analytical approach bears close resemblance to the procedure proposed by [73] such that interview transcripts were analysed and the findings were discussed and validated with a professional care support worker. Important ideas and suggestions provided by the domain expert were taken into account during the discussions. Exploiting the thematic analysis [9] approach, two hundred and ninety-four statements were examined to identify major themes and sub-themes related to the users' impressions on perception, usability, system adoption, interpersonal activity synchrony, and envisioned system benefits among others. These themes and sub-themes are now discussed.

6.1 Perceived Usefulness of Bidirectional Activity-Based Displays for Promoting Context-Awareness

The participant majority praised the system for its ability to raise context-awareness. In particular, most interviewees reported on the system's ability to trigger context-awareness owing to the following properties.

- peripheral features enabling divided attention
- information clarity
- respects privacy and dignity rights
- simplicity and effortlessness
- portability and multifunctional everyday objects
- implicit communication channel

From the quotations below, further insight can be gleaned on the implications of bidirectional for promoting social connectedness.

"I only looked at the light for a few minutes, and then I just started focusing on what I was doing while taking occasional glances." – Q

"It is rather clear what he is doing." – D

"I don't feel like someone is looking around for me. It is simple." – W

"The ability to carry the wallet around is good so you can see the activities of your partner whilst you are outside and when you in the house you can see the lamp." – A

"The cane is so cool, I can carry it around, and it serves two purposes one as a light and the other to access information anywhere. " – M

"We sit in the same office and to know what he is doing I would have to look at him, and then I can see that he is working on his computer. Now, the lamp is a bit more discrete and is a good indicator of his activities." – F

"It would be nice to see what they are doing without FaceTime or taking too much time to feel their existence." – C

6.2 Uncertainty

Although a large number of participants acknowledged the potential benefits of the system, yet, there were a few elderly participants who consistently expressed uncertainty regarding ambient technologies for social connectedness. During the investigation, it was apparent that one participant appeared to be technology-illiterate *e.g.,* he expressed his disdain for assistive devices due to technical inexperience). In addition, the significance of culture on adoption played an important role in the level of uncertainty and ultimately another participant's disapproval of peripheral technologies.

"I never use a computer, in fact, I don't know how to use it. I don't even have a smartphone. I know there are technologies to call the doctor if you need help but I would never use them, I would rather use the telephone." – X

It is also evident that culture played a significant role in the adoption of peripheral technologies. In fact, some Dutch participants reflected response patterns that were highly individualistic[4] in nature.

"I don't need to know what another person is doing every moment of the day." – X

"Okay, I see different lights showing me my partner's activities. Then, I didn't know what to do with it. What are the implications? Why do I need it? If my mother were alive then maybe when she was ill it would have been useful, but I don't need it now to keep in touch with my friend." – W

"It is not so important for me maybe there are positive effects but not for me. Most of the time, my wife and I we leave each other free, so I don't need it." – V

Moreover, another respondent perceived that the system could easily disappear in the background, which he thought to be negative especially for both context-awareness and social connectedness.

"I saw different lights, but it could be the same as having the television on and it fades in the background. If there are changes, then I wouldn't notice them and I wouldn't feel anything." – U

6.3 Role of Perceptual Processes on the Experience of Social Connectedness and Context-Awareness

Based on the responses we can infer a possible link between context-awareness and social connectedness, which is exemplified by Mr. A's comment.

[4] https://geert-hofstede.com/netherlands.html.

"Perceiving your partner's activity information makes you feel like you know their daily routines so you can form a mental pattern of what they do overtime and that can make you feel connected." – A

Also, from Mr. A's statement, we can deduce the relevance of cognitive processes discussed in [21] (*e.g.,* attention, perception, pattern recognition, and memory) as key concepts essential for facilitating context-awareness and social connectedness. Furthermore, it is imperative that the activity information received from the display is aligned with the user's mental model of their counterpart's activities. This is reflective of top-down processing as discussed by the authors in [31].

Moreover, from Mr. M's comment, we reckon the significance of habituation (*cf.* [36,85]) for social interaction in mediated environments. This is reflected in the following quotation.

"I think if I get accustomed to observing someone else's activity then over time I would feel even more connected." – M

6.4 Interactivity and Social Influence

The opportunity to exchange activity information without communication media such as Skype, FaceTime, or text messaging was highly valued among younger participants. A possible explanation for their acceptance can be attributed to multiple references to separation by geographical distance from their parents. In general, a great deal of social presence was experienced between younger interaction partners coupled with sporadic occurrences of interpersonal activity synchrony between them. Furthermore, respondents elaborated on the potential social influences of bidirectional activity-based ambient systems and highlighted the effects on engagement by virtue of the cryptic nature of the display.

Social Presence. Like the respondents in [25], most younger participants were very passionate about the system's indirect influence on social presence and by extension social connectedness. Example statements are given below.

"I liked the fact that although we were in different places, I still felt like she was quite close to me. I knew what she was doing and I was wondering what she thought about my activities. I am quite anxious for us to discuss our activities later." – B

"I feel like she is somehow with me indirectly." – O

"With ambient light even though I was alone, I didn't feel alone. I think this will be useful for lonely people." – I

Interpersonal Activity Synchrony. Most of the younger participants were captivated by the possibility of synchronizing their activities with their partner. Furthermore, the participant majority suggested that the exchange of activity levels could create intimacy and increase social interaction. This is encapsulated in the statement below.

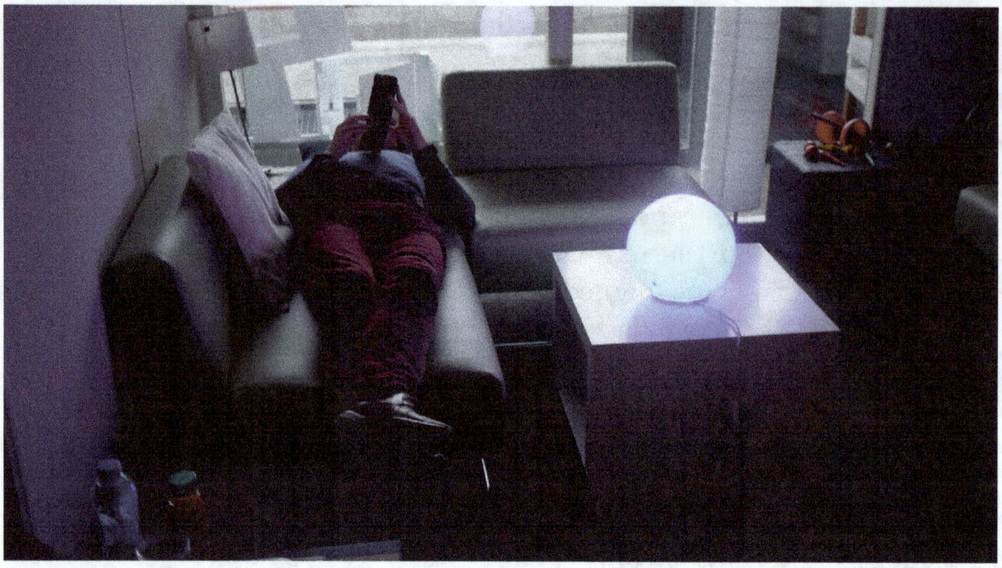

Fig. 15. Pictorial representation of interpersonal activity synchrony, the counterpart is observed in a resting state while is his caregiver is also in a resting state as depicted by the blue light. This snapshot was captured during the experiment. (Color figure online)

"It is nice to see what the other person is doing and that perhaps you can do the same things together to form some kind of bond." – R

An interesting observation reflecting interpersonal activity synchrony of two interacting partners is demonstrated below.

In one instance, the caregiver stated the following. *"There were times I had the feeling that he was doing what I was doing because when I was doing physical exercise, his light was also red."* – G

While her counterpart mentioned,

"I had the impression that she was mirroring me especially when I was resting she was resting." – S

This interaction is evidenced in Fig. 15.

Social Influence: Persuasion Versus Peer Pressure. Although synchrony appears to be intriguing, some participants argued that it could potentially have positive and negative effects on social interaction. Positive influences include the system's functional role in persuading its users to engage in the same activities. An example statement is given below.

"When I saw that my partner was active it made me feel like I should have been active as well. Also, while I was exercising and she was relaxing I felt like I wanted to relax as well." – C

On the other hand, a few participants stated that the system appeared to have adverse consequences resulting in social pressure to prevent embarrassment. In one instance, a participant mentioned that she was uncertain as to whether or not she should coordinate her activities with her partner. This is shown below.

"There was a moment when I was sitting because I already finished exercising and I was going to read, but then she was engaged in a physical activity maybe exercising. I didn't want her to feel like I wasn't doing anything. I felt a bit embarrassed. She was doing something productive, and I was just there sitting. That's not good for my reputation." – O

While another respondent was bothered by the system's persuasive effects as an implicit trigger point for stress.

"For me, my mom always wants me to exercise and also my dad is trying to lose weight. So, if we are both home and my dad is exercising, then it could influence me to exercise also. But this could be silently stressful because I can see my father is exercising and I am either sleeping or eating a hamburger or watching TV. Then, I could feel a bit stressed." – N

Mysterious Engagements. As highlighted in [25], some participants expressed a liking for the system's mysterious effects, which prompted them to mentally decrypt the exact nature of their partner's activities. This is reflected in the following statement.

"Sometimes, I was guessing what my partner was doing. In some instances, I knew she was doing some kind of mental activity but I didn't know exactly what she was doing. I would say it was a bit mysterious." – Q

The respondent further argued that the system's mysterious effects could stimulate communication through other communication media.

"For example, if I am alone at home and I am trying to figure out what my partner is doing based on the information received. Then, I may initiate further communication by calling her on Skype to determine what exactly she is doing." – Q

6.5 Relevance to the Frail Elderly – I'm Still Young I Don't Need It Now

Like the elderly respondents in [23], most elderly participants in this study commented on the relevance of the context-awareness systems for the frail elderly. These comments illustrate the tendency among our older participants to still feel young inside [2] by articulating their independence and stating how they demystified ageist stereotypes, *e.g.*, ill-health, cognitive decline, feeling sad or lonely, and the lack of vigour or vitality discussed by the authors in [77]. Example statements are presented below.

"My wife and I are very active, so we don't need it now maybe when we are older." – D

"I am alright, I am very capable of taking care of myself at home." – H

6.6 Risks and Emergency Management

As pointed out earlier, the majority of our younger participants were excited about the social connectedness benefits of the system. However, some participants were more focussed on the context-awareness features mainly for its potential in supporting the safety and monitoring of their elderly loved ones. One elderly participant was readily accepting of such systems because of her husband's current battle with dementia. As Mrs. T reflected on her husband's dementia, she stated the following.

"With lighting colour changes, I can easily observe my husband's activities while he is in another room without being present with him all the time." – T

Also, others mentioned the need for such systems for anomaly detection to identify irregular movement patterns of their elderly loved ones. These accounts are discussed below.

"If my relative is sick then is important to know if she is not moving at all." – I

"I want to know if something goes wrong" – N

Although the bidirectional activity-based ambient displays were designed to provide context-awareness and enhance social connectedness, some participants suggested that it is still necessary to provide emergency detection capabilities to complement the existing system. Additionally, a few participants suggested the need for an alarm feature for notifying caregivers in the event of an emergency.

"How can you distinguish between a person sleeping or an accident where someone has fallen on the floor? I think there is need of an extra indication for falling." – D

Also, Mr. K suggested that by introducing additional physiological measurements such as heart rate along with an alarm system could assist professional care workers.

"A supervision system for a nurse monitoring several people could detect heart rhythm and send an alarm if something is wrong." – K

Furthermore, Mrs. T pointed out that an alarm system could assist with the monitoring of her husband with dementia who tends to wander off outdoors.

"What if my husband wakes up from his sleep and starts moving? What if he wanders off outdoors? Maybe the system could signal an alarm once the front door is opened or illuminate all the colours at once to indicate some form of danger." – T

6.7 Design Suggestions

Overall, the design suggestions include ideas to offer more subtlety, humanize the display, improve aesthetics, battery life and sensor comfort, the addition of ancillary features such as vibration and sound, reduced sensitivity, and an extension of the system's scope.

Support Invisible Design. Going back to Weiser's vision of calm technology [86] ("those that disappear [...] They weave themselves into the fabric of everyday life until they are indistinguishable from it" (p. 1). A few participants made recommendations to improve the subtlety of the design. The following comments suggest how this can be achieved through simplicity, smaller LEDs, and reduced brightness for portable displays.

"Although the wallet is useful and attractive the light is quite obvious. Let's say you have to pay with the wallet then everyone says hey it's Christmas time! Therefore, a much simpler LED would be sufficient." – K

"Is it necessary to have such a long stick to receive information? Is it possible to have something smaller? I think that would be better." – W

"The cane's LED could become irritating. Maybe, it's because I really don't like LED strips it's a personal thing." – P

"The light on the wallet is very strong maybe something less bright and smaller." – D

More Explicit Communication Features. Although most participants were enthralled by the implicit communication characteristics of the light, there were two exceptions. In fact, these participants expressed interest in more explicit interpersonal communication features. This is apparent in the quotations below.

"When you are in the same room with a person, and you feel like you want to talk you can just talk to them. But in two different rooms, you cannot talk to the lights." – G

"Maybe, we can interact not only by changing activity states with the lights but also exchanging messages saying now let's get active." – C

Improve the Battery Life. Interestingly, one participant observed the battery limitations of the LED wallet. This is depicted below.

"I think it's a good system however the lifespan of the LED battery is short." – A

Recommendations for maximizing the performance of the battery life (*e.g.,* exploiting devices that work at 1.8 V) were discussed in (IWANN).

Colour. Like the experimental results in [21,23,25,26], various participants desired the freedom of colour choice based on personal preference. Moreover, a few respondents were more in favour of exploiting green for resting and blue for passive. While other younger participants were cognizant of the implicit association of red with danger and a few expressed disturbance and restlessness with the colour red. As such, warmer colours such as orange were proposed as a replacement for red. Example statements are highlighted below.

"Intuitively, I would use green for a state of calmness and blue for mental activity." – R

"For physical activity, I would use orange or yellow, something warm." – C

Position of the Smartphone. Even though all older participants expressed their satisfaction with the waist-mounted smartphone, there were a few younger participants who expressed their discomfort. In hindsight, these participants expressed discomfort during physical activities and one participant described her overall experience with the smartphone sensor as "burdensome". To rid themselves of the excess baggage, they proposed the following.

"The smartphone was a bit heavy. If it's on my personal smartphone it's okay, but if I have to carry an extra smartphone it might be too much." – F

"The smartphone could be in the pocket to prevent discomfort during exercise." – B

Vibration/Sound Effects. Although most participants were pleased with the peripheral nature of the system, a few were critical on the system's ability to sustain awareness during high periods of concentration. Accordingly, they prescribed additional sound or vibration effects to alert the user's attention and in some cases minimize the cognitive load. These recommendations are illustrated below.

"Maybe, add some vibration because when we are doing a mental activity we tend to focus and vibration could make us more alert." – E

"Maybe, I would add sound effects so that I wouldn't have to always look at the light." – L

Exploitation of Additional Everyday Objects. Although almost all the informants were positive toward our design choice of exploiting a cane and wallet, there were two respondents who suggested other everyday objects such as an ambient smartphone or an ambient id/key card. Their propositions are encapsulated within the following comments.

"You can use something that's more portable something like a mobile phone. Maybe you can use the Philips Ambilight TV as a reference." – R

"In the context of a caregiver, I wouldn't check my wallet all the time. They always carry an ID or a key card so some indication on those objects could be better." – C

Expanding the System Scope. A few participants were desirous of knowing the strength of the activity level, which could be illustrated with additional colours or changes in light intensity.

"I would increase the brightness based on the intensity of the activity." – W

However, one participant articulated her preference for only two activity levels namely (i) active or (ii) inactive to reduce any misconceptions of an intermediate activity level. Recall that a similar abstraction is implemented in [25]. Her citation is recorded below.

"Sometimes I forgot the meaning of the green and wondered whether they were engaged in mental activities or not. I think it would be better to have active or inactive states." – C

Remarkably, the temporal nature of activity information (*cf.* [21,26]) was reiterated by a young male informant when he voiced the following.

"It would be nice if I could see a summary of the data so I can see what happened in the past." – S

Moreover, one responded urged for an expansion of the system to support self-tracking.

"It's an interesting concept. However, I am more interested in knowing how I react when I am reading or sleeping or exercising. This would give me personal biofeedback." – B

6.8 Design Considerations for Bidirectional Ambient Displays for AAL

There were some key factors that emerged during the discussions with our participants, which include the following.

- Privacy and Ethics
- Context of Use
- Spatial Position
- Aesthetics

Privacy and Ethics. Generally participants were satisfied with the level of privacy offered by the system. Example accounts are given below.

"You have a feeling of connectivity indicating what the partner is doing without disturbing him with camera supervision. So, everyone is free to do what he or she wants while there is still a feeling that there is life, to say the least." – K

"It gives a good indication of what the other is doing. It is simple, and there is a certain privacy it provides. You don't feel observed." – P

Still, a few participants were fundamentally concerned with the potential privacy risks of ambient technologies. For example, Mrs. H remarked on the 'big brother is watching you' effect of the deployment of context-aware technologies in AAL environments.

"I won't like it if I lost my independence and someone can see if I feel okay or not. I would like to maintain my privacy as it's my right not to be okay. Someone else doesn't need to know. For me, it would feel like a 'big brother is watching me'. No, I wouldn't want to be constantly monitored so that someone can see how I feel. No, I don't like that." – H

Moreover, even though some participants were well aware of the privacy risks they were more willing to trade privacy for security. For example, Ms. O argued in the following statement.

"It's kind of uncomfortable for me to know that my mother always knows what I am doing right now, but for both of us to determine if we are in a 'safe' state then this system is very good. We are two far away [...] I want to her to know that I am okay." – O

Context and Purpose. From the commentaries, we observed that a few younger adults highlighted that the context and purpose of the system could affect adoption. Importantly, one young person stated that the system was only relevant for context-awareness only if her elderly relative was ill. Otherwise, it could be distracting.

"It depends on the situation if my relative is sick, then I will use it. But if I don't need to know what she is doing then it would be disturbing for my own life. So, the purpose is important." – I

With reference to situational context, another young person mentioned its relevance only in the home.

"Also, context is important if I am at home and they are at home then possibly it is okay. If I am at work and they are at work, then I don't need to know what they are doing. What's important is that they are okay." – N

However, in the home context, the user further expressed privacy concerns in the following statement.

"The thing is sometimes I sleep late and I wouldn't want them to know that. In truth, there are some things that I need to hide. I wouldn't want them to call and say why are you sleeping so late?" – N

To address privacy and situational context concerns, one participant suggested a service upon request functionality to maintain the right to control, access, and disseminate activity information at his convenience.

"I would use the lamp when it's a service on request so I should be able to control the functionality. It's a personal system so it should be visible to others only if I want to show them." – S

Reverting to N's reference on the importance of situational context, she also mentioned that consideration should be given to the time zones of two interacting partners for successful adoption.

"For me, I need to consider the time zones because sometimes when they are sleeping I am active and vice versa. Sometimes it would be disturbing for them." – N

Thus, by extension, we believe that the time-zones can affect the degree of synchrony between two interaction partners.

Spatial Position and the Stability of Social Bonds. From the remarks, we see that spatial position can change how the information is perceived and the degree of experienced social connectedness.

"In a real life situation, the positioning of the light in the room would be extremely important." – P

"I didn't really feel the connection with the light maybe because of the location of the lamp." – E

Besides, both P and E shared similar perspectives that perception and social connectedness are not only determined by the spatial position but also the stability of the emotional connection, which serves as a motive for observing the display consequently affecting how deeply the information is processed.

"In fact, I think the real connection outside the experiment will influence the results. If I don't have a good relationship with the partner, then I won't feel anything." – E

"If there is an emotional connection between the person in the other room or the person that you are taking care of. Then, there is a positive motivation to look at the lights." – P

Aesthetics. In a general sense, aesthetics was a major perceived benefit of the installation of the ambient displays. Thus, in designing bidirectional ambient technologies consideration must be given to the aesthetic needs of the participants. In retrospect, the participants postulated that the light's aesthetic properties created a pleasant atmosphere, fostered creative thinking through its mysterious effects, and led to elements of surprise, and more fun and playful interactions. Example remarks are demonstrated below. Figure 16 demonstrates a participant's interaction with the cane.

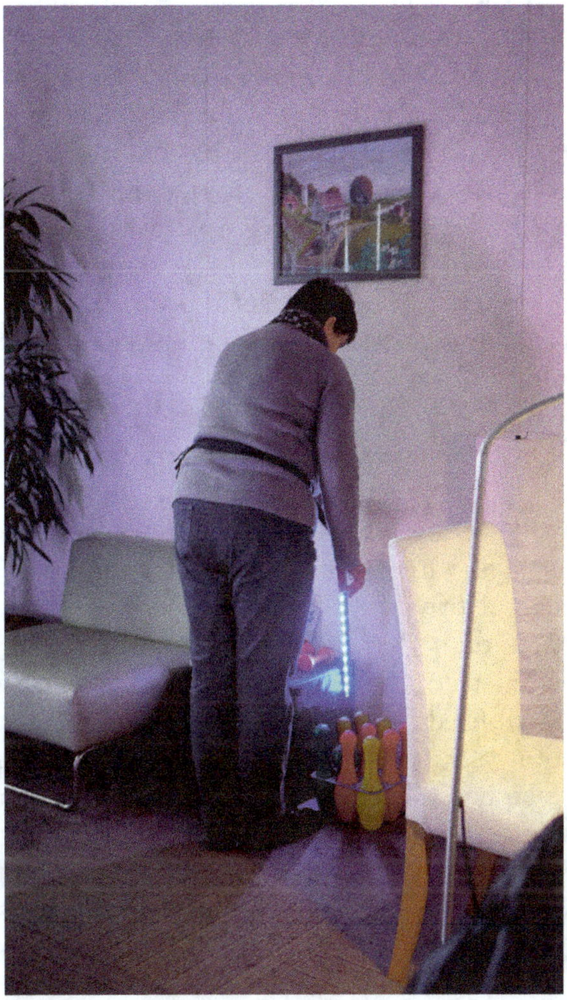

Fig. 16. Photo demonstrating a participant's interaction with the cane.

"I think the cane is an eye-catcher for the elderly. I think it's is nice and I like the fact that it surprises me." – S

"It was very fun and playful! You can use it for special activities in the home." – T

Also, C contends the prescriptive interpretation of Sullivan's notion of 'form follows function' [75] as she suggests that form is attuned to function in the statement below.

"It indicates the partner's activities and these colours add a certain ambiance to the room." – C

However, Lidwell *et al.* [48] assert that the prescriptive interpretation of 'form follows function' "aesthetic considerations in design should be secondary to functional considerations" (p. 106).

7 General Discussion

Overall, our participants identified several aspects that they found positive about the bidirectional activity-based ambient displays. Most participants could multitask, feel a sense of their partner's presence, access the activity information any and everywhere, understand the information received, enjoy an implicitly shared interaction, coordinate their activities to some extent, and maintain their privacy. Altogether, we can deduce from our findings that the process of experienced context-awareness and social connectedness among our participants included five phases: (i) visual perception, (ii) attention, (iii) memory, (iv) curiosity, and (v) habituation. Subsequently, the bidirectional exchange of activity information may consciously or unconsciously affect behavioural responses as depicted by the periodic accounts of interpersonal activity synchrony within this study. These irregular instances of coordinated actions could spark interest for further inquiry on the possibility of interpersonal activity synchrony in mediated AAL environments.

On the negative side, a few persons desired increased sensor comfort, more discreet portable displays while some felt that ambient technologies were an invasion of their personal privacy. To address privacy concerns, one informant suggested the addition of a "service upon request feature." Likewise, Hoof *et al.* [41] recommended that the user has complete control over his information collected and distributed in smart home environments.

On a different note, the most striking result to emerge from the discussion was the consistent reference to safety and monitoring systems. In fact, this was not surprising as the sense of safety and security in AAL environments has been a recurring theme throughout this doctoral research. A possible interpretation for this recurrence can be found in Maslow's hierarchy of needs, such that safety and family security needs precede the need for love and belonging [53]. Accordingly, we can infer that once our participants can guarantee the safety of their loved ones, then they can proceed to other forms of interaction to create a sense of belongingness in mediated AAL environments. As such, our design challenge has now become greater given the system scope has stretched beyond the main goal of promoting social connectedness through bidirectional ambient displays.

Going back to Mr. A's statement regarding a mental pattern of the partner's routine activities, it is clear that participants refer to their mental model as a reference for understanding their partner's activities. Consequently, this raises the challenge of designing peripheral technologies, which are coherent with the user's mental model. Norman suggests that misfortune could arise if the 'system image' is incoherent with the user's conceptual model [60]. Thus, the information portrayed should match with the user's ideology of their partner's activities. To address this, one could deploy highly accurate machine learning classification algorithms. However, system trust is critical for determining the match between the information presented and the user's conceptual model. Also, if there is no system trust then challenges with learnability and usability could emerge.

From our findings, technical literacy and cultural values can shape the users' experience of interacting with the system. Recall that our bidirectional activity-based system exploits ambient technologies and IoT to create awareness and maintain social connectedness between two interaction partners in AAL. Thus, Demiris *et al.* [29] highlight that inadequate technical literacy could impede the process "because the discussion of security and privacy concerns or issues of accuracy and reliability of sensor systems or other computing applications often require basic understanding of networking and data transfer" (p. 110). Thus, driving the need for technological literacy interventions in AAL.

8 Conclusion and Limitations

To strengthen our assessment of the behavioural implications of bidirectional activity-based displays, this chapter provides a background on interpersonal activity synchrony. Based on the knowledge acquired from prior works, it was possible to evaluate interpersonal activity synchrony by computing the cross-correlation coefficient of the counterpart's activity levels with that of their caregiver's. The results of a semi-controlled study suggest higher incidents of subjective interpersonal relationship closeness, experienced social presence, behavioural interdependence (for the counterpart only), information clarity, and the participants' willingness to adopt the technology, while utilizing minimum attentional resources with the activity-based ambient light interaction style. However, there was hardly any occurrence of interpersonal activity synchrony by using the cross-correlation approach. Nonetheless, during the post-trial interview, a few participants reported sporadic moments of synchrony during their interaction with the activity-based ambient light. Furthermore, in the said interaction style counterparts demonstrated increased tendencies to remain active in contrast to their interaction with white light.

It is plausible that some limitations could have influenced the results of this study. To begin with, we acknowledge convenience sampling as a constraint of this work. Accordingly, the findings are not entirely representative of all users within AAL community. To heighten the interest in our system, one option for future work is to specify the inclusion criteria only for the frail elderly, *e.g.*, those with (Parkinson's disease, Alzheimer's disease, or even users with epilepsy). This we know would reduce the population of our study. On the other hand, it could increase the interest in our system.

We are aware that a larger data stream of activity data is necessary to better estimate interpersonal activity synchrony in mediated environments. This can be achieved by increasing the number of participants and deploying a significantly longer experiment in the users' natural environments.

Unfortunately, the self-awareness of the wearable smart-phone sensor from [25] is still an open problem that will be addressed in future work. Notably, if our algorithms were independent to orientation and location, it could be one of the best contributions in the field of activity recognition for AAL. There are some attempts, but are very limited.

Acknowledgments. This work was supported in part by the Erasmus Mundus Joint Doctorate (EMJD) in Interactive and Cognitive Environments (ICE), which is funded by Erasmus Mundus under the FPA no. 2010–2012. Many thanks to the participants who gave useful insights and perspectives toward the design and implementation of our system. Also, we would like to express our appreciation to Mr. Geert van den Boomen, Henk Apeldoorn, Mr. Danny Jansen, Mr. Jasper Sterk, and Mr. Daniel Rodriguez-Martin for their assistance with this project.

References

1. Acampora, G., Cook, D.J., Rashidi, P., Vasilakos, A.V.: A survey on ambient intelligence in healthcare. Proc. IEEE **101**(12), 2470–2494 (2013)
2. Andrews, M.: The seductiveness of agelessness. Ageing Soc. **19**(03), 301–318 (1999)
3. Aron, A., Aron, E.N., Smollan, D.: Inclusion of other in the self scale and the structure of interpersonal closeness. J. Pers. Soc. Psychol. **63**(4), 596 (1992)
4. Bargh, J.A., Chen, M., Burrows, L.: Automaticity of social behavior: direct effects of trait construct and stereotype activation on action. J. Pers. Soc. Psychol. **71**(2), 230 (1996)
5. Baumeister, R.F., Leary, M.R.: The need to belong: desire for interpersonal attachments as a fundamental human motivation. Psychol. Bull. **117**(3), 497 (1995)
6. Bernieri, F.J.: Coordinated movement and rapport in teacher-student interactions. J. Nonverbal Behav. **12**(2), 120–138 (1988). https://doi.org/10.1007/BF00986930
7. Bian, F., Logan, J.R., Bian, Y.: Intergenerational relations in urban China: proximity, contact, and help to parents. Demography **35**(1), 115–124 (1998)
8. Biocca, F., Harms, C.: Defining and measuring social presence: contribution to the networked minds theory and measure. Proc. PRESENCE **2002**, 7–36 (2002)
9. Braun, V., Clarke, V.: Using thematic analysis in psychology. Qual. Res. Psychol. **3**(2), 77–101 (2006)
10. Chaaraoui, A.A., Florez-Revuelta, F., Harbach, M., De Luca, A., Egelman, S.: Technologies and applications for active and assisted living. Current situation. Pragmatics **27**(3), 447–474 (2017)
11. Chang, A., Resner, B., Koerner, B., Wang, X., Ishii, H.: LumiTouch: an emotional communication device. In: CHI 2001 Extended Abstracts on Human Factors in Computing Systems, CHI EA 2001, pp. 313–314. ACM, New York (2001)
12. Chartrand, T.L., Bargh, J.A.: The chameleon effect: the perception-behavior link and social interaction. J. Pers. Soc. Psychol. **76**(6), 893 (1999)
13. Chartrand, T.L., Maddux, W.W., Lakin, J.L.: Beyond the perception-behavior link: the ubiquitous utility and motivational moderators of nonconscious mimicry. In: The New Unconscious, pp. 334–361 (2005). http://www.oxfordscholarship.com/view/10.1093/acprof:oso/9780195307696.001.0001/acprof-9780195307696-chapter-14

14. Cirelli, L.K., Einarson, K.M., Trainor, L.J.: Interpersonal synchrony increases prosocial behavior in infants. Dev. Sci. **17**(6), 1003–1011 (2014)
15. Consolvo, S., Roessler, P., Shelton, B.E.: The CareNet display: lessons learned from an in home evaluation of an ambient display. In: Davies, N., Mynatt, E.D., Siio, I. (eds.) UbiComp 2004. LNCS, vol. 3205, pp. 1–17. Springer, Heidelberg (2004). https://doi.org/10.1007/978-3-540-30119-6_1
16. Cook, D.J., Augusto, J.C., Jakkula, V.R.: Review: ambient intelligence: technologies, applications, and opportunities. Pervasive Mob. Comput. **5**(4), 277–298 (2009). https://doi.org/10.1016/j.pmcj.2009.04.001
17. Cornejo, R., Favela, J., Tentori, M.: Ambient displays for integrating older adults into social networking sites. In: Kolfschoten, G., Herrmann, T., Lukosch, S. (eds.) CRIWG 2010. LNCS, vol. 6257, pp. 321–336. Springer, Heidelberg (2010). https://doi.org/10.1007/978-3-642-15714-1_24
18. Dadlani, P., Markopoulos, P., Sinitsyn, A., Aarts, E.: Supporting peace of mind and independent living with the Aurama awareness system. J. Ambient Intell. Smart Environ. **3**(1), 37–50 (2011)
19. Dadlani, P., Sinitsyn, A., Fontijn, W., Markopoulos, P.: Aurama: caregiver awareness for living independently with an augmented picture frame display. AI Soc. **25**(2), 233–245 (2010)
20. Davis, K., et al.: Activity recognition based on inertial sensors for ambient assisted living. In: 2016 19th International Conference on Information Fusion (FUSION), pp. 371–378. IEEE, July 2016
21. Davis, K., Owusu, E.B., Marcenaro, L., Feijs, L., Regazzoni, C., Hu, J.: Effects of ambient lighting displays on peripheral activity awareness. IEEE Access **5**, 9318–9335 (2017)
22. Davis, K.: Social hue: a bidirectional human activity-based system for improving social connectedness between the elderly and their caregivers. Ph.D. thesis, Technische Universiteit Eindhoven (2017)
23. Davis, K., Feijs, L., Hu, J., Marcenaro, L., Regazzoni, C.: Improving awareness and social connectedness through the social hue: insights and perspectives. In: Proceedings of the International Symposium on Interactive Technology and Ageing Populations, ITAP 2016, pp. 12–23. ACM, New York (2016)
24. Davis, K., et al.: Presenting a real-time activity-based bidirectional framework for improving social connectedness. In: Rojas, I., Joya, G., Catala, A. (eds.) IWANN 2017. LNCS, vol. 10306, pp. 356–367. Springer, Cham (2017). https://doi.org/10.1007/978-3-319-59147-6_31
25. Davis, K., Owusu, E., Hu, J., Marcenaro, L., Regazzoni, C., Feijs, L.: Promoting social connectedness through human activity-based ambient displays. In: Proceedings of the International Symposium on Interactive Technology and Ageing Populations, ITAP 2016, pp. 64–76. ACM, New York (2016)
26. Davis, K., Owusu, E., Marcenaro, L., Feijs, L., Regazzoni, C., Hu, J.: Evaluating human activity-based ambient lighting displays for effective peripheral communication. In: Proceedings of the 11th EAI International Conference on Body Area Networks, BodyNets 2016, pp. 148–154. ICST (Institute for Computer Sciences, Social-Informatics and Telecommunications Engineering), ICST, Brussels (2016). http://dl.acm.org/citation.cfm?id=3068615.3068648
27. Davis, K., Owusu, E., Marcenaro, L., Hu, J., Regazzoni, C., Feijs, L.: Pervasive Sensing for Social Connectedness. Institution of Engineering and Technology, Michael Faraday House, Stevenage (2017). Accepted for publication

28. Davis, K., Owusu, E., Regazzoni, C., Marcenaro, L., Feijs, L., Hu, J.: Perception of human activities a means to support connectedness between the elderly and their caregivers. In: Proceedings of the 1st International Conference on Information and Communication Technologies for Ageing Well and e-Health, pp. 194–199. SCITEPRESS (2015)
29. Demiris, G., Hensel, B.: "Smart homes" for patients at the end of life. J. Hous. Elderly **23**(1–2), 106–115 (2009)
30. Ekman, I., Chanel, G., Järvelä, S., Kivikangas, J.M., Salminen, M., Ravaja, N.: Social interaction in games: measuring physiological linkage and social presence. Simul. Gaming **43**(3), 321–338 (2012)
31. Engel, A.K., Fries, P., Singer, W.: Dynamic predictions: oscillations and synchrony in top-down processing. Nat. Rev. Neurosci. **2**(10), 704–716 (2001)
32. Gergle, D., Tan, D.S.: Experimental research in HCI. In: Olson, J.S., Kellogg, W.A. (eds.) Ways of Knowing in HCI, pp. 191–227. Springer, New York (2014). https://doi.org/10.1007/978-1-4939-0378-8_9
33. Gill, S.P.: Rhythmic synchrony and mediated interaction: towards a framework of rhythm in embodied interaction. AI Soc. **27**(1), 111–127 (2012). https://doi.org/10.1007/s00146-011-0362-2
34. Global Council on Brain Health: The brain and social connectedness: GCBH recommendations on social engagement and brain health. Technical report, AARP Policy, Research and International Affairs; AARP Integrated Communications and Marketing; and Age UK (2017). www.GlobalCouncilOnBrainHealth.org
35. Goleva, R.I., Garcia, N.M., Mavromoustakis, C.X., Dobre, C., Mastorakis, G., Stainov, R.: End-users testing of enhanced living environment platform and services. In: Ambient Assisted Living and Enhanced Living Environments, pp. 427–440. Elsevier (2017)
36. Gray, J.A.: Elements of a Two-Process Theory of Learning. Academic Press, Cambridge (1975)
37. Haken, H., Kelso, J.A.S., Bunz, H.: A theoretical model of phase transitions in human hand movements. Biol. Cybern. **51**(5), 347–356 (1985). https://doi.org/10.1007/BF00336922
38. Harms, C., Biocca, F.: Internal consistency and reliability of the networked minds measure of social presence. In: Alcaniz, M., Rey, B. (eds.) Proceedings of the Seventh Annual International Workshop: Presence 2004 (2004)
39. Hasson, U., Nir, Y., Levy, I., Fuhrmann, G., Malach, R.: Intersubject synchronization of cortical activity during natural vision. Science **303**(5664), 1634–1640 (2004)
40. Hatfield, E., Cacioppo, J.T., Rapson, R.L.: Emotional Contagion. Cambridge University Press, Cambridge (1994)
41. van Hoof, J., de Kort, H., Markopoulos, P., Soede, M.: Ambient intelligence, ethics and privacy. Gerontechnology **6**(3), 155–163 (2007)
42. Hove, M.J., Risen, J.L.: It's all in the timing: interpersonal synchrony increases affiliation. Soc. Cognit. **27**(6), 949–960 (2009)
43. Järvelä, S., Kätsyri, J., Ravaja, N., Chanel, G., Henttonen, P.: Intragroup emotions: physiological linkage and social presence. Front. Psychol. **7**, 105 (2016). https://www.ncbi.nlm.nih.gov/pmc/articles/PMC4746243/
44. Jivraj, S., Nazroo, J., Vanhoutte, B., Chandola, T.: Aging and subjective well-being in later life. J. Gerontol. Ser. B: Psychol. Sci. Soc. Sci. **69**(6), 930–941 (2014)
45. Julien, D., Brault, M., Chartrand, É., Bégin, J.: Immediacy behaviours and synchrony in satisfied and dissatisfied couples. Can. J. Behav. Sci./Revue canadienne des sciences du comportement **32**(2), 84 (2000)

46. Kahneman, D.: Attention and Effort. Prentice-Hall, Upper Saddle River (1973)
47. Keyes, C.L.M.: Social well-being. Soc. Psychol. Q. **61**(2), 121–140 (1998)
48. Lidwell, W., Holden, K., Butler, J.: Universal Principles of Design. Rockport Pub, Rockport (2010)
49. Lim, S., Yu, H., Kang, S., Kim, D.: Smart cane system: direction guidance system for the blind using GS1 and EPCIS system. In: Proceedings of the 11th EAI International Conference on Body Area Networks, BodyNets 2016, pp. 179–183. ICST (Institute for Computer Sciences, Social-Informatics and Telecommunications Engineering), ICST, Brussels (2016)
50. Lyyra, T.M., Heikkinen, R.L.: Perceived social support and mortality in older people. J. Gerontol. Ser. B: Psychol. Sci. Soc. Sci. **61**(3), S147–S152 (2006)
51. Mankoff, J., Dey, A.K., Hsieh, G., Kientz, J., Lederer, S., Ames, M.: Heuristic evaluation of ambient displays. In: Proceedings of the SIGCHI Conference on Human Factors in Computing Systems, CHI 2003, pp. 169–176. ACM, New York (2003)
52. Markopoulos, P., Ruyter, B.D., Mackay, W.: Awareness Systems: Advances in Theory, Methodology and Design, 1st edn. Springer, London (2009). https://doi.org/10.1007/978-1-84882-477-5
53. Maslow, A.: Motivation and Personality. Harper's Psychological Series. Harper, New York (1954)
54. Matthews, T., Rattenbury, T., Carter, S.: Defining, designing, and evaluating peripheral displays: an analysis using activity theory. Hum.-Comput. Interact. **22**(1–2), 221–261 (2007)
55. Metaxas, G., Metin, B., Schneider, J., Markopoulos, P., de Ruyter, B.: Daily Activities Diarist: supporting aging in place with semantically enriched narratives. In: Baranauskas, C., Palanque, P., Abascal, J., Barbosa, S.D.J. (eds.) INTERACT 2007. LNCS, vol. 4663, pp. 390–403. Springer, Heidelberg (2007). https://doi.org/10.1007/978-3-540-74800-7_34
56. Miles, J., Shevlin, M.: Applying Regression and Correlation: A Guide for Students and Researchers. Sage Publications, Thousand Oaks (2001)
57. Miles, L.K., Nind, L.K., Macrae, C.N.: The rhythm of rapport: interpersonal synchrony and social perception. J. Exp. Soc. Psychol. **45**(3), 585–589 (2009)
58. Mynatt, E.D., Rowan, J., Craighill, S., Jacobs, A.: Digital family portraits: supporting peace of mind for extended family members. In: Proceedings of the SIGCHI Conference on Human Factors in Computing Systems, CHI 2001, pp. 333–340. ACM, New York (2001)
59. Newberry, B.: Raising student social presence in online classes. In: WebNet 2001: World Conference on the WWW and Internet Proceedings, Orlando, FL, 23–27 October 2001, pp. 1–7. ERIC (2001)
60. Norman, D.A.: The Design of Everyday Things: Revised and Expanded Edition. The Perseus Books Group, New York (2013)
61. Pires, I.M., Garcia, N.M., Pombo, N., Flórez-Revuelta, F., Spinsante, S., Teixeira, M.C.: Identification of activities of daily living through data fusion on motion and magnetic sensors embedded on mobile devices. Pervasive Mob. Comput. **47**, 78–93 (2018)
62. Pousman, Z., Stasko, J.: A taxonomy of ambient information systems: four patterns of design. In: Proceedings of the Working Conference on Advanced Visual Interfaces, AVI 2006, pp. 67–74. ACM, New York (2006)
63. Rashidi, P., Cook, D.J., Holder, L.B., Schmitter-Edgecombe, M.: Discovering activities to recognize and track in a smart environment. IEEE Trans. Knowl. Data Eng. **23**(4), 527–539 (2011)

64. Richardson, M.J., Marsh, K.L., Isenhower, R.W., Goodman, J.R., Schmidt, R.: Rocking together: dynamics of intentional and unintentional interpersonal coordination. Hum. Mov. Sci. **26**(6), 867–891 (2007). http://www.sciencedirect.com/science/article/pii/S0167945707000528
65. Rowan, J., Mynatt, E.D.: Digital family portrait field trial: support for aging in place. In: Proceedings of the SIGCHI Conference on Human Factors in Computing Systems, CHI 2005, pp. 521–530. ACM, New York (2005)
66. Schilit, B.N., Theimer, M.M.: Disseminating active map information to mobile hosts. IEEE Netw. **8**(5), 22–32 (1994)
67. Schmidt, R.C., Carello, C., Turvey, M.T.: Phase transitions and critical fluctuations in the visual coordination of rhythmic movements between people. J. Exp. Psychol.: Hum. Percept. Perform. **16**(2), 227 (1990)
68. Scott Kelso, J., Holt, K.G., Rubin, P., Kugler, P.N.: Patterns of human interlimb coordination emerge from the properties of non-linear, limit cycle oscillatory processes: theory and data. J. Motor Behav. **13**(4), 226–261 (1981)
69. Sellen, A., Eardley, R., Izadi, S., Harper, R.: The whereabouts clock: early testing of a situated awareness device. In: CHI 2006 Extended Abstracts on Human Factors in Computing Systems, CHI EA 2006, pp. 1307–1312. ACM, New York (2006). http://doi.acm.org/10.1145/1125451.1125694
70. Short, J., Williams, E., Christie, B.: The Social Psychology of Telecommunications. Wiley, Hoboken (1976)
71. Shumway, R.H., Stoffer, D.S.: Time Series Analysis and Its Applications: With R Examples. Springer, Heidelberg (2010). https://doi.org/10.1007/978-3-319-52452-8
72. Singh, S.D.: Loneliness, depression and sociability in old age. Int. J. Indian Psychol. **2**(2), 73 (2015)
73. Steele, R., Lo, A., Secombe, C., Wong, Y.K.: Elderly persons' perception and acceptance of using wireless sensor networks to assist healthcare. Int. J. Med. Inform. **78**(12), 788–801 (2009)
74. Steptoe, A., Demakakos, P., de Oliveira, C.: The psychological well-being, health and functioning of older people in England. In: Banks, J., Nazroo, J., Steptoe, A. (eds.) The Dynamics of Ageing: Evidence from the English Longitudinal Study of Ageing 2002–2010, chap. 4, pp. 98–182. The Institute for Fiscal Studies, London (2012)
75. Sullivan, L.H.: The tall office building artistically considered. Lippincott's Mag. **57**(3), 406 (1896)
76. Thomas, K.A., Burr, R.L., Spieker, S., Lee, J., Chen, J.: Mother-infant circadian rhythm: development of individual patterns and dyadic synchrony. Early Hum. Dev. **90**(12), 885–890 (2014)
77. Thornton, J.E.: Myths of aging or ageist stereotypes. Educ. Gerontol. **28**(4), 301–312 (2002). https://doi.org/10.1080/036012702753590415
78. Tsai, S.Y., Barnard, K.E., Lentz, M.J., Thomas, K.A.: Mother-infant activity synchrony as a correlate of the emergence of circadian rhythm. Biol. Res. Nurs. **13**(1), 80–88 (2011). https://doi.org/10.1177/1099800410378889. pMID: 20798158
79. Ulzen, N.R.V., Lamoth, C.J., Daffertshofer, A., Semin, G.R., Beek, P.J.: Characteristics of instructed and uninstructed interpersonal coordination while walking side-by-side. Neurosci. Lett. **432**(2), 88–93 (2008). http://www.sciencedirect.com/science/article/pii/S0304394007012244

80. Van Bel, D.T., IJsselsteijn, W.A., de Kort, Y.A.: Interpersonal connectedness: conceptualization and directions for a measurement instrument. In: CHI 2008 Extended Abstracts on Human Factors in Computing Systems, CHI EA 2008, pp. 3129–3134. ACM, New York (2008)
81. van Bel, D.T., Smolders, K., IJsselsteijn, W.A., de Kort, Y.: Social connectedness: concept and measurement. Intell. Environ. **2**, 67–74 (2009)
82. Vasilakos, A., Pedrycz, W.: Ambient Intelligence, Wireless Networking, and Ubiquitous Computing. Artech House, Inc., Norwood (2006)
83. Vastenburg, M.H., Visser, T., Vermaas, M., Keyson, D.V.: Designing acceptable assisted living services for elderly users. In: Aarts, E., et al. (eds.) AmI 2008. LNCS, vol. 5355, pp. 1–12. Springer, Heidelberg (2008). https://doi.org/10.1007/978-3-540-89617-3_1
84. Visser, T., Vastenburg, M.H., Keyson, D.V.: Designing to support social connectedness: the case of snowglobe. Int. J. Des. **5**(3), 129–142 (2011)
85. Vogel, D.J.: Interactive public ambient displays. Ph.D. thesis, University of Toronto (2005)
86. Weiser, M.: The computer for the 21st century. Sci. Am. **265**(3), 94–104 (1991)
87. Weiser, M., Brown, J.S.: The coming age of calm technology. In: Denning, P.J., Metcalfe, R.M. (eds.) Beyond Calculation, pp. 75–85. Springer, New York (1997). https://doi.org/10.1007/978-1-4612-0685-9_6
88. Wells, M.: Resilience in older adults living in rural, suburban, and urban areas. Online J. Rural Nurs. Health Care **10**(2), 45–54 (2012)
89. Yang, Y.C., Schorpp, K., Harris, K.M.: Social support, social strain and inflammation: evidence from a national longitudinal study of US adults. Soc. Sci. Med. **107**, 124–135 (2014)
90. Zivotofsky, A.Z., Hausdorff, J.M.: The sensory feedback mechanisms enabling couples to walk synchronously: an initial investigation. J. Neuroengineering Rehabil. **4**(1), 28 (2007)

Towards Truly Affective AAL Systems

Mara Pudane[1(✉)], Sintija Petrovica[1], Egons Lavendelis[1], and Hazım Kemal Ekenel[2]

[1] Riga Technical University, Riga, Latvia
{mara.pudane, sintija.petrovica, egons.lavendelis}@rtu.lv
[2] Istanbul Technical University, Istanbul, Turkey
ekenel@itu.edu.tr

Abstract. Affective computing is a growing field of artificial intelligence. It focuses on models and strategies for detecting, obtaining, and expressing various affective states, including emotions, moods, and personality related attributes. The techniques and models developed in affective computing are applicable to various affective contexts, including Ambient Assisted Living. One of the hypotheses for the origin of emotion is that the primary purpose was to regulate social interactions. Since one of the crucial characteristics of Ambient Assisted Living systems is supporting social contact, it is unthinkable to build such systems without considering emotions. Moreover, the emotional capacity needed for Ambient Assisted Living systems exceeds simple user emotion detection and showing emotion expressions of the system. In addition, emotion generation and emotion mapping on rational thinking and behavior of a system should be considered. The chapter discusses the need and requirements for these processes in the context of various application domains of Ambient Assisted Living, i.e., healthcare, mobility, education, and social interaction.

Keywords: Affective computing · Social interaction · Healthcare Education · Mobility

1 Introduction

Ambient Assisted Living (AAL) can be described as concepts, products, and services that combine new technologies and social environment to improve the quality of life for people in all stages of their lifetime [1]. From an individual perspective, the quality of life can be considered in terms of well-being. It includes emotional (self-esteem, emotional intelligence, mindset), social (friends, family, community) and physical (health, physical safety) aspects in a person's life [2]. Humans are social beings, thus one of the most important tasks of AAL is facilitating social contact [3]. This is achievable through the implementation of affect (a generic term used to cover feelings, mood, emotions, etc.) detecting and processing mechanisms in a system. Affective data enhances a system's ability to make rational decisions and achieve its goals by serving as an extra information for detecting the context of the particular situation and as a mediator through which information can be passed.

I. Ganchev et al. (Eds.): Enhanced Living Environments, LNCS 11369, pp. 152–176, 2019.
https://doi.org/10.1007/978-3-030-10752-9_7

Integration of affective capabilities in AAL systems requires knowledge from various fields, including cognitive psychology, neuroscience, medicine, and computer science. Mentioned knowledge has been of paramount importance in such artificial field (AI) field as affective computing which mainly focuses on the study and development of systems and devices that can recognize, interpret, process, and simulate human emotions [4] which has led to significant amount of research, algorithms and methods in this area. One question that has been in the center since the first affective systems appeared is related to their affective abilities; to put it simply – what kind of emotional processes does a system need? In the studies answering this question, main affective processes of affective systems have been identified (namely, emotion recognition, emotion expression, emotion generation and emotion mapping on the rational behavior); it has been argued that depending on their focus, not all systems need all these processes [5].

Another aspect of this chapter is AAL applications that are targeted to help not only older adults but also younger people (since health disorders can affect anyone at any age) to live independently and comfortably in their living environment. However, living environments do not include only users' houses but also various environments surrounding them such as city streets, schools, shops, restaurants, and other places. Therefore, these people have needs for movement, social interaction, healthcare and acquisition of knowledge and skills not only related to specific problem domains (e.g., mathematics) but also basic skills required for everyday life like eating or cleaning. To support emerging emotional, physical and mental needs in extended AAL environments, four AAL application domains, including healthcare, education (teaching/learning), mobility (transportation), and social interaction, are analyzed in terms of previously mentioned affective processes.

The chapter starts with explanations of the complexity of affective systems and advancements in affective computing field, as well as describes affective processes and their implementations in affective computing systems. Next, the need for emotions in existing AAL application areas has been discussed and a short analysis of AAL systems in the context of basic emotional processes has been provided.

2 General Emotional Processes of Affective Systems

Affective computing (AC), which started its advancement in 1997 [4], aims to endow computers with abilities to detect, recognize, interpret, process, simulate human emotions from visual, textual, and auditory sources, as well as respond appropriately [6]. AC humanizes human-computer interactions by building artificial emotional intelligence. As natural language interactions with technology continue to evolve (examples include search, bots, and personal assistants), emotion recognition is already emerging to improve advertising, marketing, entertainment, travel, customer service, and healthcare [7].

Advances in data processing speeds and disciplines of computer science, AI, machine learning, psychology, and neuroscience, are all leading to expanding of AC field [8]. Computers, cameras, and sensors can capture facial expressions, gaze, posture, gestures, tone of voice, speech, patterns of keyboard and/or mouse usage, as well as physiological states (e.g., skin temperature or conductance, heart rate and blood volume pulse) to register changes in a user's emotional state [6].

Analysis of existing studies shows that numerous computational models of emotions have been developed and applied by researchers working in the AC area. An abundant amount of various systems and applications has facilitated discussion of main affective processes and system's affective abilities in general.

One of fundamental works in this direction has been done by Hudlicka who proposed a general affective system framework [9]. The framework focuses on the roles of emotions and their fulfillment in artificial units. Such general approach allows systematic and organized design and implementation of necessary processes and functions, as well as enables comparison of affective mechanisms of various systems. According to AC, an abstract affective component can be identified, which executes three processes: affect recognition, affect calculation as well as affect expression [4]. Affect calculation may include two separate processes: emotion generation and emotion mapping on behavior [9]. By combining these ideas, Petrovica and Pudane [10] have defined processes that are needed specifically for a fully affective system that interacts with a user (see Fig. 1).

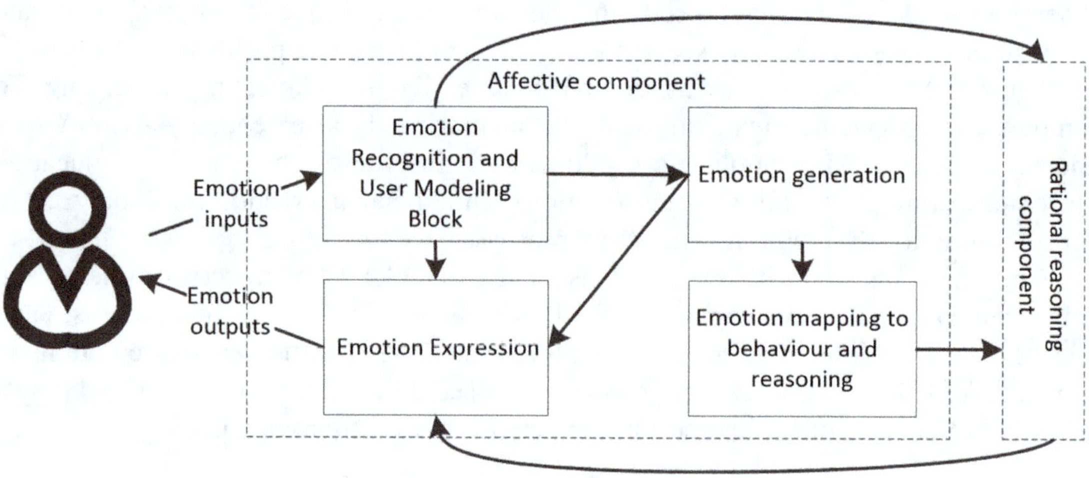

Fig. 1. Affective processes performed by an emotion-aware system (only affective interactions with a user are shown) (adapted from [10]).

Emotion recognition is usually done by extracting emotional cues from one or more modalities, i.e., facial expressions [11], gestures [12], body postures [13], voice [14], etc. Perception of various modalities is a precondition in order to automatically detect emotions and accordingly adapt the behavior of AAL systems. In the AC field, affect detection is commonly achieved both through non-intrusive sensors, which do not require physical contact, e.g., video cameras, eye trackers, and microphones, and intrusive sensors which require physical contact with human body, e.g., physiological sensors or haptic (touch) sensors. Since the main goal of AAL field is the development of non-intrusive intelligent systems that are able to proactively support people with special needs in their daily activities, non-invasive user monitoring is an important aspect of AAL systems [15].

Emotional state generation is related to the appraisal of stimuli causing subjective emotional experience. Emotional responses are triggered by various events that are evaluated as being significant for a person's (or robot's/agent's) expectations, needs, or goals. Therefore, the same stimulus can produce distinct emotions, depending on differences in the person's interpretations [9]. In AC field, affect generation is achieved by computational emotion modeling. One of the goals for computational emotion modeling is to enrich the architecture of intelligent systems with emotion mechanisms similar to those of humans, and thus endow them with the capacity to "have" emotions. In the context of AAL, some studies exist in this direction, e.g., in [16] authors describe need-inspired emotion model applied in a HiFi agent whose emotions are generated by evaluating the situation and comparing it to agent's different needs.

Emotion mapping on cognition and behavior means defining reasoning or behavior changes caused by an emotional experience. Emotions can lead to the expression and communication of different reactions or the activation of specific actions in a person's (or agent's/robot's) body. Thus, models of emotion effects should deal with the multimodal nature of emotion. Systems with embodied agents need to express emotions not only through behavior, but also through other modalities available in their particular embodiment (e.g., facial expressions, speech, or gestures). One of the possible approaches that can be used for mapping emotions to behavioral reactions is the application of a behavior-consequent model that allows aligning emotional state to physical actions or other direct outward or social expressions, for instance smiling when happy. Behavioral-consequent models are often used to synthesize human-like emotional or social behavior in embodied robots like Kismet [17] or in virtual agents such as Max [18]. Regarding AAL developments that are able to link emotions with behavioral effects, few projects can be found. For example, in a NICA project [19] a behavioral architecture is developed for a social empathic robot which can assist a user in the interaction with a smart home environment.

Emotion expression is focused on the system's ability to express emotions as responses to people's personality, emotions, moods, attitudes, and actions. For AAL systems, such ability could improve their functionality since many AAL systems are developed as personal assistants fulfilling two functions:

1. facilitation of the completion of daily tasks [20]
2. maintenance of social interaction and communication to prevent social isolation of people [21].

To make the virtual companions or assistants not only look realistic but also have natural and human-like behaviors, one of the key characteristics is personality and the ability to exhibit human traits and characteristics, including emotions [22]. In AC field, such functionality is achieved mainly through affective conversational agents or affective robots; in AAL systems, it is implemented in a similar way – through virtual agents embodied into a system's interface or robots. Thus, ways how emotions are expressed by AAL systems (or virtual agents) can be similar to those used by humans, i.e., facial expressions [23], voice and speech [24], behavior and body posture [25]. In other cases, a reaction to human emotions can be expressed through changes in music, color, and lighting [2].

While all four functional blocks (emotion recognition, emotion generation, emotion mapping on the rational behavior and emotion expression) if implemented properly ensure that a system is fully affective, it is assumed that a system still can perform well if it has just a few functional blocks. For example, if a system needs to adapt to a user's emotions, it will achieve its goals just by recognizing emotions and expressing them as a response to a user's emotions. Such approach is often used in intelligent tutoring systems [5].

AAL systems, in general, are complex in the sense that they need to support social interaction as well as carry out rational functions. This leads to thinking that in AAL systems, all four processes are needed: to detect emotion, to generate emotion, to map emotion on rational processes ("feel" emotion) and to express emotion.

While these components are already recognizable in existing systems, we argue that depending on the application area of AAL (as opposed to AAL systems as a whole), requirements for affective abilities differ. While rich affective model might be crucial in other cases, such as when dealing with older adults or targeting long-term interaction and/or companionship, for more specific AAL systems, full set of identified functions is not necessary. To prove this, we analyze four different areas where AAL can be used. To compare these areas, we use affective processes as a reference. It provides main functions required for AAL systems.

In the next section, various AAL application domains corresponding to requirements of AAL systems are reviewed and analyzed. Main characteristics are described for all listed application areas, as well as these characteristics are analyzed in the context of AC processes. Analysis of basic affective processes in existing AAL applications would help to develop truly affective systems supporting users not only physically but also mentally.

3 Affective Computing in AAL

AAL systems are aimed at satisfying the needs of those in care. In the research on older adults [6], needs have been divided into four kinds: Errand, Life curation, Emotional health and Comfort needs. Older adults are one of the major user groups of AAL, however, additional need for younger generation appears – a need for education, e.g., in autistic children cases [26]. We have chosen the following application areas in which AAL systems should support specific user needs:

- *education* which supports life comfort in long-term by ensuring that basic life skills are learned;
- *the social interaction* that supports emotional and comfort needs;
- *mobility* supporting errand needs as well as comfort since the ability to move freely increases independence;
- *healthcare* supporting physical (life curation) needs.

3.1 Emotions as Part of AAL in Education

Emotions play a central role as they ensure our survival and support all activities from the most basic to the most elaborated tasks, including education [27]. Studies have shown that emotions can influence various aspects of human behavior and cognitive processes, such as attention, long-term memorizing, decision making, understanding, remembering, analyzing, reasoning, and application of knowledge [28]. Emotions and cognition are complementary processes in learning situations when learners have to make conclusions, answer causal questions, identify problems, solve tasks, make knowledge-based comparisons, provide logical explanations, as well as demonstrate a usage of acquired knowledge and transfer it to others [29]. Emotional states of a learner can influence his/her problem-solving abilities and even leave an impact on a willingness to engage in the learning process, as well as they can affect motivation to learn. It is considered that positive emotions play an important role in the development of creativity and ability to adapt to different problems during their solving, conversely, negative emotions can hinder thinking processes, abilities to concentrate, remember, memorize, solve tasks, reason, and make conclusions [30].

Learning environments utilizing AC (i.e., monitoring of learner's emotions and/or responding to them [31]) can create different scenarios that help and improve educational conditions. A system for emotion identification may detect signals of frustration during the learning process or lack of understanding during the study of concepts and definitions [27]. With such identification at the beginning of processes, the educational staff can start individual psychological assistance for learners, avoiding future problems that interfere in the learning process, and even more, in their lives. Currently, many examples of AC in educational settings already exist, e.g., *AutoTutor* [32], *MathSpring* [33], *MetaTutor* [34], etc. However, most of them focus on normally developing individuals and provide knowledge in specific problem domains, e.g., physics, mathematics, medicine, etc. Therefore, such developments might be applicable in cases when learners are not able to attend schools, for example, children with movement disorders.

If we are focusing particularly on AAL field and children with special educational needs, including those that have emotional, behavioral, sensory, physical, or mental disabilities, like children with autism, then previously mentioned affective learning environments (e.g., *MetaTutor*) developed for teaching specific problem domain are not applicable. This is due to the fact that most of the children suffering from autism have problems with learning even the basic skills required for everyday life [26]. In general, autism is a communication disorder that requires early and continuous educational interventions on various levels like everyday social interaction, communication and reasoning skills, language, understanding norms of social behavior, imagination, etc. [35]. Usually, these skills are relatively self-evident or easy to develop for other children. Basic social interaction skills are generally acquired from a very early age through an ongoing experience with the world and interactions with the people around us. Children with autism experience difficulties in this domain [36]. A social-emotional domain is strictly interrelated with cognitive and motor development, as it consists of the acquisition of capacities for personal relationships, emotional expression, motivation and engagement [36]. From an affective perspective, children with autism often have difficulty recognizing emotions in others and sharing enjoyment, interests, or accomplishments, as well as in interpreting facial cues to understand emotional expressions of others [37]. Without this understanding, they will remain oblivious to other people's intentions and emotions. A lack of such an important prior knowledge about the environment hinders children to make informed decisions [38].

In general, the education is considered as the most proper solution for the autism, however, planning of the learning process for learners with autism is complex, because these learners have significant differences from most other learners in learning style, communication, and social skill development, and often have challenging behaviors [39]. Such differences may strongly influence the educational process and often lead to social exclusion from meaningful participation in learning activities and community life. Exclusion, in turn, further reduces learners' perspectives to learn, grow, and develop [27]. Adapted educational systems facilitating an acquisition of knowledge and skills through the use of AC are crucial if the objective is successful development of the society where equal opportunities are provided for all children, youth, and adults.

Analysis of existing learning environments targeting AAL domain allows concluding that most of the developed solutions are particularly aimed at assisting autistic children in communication and interaction with other people. For example, mobile application *CaptureMyEmotion* [40] helps to teach children to recognize their emotions in the moment of taking photos, recording videos or sounds. Later emotions can be discussed with a caregiver thus helping children to learn their emotions. Another solution called *Emotional Advisor* has been proposed to help autistic children to engage in meaningful conversations where people are able to recognize their own or other people's emotions. *Emotional Advisor* is capable of teaching and guiding autistic people on how to respond appropriately based on how the other person is feeling or expressing emotions during verbal communication [38]. In [41], the educational system called *Face3D* has been proposed for autistic children to help them in understanding and reasoning about other people's (for example, relatives') mental and emotional states by use of virtual agents representing real people, their performance, emotions, and behavior.

A robotic solution called *IROMEC* (Interactive Robotic Social Mediators as Companions) has been developed to teach autistic children basic social interaction skills [36]. During playing with *IROMEC*, children's specific strengths and needs are taken into consideration and a wide range of objectives are covered regarding the development of different child's skills (sensory, communicational and interaction, motor, cognitive, social, and emotional) [42]. The robot allows the use of different inputs (e.g. direct operation on touchscreen, buttons, remotely controlled switches, etc.) which can be changed according to child's abilities and provides personalized feedback according to child's and therapist's preferences, therefore *IROMEC* adapts itself and develops along with a child [36]. Regarding the emotional factor covered by the system, *IROMEC* can display a set of basic emotions such as happiness, sadness, fear, surprise, disgust, anger. In addition, various scenarios of *IROMEC* are aimed at improving child's self-esteem and regulation of emotions, as well as it enables teaching a range of basic emotions [42].

Even though many educational environments are targeting autistic children, more general solutions for people with disabilities also exist (however, not many). For example, an Ambient Intelligence Context-aware Affective Recommender Platform (*AICARP*) has been built to support learner's needs through personalizing and adapting the learning environment during language learning [43]. *AICARP* ensures personalized feedback (e.g., playing different songs or sending some signals using a light and a buzzer) when particular learner's emotional states, i.e., relaxed or nervous, are detected [44].

Overall, it can be concluded that AAL systems aiming at helping children during the learning process will not be able to provide full-fledged support if emotional aspects will not be considered during the development of the particular system. Emotions directly affect human cognitive abilities, including learning skills, therefore non-intrusive detection of learner's emotional states and appropriate response (or adaptation) to these emotions are those capabilities which should be considered during the design of such AAL systems.

3.2 Emotions as Part of AAL in the Social Interaction

One of AAL goals is to ensure people's wellbeing which includes not only satisfying physical needs or running errands but also making sure a person is, putting it simply, happy [45]. This is especially important in a case when a person uses a system in a long term, i.e., service robots for older adults and artificial nannies for kids [46]. Moreover, research shows that people are more open to system's suggestions if it uses emotional words [47]. This leads to conclusion that a user would be more interested to engage with a system if it would fulfill their emotional expectations as a result supporting the main functions of AAL as well. A system that satisfies emotional needs has its advantages, and yet not many AAL systems exist in this direction.

The most straight-forward way for implementing social and emotional behaviors in an AAL system is through artificial companions. Developing such systems present multiple challenges such as unmistakable expressions of emotions, the ability to conduct high-level dialogue, abilities to learn, to adapt, to develop a personality, to use natural cues, and to develop social competencies [48, 49]. While it is not an easy task, research suggests that aside from already mentioned benefits – satisfying emotional needs and reducing loneliness and supporting "rational" tasks – companions also reduce stress and as a consequence can improve physical health [50]. However, for the companions to achieve these goals an important characteristic is a believability – i.e., a user needs to perceive them as if they act on their own; emotions are crucial for a companion to be believable [51].

Believable artificial companions have been researched in several areas, including social robotics, virtual assistants both as chatbots and as characters that provide other activities [52]. In an AAL environment, mobile robots provide more possibilities in terms of running errands or physically helping a user. Moreover, the research shows that people tend to empathize and attach to a robotic companion compared to its simulation [53]; robotic pets can be involved in therapy and achieve effect similarly as real pets [54] that cannot be done on 2D screen.

In the field of AC, however, several frameworks and projects for virtual agents have been developed that in terms of behavior are believable. One of such developments is *WASABI* – an architecture that is implemented as a virtual reality companion for playing a card game [18]. For this reason, this subsection reviews different types of assistants; it does not focus on "practical" functions (such as running errands, reminding drinking pills, etc.) of the companions but rather on their emotional abilities and behaviors that enable them to become emotionally believable.

In general, there are two types of companions: virtual and robotic [52]. Virtual assistants have no physical embodiment and they can have no virtual body as well (e.g., a chatbot). Emotions in companions, however, are closely related to expression through the body which helps them to be readable without misunderstandings [48] so a companion needs at least some kind of body – even if it is a virtual agent.

Robotic companions are researched by a field called social robotics [17]. Social robots are autonomous robots that can interact with a user in a socially believable manner [17]. Social robots are grouped into the ones that use strong approaches and those that use weak approaches. The strong approach means that a robot evolves its abilities over time; on the contrary the weak approach means a robot is just imitating emotions [49]. In the context of companions, this classification can be extended to virtual assistants as well.

Several researchers have noted that for companions to be able to adapt to a user, to form a personality and display believable behavior in long-term, they need to be able to learn [48, 55]. In [55], it is especially accented that in the future social robots will need to be personalized for which sophisticated user model might be needed. This leads to the conclusion that weak approaches will be left to narrow applications and currently the development of strong approaches is needed.

The weak approach is often used in robots that are zoomorphic, i.e., remind animals; some of these animals have no emotions at all e.g., robotic parrot *RoboParrot* that is used for educational purposes and therapy [56] or robotic seal *PARO* which is also used for therapy [57]. Sony's robotic dog *AIBO*, on the other hand, can express six emotions: happiness, anger, fear, sadness, surprise, and dislike [46] but lately Sony has moved towards strong approaches claiming that dog can form an emotional bond with a user [58].

The strong approach in zoomorphic agents has been developed already almost two decades ago in *FLAME* which is a virtual agent [59]. *FLAME* is a fuzzy logic adaptive model of emotions which was implemented as a pet dog. A user can give his feedback to the pet, thus forming his behavior and teaching new rules. The author claims that such learning adapts the pet to the user.

Another group of robots and agents are the ones that are not similar neither to animals nor humans. They rely on different forms of emotion expression [48]. A well-known example of such social robots is Mung that has a simple body and LED lights that allows expressing emotion through colors [60]. An interesting experiment was done to investigate if movement-based emotions (without e.g. facial features) can be recognized [61]. The results showed that users still recognize emotions with sufficient accuracy. Such studies are important also for humanoid robots since implementing facial features is a complex task from both, hardware and software perspective, and for this reason, other approaches are often chosen. One example of that is Nao – widely used social robot (see e.g. [62] where Nao is used to investigate interaction with users or [63] where Nao is used to interact with autistic children) which relies on emotion expression through the body movements and lights [64].

Humanoids or robots with human-like expressions are often used for emotion expression [52]. Not all of them, however, express emotions through complex channels and not all of them use the strong approach. In [65] a human-like robot *Daryl* is described. While it shows its emotions through verbal cues and movement, the approach used in *Daryl* cannot be considered as strong since (a) the robot does not learn anything and (b) it reacts to the onlooker's shirts color, and emotions are assigned arbitrarily to colors.

One of the first anthropomorphic robots was *Kismet*. Despite the fact that the author claimed that in theory, *Kismet* could learn, in the reality, it did not do so [66]. On its basis, *Leonardo* who uses the strong approach was developed. *Leonardo* uses gestures and facial expressions for social communication, can learn about objects and form affective memories which in turn underlies his likes and dislikes [67, 68]. Already mentioned *WASABI* has a human life-size body and sophisticated internal models that allows displaying mood, emotions and build attitude [18].

The strong approach is currently making its way into the social virtual agent's world. One can see it in robots developed by the industry, the most sophisticated and publicly known being *Sophia* [69], and also in papers recently published which are focused on developing methods that solve different learning issues. A model for learning emotional reactions from humans and the environment, similarly as humans do, has been developed in [70]. Similarly, in [71], a method for learning facial expressions from humans has been implemented and tested. This all leads to the conclusion that the research on companions indeed has made rapid development since 2009 when social robotics was considered to be "very young" [68] and is on a track toward long-term companions that are able to adapt and learn from a user.

Currently, there are many advanced approaches in AC that allows modeling advanced user states which are not yet implemented into the area of social robotics, mostly because robots have other challenges that slow down development of emotional models (such as mechanical limitations, materials used, etc.) [48]. However, it can be concluded that due to practical functions and emotional attachment to robotic companions compared to virtual companions, social robots are the future of artificial companionship.

3.3 Emotions as Part of AAL in Mobility

AAL applications are targeted to help older adults or people with disabilities to live independently and comfortably in their living environment; however, living environments do not include only home, but also various environments such as neighborhood, shopping mall and other public places [72]. The best way to help people with disabilities is to give them autonomy and independence [73]; therefore, mobility that includes movement by private cars, public transport, wheelchairs and walking (by person itself or using walking sticks or exoskeletons) has become one of the most important areas for AAL solutions [74]. For example, older adults prefer to live as independently as possible at home, but living independently involves many possible risks, such as falling, weakening bodies, memory loss, and wandering that limit mobility and activities [75]. The main objective to be achieved regarding people with disabilities is providing them with an access to information resources and ability to move safely and autonomously in any environment. So far, many environments are not easily accessible for these people by themselves and without a guide [72].

In parallel to the development of AAL systems for the mobility, AC has also entered this domain. Emotional factors and affective states are crucial for enhanced safety and comfort [76] since essential driver abilities and attributes are affected by emotions, including perception and organization of memory, goal generation, evaluation, decision-making, strategic planning, focus and attention, motivation and performance, intentions and communication [77]. Furthermore, the mobility of older adults can be affected by emotional factors, e.g., the fear of getting lost or hurt [78]. Current predictions show that average population's age is increasing and within 50 years one-third of the population in regions like Japan, Europe, China, and North America, will be over 60 years old [24]. Therefore, a great number of drivers will be older adults in the future.

Aggressiveness and anger are emotional states that extremely influence driving behavior and increase the risk of causing an accident [77]. As reported in a literature, aggressive or angry behaviors may occur in people with Alzheimer's or other with dementias quite easily [79]. Furthermore, aging has been found to have negative effects on dual-task performance and older drivers present declines in information processing and driving performance [24]. Even healthy people can experience a wide range of emotions during driving, e.g., stress (caused by rush hour traffic congestion), confusion (caused by confusing road signs), nervousness or fear (e.g., for novice drivers), sadness (caused by negative event), etc. [77]. While driving, these emotions can have very harmful effects on the road, or even cause death. For instance, anger can lead to sudden driving reactions, often involving car accidents. Sadness or an excess of joy can lead to a loss of attention [80]. Considering the great responsibility, a driver has for his/her passengers, other road users, and her- or himself, as well as the fact that steering a car is an activity where even the smallest disturbance potentially has grave repercussions, keeping the driver in an emotional state that is the most suited for a driving is of enormous importance. Too low level of activation (e.g., resulting from emotional states like sadness or fatigue) also leads to reduced attention as well as prolonged reaction time and therefore lowers driving performance. In general, loss of mobility as a consequence of any illnesses puts people at an increased risk of social isolation and lower levels of physical activity [81].

By analyzing existing AAL solutions related to mobility and AC, it is possible to distinguish at least three application categories: intelligent solutions for walking, virtual environments for driving, and systems leading to affect-aware cars. All the mentioned categories and examples will be discussed further.

A support during the walking is of particular importance for older adults, people having problems with vision or movement in general. Currently, several developments (including robotic solutions and mobile applications) have been proposed to provide walking assistance or motivate people to go out and do physical activities. In [82], the *Elderly-assistant & Walking-assistant robot* has been described which is able to determine an intention of a user and identify a walking-mode. Its purpose is to provide physical support and walking assistance for older adults to meet their needs for walking autonomy, friendliness, and security [83].

For example, *iWalkActive* has been developed [84] to offer people a highly innovative, attractive and open walker platform that greatly improves a user's mobility in an enjoyable and motivating way at the same time supporting physical activities that are either impossible or very difficult to perform with traditional non-motorized walkers, e.g., rollators. *iWalkActive* offers community services such as recording, sharing and rating walking routes, thus proving a possibility to stay socially connected.

DALi (Devices for Assisted Living) project was aimed at developing a semi-autonomous, intelligent mobility aid for older adults, which supports navigation in crowded and unstructured environments, i.e., public urban places such as shopping malls, airports, and hospitals [85]. This project takes into account also psychological and socio-emotional needs of older users, including self-consciousness, pride, and fear of embarrassment because older adults are more focused on achieving emotional goals compared to younger adults. Thus, this project focuses on emotional benefits achieved by improving a sense of safety and reducing the fear of falling. The use of the *DALi* also leads to the renewal of confidence and contribute to a belief in mastery [85].

Eyewalker project targets the development of an independent solution that can be simply clipped on a rollator [86]. *Eyewalker* involves the determination of a user's emotional state based on movement analysis since gait itself provides relevant information about a person's affective state. For the emotion detection, an acceleration data is analyzed.

Besides already mentioned physical solutions, various mobile or software applications have been developed focused on a facilitation of physical activities, including walking since regular walking is beneficial for enhancing mental health, for example, reducing physical symptoms and anxiety associated with minor stress. *Ambient Walk* is a mobile application that aims to explore how ambient sound generated by walking and meditative breathing, and the practice itself impacts user's affective states [87]. *Ambient Walk* is designed to use audio-visual interaction as an interventional medium that provides novel means to foster mindfulness and relaxation. A similar mobile application has been proposed in [88]. This mobile tool supports mindful walking to reduce stress and to target such diseases as diabetes or depression. It is a mobile personalized tool that senses the walking speed and provides haptic feedback.

Next category regarding developed AAL mobility solutions includes various virtual environments (e.g., driving simulators) aimed at analyzing emotions during the driving process [89]. For example, young adults with autism have difficulties in learning safe driving skills. Furthermore, they demonstrate unsafe gaze patterns and higher levels of anxiety [90]. One of such virtual reality-based environments has been described in [91]. Environment operating as a driving simulator integrates electroencephalogram sensor, eye tracker and physiological data acquisition system for the recognition of several affective states and the mental workload of autistic individuals when they performed driving tasks. Based on acquired affective data, interventions of the system are adapted to keep users in a flow state. A similar solution called *Driving Simulator* has been designed to elicit driving related emotions and states, i.e., panic, fear, frustration, anger, boredom, and sleepiness [92]. Detection of mentioned affective states is carried out based on the analysis of various physiological body signals (GSR, temperature, and heart rate). *Emotional Car* simulator described in [80] has been developed with an aim to control and reduce the negative impact of emotions during the driving. The simulator can capture physiological data through EEG systems and recognize such affective states as excitement, engagement, boredom, meditation, and frustration. Besides emotion recognition, this environment integrates a virtual agent which intervenes to reduce an emotional impact so that a driver can return to a neutral emotion.

Another area where mobility will be improved in the near future is the use of autonomous cars. As such cars will not require attention from a driver, their use by older users or people with disabilities will be facilitated [74]. Therefore, researchers have been working on various solutions which can be integrated into a car to make it affect-aware. An extensive work has been done in the direction of car-voice integration since speech is a powerful carrier of emotional information [93]. This is also due to the fact that speech-controlled systems are already integrated into existing cars. Besides emotion recognition from voice, this process can be carried out based on other modalities, e.g., facial expressions and/or body posture [95], physiological signals [96], and even driving style [77]. However, the best way how a car can respond to the emotional state of a driver is through the voice. An appropriate voice response can be provided in terms of words used, presentation of a message by stressing particular words in the message and speaking in an appropriate emotional state [93]. Adapting a personality of an automated in-car assistant to a mood of a driver can also be important. A badly synthesized voice or an overly friendly, notoriously the same voice is likely to annoy the driver which soon would lead to distraction. Therefore, as an important adaptation strategy, matching in-car voice with the driver's emotion is beneficial [77]. A solution called Voice User Help has been implemented and described in [24]. It is a smart voice-operated system that utilizes natural language understanding and emotional adaptive interfaces to assist drivers when looking for vehicle information with minimal effect on their driving performance. Additionally, the system presents an opportunity for older adult drivers to reduce the learning curve of new in-vehicle technologies and improve efficiency. In parallel to the speech recognition engine, an emotion recognition engine estimates the current emotional state of the user (e.g., angry, annoyed, joyful, happy, confused, bored, neutral) based on prosodic cues. Later, this information is used by a dialog manager to modify its responses.

Another research related to emotionally responsive cars has been proposed in [76]. A car can detect abnormal levels of stress and use this information to automatically adapt its interactions with a driver and increase individual and social awareness. Thus, the car is able to help the driver to better manage stress through adaptive music, calming temperature, corrective headlights, an empathetic voice of GPS, etc.

3.4 Emotions as Part of AAL in Healthcare

One of the primary applications for AAL systems is healthcare so it is not a surprise that there exists a remarkable number of various solutions. The overall benefits of using technology in healthcare include increased accessibility and cost-effectiveness, exclusion of human factor from the treatment (including infinite patience, diminishing variability) as well as tailoring communication to users' needs [97].

Healthcare applications are intended not only to take care of older adults or people with disabilities but also to monitor users with chronic health conditions [98, 99]. Besides, healthcare in AAL systems is related not only to maintaining physical health but also to nurturing mental health. For this reason, it is closely related to cyberpsychology – a research area that has originated in psychology and focuses on treating and preventing mental illnesses through technology [97].

Specifically, some of the developments have been proven to increase the safety of older adults [100], improve the mental safety of chronic patients [101] and to enhance the quality of life for autistic children via accurately recognizing their emotions [102]. Healthcare applications also help to prevent habits that may lead to health problems in the future, such as overeating [103] and excessive drinking [104].

One can easily see that emotions have a crucial role in healthcare applications. Emotions are related to both causes and curing of physiological and mental illnesses [97] thus manipulations with a person's emotional state can help with preventing illnesses as well as in the treatment of health problems.

Researchers have found that emotional responses towards various emotion elicitors can mitigate or enhance stress-related conditions. One example of physical disease prevention is Cardiac Defence Response detection which is a health risk that is not associated with dangerous stimuli. In [105], an algorithm has been designed for automatic recognition of such condition; it can help a patient to self-regulate as well as it notifies medical staff of the user's health state. Physical diseases are particularly closely related to emotions when dealing with older adults and yet it is one of the groups that are susceptible towards depression; for this reason, a solution called a *SENTIENT* has been developed [106]. It monitors a user with the aim to detect negative or positive emotional valence in real-time thus enabling detecting and curing depression at its early stages.

As mentioned before, detection of affective state can also help with a treatment which in case of AAL systems can mean one of two things, i.e., there are two types of systems interventions in case of problems: in one case, system monitors a user and if abnormality is detected, calls caretaker, in the other system intervenes itself [97]. In case of life-threatening conditions, it is crucial for a system's communication with caretakers to be failsafe; for this reason, researchers look for such solutions both from abnormality detection and messaging [107] perspectives. Abnormality detection is closely related to how well a system can detect user's emotional states which is why several sensor data fusion solutions have been developed (see, e.g. [108] where a method to fuse image and sound have been invented). A question of sensors used in AAL systems is still open since they need, on one hand, to be unobtrusive, and on the other hand, informative enough. For this reason, wearable sensors and mobile phones are often used (see, e.g., [109]).

A system can intervene with the user itself and try to help in various ways. One such way is through changing conditions, e.g., switching on the light at night when distress is noticed [110]. In [111], based on pitch and speed while talking on the phone, depressive and manic states of patients suffering from bipolar disorder have been detected which then can be used for a treatment. Emotion detection and analysis can also be used not only with an aim to detect existing emotional state of a user but also to predict and automatically analyze behavior of involved humans [112].

While there are a lot of systems that monitor and analyze user's states, the vast majority of them contact human caretakers once the intervention is needed. A current trend in the health applications is moving towards ubiquitous healthcare which means monitoring patients in all environments [107]. One such novel approach is monitoring older adults via the community [113]. Another promising research direction is personalization of a treatment for similar diseases [114].

4 Analysis of Affective Requirements for AAL Application Domains

As it was described in Sect. 2, four basic affective processes (emotion recognition, affect calculation consisting of emotion generation and emotion mapping on cognition and behavior, as well as emotion expression) can be fulfilled by an affective component, a unit or a system. The main goal of this section is to provide analysis and summary of previously considered AAL systems in terms of mentioned processes.

In general, the relationship between previously analyzed AAL application domains and all four affective processes is represented in Table 1. If the specific affective process is of *high* importance and should be included in the development of AAL systems as a functional requirement then it is depicted with black color. If not all solutions of the specific AAL application domain require the corresponding functionality then dark grey color is used (*medium* importance). Light grey color represents cases when the process is not essential to ensure the intended functionality of the AAL system (*low* importance).

Table 1. The relationship between affective processes and AAL application domains.

Processes \ Domain	Education	Social Interaction	Mobility	Healthcare
Emotion recognition	High	High	Medium	High
Emotion generation	Medium	High	Medium	Medium
Emotion mapping on cognition and behavior	Low	Medium	Low	Low
Emotion expression	High	High	Medium	Medium

high - the process should be included obligatory in the development of AAL systems
medium - the process is not necessary for all AAL systems in the specific domain
low - the process is not essential to ensure the intended functionality of AAL systems

Education. Emotion recognition and creation of a user model is an essential task of AAL systems targeting provision of educational activities since reasoning about learner's emotions and adaptation of a system's behavior (including emotion expressions of the system itself) is further required as a feedback. As an example, previously described *IROMEC* robot can be mentioned. It carries out user modeling (models child's abilities and emotions) and accordingly adapts itself and provides personalized feedback. In general, emotion recognition is carried out through various modalities. The most popular one, of course, is the identification of facial expressions via cameras because it is considered a non-intrusive method. However, intrusive approaches (for example, analysis of physiological data) are applied as well for emotion recognition purposes.

If we return to affective processes, in particular, to emotion generation, then for AAL applications aimed at teaching specific knowledge or skills for a short-term period it is not of particular importance to actually "feel" or generate emotions based on system's own emotion model. It can be just an imitation of emotions (e.g., feeling empathy towards learners) as predefined reactions to learner's emotions, actions and/or learning outcomes in order to increase system's (or pedagogical agent's) believability and gain learners' trust. Thus, there is no need to generate further changes in the system's rational processes and/or behavior according to felt system's emotions.

The Social Interaction. A significant amount of effort has been dedicated to emotion recognition. Particularly, a challenge for social robots is emotion identification outside of the laboratory, i.e., "in the wild". While the most social robots recognize user's emotions from the camera, several use audio signals and body postures as well. In general, emotion recognition in AAL environment does not differ from emotion recognition that is being done away from a computer. A more interesting task is user modeling which is crucial for adapting to a user and forming a long-term friendship. While user modeling is also one of the key factors for education and healthcare, for companions it is especially crucial to develop long-term affective models, structures about a user, his interests and user's affective attitudes towards various things.

Emotion expression is also very important for companions from two aspects: first, emotional expressions should be clearly understandable for a user; secondly, they should be socially appropriate. Expressivity, in general, is much-researched topic that has resulted in the aforementioned robot *Leonardo* as well as other developments.

An affective ability that differs social interaction from other areas is the necessity for the calculation of a system's internal affective states, including emotion generation and mapping on cognition and behavior. Such approach allows the system to be more believable over a long time since emotional displays and emotion influence on behavior is the key to affection formation and life illusion (i.e. belief that the artificial companion is actually alive).

Mobility. Regarding mobility and transportation in general, there can be various options depending on a system's specificity. If the solution is aimed at supporting just a walking then there is no need for the emotion integration, however, if some form of interaction is involved then emotion inclusion can become an essential task.

In case of walking assistants, emotion recognition as a system's capability not always is required since most of these developments aim to promote positive emotional outcomes (e.g., reducing the fear of getting lost) through specific actions (for example, the *DALi* project). The most important would be a creation of a user profile according to which a system would adapt its actions targeting emotional benefits.

If the aim is a long-term interaction and/or communication which could be the case of affect-sensitive cars, then recognition of user's emotions and generation of appropriate emotional responses for an in-car assistant via voice or facial expressions may be required. However, behavior and rational thinking of such systems should not submit to emotions since this can lead to negative outcomes, for example, car accidents, injuries, etc.

Currently, a great amount of work is already devoted to the emotion recognition from driver's voice since many cars use voice analysis and speech recognition services. Therefore, a possibility to acquire affective data in many cases is already integrated into cars only analysis of the collected data in the context of emotions should be applied. Regarding this issue, results of studies and experiments carried out with driving simulators can be used as well to analyze driver's emotions in particular situations with an aim to create corresponding drivers' profiles.

Healthcare. When it comes to the affect integration into healthcare applications, the largest amount of research and practical studies has been linked to affect recognition. It is a logical consequence of field specifics: accurate affective state recognition underlies the entire chain of procedures that healthcare applications carry out. However, emotion recognition is not the only thing in the center of attention. User modeling and possibly forecasting his or her emotional reactions and consequently the behavior is of uttermost importance. Accurate and personalized user models would enable more precise detection of affective state and consequently would lead to more accurate evaluation of user's health condition.

In the healthcare, similarly as in educational systems it is not needed for a system to have its own affective state but rather system should be able to tailor the affective reaction for achieving particular emotion from a user. System's reasoning and decision-making processes, as can be seen from existing research, closely interact with user's emotions, monitoring and forecasting them as well as adjusting system's behavior.

Finally, some emotion expression capacities might be needed if a system performs interventions when required. In this case, functions of a healthcare system are merged with companionship functions so the system might need affective abilities vital for companions.

5 Conclusions

The chapter discusses a need of integration of AC approaches and methods in the context of AAL systems to improve their functionality in terms of rational decision making and enhancement of social interaction with people requiring the use of these systems. Four basic emotional processes forming general affective system framework have been described and analysis of various AAL systems application areas (i.e., education, social interaction, mobility, and healthcare) have been done to identify current capabilities of AAL systems in terms of listed processes.

Overall, it can be concluded that the existence of truly affective AAL system is not in the far future – separate parts of such systems already exist. Emotion detection is the most studied process in AC, therefore, various methods and algorithms have been developed which can be applied in the development of AAL systems. The analyzed AAL areas are closely merged together; it can be clearly seen that one system can have multiple functions.

Processes related to system's emotion expression can be considered as a second most developed direction not only in AC but also in the field of AAL. Many researchers are working towards intelligent and expressive social agents which display believable behavior and can be used as personal assistants, teachers, companions, etc. In many cases, such agents represent a system itself and carry out most of the system's functions aimed at direct interaction with a user, thus improving system's communicative abilities.

The research focused on affect generation and consequently – the system's endowment with abilities to "feel" emotions already exists, although it is at the very beginning of its development. Currently, most part of AAL systems just imitates abilities to "feel" emotions by using predefined emotion and/or behavior patterns as responses to user's emotions. However, one direction where "feeling" real emotions is of primary interest, is companionship and long-term social interaction. While in some areas, such as healthcare, the system's dependency on its own emotions can be unnecessary or even dangerous, in the social interaction "emotional glitches", e.g., being offended, can make companion more believable and life-like. It can be concluded that this is one of future research directions.

Another trend that is closely related to the future of AAL is personalization – personal services and personal communication with a user. This means that there is a need to store not only "rational" data, such as health condition, but also affective data and attitudes of a user – which puts various user modeling techniques (including machine learning) as a top-interest research.

References

1. Eichelberg, M., Rölker-Denker, L.: Action Aimed at Promoting Standards and Interoperability in the Field of AAL (Deliverable D5). AAL Joint Programme (2014)
2. Castillo, J.C., et al.: Software architecture for smart emotion recognition and regulation of the ageing adult. Cogn. Comput. **8**(2), 357–367 (2016)
3. Takács, B., Hanák, D.: A mobile system for assisted living with ambient facial interfaces. Int. J. Comput. Sci. Inf. Syst. **2**(2), 33–50 (2007)
4. Picard, W.: Affective Computing. MIT Press, Cambridge (1997)
5. Pudane, M., Lavendelis, E.: General guidelines for design of affective multi-agent systems. Appl. Comput. Syst. **22**, 5–12 (2017)
6. Lee, W., Norman, M.D.: Affective computing as complex systems science. Procedia Comput. Sci. **95**, 18–23 (2016)
7. Page, T.: Affective computing in the design of interactive systems. i-Manager's J. Mob. Appl. Technol. **2**(2), 1–18 (2015)
8. Carrie, C.: On Affective Computing: Past Imperfect, Future Impactful. https://hackernoon.com/affective-computing-past-imperfect-future-impactful-13e4a8836137. Accessed 31 Aug 2018
9. Hudlicka, E.: Computational analytical framework for affective modeling: towards guidelines for designing computational models of emotions. In: Handbook of Research on Synthesizing Human Emotion in Intelligent Systems and Robotics, pp. 1–62. IGI Global, USA (2015)

10. Petrovica, S., Pudane, M.: Emotion modeling for simulation of affective student-tutor interaction: personality matching. Int. J. Educ. Inf. Technol. **10**, 159–167 (2016)
11. Chen, J., Chen, Z., Chi, Z., Fu, H.: Facial expression recognition in video with multiple feature fusion. IEEE Trans. Affect. Comput. **9**(1), 38–50 (2018)
12. Zen, G., Porzi, L., Sangineto, E., Ricci, E., Sebe, N.: Learning personalized models for facial expression analysis and gesture recognition. IEEE Trans. Multimedia **18**(4), 775–788 (2016)
13. Zacharatos, H., Gatzoulis, C., Chrysanthou, Y.L.: Automatic emotion recognition based on body movement analysis: a survey. IEEE Comput. Graph. Appl. **34**(6), 35–45 (2014)
14. Rojas, V., Ochoa, S.F., Hervás, R.: Monitoring moods in elderly people through voice processing. In: Pecchia, L., Chen, L.L., Nugent, C., Bravo, J. (eds.) IWAAL 2014. LNCS, vol. 8868, pp. 139–146. Springer, Cham (2014). https://doi.org/10.1007/978-3-319-13105-4_22
15. Capineri, L.: Resistive sensors with smart textiles for wearable technology: from fabrication processes to integration with electronics. Procedia Eng. **87**, 724–727 (2014)
16. Lutfi, S.L., Fernández-Martínez, F., Lorenzo-Trueba, J., Barra-Chicote, R., Montero, J.M.: I feel you: the design and evaluation of a domotic affect-sensitive spoken conversational agent. Sens. (Basel, Switzerland) **13**(8), 10519–10538 (2013)
17. Breazeal, C.: Designing Sociable Robots. MIT Press, Cambridge (2002)
18. Becker-Asano, C.: WASABI: Affect Simulation for Agents with Believable Interactivity. IOS Press, USA (2008)
19. Carolis, B.D., Ferilli, S., Palestra, G., Carofiglio, V.: Towards an empathic social robot for ambient assisted living. In: Proceedings of the 2nd International Workshop on Emotion and Sentiment in Social and Expressive Media: Opportunities and Challenges for Emotion-Aware Multiagent Systems, pp. 19–34 (2015)
20. Brumitt, B., Meyers, B., Krumm, J., Kern, A., Shafer, S.: EasyLiving: technologies for intelligent environments. In: Thomas, P., Gellersen, Hans-W. (eds.) HUC 2000. LNCS, vol. 1927, pp. 12–29. Springer, Heidelberg (2000). https://doi.org/10.1007/3-540-39959-3_2
21. Doyle, J., Skrba, Z., McDonnell, R., Arent, B.: Designing a touch screen communication device to support social interaction amongst older adults. In: Proceedings of the 24th BCS Interaction Specialist Group Conference, pp. 177–185. BCS Learning & Development Ltd., Swindon (2010)
22. Wang, D., Subagdja, B., Kang, Y., Tan, A. H., Zhang, D.: Towards intelligent caring agents for aging-in-place: issues and challenges. In: Proceedings of 2014 IEEE Symposium on Computational Intelligence for Human-Like Intelligence, pp. 1–8. IEEE Computer Society (2015)
23. Tsiourti, C., Joly, E., Wings, C., Moussa, M.B., Wac, K.: Virtual assistive companion for older adults: field study and design implications. In: Proceedings of 8th International Conference on Pervasive Computing Technologies for Healthcare (PervasiveHealth), pp. 57–64 (2014)
24. Alvarez, I., López-de-Ipiña, M.K., Gilbert, J.E.: The voice user help, a smart vehicle assistant for the elderly. In: Bravo, J., López-de-Ipiña, D., Moya, F. (eds.) UCAmI 2012. LNCS, vol. 7656, pp. 314–321. Springer, Heidelberg (2012). https://doi.org/10.1007/978-3-642-35377-2_43
25. Hanke, S., Tsiourti, C., Sili, M., Christodoulou, E.: Embodied ambient intelligent systems. Ambient Intelligence and Smart Environments: Recent Advances in Ambient Assisted Living – Bridging Assistive Technologies. e-Health and Personalized Health Care, pp. 65–85. IOS Press, Netherlands (2015)

26. Tang, Z., Guo, J., Miao, S., Acharya, S., Feng, J.: Ambient intelligence based context-aware assistive system to improve independence for people with autism spectrum disorder. In: Proceedings of Hawaii International Conference on System Sciences, Koloa, HI, USA, pp. 3339–3348 (2016)
27. Kadar, M., Ferreira, F., Calado, J., Artifice, A., Sarraipa, J., Jardim-Goncalves, R.: Affective computing to enhance emotional sustainability of students in dropout prevention. In: Proceedings of the 7th International Conference on Software Development and Technologies for Enhancing Accessibility and Fighting Info-exclusion, pp. 85–91. ACM Press, New York (2016)
28. Schwarz, N.: Emotion, cognition, and decision making. J. Cogn. Emot. **14**(4), 440–443 (2000)
29. Lehman, B., D'Mello, S., Person, N.: The Intricate Dance between Cognition and Emotion during Expert Tutoring. In: Aleven, V., Kay, J., Mostow, J. (eds.) ITS 2010. LNCS, vol. 6095, pp. 1–10. Springer, Heidelberg (2010). https://doi.org/10.1007/978-3-642-13437-1_1
30. Forbes-Riley, K., Rotaru, M., Litman, D.J.: The relative impact of student affect on performance models in a spoken dialogue tutoring system. User Model. User-Adap. Inter. **18**(1–2), 11–43 (2008)
31. Luneski, A., Bamidis, P.D., Hitoglou-Antoniadou, M.: Affective computing and medical informatics: state of the art in emotion-aware medical applications. Stud. Health Technol. Inf. **136**, 517–522 (2008)
32. D'Mello, S.K., Graesser, A.C.: AutoTutor and affective autotutor: learning by talking with cognitively and emotionally intelligent computers that talk back. ACM Trans. Interact. Intell. Syst. **2**(4), 23:2–23:39 (2012)
33. Woolf, B.P.: Building Intelligent Interactive Tutors: Student-Centered Strategies for Revolutionizing E-Learning. Morgan Kaufmann Publishers, San Francisco (2009)
34. Taub, M., Azevedo, R., Bouchet, F., Khosravifar, B.: Can the use of cognitive and metacognitive self-regulated learning strategies be predicted by learners' levels of prior knowledge in hypermedia-learning environments? Comput. Hum. Behav. **39**, 356–367 (2014)
35. Konstantinidis, E.I., Luneski, A., Nikolaidou, M.M.: Using affective avatars and rich multimedia content for education of children with autism. In: Proceedings of the 2nd International Conference on Pervasive Technologies Related to Assistive Environments, pp. 1–6. ACM Press, New York (2009)
36. Ferrari, E., Robins, B., Dautenhahn, K.: Therapeutic and educational objectives in robot assisted play for children with autism. In: Proceedings of the 18th IEEE International Symposium on Robot and Human Interactive Communication, pp. 108–114. IEEE Computer Society (2009)
37. Messinger, D.S., et al.: Affective computing, emotional development, and autism. In: The Oxford Handbook of Affective Computing, pp. 516–536. Oxford University Press (2015)
38. Teoh, T.T., Lim, S.M., Cho, S.Y., Nguwi, Y.Y.: Emotional advisor to help children with autism in social communication. In: Proceedings of the 6th International Conference on Computer Sciences and Convergence Information Technology, Jeju, South Korea, pp. 278–283 (2011)
39. Judy, M.V., Krishnakumar, U., Hari Narayanan, A.G.: Constructing a personalized e-learning system for students with autism based on soft semantic web technologies. In: Proceedings of IEEE International Conference on Technology Enhanced Education, pp. 1–5. IEEE Computer Society (2012)

40. Leijdekkers, P., Gay, V., Frederick, W.: CaptureMyEmotion: a mobile app to improve emotion learning for autistic children using sensors. In: Proceedings of the 26th IEEE International Symposium on Computer-Based Medical Systems, pp. 381–384. IEEE Computer Society (2013)
41. Bertacchini, F., et al.: An emotional learning environment for subjects with autism spectrum disorder. In: Proceedings of International Conference on Interactive Collaborative Learning, pp. 653–659. IEEE Computer Society (2013)
42. Robins, B., et al.: Scenarios of robot assisted play for children with cognitive and physical disabilities. Interact. Stud. **13**(2), 189–234 (2012)
43. Santos, O.C., Saneiro, M., Rodriguez-Sanchez, M., Boticario, J.G., Uria-Rivas R., Salmeron-Majadas S.: The potential of ambient intelligence to deliver interactive context-aware affective educational support through recommendations. In: Proceedings of the Workshops at the 17th International Conference on Artificial Intelligence in Education, pp. 1–3. Springer, Switzerland (2015)
44. Santos, O.C., Saneiro, M., Boticario, J.G., Rodriguez-Sanchez, M.: Toward interactive context-aware affective educational recommendations in computer assisted language learning. New Rev. Hypermedia Multimed. **22**(1–2), 27–57 (2016)
45. Ivanova Goleva, R., et al.: AALaaS and ELEaaS platforms. In: Enhanced Living Environments: From Models to Technologies, pp. 207–234. The IET (2017)
46. Sharkey, A., Sharkey, N.: Children, the elderly, and interactive robots: anthropomorphism and deception in robot care and companionship. IEEE Robot. Autom. Mag. **18**(1), 32–38 (2011)
47. Hosseini, S.M.F., et al.: Both look and feel matter: essential factors for robotic companionship. In: Proceedings of 26th IEEE International Symposium on Robot and Human Interactive Communication, pp. 150–155. IEEE Computer Society (2017)
48. Paiva, A., Leite, I., Ribeiro, T.: Emotion modelling for social robots. In: The Oxford Handbook of Affective Computing, pp. 296–419. Oxford University Press (2015)
49. Weber, J.: Human-robot interaction. In: Handbook of Research on Computer Mediated Communication, pp. 855–867. IGI Global (2008)
50. Aminuddin, R., Sharkey, A., Levita, L.: Interaction with the Paro robot may reduce psychophysiological stress responses. In: ACM/IEEE International Conference on Human-Robot Interaction, pp. 593–594. IEEE Computer Society (2016)
51. Selvarajah, K., Richards, D.: The use of emotions to create believable agents in a virtual environment. In: Proceedings of the Fourth International Joint Conference on Autonomous Agents and Multiagent Systems, pp. 13–20. ACM Press, New York (2005)
52. Hortensius, R., Hekele, F., Cross, E.S.: The perception of emotions in artificial agents. IEEE Trans. Cogn. Dev. Syst., 1 (2018)
53. Seo, S.H., Geiskkovitch, D., Nakane, M., King, C., Young, J.E.: Poor thing! would you feel sorry for a simulated robot? In: Proceedings of the 10th Annual ACM/IEEE International Conference on Human-Robot Interaction, pp. 125–132. ACM Press, New York (2015)
54. Robinson, H., Macdonald, B., Kerse, N., Broadbent, E.: The psychosocial effects of a companion robot: a randomized controlled trial. J. Am. Med. Dir. Assoc. **14**(9), 661–667 (2013)
55. Dautenhahn, K.: Robots we like to live with?! a developmental perspective on a personalized, life-long robot companion. In: Proceedings of the 2004 IEEE International Workshop on Robot and Human Interactive Communication, pp. 17–22. IEEE Computer Society (2004)
56. Shayan, A.M., Sarmadi, A., Pirastehzad, A., Moradi, H., Soleiman, P.: RoboParrot 2.0: a multi-purpose social robot. In: Proceedings of IEEE International Conference on Robotics and Mechatronics, pp. 422–427. IEEE Computer Society (2016)

57. PARO Robots, PARO Therapeutic Robot, http://www.parorobots.com/. Accessed 28 Aug 2018
58. Entertainment Robot "AIBO". https://www.sony.net/SonyInfo/News/Press/201711/17-105E/index.html. Accessed 29 Aug 2018
59. Seif El-Nasr, M., Yen, J., Ioerger, T.R.: FLAME – fuzzy logic adaptive model of emotions. Auton. Agents Multi-Agent Syst. **3**(3), 219–257 (2000)
60. Kim, E.H., Kwak, S.S., Han, J., Kwak, Y.K.: Evaluation of the expressions of robotic emotions of the emotional robot "Mung". In: Proceedings of the 3rd International Conference on Ubiquitous Information Management and Communication, pp. 362–365. ACM Press, New York (2009)
61. Embgen, S., Luber, M., Becker-Asano, C., Ragni, M., Evers, V., Arras, K.O.: Robot-specific social cues in emotional body language. In: Proceedings of IEEE International Workshop on Robot and Human Interactive Communication, pp. 1019–1025. IEEE Computer Society (2012)
62. Rehm, M., Krogsager, A.: Negative affect in human robot interaction - Impoliteness in unexpected encounters with robots. In: Proceedings of IEEE International Workshop on Robot and Human Interactive Communication, pp. 45–50. IEEE Computer Society (2013)
63. Shamsuddin, S., Yussof, H., Ismail, L.I., Mohamed, S., Hanapiah, F.A., Zahari, N.I.: Humanoid robot NAO interacting with autistic children of moderately impaired intelligence to augment communication skills. Procedia Eng. **41**, 1533–1538 (2012)
64. SoftBank Robotics, Who is Nao? https://www.softbankrobotics.com/emea/en/robots/nao. Accessed 29 Aug 2018
65. Hollinger, G.A., Georgiev, Y., Manfredi, A., Maxwell, B.A., Pezzementi, Z.A., Mitchell, B.: Design of a social mobile robot using emotion-based decision mechanisms. In: Proceedings of IEEE International Conference on Intelligent Robots and Systems, pp. 3093–3098. IEEE Computer Society (2006)
66. Breazeal, C.: Sociable Machines: Expressive Social Exchange Between Humans and Robots. MIT Press, Cambridge (2000)
67. Thomaz, A.L., Breazeal, C.: Asymmetric interpretations of positive and negative human feedback for a social learning agent. In: Proceedings of IEEE International Workshop on Robot and Human Interactive Communication, pp. 720–725. IEEE Computer Society (2007)
68. Breazeal, C.: Role of expressive behaviour for robots that learn from people. Philos. Trans. R. Soc. B: Biol. Sci. **364**(1535), 3527–3538 (2009)
69. Hanson Robotics, Sophia. http://www.hansonrobotics.com/robot/sophia/. Accessed 28 Aug 2018
70. Dang, T.L.Q., Jeong, S., Chong, N.Y.: Personalized robot emotion representation through retrieval of memories. In: Proceedings of the 3rd International Conference on Control, Automation and Robotics, pp. 65–70. IEEE Computer Society (2017)
71. Chen, C., Garrod, O.G.B., Zhan, J., Beskow, J., Schyns, P.G., Jack, R.E.: Reverse engineering psychologically valid facial expressions of emotion into social robots. In: Proceedings of 13th IEEE International Conference on Automatic Face and Gesture Recognition, pp. 448–452. IEEE Computer Society (2018)
72. Li, R., Lu, B., McDonald-Maier, K.D.: Cognitive assisted living ambient system: a survey. Digit. Commun. Netw. **1**(4), 229–252 (2015)
73. Favela, J., Alamán, X.: Special theme: ambient assisted living for mobility: safety, well-being and inclusion. Pers. Ubiquitous Comput. **17**, 1061–1602 (2013)
74. Flórez-Revuelta, F., Chaaraoui, A.A.: Technologies and applications for active and assisted living. what's next? In: Active and Assisted Living: Technologies and Applications, pp. 1–8. The IET (2016)

75. Chan, M., Campo, E., Bourennane, W., Bettahar, F., Charlon, Y.: Mobility behavior assessment using a smart-monitoring system to care for the elderly in a hospital environment. In: Proceedings of the 7th International Conference on Pervasive Technologies Related to Assistive Environments, Article No. 51. ACM Press, New York (2014)
76. Hernandez, J., McDuff, D., Benavides, X., Amores, J., Maes, P., Picard, R.: AutoEmotive: bringing empathy to the driving experience to manage stress. In: Proceedings of the Companion Publication on Designing Interactive Systems, pp. 53–56. ACM Press, New York (2014)
77. Eyben, F., Wöllmer, M., Poitschke, T., Schuller, B., Blaschke, C., Färber, B., Nguyen-Thien, N.: Emotion on the road–necessity, acceptance, and feasibility of affective computing in the car. Adv. Hum.-Comput. Interact. **2010**, 1–17 (2010)
78. GOAL Consortium: Deliverable D2.1. Profiles of Older People. Growing Older, staying mobile: Transport needs for an ageing society (GOAL). http://www.goal-project.eu/images/reports/d2-1_goal_final_20120725.pdf. Accessed 29 Aug 2018
79. Alzheimer's Association: Behaviors. How to respond when dementia causes unpredictable behaviors. https://www.alz.org/media/Documents/alzheimers-dementia-unpredictable-behaviors-b.pdf. Accessed 29 Aug 2018
80. Frasson, C., Brosseau, P.O., Tran, T.H.D.: Virtual environment for monitoring emotional behaviour in driving. In: Trausan-Matu, S., Boyer, K.E., Crosby, M., Panourgia, K. (eds.) ITS 2014. LNCS, vol. 8474, pp. 75–83. Springer, Cham (2014). https://doi.org/10.1007/978-3-319-07221-0_10
81. Shumway-Cook, A., Ciol, M.A., Yorkston, K.M., Hoffman, J.M., Chan, L.: Mobility limitations in the medicare population: prevalence and sociodemographic and clinical correlates. J. Am. Geriatr. Soc. **53**(7), 1217–1221 (2005)
82. Han, H., Zhang, X., Mu, X.: An approach for fuzzy control of elderly-assistant & walking-assistant robot. In: Proceeding of the 14th International Conference on Ubiquitous Robots and Ambient Intelligence, pp. 263–267. IEEE Computer Society (2017)
83. Wei, X., Zhang, X., Yi, P.: Design of control system for elderly-assistant & walking-assistant robot based on fuzzy adaptive method. In: Proceedings of the 2012 IEEE International Conference on Mechatronics and Automation, pp. 2083–2087. IEEE Computer Society (2012)
84. Morandell, M., et al.: iWalkActive: an active walker for active people. In: Assistive Technology: From Research to Practice, pp. 216–221. IOS Press (2013)
85. Bright, A.K., Coventry, L.: Assistive technology for older adults: psychological and socio-emotional design requirements. In: Proceedings of the 6th International Conference on PErvasive Technologies Related to Assistive Environments, Article No. 9. ACM Press, New York (2013)
86. Weiss, V., Bologna, G., Cloix, S., Hasler, D., Pun, T.: Walking behavior change detector for a "smart" walker. Procedia Comput. Sci. **39**, 43–50 (2014)
87. Chen, S., Bowers, J., Durrant, A.: "Ambient walk": a mobile application for mindful walking with sonification of biophysical data. In: Proceedings of the 2015 British HCI Conference, pp. 315–315. ACM Press, New York (2015)
88. Pryss, R., Reichert, M., John, D., Frank, J., Schlee, W., Probst, T.: A personalized sensor support tool for the training of mindful walking. In: Proceeding of the 15th IEEE International Conference on Wearable and Implantable Body Sensor Networks, pp. 114–117. IEEE Computer Society (2018)

89. Jeon, M., Yim, J.-B., Walker, B.N.: An angry driver is not the same as a fearful driver: effects of specific negative emotions on risk perception, driving performance, and workload. In: Proceedings of the 3rd International Conference on Automotive User Interfaces and Interactive Vehicular Applications, pp. 137–140. ACM Press, New York (2011)
90. Reimer, B., et al.: Brief report: examining driving behavior in young adults with high functioning autism spectrum disorders: a pilot study using a driving simulation paradigm. J. Autism Dev. Disord. **43**(9), 2211–2217 (2013)
91. Fan, J., Wade, J., Key, A., Warren, Z., Sarkar, N.: EEG-based affect and workload recognition in a virtual driving environment for ASD intervention. IEEE Trans. Biomed. Eng. **65**(1), 43–51 (2018)
92. Lisetti, C.L., Nasoz, F.: Affective intelligent car interfaces with emotion recognition. In: Proceedings of the 11th International Conference on Human Computer Interaction, pp. 1–10. ACM Press, New York (2005)
93. Jones, C.M., Jonsson, I.: Automatic recognition of affective cues in the speech of car drivers to allow appropriate responses. In: Proceedings of the 17th Australia conference on Computer-Human Interaction: Citizens Online: Considerations for Today and the Future, pp. 1–10. Computer-Human Interaction Special Interest Group (2005)
94. Jonsson, I.M., Nass, C., Harris, H., Takayama, L.: Matching in-car voice with drivers state: impact on attitude and driving performance. In: Proceedings of the 3rd International Driving Symposium on Human Factors in Driver Assessment, Training and Vehicle Design, pp. 173–181. University of Iowa (2005)
95. Caridakis, G.: Multimodal emotion recognition from expressive faces, body gestures and speech. In: Boukis, C., Pnevmatikakis, A., Polymenakos, L. (eds.) AIAI 2007. ITIFIP, vol. 247, pp. 375–388. Springer, Boston (2007). https://doi.org/10.1007/978-0-387-74161-1_41
96. Hönig, F., Wagner, J., Batliner, A., Nöth, E.: Classification of user states with physiological signals: on-line generic features vs. specialized. In: Proceedings of the 17th European Signal Processing Conference, pp. 2357–2316. The University of Strathclyde (2009)
97. Calvo, R., et al.: Cyberpsychology and affective computing. In: The Oxford Handbook of Affective Computing, pp. 547–558. Oxford University Press (2015)
98. Breazeal, C.: Social robots for health applications. In: Proceedings of 2011 Annual International Conference of the IEEE Engineering in Medicine and Biology Society, pp. 5368–5371. IEEE Computer Society (2011)
99. Memon, M., Wagner, S.R., Pedersen, C.F., Aysha Beevi, F.H., Hansen, F.O.: Ambient assisted living healthcare frameworks, platforms, standards, and quality attributes. Sens. (Basel, Switzerland) **14**, 4312–4341 (2014)
100. Coradeschi, S., et al.: GiraffPlus: combining social interaction and long term monitoring for promoting independent living. In: Proceedings of 2013 6th International Conference on Human System Interactions, pp. 578–585. IEEE Computer Society (2013)
101. Khalil, R.M., Al-Jumaily, A.: Machine learning based prediction of depression among type 2 diabetic patients. In: Proceedings of 12th International Conference on Intelligent Systems and Knowledge Engineering, pp. 1–5. IEEE Computer Society (2017)
102. Kashanian, H., Ajami, N.B., Deghati, M.: Communication with autistic people through wearable sensors and cloud technology. In: Proceedings of 2017 5th Iranian Joint Congress on Fuzzy and Intelligent Systems, pp. 139–143 (2017)
103. Carroll, E.A., et al.: Food and mood: Just-in-time support for emotional eating. In: Proceedings of 2013 Humaine Association Conference on Affective Computing and Intelligent Interaction, pp. 252–257. IEEE Computer Society (2013)

104. Shi, R., Chen, Z., Wang, H., Sun, P., Trull, T., Shang, Y.: MAAS - a mobile ambulatory assessment system for alcohol craving studies. In: Proceedings of International Computer Software and Applications Conference, pp. 282–287. IEEE Computer Society (2015)
105. Gravina, R., Fortino, G.: Automatic methods for the detection of accelerative cardiac defense response. IEEE Trans. Affect. Comput. **7**(3), 286–298 (2016)
106. Leon, E., Montejo, M., Dorronsoro, I.: Prospect of smart home-based detection of subclinical depressive disorders. In: Proceedings of 5th International Conference on Pervasive Computing Technologies for Healthcare (PervasiveHealth) and Workshops, pp. 452–457. IEEE Computer Society (2011)
107. Taleb, T., Bottazzi, D., Nasser, N.: A novel middleware solution to improve ubiquitous healthcare systems aided by affective information. IEEE Trans. Inf Technol. Biomed. **14**(2), 335–349 (2010)
108. Alamri, A.: Monitoring system for patients using multimedia for smart healthcare. IEEE Access **6**, 23271–23276 (2018)
109. Sano, A., Picard, R.W.: Stress recognition using wearable sensors and mobile phones. In: Proceedings of 2013 Humaine Association Conference on Affective Computing and Intelligent Interaction, pp. 671–676. IEEE Computer Society (2013)
110. Martin, S., et al.: Participatory research to design a novel telehealth system to support the night-time needs of people with dementia: NOCTURNAL. Int. J. Environ. Res. Public Health **10**(12), 6764–6782 (2013)
111. Grünerbl, A., et al.: Smart-phone based recognition of states and state changes in bipolar disorder patients. IEEE J. Biomed. Health Inform. **19**(1), 140–148 (2015)
112. Banos, O., et al.: Mining human behavior for health promotion, pp. 5062–5065 (2015)
113. Garcia, A.C., Vivacqua, A.S., Pi, N.S., Martí, L., López, J.M.: Crowd-based ambient assisted living to monitor the elderly's health outdoors. IEEE Softw. **34**, 53–57 (2017)
114. Billis, A.S., et al.: A decision-support framework for promoting independent living and ageing well. IEEE J. Biomed. Health Inform. **19**(1), 199–209 (2015)

Maintaining Mental Wellbeing of Elderly at Home

Emmanouela Vogiatzaki[1] and Artur Krukowski[2](✉)

[1] Research for Science, Art and Technology (RFSAT) Ltd., Sheffield, UK
[2] Intracom S. A. Telecom Solutions, Athens, Greece
krukowa@intracom-telecom.com

Abstract. We describe herein the problem of providing the most cost efficient and effective ways of supporting mental wellbeing as well as methods for physical and mental rehabilitation for elderly at home including a recovery from accidents, particularly concentrating on those impacting brain activities, such as aging-related dementia and stroke, illnesses with very high socio-economic influence. Technologies built in several EU funded projects, e.g. FP7-ICT-StrokeBack, FP7-ICT-ARMOR, Artemis-CHIRON, FP7-SEC-AF3 and other ones, are suitable also for other kinds of health issues, such as recovery from injuries, restoring mobility etc. A common part is stimulating engagement through entertainment, rivalry and "real feeling" of gaming environment, motivating compliance with rehabilitation rules. The automated home system combining progress in ICT and applied clinical know-how allows patients, their direct care providers and family to back the effective use of rehabilitation procedures in their familiar home surroundings instead of unfriendly clinical settings. Our system integrates a set of state of art technologies ranging from augmented/virtual reality gaming, merged with immersive user interfaces for providing mixed reality exercise setting, innovative embedded micro sensor devices with improved power autonomy through use of the newest Bluetooth Smart communication transceivers, combined together into a Personal Health Record (PHR) system supporting the delivery of individual, patient-centred e-health services both at home, at hospital or when mobile. The use of mixed-reality systems, merging interactive virtual components with realistic settings of patient's home, is linked with multi-modal user interfaces stimulating operation of his/her body to accomplish the objective of the exercise, while self-motivation is inspired by rivalry with oneself and other people. This gears to achieving better individual's contribution to rehabilitation procedure, leading to attaining meaningfully quicker regaining of one's earlier abilities. The physiological data is combined with and related to the detected body motion sensing using novel feature extraction and classification procedures handled within a wearable unit, to determine the precision of performed workouts. By using physical intervention only when essential, this disregards expensive human involvement and thus significantly decreases related expenses of Public Health Care services.

We start with describing the motivation and needs for such system in Sect. 2, which gives raise to deriving system specifications and architecture as described in Sect. 3. In following Sects. 4 and 5 we described specific technologies developed in our projects, namely Mixed-Reality Rehabilitation Training

I. Ganchev et al. (Eds.): Enhanced Living Environments, LNCS 11369, pp. 177–209, 2019.
https://doi.org/10.1007/978-3-030-10752-9_8

System integrated into a Personal Health Record (PHR) platform. We then provide the overview of the overall system integrated into a portable unit in Sect. 6, concluding with report on evaluations with users in Sect. 7.

1 Motivation and Objectives

The Public Health Care devotes more than 3% of their whole healthcare spending for dealing with effects of brain associated diseases among diverse countries in Europe and USA. The usual retirement age and life expectation has increased over recent years, whereas risk of evolving mental issues have raised to almost 40–50% of population in and over the retiring age. Investigations show that expenses of long-term care have raised from 13% to 49% of average global expenses over recent years. Hence, creating an effective policy for sustaining mental wellbeing, providing continuing care and rehabilitation approach for people at risk, actively engaging patients in this process, at the same time lowering expensive human involvement turn out to be a matter of urgency.

The pervasiveness of getting old in the European civilizations is projected to lead to enlarged population suffering from mental illnesses, where peak risk of dementia may reach almost 40% of the retired population and a raising risk of strokes for elderly. For instance, [2] forecasts that the total stroke patients in Hessen (Germany); may rise from 20,846 in 2005 to over 35,000 in 2050 that equals a surge of near 70% during the next four decades. The German Aerztezeitung forecasts a growth of more than 2.5 times, meaning a vast burden on expenditure of healthcare organisations. The consequence on healthcare could be even more important as the present tendency shows a ratio of young and healthy peoples to elderly folks also lowers, such that the casual care price could be reducing and thus directly pointing to raised direct healthcare expenses. This could become a weight for economies.

Consequently, there is a serious need for improving medical care, specifically at home, engaging elderly into their care process for accomplishing best result in terms of both medical care and quality of life. Furthermore, the results of individual strokes have significant effect on our society too. The entire expense of stroke care within EU has been estimated over 38 billion euros in 2006. This amount involved healthcare expenses (about 49% of entire cost), production loss due to incapacity and deaths (23% whole cost) and casual care charges (29% of whole cost).

Our work targets both of the mentioned difficulties. The target was to develop a telemedicine system that would provide medical recuperation at home for elderly with negligible human involvement. Using StrokeBack services, elderly could perform therapy at their home, a place where they feel emotionally more comfortable than at clinics. Furthermore, interactions with physiotherapists could be reduced thus reducing costs of medical care. By helping in appropriately performing the physiotherapy with automatic guidance enhanced by suitable medical data and overseen by professionals only when necessary, we intended to stimulate elderly to train more and more efficiently than it is likely nowadays. Henceforth, we aimed to improve the speed of rehabilitation, as well as the quality of life for the elderly, at the same time reducing overall costs of healthcare. The system has been accompanied with a Patient Health

Record (PHR), in which exercise parameters and important patient data would be stored. Therefore, the PHR delivers all essential medical info that rehabilitation professionals might require to assess success of the rehabilitation exercises, for example to presume links between chosen trainings and rehabilitation results for various people. Also, to assess a general patient wellbeing. Moreover, PHR is used to offer mid-term feedback to patients, such as speed and effect of therapy related to usual and recent progress, thus maintaining high motivation.

We intended to improve keeping mental fitness and where mental illness develops, speeding up a recovery in case of stroke and reducing progress of age-related mental degradation for elderly living alone. We expected a twofold advantage from using our system. Most people feel emotionally healthier in their familiar home setting rather than in hospices while recovery speed is much faster. Moreover, we intended to exploit an improved enthusiasm of elderly during training with tools resembling game consoles. An ability to perform workouts without supervision by physiotherapists benefits the reduction of medical expenses by lowering costly human interaction time. Nowadays, amount of time needed for conducting occupational (means therapeutic) and physiotherapeutic sessions are constrained by costs for patient's lodging, transportation for therapists visiting patients' homes. Our objective is to provide new technological capabilities and service assemblies for enabling elderly to improve their wellbeing through increase of the amount of exercises.

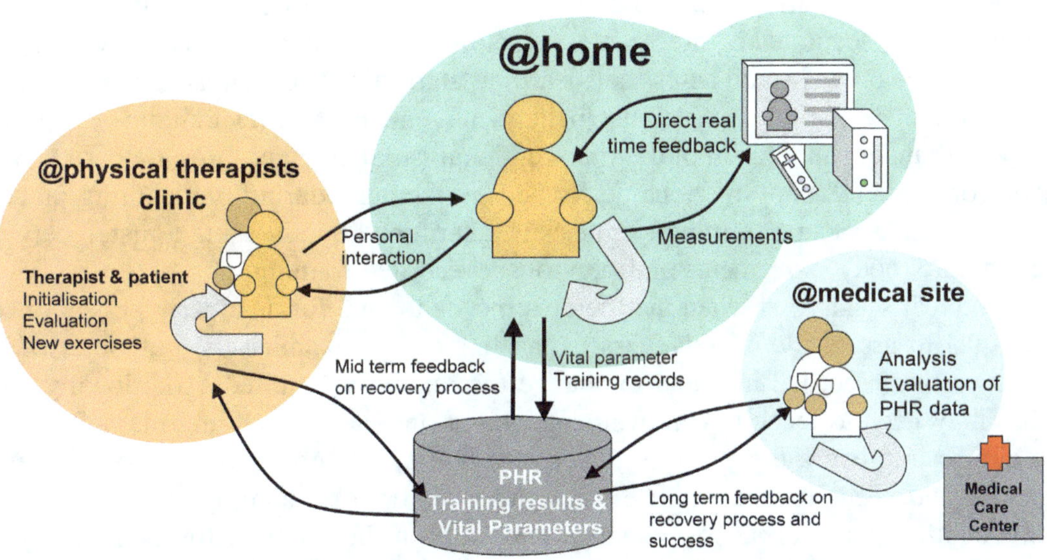

Fig. 1. The overall architecture of the foreseen therapy system

Over recent years game consoles attracted much attention when used for rehabilitation trainings. Articles prove achieving significant improvement in speeding up rehabilitation process and mostly being an incentive for patients [1, 2, 14, 26]. We target mostly elderly people at early phases of cerebral decay, supporting them with initial therapy whereas empowering also more affected ones to benefit from using our specialist care services too. We designed our services with clinical use in mind with aim to be adjustable to ones' capabilities (patient-oriented). This could be used both by hemiplegic and paretic persons, as well as those using wheelchairs. This way we intended to decrease the time, static therapy and treatment process, allowing elderly to maintain conducting their normal life for as long as possible.

The concept of the described system centres on patients treated as subjects of the recovery process (Fig. 1), based on a proven premise that elderly feel more comfortable at home. It is known that people in general train more and better within stimulating surroundings. A person follows more instructions from a therapist. They can exercise at home and the system oversees their workout, providing feedback in real time if they execute them properly or not. The system saves results and core physiological data, which is then examined by medical professionals to evaluate ones' progress. The elderly may get immediate response about their individual condition. To guarantee correct guidance, therapists also receive information from the PHR about patient progress to be able to assess the recovery and decide if to use alternative training exercises, being introduced to one's training regime.

For remote therapy training at gold standard, that is as good as during face-to-face exercise with therapists, advanced sensor body area networks (BAN) were employed. The BAN worn by elderly supports continuous supervision of elderly's movement and main body measurements. The objective is to check and save patients' condition such that they can regularly, train autonomously without instructions from therapists. Using appropriate sensors, we can assume to detect also undesirable extra actions. Elderly may wear sensors during a whole day that permits professionals to relate ones' daily activities with accurate required patterns defined by trainings. To ease system configuration, we only use and assess self-learning algorithms for analysing exercises, that is the system learns correct actions (patient movements) during training as they are performed under supervision of the training therapist. Such algorithms are based on the record of "correct" body motions performed by therapist during the learning process, while correctness of performing exercises is determined by assessing a match between the patient's body movements and previously recorded training data.

A typical scenario is when the therapist needs to care for an elderly person once a week just to assess the effectiveness of the therapy, to examine the outcomes of last training using recorded info and to change the regime if required. Additionally, therapists may need to teach new movements and arrange a new training plan. This way, we aim to improve a therapy effectiveness at home. Our objective is also to assess a viability and needs for making use of electronic PHR for recording and documenting one's condition as well as to remotely follow up on the training, for example by the visiting physician. This contains the data captured during training workouts and during everyday activities. Such an information is kept in database and can then be examined by medical experts. The assessment may be exploited for determining actual effects of personal training. Such an advice may be beneficial for choosing training plans for other persons, for reviewing efficiency of training for given groups of people etc. Physiological data could be helpful in assessing one's condition and could help in examining chances of future events.

2 Specifications and Architecture

Many articles have been published from user point of view about home-based rehabilitation systems. When building such a system for elderly suffering from age-caused cerebral problems, it is important to consider how to promote them to such target audience, developing and evaluating home training platforms, form of user interface, types of wearable sensors and a feasibility of the home-based therapy technologies. User needs and requirements, sensor accessories and usability constraints have been identified through interviews with target user groups including a total of 16 physiotherapists, 39 patients and 13 care takers. Consultations have been done with new volunteers and some experienced ones, who were already familiar with the system and could suggest new features. The first system prototype was evaluated with 5 therapists and 4 patients who had used the system over the period of two-weeks. Clinical requirements were assessed based on responses to a postal investigation from 28 therapists. The subsequent version has been evaluated on 8 patients. The result of this investigation was that home-based therapy needs to:

- Supplement a therapy – patients did not like it as alternative type of therapy
- not to be focussed on one “type of rehabilitation”
- be adaptable to personal needs as no two people are the same
- be simple and small to use, flexible to fit personal requirements of one’s home
- anticipate problems with memory, awareness, language, understanding info and losses of attention linked with old-age dementia
- provide response on outcome of therapy, even if progress may be slow

The developed system comprises two components:

1. “**Expert clinical system**” installed at the clinic, although it might be portable as well. This might require technicians with expert clinical knowledge to set it up to fit the needs of a particular patient.
2. “**Home system**” significantly less complex and easier to use, permitting to be installed and configured by anyone, such as family or care takers.

Our system was produced and its performance evaluated on the subset of ‘Wolf Motor Function Test’ (WMFT). The actions involved a variety of skill levels and practical activities. The system produced extra impairment information such as: spasticity versus stiffness, motor control, rapidity, smoothness of movements, repeatability, fatigue and endurance, as well as the effort put in. The essential assumption was for the expert system to evolve into an analytic tool for recognition of core impairments, flagged through study of data created during execution of common activities. It incorporates a BAN of wearable physiological and activity checking sensors with objective to gather rich and highly useful data for real time data examination. Real-time advice and power autonomy were not critical at the time. The essential objective of a home-based system was usability as crucial to ensuring user compliance with prescribed therapies. It was anticipated to be as small as possible and employ only the most necessary set of sensors permitting elderly to easily interact with it. Here the power consumption was critical, similarly to real-time data examination and display. It included immersive user interfaces such as Leap Motion [4], MS Kinect [3], EEG from Emotiv [5] and others, integrated with many virtual and augmentation technologies to allow fully immersive gaming experience, through e.g. supported Smart 3D TVs, 3D projectors and AR/VR visors (Fig. 2).

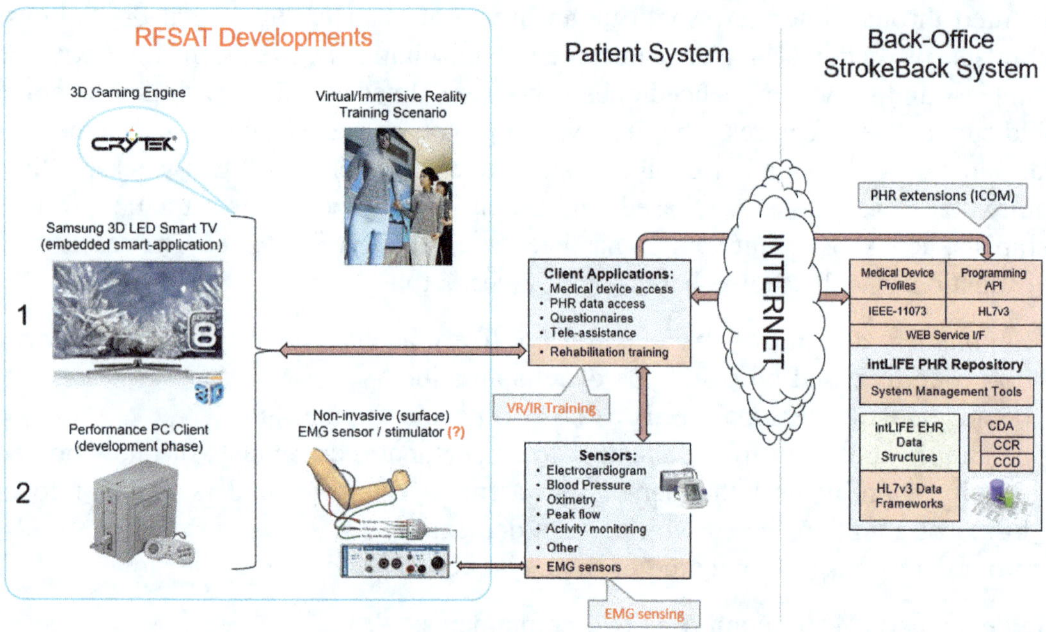

Fig. 2. Physical composition of a gaming sub-system

There is a general resistance observed among elderly to using technologies on their bodies, to some level accepted when part of the medical process. The highest problem with acceptance is when it comes to visors, especially closed Virtual Reality ones. In many cases users accept such technologies when used of short periods of time and being part of a routine medical examination and/or a test, but they tend to avoid using it alone when performing training at home. On the other hand, open Augmented Reality glasses, though generally more expensive, are more accepted by elderly since they resemble more standard prescription glasses. In such cases acceptance and compliance with prescribed exercise regimes is much higher.

A generic architecture of the rehabilitation system is presented in Fig. 3. It shows a Patient Module installed at home and offering remote physiological supervision of one's health signs, running therapeutical games and offering a full integration with the online PHR service used as a database for sharing information among the elderly and their leading physician(s).

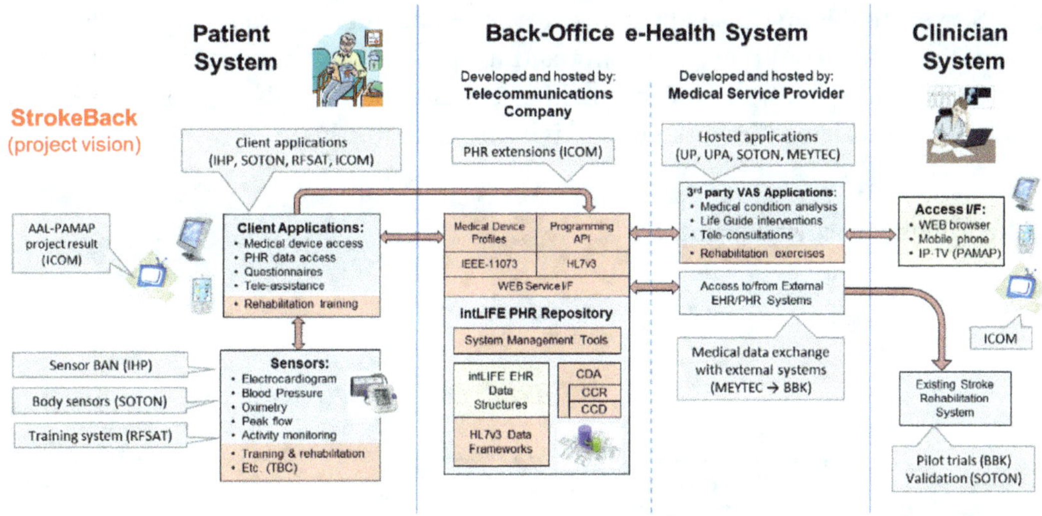

Fig. 3. Overall rehabilitation system architecture

The architecture has been aimed to support also use of mobile devices such as tablets, smartphones, portables etc. We developed an inexpensive combined gaming solution suitable both for full-body and near-field trainings. The clinician sub-system offers link to back-office PHR database for continuous supervision of patients' well-being. Current version combined two sections, both including Kinect and Leap Motion depth sensor (refer to Sect. 6 for more details). One set of sensors is integrated into the horizontal table and is aimed for tracking the use of physical objects and another one is built into a vertical section for tracing body movements. Two displays have been used, a horizontal one for physical objects and a vertical one for displaying conventional board games controlled either through Kinect sensor or other user interfaces. A progress of therapy and other relevant physical information, such as audio-visual teleconferencing, are supported as required. Back-office services were open-source based platforms like Open EMR [6] services.

Eventually, all those services have been migrated to intLIFE core PHR service platform from Intracom Telecom. The overall gaming platform used a client-server approach composed of a repository for games and serving them directly from the PHR server, in such a way greatly reducing load on client devices. This permitted us both to execute games on common everyday devices such as Smart TVs or Smartphones, at the same time allowing to maintain the most recent versions of games with no need for updating them on client devices. Still, as with all network connected system, one needs to expect that connection among networked devices may not always be sustained. Therefore, we have anticipated two operational scenarios in our system: one when network is persistent and another one when it is not (Fig. 4). In the former case when the network is continuously available, the server is built into a home gateway, while the client device was a game unit including a game server (repository of games and results for each user) operates remotely from the same physical server as the one hosting PHR services. The home unit did not need to bother about updating games to their latest versions or managing game results. Nevertheless, when network may or may not be available at all times, the game server needs to be hosted locally on a home gateway, together with the

Kinect Server. In the first case, the game server can be operated remotely. In the second scenario, the server could be run locally and use games downloaded earlier. Similarly, physical data and game results can be either uploaded on the fly or stored locally and uploaded as soon as the network connectivity is re-established.

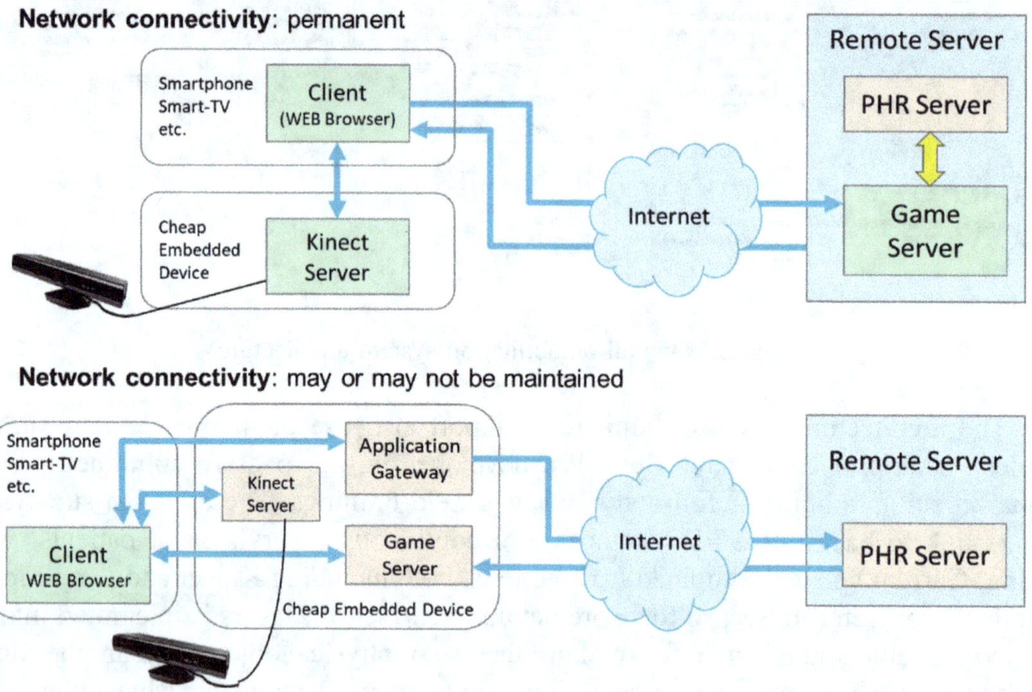

Fig. 4. Online & offline use of Kinect Server for "game" management

An expert system has been designed to be working in a controlled environment under the supervision of a physiotherapist, or other suitably competent clinician, trained in its use. This will normally take place at a medical centre though it might be used in a home environment too if suitable personnel are present. The expert system consists of a range of body-worn wireless sensors (sensor BAN) and a Motion Capture (MoCap) system using depth sensing devices (Kinect or ASUS [7]) deployed on a PC. A choice of sensors includes kinematic sensor units (containing tri-axial accelerometers, tri-axial gyroscopes and tri-axial magnetometers. When combined they give 9 degrees of freedom of measurements). Electromyography (EMG) sensors monitor muscle motion in biceps and triceps, while electrocardiograph (ECG) sensors monitor the heart rate. A kinetic sensor unit are positioned both on forearms just above the wrist and on upper arms just above the elbow as well as on the sternum. The motion capture module is used to trace patients as they complete given tasks and exercises, whereas video records are used as qualitative measures of the progress of patient's therapy. Suitable ways to secure and achieve repeatability of sensor placement on the body was investigated during research phase as well as possible effects of sensor orientation and misalignment.

Evaluations with expert system starts with a face-to-face discussion of the patient with a clinician. Based on this, clinician can assess patient's level of impairment, while the patient informs the clinician about their personal expectations from rehabilitation training. Such a process allows the clinician to choose a range of upper limb training tasks and exercises that might be most suitable for a particular patient. Then measurement phase starts with a patient stimulated to complete a set of exercises and training tasks selected from the WMFT database that have been explicitly selected by clinicians to for the patient's needs and apparent abilities.

A motion capture system keeps a history of patient's actions during trainings. Via appropriate signal processing, a motion capture system produces temporal and spatial-kinetic data, such as limb placement in space, limb velocity and acceleration, joint angles and time required to complete particular tasks. Hence, motion capture system could be perceived as a 'standard' against which the data resulting from other sensors could be compared with. During the training, physiological data from body-worn wireless sensors is transmitted to server PC in real-time and processed in two different ways. Raw sensor data is converted into 3-dimensional spatial info that can be immediately compared against data generated from motion capture unit. With depth-based sensing and taking advantage of extra information from wearable Shimmer accelerometers, body motion sensing accuracy of movements with centimetre accuracies can be practically achieved from a distance of 2–3 m. Subsequent data processing approach includes looking for patterns in the sensor data, which shows a high correlation with expected actions of the upper limb or specific training tasks that are performed. Home-based system uses such a data as templates for determining if such actions are performed by patients as part of their everyday activities. Other features are also used as indexes for assessing progress and effectiveness of the training, e.g. including calculation of energy spending out of EMG data or assessing metabolic rate out of ECG data. A clinician can judge patients' condition when they perform prescribed training and make professional judgement of the patient state according to the WMFT scoring scheme. Such a score is sent to PHR database. All raw data gathered by body-worn wireless sensors and motion capture unit, including processed data are saved in PHR as well [8, 14].

Subsequent visits to leading physicians may re-assess patient's performance for the prescribed set of training tasks out of the WMFT, permitting a long-term assessment of the progress of rehabilitation to be determined with clinical reliability, in our case corresponding to measure of progress of rehabilitation as determined by physiotherapists though classical set of training exercises. Since home-based systems are needed to be used without professional involvement, they may be less complex than expert ones and use less sensors. For example, EMG and ECG sensors may not be incorporated into home-based BAN. Ease of use is most important as such a system needs to be run exclusively by patients, with a support of their carers or family members.

3 Mixed-Reality Training System

The core idea of the telemedicine platform for supporting clinical training at home for elderly people with negligible professional support has been supplemented with a Patient Health Record (PHR) platform where training data, vital physiological and personal data of the patients were stored. Thus, the PHR offered required medical and personal info about the patient, which rehabilitators might require for evaluating effectiveness and progress of the training. This means to assess the relation between chosen exercises and speed of rehabilitation for various persons and to determine their overall wellbeing. The PHR could be employed to inform patients about their mid-term performance e.g. her/his, speed of rehabilitation as compared to a clinical one involving visits to physiotherapists, including their progress over last day/weeks, thus keeping patients' enthusiasm high.

Benefits we expected from our method is twofold, since most people feel emotionally easier training in their familiar environment, this improves and speeds up their rehabilitation. Moreover, focusing on exercising with tools resembling game consoles, we are able to maintain patients' motivation. A proposed notion puts patients into a centre of the training procedure, exploiting the fact that people feel more comfortable at home. It has been proven that patients exercise more when training is linked with attractive atmospheres [1]. Firstly, elderly may learn physical training exercises from therapists at care centres. Subsequently, patients can train at home while the system monitors their progress and provides real-time response if they perform their exercises correctly or not. Furthermore, recorded results of the training and vital parameters of the patient are readily available to physicians. Such a data may be then analysed for assessing patient's progress and determine the level of recovery. Patients can also obtain midterm feedback about their individual recovery process. To warrant suitable supervision, therapists get information from the PHR allowing them to assess progress of recovery allowing them to decide if other types of exercises may need to be introduced into the patient's training schedule.

3.1 Game-Based Training System

Using virtual, augmented and mixed-reality immersive systems for training at home unlocks an attractive path to improving several adverse effects happening due to brain traumas. Such comprise assisting in a recovery of motor skills, limb-eye coordination, orientation in space, daily routines etc. Exercises can vary from simple goal-oriented limb moves intended to achieve a specific goal (e.g. to put a coffee cup on a table), improving decreased motor skills (e.g. simulated driving), and many other ones. In order to boost effectiveness of training exercises, cutting-edge haptic user interfaces have been produced, permitting a direct body stimulus and using physical items inside of the virtual environments, complementing visual stimulus.

Immersive interfaces have quickly found to be attractive for remote home-based training, both performed independently and remotely supervised by therapists. Dependent on physical interfaces, several training approaches are possible. User interfaces like Cyber Glove [10] or Rutgers RMII Master [11] permit a handover of patient's limb moves to virtual gaming environments. They use pressure-sensing servos, one per finger, integrated with motion sensors. This lets therapists to accomplish a range of motions with variable speed, fractionation (e.g. moving separate fingers) and strength (through pressure sensors). Games consist of two main classes: physical training (e.g. DigiKey, Power Putty) and practical training (e.g. Peg Board where objects of different shapes and sizes need to be fitted into matching holes or Ball Game requiring manipulation of different balls). Computer monitors the progress of exercises and is used for providing a visual feedback. Cyber Gloves have been used by the

Rehabilitation Institute of Chicago [8] for evaluating patterns of finger actions when grasping and for assessing a space of movement for diverse circumstances after stroke. Virtual environments are gradually introduced for practical exercises and simulation of natural surroundings, e.g. home, work, etc. Training types can include simple goal-oriented movements [9] for recovering ability to execute everyday activities.

Modern rehabilitation systems, though taking advantage of the latest immersive technologies appear to focus on proprietary and closed range of exercises, missing comprehensively addressing a complete range of disabilities and providing a all-inclusive set of rehabilitation setups. Use of technologies is also limited and fluctuates from one system to another. Though there are systems of using avatars aimed to provide more intuitive feedback, using many complex wearable devices (as in Fig. 2) might become tiring for users and could reduce an effectiveness of the rehabilitation. In our method we provided novel technologies for body motion tracking that take advantage of the information captured by correlating info from wearable sensors with visual feedback that have been recently available commercially, such as MS Kinect [3], Leap Motion [4] user interfaces, and 3D mixed reality visors.

The developed system provides a full 3D visual and physical feedback via Mixed-Reality interface and visor technologies, putting the user into a training space. Since detecting muscle activity may not be achieved without wearable sensors, IHP GmbH has developed a custom embedded lightweight sensor for short-range wireless communication of most common parameters such as EMG, critical medical signs like ECG, Blood Pressure, heart rate etc. This way, rehabilitation exercises became more intuitive by using exercise templates with feedback displaying level of compliance with prescribed exercises. Therapists are able to prescribe exercises as treatments in the EHR/PHR platform, offering means of correlating data with changes of patient's condition, improving efficiency of patients' recovery.

3.2 Body Sensing and User Interfaces

We developed an automated way to automatically track the correctness of performed exercises and be able to compare patient's body movement against correct ones (templates). Most of the existing methods use complex sets of wearable sensors and/or expensive visual monitoring methods. In our project we investigated modern commercial 3D scanning sensors using IR-LED technologies, such as MS Kinect [3] released in version 2 and recently being commonly phased out by Intel's RealSense depth cameras [30], Prime Sense [31] and Leap Motion [4] devices. For improved accuracy additional embedded micro sensors can be used, such as gyroscopes (often at a price of a need for frequent position and tilt calibration) as well as more common inertial sensors and accelerometers, detecting changes in speed. Many of such sensors are available on the market. Furthermore, brain wave sensing with devices like EPOC EEG U/I from Emotiv, currently used in our system as user interface, although also beneficial for detecting brain problems such as risk of seizures, while generic sensors devices like Shimmer allow deploying a range of other modalities including electromyographic (EMG) ones used for detecting activity of muscles during training. Bearing in mind their very small sizes (often less than 5×5 mm in case of gyros and accelerometers, while sensor boards often smaller than 3×4 cm) a development of wireless and very low weight wearable sensors is feasible, able to be energy-autonomous by using energy harvesting techniques.

Monitoring activity of muscles poses a problem with sensing since it has been well known since long ago [26] that EMG represents exertion rather than the result. Therefore, it may be unreliable as an indicator of muscle strength when they get fatigued. As a result, measuring the force, alongside the EMG, is a significant advancement in determining the efficiency of rehabilitation plans and may show that not only the fatigue occurs, but also if the origin of the process is central or peripheral [12]. Standard surface EMG sensing needs precise placing of sensors over target muscles, and so placing them in "smart" clothes for home use could make it simpler for patients to use them and avoid wrong placement of electrodes. Electrode arrays are commonly being developed for sensing and processing of EMG signals and can be used to optimise received signals. Various options have been researched to provide adequately reliable, though economic muscle activity sensing as well. We decided therefore to employ EMG sensors on 2R Shimmer device for development purposes, whereby use a purpose devised sensor from IHP GmbH.

Nevertheless, more types of sensors are needed for providing reliable home care for patients apart of the EMG ones. Novel approaches are required to combine construction nodes in a body sensor network. Commercial systems in existence offer basic info about activity, e.g. movement and direction of speed and postures. Offering reliable info about performance, e.g. corresponding to movement and muscle activity during a specific task and sensing abnormalities, anticipated patterns or small changes related to recovery, needs a higher level of complexity of data acquisition, interpretation and processing. The challenge is to devise and build a unified multi-modal system together with high-level analysis algorithms for extracted signal and data optimisation. The Kinect device shows a potential for being employed as a haptic user interface [23]. It has been used in many earlier projects, with Open Source libraries available for various browsers, like Chrome [13], and demos compatible with Windows 7 and higher [14] platforms. Subsequent versions improved compatibility and performance of Kinect drivers on Windows platforms. Even that Kinect itself has been discontinued, its technology has been transferred to such systems like HoloLens, Cortana, Intel Real-Sense, Windows Hello biometric facial ID system, as well as context-aware user interfaces. Microsoft tends to suggests users to move to Intel Prime Sensor cameras for using their cloud-powered solutions, based on Project Kinect for Azure, which combines the next generation of Microsoft's category-defining depth sensor with Azure AI services [32].

Existing body-wearable approaches to acquiring physiological measurements are commonly considered quite adequate though they are frequently bulky and awkward to mount, for example electro-goniometers. They may be also expensive to implement, for example the VIACON camera. Capabilities for being used at home is then quite limited. Consequently, we decided to resolve those disadvantages by:

- Expanding the usability of current sensor technologies: for example, by using MEMS accelerometers with wireless capabilities that are readily available on the market for measuring joint angles for upper and lower limbs, thus enabling us to offer low-cost sensors without cabling, optimized with respect to their info-content and spatial position.
- Innovation in sensing procedures thus to lower the number of sensors that needs to be worn on a body, at the same sustaining sufficiently good quality of data received. Since many users have games consoles at home (e.g. Xbox, Nintendo Wii etc.) for family entertainment, they can be also used to host rehabilitation applications. With evolution of home game consoles like Xbox, human body motion will be easily to monitor with low-cost cameras fitted to e.g. Smart TV sets.
- Effortless installation and calibration even by not technically skilled users for home use, making such a solution applicable for home use even for first timers who are care for by untrained family members and/or unskilled caretakers.
- Seamless validation if exercises are done correctly by patients could be based on data captured by Body Area Networks (BAN). Those would be correlated with treatments prescribed for individual medical condition, allowing for determining the effectiveness of patient's training, if it is negative or positive.

3.3 The Prototype

A prototype system implementation, integrating a range of technologies, such as physiological monitoring with both Shimmer and Ghost sensors, user interfaces for controlling games, not to mention rehabilitation games themselves, built using Unity3D engine. Assembly of individual sub-systems of the "Patients home training place" is shown in Fig. 5, and its placement on a patient in Fig. 6.

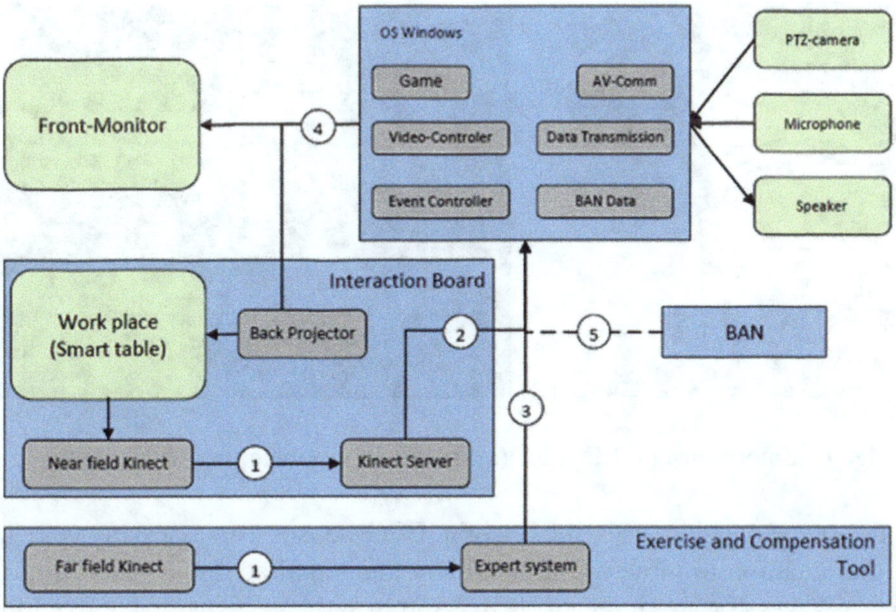

Fig. 5. Integration of the overall "home" system

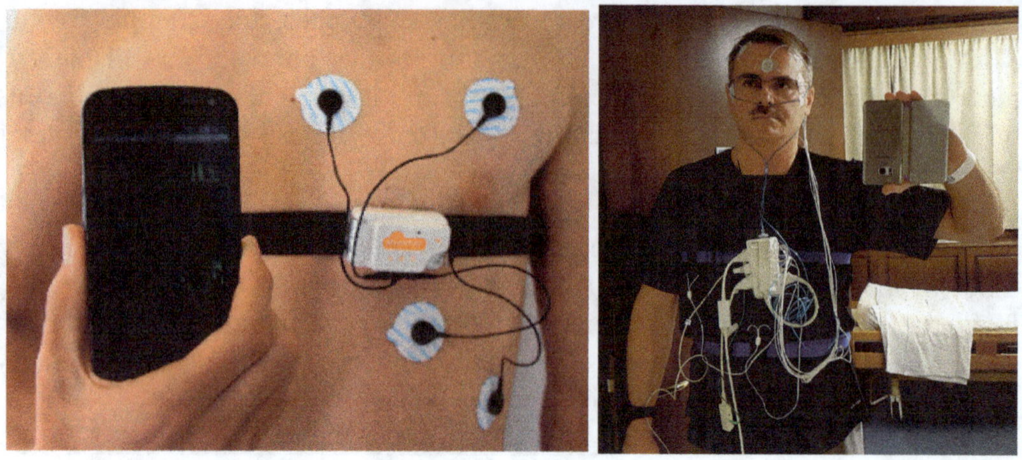

Fig. 6. ECG sensing with Shimmer2R (L) and wearable EEG system (R)

The PTZ-camera used for supervision of the patient during exercises has pan-tilt-zoom capabilities. Considering that very intensive training may in some cases of recovering patients increase a risk of causing traumas, such as stroke or epilepsy, for safety reasons we included an EEG Insight sensor from Emotiv, monitoring the brain waves and searching for "flashes" of activity between two brain spheres, being indicated by our involved physiotherapists as signs of increased risk of pre-event condition (Fig. 7). Such a sensor has an extra benefit to be used as a catchy gaming interface, shifting patient's perception from its intended use as a preventive sensor to enjoying playing games free-hands using the "power of the mind". Emotiv offers a Unity3D support, not to mention a more powerful INSIGHT [5] EEG sensor with smaller number of detectors than earlier EPOCH one, 5 + 2 compared to 14 + 2.

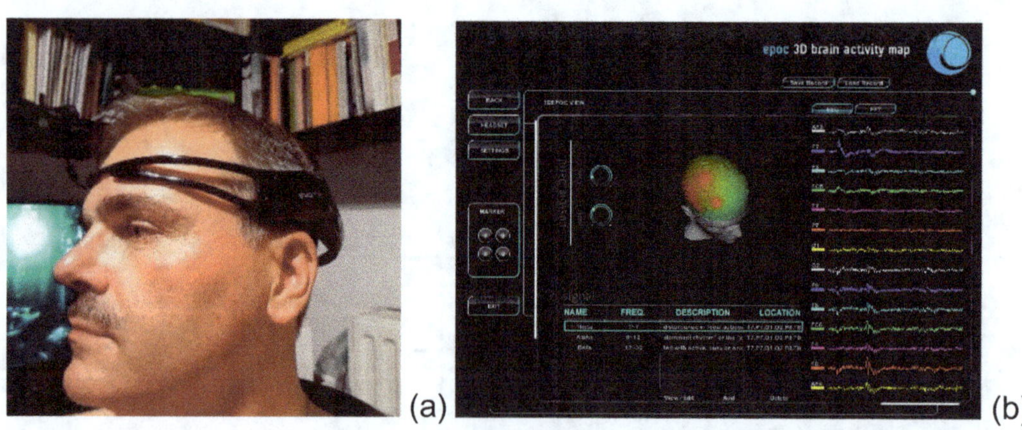

Fig. 7. Emotiv Insight EEG U/I (a), brain activity mapping with Emotiv (b)

The prototype version uses the Insight EEG sensor for assessing a relationship between the intention to move e.g. a hand and the actual action, in addition to seeking within brain waves for any indications that might indicate risks of approaching stroke as well as being used as a user interface similar to a "mouse". Correlating with data obtained from EMG sensors allows to detect instances when patient's brain correctly sends a signal to e.g. move an hand, which could not be executed because of a broken nerve links.

3.3.1 The "Kinect Server"

The primary user interface for controlling rehabilitation games in our system is MS Kinect. We take advantage of its distance sensing capabilities combined with RGB camera, which have shown to be effective both for full body motion tracking (using its skeleton matching algorithm) and for near-field training e.g. for hands and legs. As Kinect had not been originally indented to be used for close range detection and only parts of the bodies being visible, such a skeleton tracing is not effective enough and therefore we developed a custom algorithm for being able to determine reliably movements of arms, hands and fingers, being also able to separate those from the objects behind. This led to building a "Kinect server", extending available open source algorithms. The application used Open NI drivers for Linux at the beginning, then transcoded to MS Kinect 2 drivers for Windows operating systems. The "Kinect Server" enables connections remotely to MS Kinect device and then making use of the sensor data from a variety of client devices, which have previously not been supported by the MS Kinect SDK. The Kinect Server prototype used initially Open NI drivers for Xbox, later transcoded to more generic drivers provided by Microsoft in Kinect SDK 1.7 and later versions. The Kinect Server based system is composed out of two sub-modules:

- **Server** – requires to run on an operating system supported by MS Kinect drivers. Its role is to receive the data from the Kinect sensor and provide it in a suitable form via network to remote client devices.
- **Client** – can be installed and executed on ANY device and operating system as long as it offers WEB accessibility with support for Java Scripts. This implies that nearly any device able to access the WEB, such as tablets and smartphones, not to mention Smart TVs, and other devices are therefore natively supported and can take advantage of MS Kinect sensor capabilities.

Range of data and info available from Kinect Server by connected clients includes: RGB feeds, depth maps (both natively offered by Kinect sensor) and a list of detected objects (custom data offered by Kinect Server). Custom options are offered, e.g. ability to limit the area in which objects are detected, permitting applications to remove background objects and be able to focus only on objects of interest (e.g. directly in front and/or closest ones to the sensor). As the sever was built as a generic enabler, additional gesture recognition capability has been offered as well. To enable interoperability with various commercial devices and operating systems, we selected Python for developing our "palm_controls" scripts that are able to detect explicit motions and map those to selected keystrokes and mouse "clicks".

3.3.2 Embedded Kinect Server (EKS)

The disadvantages of the Kinect sensor related to the lack of seamless compatibility with many Operating Systems, vide range of drivers that are often incompatible with one another, need to be connected to two USB ports on different physical controllers, as well as the requirement to be run-on high-performance workstations, made us to investigate different ways to interact with MS Kinect sensors. Initially we aimed to run our Embedded Kinect Server (EKS) on embedded microcomputers, such as the Raspberry PI [28] or similar ones, thus enabling client devices to run games while taking advantage of data received directly from EKS via local wireless network or Ethernet. This allowed us to "break" the restriction of the physical (wired) connection between the Kinect sensor and the game console, thus allowing 3D sensing capabilities to be available on any networked device.

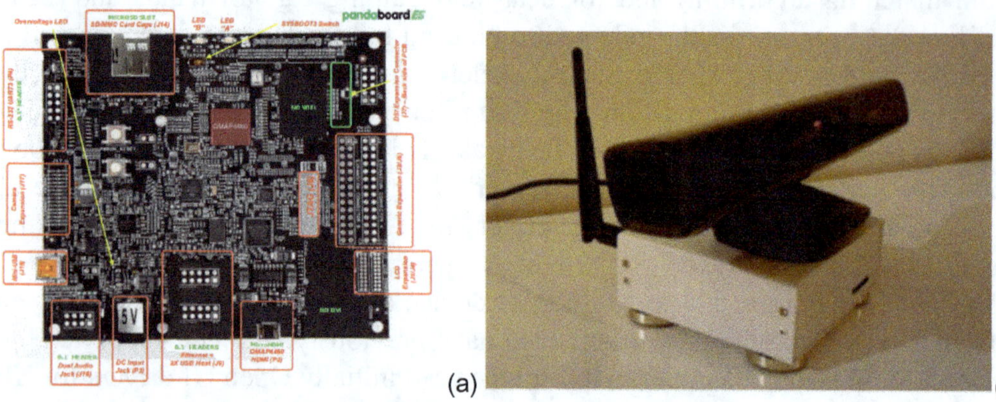

(a) (b)

Fig. 8. Embedded Kinect Server deployment: Panda board (a) and physical prototype integrated with the MS Kinect for Windows sensor (b)

A range of embedded devices have been examined: from Raspberry PI and eBox 3350 [15], to Panda boards (Fig. 8) [16] and a number of other ones. We discovered though our trials that there was an inherent issue with Kinect's design existing in all versions, starting from Xbox one to later Windows one. The USB ports could not supply sufficient amount of current and so additional power supply was required. Attempts to increase current supplied by USB ports on Raspberry PI devices, using external powered USB hubs, not to mention other work-arounds, they were all unsuccessful. Until recently, the only embedded platform able to stably operate the Kinect sensor (keeping connectivity and be able to run EKS) was Panda Board. It has been successfully used in our tests to execute the Mario Bros game on various Android operated smartphones and Samsung Smart TVs, which could wirelessly connect to the Kinect sensor for controlling the game with body gestures [35].

3.3.3 Rehabilitation Games Using the "Kinect Server"

The core functionalities supported by our Kinect Server enable limiting the field of view, removing background outside pre-defined area, separating and classifying between individual objects etc. This enabled us to build a Kinect-based user interface, where compliant with needs and requirements of physiotherapists, we traded classical keyboard keys and mouse strokes with hand gestures equivalent to arrows up/down/left/right and mouse clicks action by making a fist. This way we were able to develop our game-based training system, the first of its kind, for rehabilitation of stroke patients who had mobility issues after their stroke episodes. We conducted evaluations, first using Mario Bros game controlled entirely using hand movements. Algorithms detecting position of the hand and producing fake key presses were first developed with Matlab and subsequently ported to PERL for distribution together with Kinect server to embedded devices. They assumed that hand(s) were fixed at a known distance from the sensor on a stable support (requirement from physiotherapists) support, thus we knew the common position of the hand with fingers facing the Kinect sensor. This allowed for easy recognition of the direction and movements of fingertips. This way no calibration of the Kinect sensor was ever required, being a commonly known problem for this device. Removal of the surrounding objects was also simplified by ignoring anything more or less distant from the hand and allowing us to focus our attention entirely on monitoring a 3D space from the fingertip to the end of the wrist. The position of the bounding box around the hand allowed detecting changes in hand position, while horizontal and vertical direction to the hand section mostly extruding from the centre of gravity allowed to determine which finger was moved, in which direction and how far. We then extended the algorithm to more elaborated hand gestures and various combinations of movements. A custom delay between "reads" was used to set the detection "speed". Such a recognition algorithm, enhanced with recognition of full arm movement, could be easily adapted to e.g. sign language recognition. To evaluate such a capability and to allow patients to play with their full body, we have developed a test game mixing real and virtual objects to form a mixed-reality gaming environment. In this game we requested patients to throw a ball made of paper at the imaginary balloons (circles projected on to the wall) as presented in Fig. 9. The Kinect device was easily able to detect the paper ball leaving the hand and hitting a specific area of the wall. This was correlated with projections to determine a collision, which was rewarded with "balloons" being loudly blown into pieces to a great joy of the gamers.

Fig. 9. Throwing real paper ball at virtual targets

Such games enabled our test patients to rehabilitate their entire body, not only their limbs. It was very entertaining not only for our users, but for their care takers alike. It had significant benefit for rehabilitation, allowing patients to focus on improving movements of their hand and the whole body and forgetting their disabilities at least for some time, resulting in the increased effectiveness of their training.

3.3.4 Full-Body Exercising Through "Avateering"

We subsequently examined various other, more advanced games that could be used for full-body rehabilitation. They were developed using 3D gaming engines and took advantage of the avateering, i.e. featuring transfer of the physical body movements to the virtual character in the game (avatar). Our first approach required "hacks" built by Kinect developer communities to enable embedding games into WEB pages. The most suitable one for our use was ZigFu [17]. Its advantage was that it was compatible with Open NI drivers Unity3D [18] gaming engine.

Fig. 10. Avateering in a "home" environment

It was simpler in use than other commercial ones like Brekel [19] or Autodesk Motion Builder [20]. To make games more intuitive and familiar for our users (often elderly and people unfamiliar with computer games) we modelled gaming environments to resemble natural spaces with photorealistic quality [21]. The example presented in Fig. 10 (left) shows a "Virtual Room" built in Unity3D [24], with test subject testing avateering algorithm in Fig. 10 (right).

An inherent benefit from using 3D gaming engines such as Unity3D, Cry Engine or Unreal Engine was an opportunity to produce games that could be executed both as stand-alone applications on supported computers and consoles, or embedded into WEB pages and executed using a classical WEB browser. This made it easier to integrate games into the PHR platform, where they were prescribed by physicians and physiotherapists as therapies, distributed and operated using WEB browsers on any networked client device. Games contained embedded versions of custom-built Kinect Server plug-ins. More recently we integrated also the electromyographic (EMG) "Myo" [22] sensor from Thalmic Labs. It allowed us to detect electrical signals on the skin that were caused by movement of the muscles. This offered two main advantages, one to allow physiotherapists to get an indication if control signals from the brain reach the muscles.

Furthermore, this offered us additional data for being used as an additional user interface. With provision of various support software by the manufacturer, offering support for programming 3rd-party applications making use of this sensors, with plugin for Unity3D and the application translating various muscle signals to gestures, we were able to map them subsequently to keystrokes and mouse clicks for explicit use in our games. Furthermore, the SDK gives direct access to raw signals from all eight EMG sensors (around a band that can be placed on a forearm or an arm), which enabled us to process raw signals as well in order to improve the accuracy and reliability of our user interface. Using such an approach we adapted the "Amazing Skater" game template from Ace Games [23] that was built in Unity3D and added the EMG as a user interface (screenshots are presented in Fig. 11). This was an incentive-based game combining rehabilitation with entertainment, allowing to avoid using Kinect sensor in favour of a more compact and easier controlled user interface, detecting muscle activities.

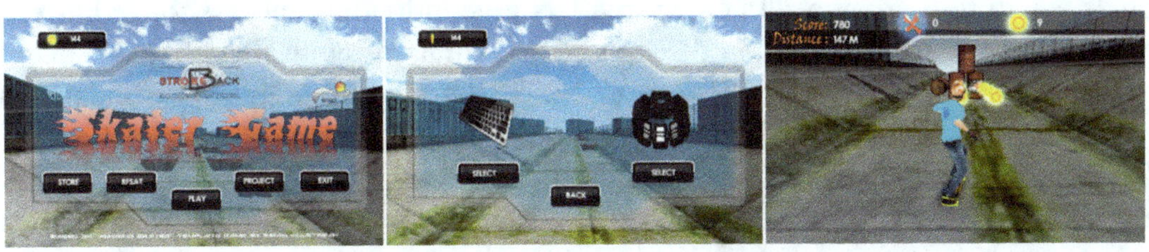

Fig. 11. The "Skater Game" adapted from a template by Ace Games

The game can be played using either a keyboard or a Myo sensor. The latter is supported through a Unity3D plugin, though it can be also operated using custom StrokeBack application profile via Myo Application Manager.

4 Personal Health Record Systems

The Personal Health Record (PHR) solutions define a manageable, integrated, flexible and expandable system for provision of care management services and management of patient data. According to NAHIT report [36] regarding definition of key technological terms related to e-health, the following definitions apply:

- Electronic Medical Record (EMR): An electronic record of health-related information on an individual that can be created, gathered, managed, and consulted by authorized clinicians and staff within one health care organization.
- Electronic Health Record (EHR): An electronic record of health-related information on an individual that conforms to nationally recognized interoperability standards and that can be created, managed, and consulted by authorized clinicians and staff across more than one health care organization.
- Personal Health Record (PHR): An electronic record of health-related information on an individual that conforms to nationally recognized interoperability standards and that can be drawn from multiple sources while being managed, shared, and controlled by the individual.

The core feature of the PHR, which distinguishes it from the EMR and EHR, is that info contained within it is under the control of the individual. The above definition names such individuals as controllers, but leaves room for other bodies to act in the individual's interest, having a control over the access to PHR. Such agents may be expressly declared by the individual, though not in all cases. For example, agents acting on behalf of an individual include parents for their children, and later in life, children acting for parents. The individual is distinctively a guardian of information stored or accessible within a PHR, who decides what volumes of information to include, how it is maintained and ordered, and who can read it or "check it out". Standards and policy will need to determine if and how individuals can delete or modify information in a PHR that originated from an EHR and how these modifications are communicated to other providers with whom the data in the PHR are shared. Having control also means that an individual's PHR can exist independently of the entity that sponsors it—the PHR is portable. This requirement for portability excludes models in which sponsors such as health insurers or health care providers give individuals access to health-related information that is dependent on the individual remaining with that sponsor.

The long-term goal of a PHR is to be a lifelong resource of pertinent health information for an individual. Thus, it should have both the depth and breadth of information to enable individuals to become more engaged in their own healthcare as they move from being passive recipients to active participants in their personal health management. The health information in a PHR can be drawn from a broad range of possible sources. The sum of these and other inputs is a well-rounded picture comprising clinical information, administrative information, and wellness information for individuals to employ and impart to others at their discretion. Significant sources may include, but are not limited to:

- Individuals—Self-generated information for personal management or information for care providers, including information about allergies, prescribed medications, eating habits, exercise objectives, the progression of an illness or recovery from it, and preferences regarding care in various circumstances.
- Health care providers—Including hospitals, skilled nursing homes, long term care, and other facilities; pharmacies, lab, and facilities reporting test results.
- Health care clinicians—Including physicians, nurses, behavioural health professionals, registered dieticians, chiropractors, and other licensed or certified care providers.
- Medical devices—Instruments, machines and implanted devices monitoring clinical indices, for immediate use as well as for historical purposes.
- Wellness promoters—Entities supplying services or information to generate and maintain good health, such as proactive medicine centres, fitness centres, rehabilitation experts, and complementary/alternative medicine practitioners.
- Health insurers—Information arising from claims for insurance payments, disease management programs recommending certain actions and collecting results, updated information on drugs in a formulary, and other coverage policies specific to an individual.

- Public health—Government health departments, disease surveillance and immunization programs, school-based care providers and social workers, and non-governmental organizations engaged in health and wellness.
- Research institutions—Information about opportunities to engage in clinical trials and studies, and recently published results of interest to the individual.

The HL7 [8] standard from the HL7 EHR Work Group [9], describes PHR as the patient-centric system that is mostly controlled by the individual and governs the form and technical development of interoperable PHR/EHR systems.

The overarching theme of a PHR-S involves a patient centric tool that is controlled for the most part, by the individual. It should be immediately available electronically, and able to link to other systems, either in a "pull-push" or "push-pull" method. The PHR-S is intended to provide functionality to help an individual maintain a longitudinal view of his or her health history, and may be comprised of information from a plethora of sources—i.e., from providers and health plans, as well as from the individual. Data collected by the system is administrative and/or clinical, and the tool may provide access to a wealth of forms (advance directives) and advice (diet, exercise, disease management). A PHR-S would help the individual collect behavioural health, public health, patient entered and patient accessed data (including medical monitoring devices), medication information, care management plans and the like, and could be connected to providers, laboratories, pharmacies, nursing homes, hospitals and other institutions and clinical resources. At its core, the PHR-S should provide the ability for the individual to capture and maintain demographic, insurance coverage, and provider information. It should also provide the ability to capture health history in the form of a health summary, problems, conditions, symptoms, allergies, medications, laboratory and other test results, immunizations and encounters. Additionally, personal care planning features such as advance directives and care plans should be available. The system must be secure and have appropriate identity and access management capabilities, and use standard nomenclature, coding and data exchange standards for consistency and interoperability. A host of optional features have been addressed over the course of this initiative, including secure messaging, graphing for test results, patient education, guideline-based reminders, appointment scheduling and reminders, drug-drug interactions, formulary management, health care cost comparisons, document storage and clinical trial eligibility. The effective use of a PHR-S is a key point for improving healthcare in terms of self-management, patient-provider communication and quality outcomes.

The PHR provides all necessary functionalities to assist the individual in maintaining a continuous insight into his/her medical history, including info coming from a number of sources. It assists an individual in collecting vital physiological data (e.g. from medical monitoring devices), health info, care management plans and alike, potentially connecting also to providers, labs, pharmacies, nursing homes, clinics and similar organisations and medical resources. The PHR encompasses the whole health history, including health issues, conditions, symptoms, allergies, medicines, lab test results, immunizations and visits. Considering the sensitivity of data on record, such platforms need to be secure and employ sufficient access management, authentication and authorisation mechanisms. There are two distinct dimensions to be highlighted:

- Integrated care management plans or integration with related third-party systems: Current PHR systems do not adequately support this need. Take for example Google Health or Microsoft Health Vault: notwithstanding the fact that these products offer very attractive web interfaces for the patients to edit and store their personal record of health-related information they lack of any functionality related to the lay out and maintenance of a rehabilitation plan. Typically, this need is covered by special purpose software solutions that are entirely clinicians-oriented and do not actively put the patients in the loop (i.e. not Personal Health Systems). In contrast, our approach is patient-centric: the intention of the project is to build a PHR-S that facilitates personal care planning. This does not mean that the clinicians are made subordinates in the rehabilitation process: the proposed PHR-S facilitates their tele-supervision, if granted such a right by the patients.
- Standard nomenclature, coding and data exchange standards for consistency and interoperability: The significance of these parameters is that they ensure human readability and machine processability of health-related data. In HL7, the former is guaranteed by a Clinical Document Architecture (CDA) HL7 standard, while the latter is guaranteed by v2.x or v3 HL7 Messaging standard. HL7 CDA is an XML-based mark-up standard intended to specify the encoding, structure and semantics of clinical documents for exchange. The CDA specifies that the content of the document consist of a mandatory textual part (which ensures human interpretation of the document contents) and optional structured parts (for software processing). The structured part relies on coding systems (such as from SNOMED and LOINC) to represent concepts. The consortium is not aware of any PHR-S that claims full adoption of the HL7 CDA. For example, Google Health supports a subset of CCR [3], a competing standard to CDA, while Microsoft Health Vault claims to support a subset of CCR and CDA [4], but actually only for importing information from other systems, and not for exporting [5]. As for the underlying messaging scheme, to our knowledge, none of these PHR-S claim support of a widely used standard messaging scheme, such as those of HL7.

On top of the above one should add the need for a controllable, integrated, yet fully open ICT solution that ensures the smooth execution of the project trials. The accumulated experience indicates that while a significant amount of yet unmet ICT-related end-user related requirements arise whenever a new medical issue is examined within an R&D project, in most of the cases neither the legacy ICT systems in the trials sites are open and accessible nor the IT personnel easily accepts intervention and links to such systems. From this perspective, by embedding within the project ICT environment a novel, open PHR-S allows StrokeBack to deliver a self-contained ICT solution able to be deployed in both rich and virgin e-Health environments.

4.1 Overview of Personal Health Record (PHR) Systems

There are various open-source as well as commercial implementations of PHR platforms available in the market. One of the most well-known ones is Microsoft HealthVault [27], which offers online service for storing and maintaining various types of health-related information. The HealthVault platform has capabilities of a typical search engine, permitting users to scan specifically for medical information. Patients may store their personal medical records as well as the prescription history, manage their records, upload medical data from such devices as blood pressure monitors, glucose meters, weights, thermometers and then process this and manage this data. The information can be then shared with other types of medical and health management WEB portals and/or immediately with their physicians or general practitioners. The HealthVault includes also a desktop client allowing medical information to be received from various types of personal physiological measuring devices to be then sent to the PHR. From most common open source implementations, Tolven [21] is the most characteristic one that focuses on providing an electronic Personal Health Record (PHR) enabling users to capture and individually share their health information in a secure way. Another open-source PHR solution one is Indivo X [25], which is promoted as Personally-Controlled Health Record (PCHR), a system, which offers means of creating a PHR, with links to other PHRs as well.

4.2 Generic Architecture of the PHR System

The functions are supported by a Personal Health Record (PHR) system enable individuals to manage information about his or her healthcare. They provide direction as to the individual's ability to interact with a Personal Health Record in such a way to individualize the record and maintain a current and accurate record of his or her healthcare activities. They include activities such as managing wellness, prevention and encounters. Such functions are designed to encourage and allow an individual to participate actively in his/her healthcare and better access the resources that allow for self-education and monitoring [8]. The principal users of these functions are expected to be individuals referenced as account holders; the patient or subject of care and healthcare providers will have access to certain functions to view, update or make corrections to their Personal Health Record. The Account Holder will receive appropriate decision support, as well as support from the PHR-S to enable effective electronic communication between providers, and between the provider and the account holder or account holder's designated representative.

Intracom Telecom has implemented its own proprietary version of the PHR platform, named intLIFE, which integrates a range of healthcare application, targeting a number of chronic diseases as well as supports generic wellbeing services. Custom-made adaptations were made to ensure safe sharing of users' medical data with proper procedures, ensuring sufficient level of private data protection. It secures a controlled access to such data via custom authentication ad authorisation mechanisms, thus guaranteeing that all data that may be circulated around, could neither be traced back to nor be used to identify the person from whom such data had been obtained from. In such a way, a health system that is based on Intracom's PHR services can be used securely and safely for production of clinical models created from massive amounts of raw data from vast number of patients. This permits a more reliable feature-based medical diagnosis for other patients and determining a range of conditions that had not been possible before. In order to safeguard the privacy and security of information stored within the EHR/PHR to essential levels, both the Management subsystem and the Vital Signs Monitoring one are linked together via encrypted interfaces employing authentication, authorisation and data anonymization modules. The PHR developed by Intracom has a modular architecture supporting effortlessly adding and removing any functional sub-systems. This was achieved by separating business layers from underlying technical frameworks. The former one corresponds to end user needs in a given domain, whereby the latter horizontal layers offer generic, business agnostic functionalities (Fig. 12).

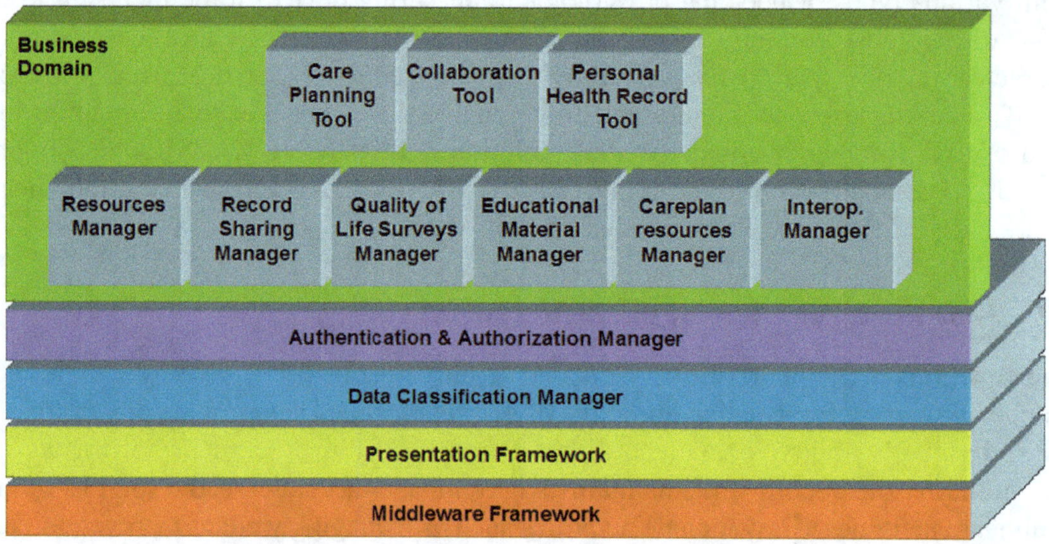

Fig. 12. PHR-S platform architecture

The *Middleware Framework* provides a flexible and configurable link between internal and external modules. The capability maintained by this layer is associated with API management, rights management, user interfaces and the presentation layer. The *Presentation Framework* provides auxiliary application guidance and access from various WEB browsers. The foundation for the design of this layer was ensuring independence of the graphical user interface from the business domain.

In order to facilitate the independent development of applications and services by third parties that can be easily integrated and glued with the core PHR system, we will follow a modular programming approach. The advantage of this approach is that it provides us with great flexibility in assigning discrete functions to each of the modules and allows easy integration through appropriate interfaces. The PHR includes a set of core modules that are necessary independently of the value-added services that are provided to end users. Such core modules include:

- **External adapter controller module** responsible for directing calls to appropriate ESPs components; it also includes libraries for translation to HL7 messages, so as to support standard based communication with external systems.
- **User management module** providing functionalities related to the administration and management of the users who have access to the PHR-S and the various applications and services built on top of it. It includes aspects related to access rules and user roles. Appropriate interfaces of the User Management Module

enable access by third party applications and facilitate a centralized approach in users management.

- **Permission management module** enabling account holders (health record owners or their designees) to manage access rights (permissions) to their PHR. and controls access to protected resources.
- **Audit management module** enabling logging of information related to the transactions being executed in the PHR-S. Such transactions may include log in attempts, modifications of permissions, modification of PHR content, etc. It logs timestamps and respective user who is involved for each transaction.

On top of the above, one can easily build independent business services around the core PHR-S. The exact services to be built will be based on the outcome of the end user requirements collection and elicitation process. Nevertheless, we can rather safely present in this paragraph some indicative services that are in line with the general objectives of the project as apposed in the Description of Work:

- General Health Record Service providing patients with access to their medical data (general demographics, family history data, vaccinations, allergies, etc.).
- General Health Record Service Extensions providing extra functionality to the patients, correlated with disease-specific aspects. Indicative such extensions provide functionality related to the management of post-incident health interventions, diabetes, COPD, nutrition and general lifestyle, etc.
- Exercise Guidance Service guiding patients while executing a predefined set of activities and/or physical exercises –possibly set up by the clinician using the Care Management Service Module see below-. It may provide direct –online- feedback to the subject, during the execution of the activities or offline feedback, after the end of an activity session.
- Care Management Service providing clinicians with the necessary functionality in order to set up and monitor plans related to the management of the disease of their patient. This module has different extensions, depending on the disease: e.g. it is different for stroke patients, diabetics, COPDs, etc.
- Videoconference Service enabling patients and clinicians to keep undergo live videoconference sessions. Service configuration parameters are dedicated to defining who and how often can establish such a session. This feature addresses the need described by the clinicians to be able to put relatively strict rules as to how often their patients may call them in the course of the day.
- Quality of Life Surveys Service: This service enables the patient to participate in questionnaire-based surveys related to her quality of life.

5 Overall System Integration

The prototype architecture compliant with expressed user requirements, led to te selection of relevant use cases and a range of components needed for each of those use cases. Moreover, features of the "look and feel" for the developed system and the deployment at patient's homes and within their life has been built into the design. As a consequence of additional research on the minimum space between patient and distance sensors, the first prototype of the home unit for patients' use has been created. This server as a reference for matching advances in other subsystems.

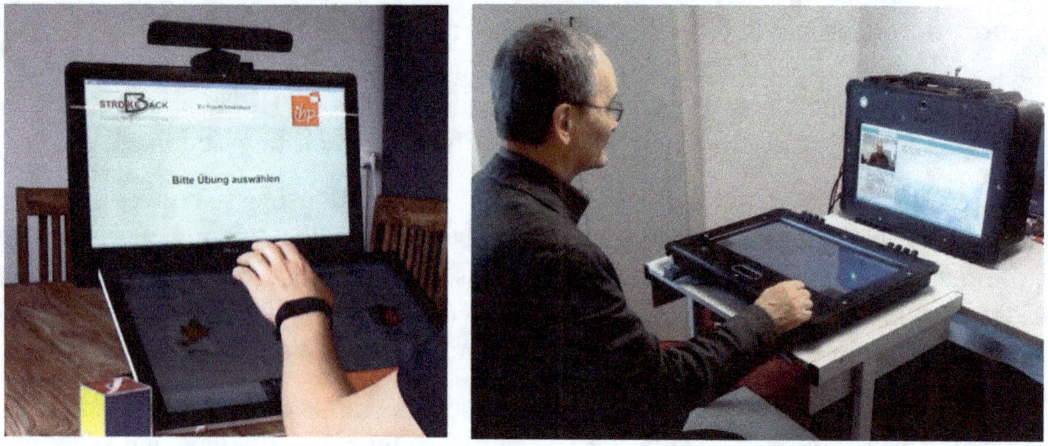

Fig. 13. Prototypes of the mobile patient station for home use.

Various versions of training games were tested and have been enhanced following a feedback from physiotherapists and end users. Similar approach has been followed in the development of PHR services, "Exercise and Compensation Analyse (ECA)" tool as well as user interfaces embedded into the mobile unit. Regarding events envisaged to be used for using rehabilitation games, an event capture algorithm has been created using close-range distance sensors, including Kinect and Leap Motion, which concentrated on movements of wrists and palms, such as open and close actions for the latter ones, both being indicated by clinicians as most important for the effective rehabilitation of post-stroke patients. After putting together all components into the integrated system, combining range/distance sensors with ECA tool for body motion capture, the performance of the close-range Kinect devices reduced significantly when both were used at the same time. Therefore, we decided to make all components to use data from just one Kinect device, integrating it as far-field sensor while applying Leap-Motion one for detection of near-field motions and interactions with games.

The experimental assessment of the integrated Mobile Patient Unit and its corresponding training regimes started from the review of the overall physical design with vertical and horizontal displays. The first version of the system was bulky and weighty; therefore, a second smaller variant was built (Fig. 13). The former one has been designed with clinical (stationary) use in mind, while the latter one offers few innovative technical enhancements. Specifically, the close-range detection with Kinect sensor was replaced with the Leap Motion one built into the base of the unit, to take over the tracking and recognition of hand gestures. In this way, the overall size of the mobile unit could be lowered by 30 to 40% with weight 50% lower.

6 Deployment and Validation

A dedicated pilot study has been organized in Germany in order to validate the usability and practicality of the developed PHR system and the Care Management services. The system has been installed at the Brandenburg Klinik Berlin-Brandenburg [29] and evaluated with a control group of 25 patients. The aims of those evaluations were to check if the developed framework was *"usable* and *useful"*, and if the implemented Care Management services are beneficial for the physiotherapists in conducting their rehabilitation work and help patients in achieving improvement of their motor functions. Project participants were all involved in performing both the technical validation of the system functionalities and the initial assessments with end users. We followed a specific process to validate the rehabilitation system:

- Users switching on the rehabilitation unit.
- Users launching "Tele-rehabilitation" process with the "touch table".
- Users selecting "autonomous training" that is the training mode when exercises are performed without direct involvement of physiotherapists. The "auto training" mode was selected automatically in case of no connection to server.
- User selected a game and executed it, custom selection depending on earlier scores and adjusted a level of difficulty. In case that exercises included background music, user could select a favourite one. The whole selection process had been configured earlier by physiotherapists who decoded which options were to be made available to patients.
- Users started the exercise in an autonomous mode. The PHR physiological monitoring sub-system assessed and analysed user operation and generated feedback. In the end, results and scores achieved were sent to the PHR.
- Users run exercises with online supervision by physiotherapists. They were constantly supervised, could see their clinicians via teleconferencing and could instantly receive instructions how to correctly perform their exercises.
- Users could check their scores and evaluation results after completing them.

Evaluation results confirmed our earlier expectations that Kinect could not be used reliably at close range and for tracking movement of upper limbs, especially when it concerned movements of fingers and even hand gestures. It also required calibration every so often. On the other hand, the Leap Motion sensor has proven more beneficial in such situations, providing a reliable and precise tracking of hands and fingers. Based on such results, the final (commercial) solution combining advantage of both sensors and certainly reducing their respective disadvantages, could be produced, in which Kinect was placed in vertical section of the mobile unit to monitor full body motion and interaction with the surrounding environment, while the Leap Motion being installed in the flat part of the unit was used for short range interactions with games using hand gestures and interaction with virtual objects using fingers, whose movements were transferred via avateering to virtual hands.

We integrated a teleconferencing functionality into our system to evaluate benefits of teletherapeutic interventions. In most cases, young users could achieve better results, whereby interactions with aphasic users has proven more complex, in some cases impossible, with neuropsychological issues causing a barrier. Specifically, complicated verbal directions were often misinterpreted by users. In this context the "Selective Repetitive Movements" and "Arm Ability Training" types of exercises have shown best user compliance, which could be explained by exercises being easier to demonstrate visually. Therapists used the following procedures:

1. Restricting rehabilitation games to upper limbs
2. Employing evidence-based interventions during exercises
3. Focusing on motor functions, cognitive skills and fast system response

The produced three types of tests based on earlier defined technical specs:

- "Selective Repetitive Movements", a set involving joints and movements of upper limbs with main attention to hands, especially distal movements. We postulate that such exercises could be readily linked with mixed-reality games. Using such gaming methodology helps in overcoming the problem of high number of monotonous repetitions, thus improving users' motivation, compliance and attention on correctly performing their rehabilitation exercises.
- "Arm Ability Training", a set where we promote use of everyday objects, where we see a potential to motivate our users. Specifically, we address here problems with users who lacking everyday exercises as part of their daily routines. Therefore, interventions considered here required focussed attention not only to motor capabilities, but also to cognitive and sensitivity ones.
- "Music Supported Training", asset not needing any previous musical tutoring. It uses music as means of improving user motivation. Various musical devices may be used, whereby for simplicity of use we chose a synthesiser keyboard.

The three above mentioned types of training procedures made it possible to combine patients with different impairments into the same intervention group and apply the same types of telerehabilitation exercises. This also provide sufficient variability in case that some users might chose other rehabilitation exercises, while ensuring maintaining his/her motivation and compliance. We provide a full set of guidelines to users to ensure that they can follow correctly the rehabilitation training routines.

In order to speed up rehabilitation speed, exercises require investigation from point of view of: visual and interaction attractiveness, effective operation of the exercises and probably the most difficult one to achieve, the real time assessment of the correctness of performing exercises by end users. Constraints to be taken into consideration are mainly how well patients perform their rehabilitation and how much improvement is achieved, physiological data taken both during exercises and in daily living activities, cognitive abilities and so on. The analysis we do follows clinical models relating wellbeing with physiological data, based on the results from Virtual Physiological Human (VPH) project [33], to which we have added new variables corresponding to the improvement of physical and cognitive capabilities based on clinical experiences and used as indicators for remote rehabilitation, periodically verified in clinical environments by medical professionals. An extensive historical overview of physiological models can be found in [34].

Since using only few classical rehabilitation exercises was not suitable from therapeutic perspective because of the complex nature and varying types of impairments faced by individuals, we opted for creating a system where it could be individually configured and geared to fit specific clinical rehabilitation needs of the patients. The system had to be able to "learn" new training types in real-time, meaning adaptation to changing movements of the patient, thus allowing the system to assess body motion with respect to pre-defined exercises at a later time.

We appreciate the fact that patients may not always perform in the similar manner and movements may not be repeated exactly as they had been recorded. Furthermore, assessment and measuring of the position of joints using Kinect exhibits certain level of inaccuracies. Therefore, the system needs to be adjustable to user's rehabilitation conditions and level of progress, including custom precision of detecting movements. The latest prototype calculates a deviation from the reference set of body motions as a variation in the off-axis angles for every vector associated with a specific part of the body, e.g. upper or lower limbs. The acceptable deviation from the reference movements in the pre-recorded training may be customised, before launching the supervisory application. The latter one was enhanced with a support for overseeing several exercises simultaneously. Each of them may be adjusted to provide a pre-defined type of feedback when performing correctly the exercise.

6.1 Execution of Rehabilitation Studies

To ensure high reliability of study results, we strictly followed a certain set of procedures and had provided guides to patients and physiotherapists before starting the evaluations. They comprised relevant info for patients and "informed consent forms" outlining the scope of the tests and requesting permission to e.g. capture and use personal data for the sole purpose of the tests. This has followed a face-to-face interview after which users were requested to sign the "informed consent forms" before being able to take part in the evaluation tests. Following the tests, a separate set of questionnaires was filled for each patient to individually assess their performance during the studies. Their responses provided a base for assessing the results of the rehabilitation from the perspective of achieved outcomes, usability and technical practicability of our proposed method.

6.2 Evaluation of Pilot Results

The evaluations were combined with a number of classical rehabilitation exercises and means to judge the effectiveness of the newly adopted procedures. Each user from the group of 25 patients engaged in the evaluations took part in the trials for a period of six weeks. Over this period, evaluations have been performed 4 times every two weeks throughout the whole evaluation period. We employed the WMFT as standard means of evaluating patients' physical capabilities. The WMFT process that we used consisted out of 17 smaller tasks that each patient was expected to execute, while the physiotherapist rated their performance in a scale from 0, corresponding to very bad achievements, to 5, representing normal scores, towards perfect achievement. The aim of the task was to place nine (9) little timber slats into corresponding holes on a flat board. Then they were to place them back at their original places. The goal was for patient to achieve this task as quickly as they could.

The second test has been performed when seated and its purpose was to move dices from one box to another one over a small obstruction wall within one minute, from right to left and back again. The score was calculated as the number of dices moved during the time limit. The Barthel Index was used to assess patient's motor skills and as a result also the effectiveness of the rehabilitation. This is a kind of analysis using an observer judging and providing a score for a trainee, in this case by the physiotherapist or a clinician. It offers a way to evaluate patient capabilities associated with daily activities. It includes such common tasks as going to toilet, eating and drinking, movability, personal hygiene, dressing and undressing, incontinence and ability to climb staircases. The tests of this kind were assessed in scale between 0 corresponding to a person completely independent to 10 representing worst case scenario of a person totally dependent of care from third persons. The total of the scores from all tests provided the final evaluation results and the actual condition of the person. The rating has been performed by interviewer by filling a specific questionnaire. The questionnaire was filled by the patient who was expected to answer 49 questions about their everyday activities, personal characteristics, family relations, speech abilities, movability, social activities etc. Every question was scored from 0 to 5, corresponding to bad and normal respectively. The higher the score was, the better the effectiveness of the rehabilitation was.

7 Conclusions

The development of the Electronic Health Record (EHR) clinical systems and the Personal Health Record (PHR) ones were the outcome of the intrinsic problem of the medical professionals in effectively managing the increasing amount of paper archives and all types of printed medical records. The absence of unified way of transferring information among electronic medical systems made the situation even more difficult. The introduction of the HL7 standard [8, 9] provided reference rules and procedures as a means to resolve this situation, though since the beginning the HL7 was treated only as guidelines and not a factual standard of rules to be strictly followed. This caused electronic systems to be developed and used that employed only different subsets of the HL7 specification [9] that suited the given medical service provider and not the complete standard. Transferring information among systems build in such a way proved to be difficult, causing much information to be misinterpreted or made incomplete. This issue has been identified early as a critical one for future wide-spread of electronic communication among clinical systems. Now the HL7 is considered more as a factual base for providing interoperability criteria for smooth operation of medical systems. However, since it still misses device level interoperability, more work is still needed for ensuring seamless mobile physiological monitoring with links to diverse clinical systems. In our projects, the work progressed towards merging both areas of electronic health record interoperability with device level certification, which has resulted in creation of the proprietary implementation of the PHR core services by Intracom, the intLIFE core platform, where core interoperability components are fully compatible with HL7 specification, with remote monitoring ensured to be performed with devices certified for use for critical medical applications. The intLIFE platform embeds purpose defined device profiles allowing linking any certified medical device with its electronic repository of medical measurements and clinical information.

The formal technical validation tests confirmed the usability of the developed system. It proves to be beneficial to clinicians for acquiring and storage of physiological information about their patients, not to mention integration of various applications and services for processing and assessment of such a data. We specifically validated the usability of user interfaces such as Leap Motion operating gaming application, especially for those using immersive and natural interactions within virtual and mixed reality 3D environments. After the successful technical validation tests, the evaluations with real users, patients and clinicians have been conducted. They concentrated on body motion capture and acquiring movements of the real person (physiotherapist) to be used later for demonstrating the correct way of performing exercises by avateering as presented in Fig. 10. Those were integrated into the complete system along with server offering custom selection of games, treated as therapies prescribed by clinicians in the same way that medicines are. Links with PHR online platform provided a clinical base for managing both the game selections, personal and clinical patient data as well as games scores and physiological data obtained from medical devices. It also offered means for correlating all this data to produce the best overall view of the current condition of the patient, both physical and mental.

Evaluations with real users allowed to refine all aspects of therapeutic interventions. Although physiotherapists may still strongly depend on classical occupational therapies and focussing on personal rehabilitation, they commonly agree with the added benefits from employing the automatic clinical assessment of subjcts' motor skills and progress of recovery compliant with WMFT, as well as computer-based occupational exercises with both real and physical objects in mixed-reality environments. Apart from classical exercises, everyday activities can be effortlessly supervised using Body Area Networks (BAN) of sensors throughout the day with proper consideration for rights to privacy of the individuals, by restricting direct access to certain private raw data by physicians and care takers, instead offering processed diagnosis and relevant physiological data only. Data gathered from long-term monitoring of basic movements in semi-natural scenarios (over three weeks period) has been used to improve the accuracy of ADL recognition algorithms. They were employed as basis for developing novel application-specific integrated circuits (ASIC) used for automated detection of various types of movements. Individualized training and novel compensational analysis components have also been integrated into a single Exercise Evaluation Tool (EET). The EET offers benefits for exercising e.g. upper limbs with recorded movement traces, which patients are expected to follow. The EET can automatically analyse the correctness of such exercises. The previous version has been extended by fine-tuning for individual sections of the limbs (e.g. shoulder, upper and lower arm, etc.). For examples we can determine how much the patient's movement varies from the correct ones. Similar features were also implemented for detecting compensational moves during exercises, such as if patient remains standing during exercises with specific objects.

In conclusion we could notice significant changes among medical communities fter the introduction of electronic health records, enhancing the efficiency of medical services at a lower cost, while continuing to offer a wide range of research challenges, which we expect to be pursued and likely resolved in the near future.

Acknowledgements. The work leading to the results presented in this chapter originated from a number of projects and have received funding from such sources as the "European Union's Seventh Framework Programme" for research, technological development and demonstration under grant agreement no 288692-StrokeBack ("Telemedicine System Empowering Stroke Patients to Fight Back") and COST Action under grant agreement no IC1303-AAPELE ("Algorithms, Architectures and Platforms for Enhanced Living Environments").

References

1. Kirchhof, P., Adamou, A., Knight, E., Lip, G.Y.H., Norrving, B., de Pouvourville, G.: How Can We Avoid a Stroke Crisis? (2009). ISBN 978-1-903539-09-5
2. Foerch, C., Misselwitz, B., Sitzer, M., Steinmetz, H., Neumann-Haefelin, T.: Die Schlaganfallzahlen bis zum Jahr 2050. Deutsches Ärzteblatt **105**(26), 467–473 (2008)
3. Microsoft Kinect sensor. http://www.microsoft.com/en-us/kinectforwindows
4. Leap Motion sensor (2018). https://www.leapmotion.com
5. Emotiv EEG interfaces (2018). http://emotiv.com
6. Open EMR project (2017). http://www.open-emr.org
7. ASUS sensor (2018). http://www.asus.com/Multimedia/Xtion
8. HL7 EHR System Functional Model: A Major Development towards Consensus on Electronic Health Record System Functionality, White Paper (2004)
9. HL7: Health Level Seven International (2007). www.hl7.org
10. Virtual Technologies (2018). http://www.cyberglovesystems.com/all-products
11. Bouzit, M., Burdea, G., Popescu, G., Boian, R.: The Rutgers Master II—new design force-feedback glove. IEEE/ASME Trans. Mechatron. **7**(2), 256–263 (2002)
12. Giles, J.: Inside the race to hack the Kinect. New Sci. **208**(2789), 22–23 (2010). ISSN 0262-4079
13. MIT Media Lab Hacks the Kinect for Browser Navigation with Gestures (2017). http://www.readwriteweb.com/2010/11/24/kinect_browser_navigation
14. Krukowski, A., Barca, C.C., Vogiatzaki, E., Rodríguez, J.M.: Patient health record (PHR) system. In: Maharatna, K., Bonfiglio, S. (eds.) Systems Design for Remote Healthcare, pp. 173–200. Springer, New York (2014). https://doi.org/10.1007/978-1-4614-8842-2_6
15. eBox (2017). http://robosavvy.com/store/product_info.php/products_id/1704
16. Panda Board (2018). http://www.pandaboard.org
17. ZigFu for Unity3D (2017). http://zigfu.com
18. Unity3D game engine (2017). http://unity3d.com
19. Kinect marker-less motion capture (Brekel) (2018). http://www.brekel.com
20. Motion Builder (2018). http://www.autodesk.com/products/motionbuilder
21. Tolven Open Source Project. http://home.tolven.org. Accessed 6 Apr 2015
22. Myo Gesture Control Armband (2018). https://www.thalmic.com/en/myo
23. "Amazing Skater" from Ace Games (2017). http://www.acegames.in
24. Virtual Room (2017). https://www.assetstore.unity3d.com/en/#!/content/6468
25. INDIVO Personally Controlled Health Record (2017). http://indivohealth.org
26. Bütefisch, C., Hummelsheim, H., Denzler, P., Mauritz, K.H.: Repetitive training of isolated movements improves the outcome of motor rehabilitation of the centrally paretic hand. J. Neurol. Sci. **130**, 59–68 (1995)
27. MS Health Vault (2017). https://www.healthvault.com
28. Raspberry PI (2018). http://www.raspberrypi.org

29. Brandenburgklinik (2018). http://www.brandenburgklinik.de
30. Intel Real Sense camera (2018). https://software.intel.com/realsense
31. Prime Sense sensors (2018). https://en.wikipedia.org/wiki/PrimeSense
32. MS Project Kinect for Azure (2017). https://developer.microsoft.com/en-us/windows/kinect
33. Virtual Physiological Human (VPH) (2018). http://www.vph-institute.org/
34. Michmizos, K., Nikita, K.: Physiological systems modelling, simulation, and control. In: Abu-Faraj, Z.O. (ed.) Handbook of Research on Biomedical Engineering Education and Advanced Bioengineering Learning: Interdisciplinary Concepts. IGI Global, June 2012. https://doi.org/10.4018/978-1-4666-0122-2.ch017
35. Cipitelli, E., Gasparrini, S., et al.: Depth stream compressions for enhanced real time fall detection by multiple sensors. In: IEEE 4th International Conference on Consumer Electronics Berlin (ICCE-Berlin), Berlin, pp. 29–30 (2014). https://doi.org/10.1109/icce-belin.2014.7034215
36. National Alliance for Health Information Technology Report to the Office of the National Coordinator for Health Information Technology on Defining Key Health Information Technology Terms, 28 April 2008

System Development for Monitoring Physiological Parameters in Living Environment

Oliver Mladenovski[1], Jugoslav Achkoski[1], and Rossitza Goleva[2(✉)]

[1] Military Academy "General Mihailo Apostolski", Skopje, Former Yugoslav Republic of Macedonia
oliver.mladenovski@yahoo.com, jugoslav.ackoski@ugd.edu.mk

[2] New Bulgarian University, Sofia, Bulgaria
rgoleva@gmail.com

Abstract. Nowadays, sensors, algorithms and software applications are embedded in people's everyday lives. To be more precise, living environment is significantly dependent on previously mentioned technology especially in the field of medicine.

The ultimate goal of this research is to collect data from different medical sensors platform, which can be used in initial medical assessment and management in the living environment. Furthermore, collected data from sport's activity were analysed in order to measure the strength of linear association between variables.

First, research on market available equipment is performed which is focused on medical sensors for assisted living in people's everyday environment. Second, research on hardware in terms of tablet, desktop machines, iPad etc. is conducted and scenarios of using the hardware are elaborated. Regarding the scenarios, the concept that demonstrates the advantages and disadvantages of the system for ambient assisted living is shown. The architecture of the system followed by sensors, computer networks, terminals is included and the technology for achieving the system's functionality is presented. Next, the Zephyr Bioharness 3 sensor for measuring physiological data is used for collecting data in the living environment. Finally, integration of the sensor with the most convenient terminal in the living environment is done and collected data are visualized via MATLAB. The parameters monitored are Heart Rate (HR), Respiratory Rate (RR), Peak Acceleration (PkAcc). The proof of the correlation between listed parameters describes the physiological status in the living environment.

The ratio between HR and PkAcc is 0.91. It is a strong positive correlation. It means that changes in heart beats are linearly followed by the peak acceleration. Next, the ratio between HR and RR is 0.88. It is also a strong positive correlation. It means that changes in heart beats are linearly followed by the respiratory rate. The ratio between RR and PkAcc is 0.84. Again, it is a strong positive correlation. It means that changes in respiratory rate are linearly followed by the peak acceleration.

I. Ganchev et al. (Eds.): Enhanced Living Environments, LNCS 11369, pp. 210–225, 2019.
https://doi.org/10.1007/978-3-030-10752-9_9

Keywords: Zephyr Bioharness 3 sensor · Smart device
Physiological parameters · Android application development
Data visualization

1 Introduction

This chapter contributes in system development for physiological parameters monitoring in living environment. It describes the integration of different technologies in terms of collecting physiological data, algorithms for processing collected data and software application for visualization.

The main problem that this research highlights is the creation of a system that could response on the problems that health caring institutions face nowadays during their primary tasks. The goal is to create a system that could decrease the risk of losing personnel or suffering damage through checking and monitoring of the physiological status. The technological approach for solving a medical problem and assessing a patient's status in ambient living environment is introduced in a more efficient and accurate manner. It means that certain medical algorithms used for initial assessment are researched in the creation of models for assessing (i.e. triage) the medical status. It is based on a Machine Learning (ML) algorithm.

There are many articles that illustrate the use of machine learning algorithms in decision making while assessing the medical status, but the contemporary technological development in terms of hardware, software, operating systems, computer networks, and processing power influence on their extended use in the fields (i.e. initial medical assessment) where they are not sufficiently exploited.

Although ML algorithms are used in numerous medical applications for supporting physicians' decisions, the implementation in medical emergency has not been enough yet. In addition, automated prediction for the patient's status in real-time based on ML algorithm and patient vital signs monitoring supports medical centers preparations for the level of treating patients after pre-hospital triage.

The paper is structured as follows. The second section presents related work in the field. The third section talks about the equipment related to measuring psychophysiological parameters, problems with reports of conducted statistical analysis. The fourth section shows the architecture of the whole system that has being developed. Fifth section presents proof from the field experiment. Sixth section presents the approaches in terms of conducted multiple linear regression analysis and correlation over created dataset. At the end there are future research plan and conclusion.

2 Related Works

The paper has been inspired by the needs to have developed system that can collect data from living environment including live streaming monitoring [1]. During the research it has been found that some similar works exists [2]. Hailstone et al. [2] were testing the sensor Zephyr BioHarness™ and they have done a research with study case and experimental proof. The accuracy of their research motivated the presented implementation in living environment.

On the other hand, the authors in [3] have compared the accuracy of the BioHarness™ and Vmax metabolic cart as well as the K4 b^2 portable metabolic measurement system in health environment. The present chapter shows a collection of data in different conditions like sport, military exercises, everyday activity. Devices such as the Bioharness™ are being used in a variety of situations including physical activity, exercise monitoring, and emergency professions. The authors in [4] were testing the dates from the Bioharness in abnormal Heart Rate (HR) conditions which is a one of the expected scenarios in living environment. There are also several authors who are talking about the same topic but they are using some different sensors and methods, like in [5–7]. New generation smart watches have been used to measure the physiological parameters as HR, Galvanic Skin Resistance (GSR), temperature and EQ02 in a multi parameter body-worn system [7]. There are capable to log and transmit the physiological data describing a wearer's cardiorespiratory and thermal status. About the monitoring there are works that describe different techniques actually known to monitor HR. In the [8, 9] the authors are focusing in particular on the so-called photo plethysmography (PPG) technique.

An assessment of the reliability of five Bioharness™ variables using a treadmill based protocol is studied in [10]. The authors also describe the correlation coefficient that are used between the variables.

In [11], an application is developed for improving male/female sports condition dependable on their body profile with the e-health platform. There are some authors that compare different sensors for measuring the physiological parameters on older people. They have found that the creation of an acceptable monitoring device for older persons requires from designers and developers to consider the special demands and abilities of the target group [12–16].

In [17] the authors validate cardiovascular alarms in critically ill patients in an experimental setting by generating a database of physiological data and clinical alarm annotations. They report the current rate of alarms and their clinical validity having collected physiological data at one second intervals while monitoring alarms. It was reported during 982 h of observation to have 5934 alarms, i.e. six alarms per hour. They find out that about 40% of all alarms did not correctly describe the patient condition and were classified as technically false; while 68% of those were caused by manipulation. Only 885 (15%) of all alarms were considered clinically relevant. Most of the generated alarms were threshold alarms (70%) and were related to arterial blood pressure (45%).

In [18] the authors describe the development of a computer system for long-term large-scale recording and storage of multichannel physiological signals that was built using commercial solutions (software and hardware) and existing hospital IT infrastructure. Both numeric (1 Hz) and waveform (62.5–500 Hz) data were captured from 24 Surgical Intensive Care Unit (SICU) bedside monitors simultaneously and stored in a file-based Vital Sign Data Bank (VSDB) during one-year period. The database size is 4.21 TB. Vital signs were recorded from 1175 critically ill patients and up to six Electro Cardiographs (ECG). All type of monitored waveforms and all monitored numeric data were recorded in most of the cases.

Factors and predictors that influence nurses' intention to use the Electronic Intensive Care Unit (eICU) are presented in [19]. The aim is to analyse the applicability of the Technology Acceptance Model in healthcare settings, and to provide psychometric evidence of the measurement scales used in the study. The study involved 117 participants from two healthcare systems. The acceptance survey on the use of eICU was conducted as a studying instrument. The results show that perceived usefulness is the most influential factor. The merge between tele–intensive care units, informatics, telecommunication technology, tele nursing, and telemedicine is used in [20] to provide expert, evidence-based, and cutting-edge services to critically ill patients.

The book on enhanced living environments [21] presents the theory and the practice in the field using the up-to-date technological solutions. The main aspects of assistive care systems and applications relevant to the highly positive and dynamic scientific domain have attracted much interest in the world of Internet technology in the last decade.

3 System Architecture for Collecting Physiological Data

The purpose of this section is to show the data collection from different multisensory platform, which collect bio signals in terms of ECG, Heart Rate, Respiratory Rate. The architecture is shown in Fig. 1.

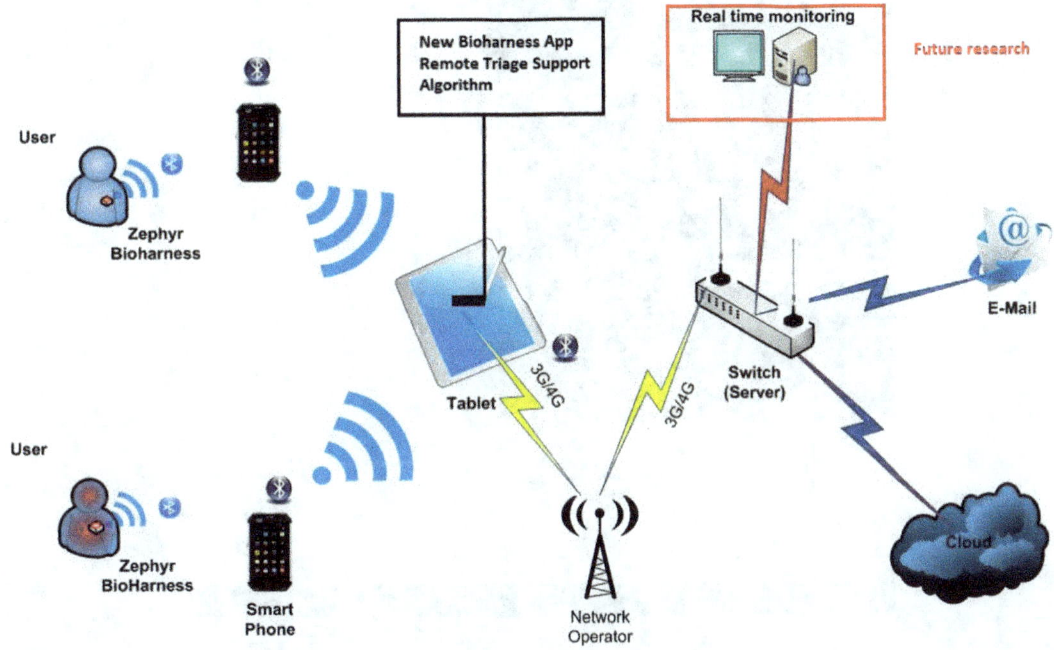

Fig. 1. System structure

The data floating is "wireless" and it is a mobile system with fast data transfer. The use of Bluetooth technology introduced acceptable latency for the measured signals. The data is sent from the user (from the sensor in Fig. 2a) via Bluetooth connection to the smartphone. Also, it can be connected directly to the tablet, where the data is processing by the algorithm that has been used to create the BioHarness App. It could be seen in Fig. 2b and c.

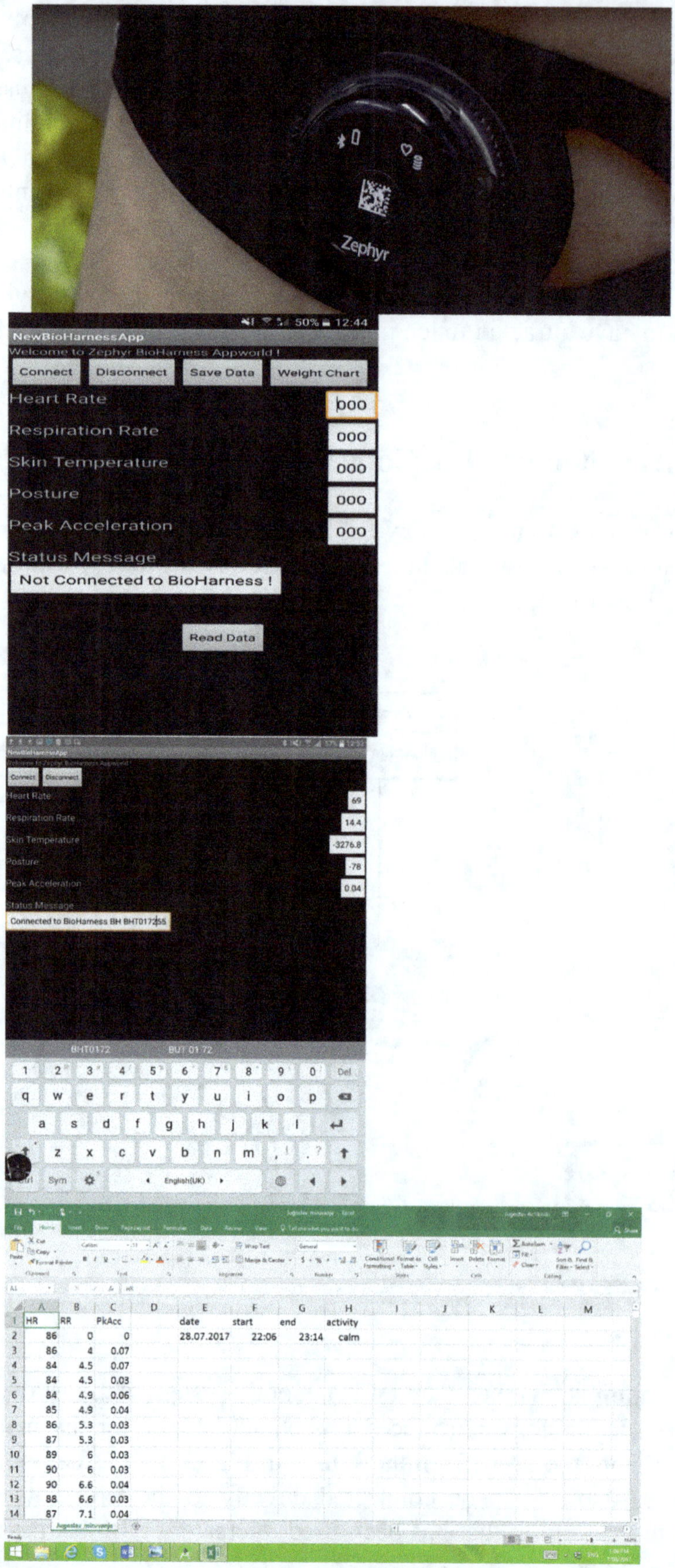

Fig. 2. (a) Zephyr Bioharness 3 sensor; (b) API for Android operating system; (c) Upgraded API; (d) Comma Separated Value (CSV) file

Processed data via 3G/4G have been transferred to the switch and multicasted to the monitoring center with medical personnel and the cloud.

The Bluetooth Connection

The Bluetooth technology allows maximum 7 users (devices) to communicate in one piconet (an ad-hoc network) in a master/slave mode. At any time, the data can be transferred between the devices and the master or the "initiator". It decides where the data should be transferred. It is also possible one "slave" to receive data from another "master", i.e. two devices are sending data to one ("slave") at the same time. The technology is being used in industry, Personal Area Networks, smartphones, gaming consoles, Wireless Audio Devices etc. The range and reliability of the systems depend on the firmware, software and hardware of the device but typically it is between 10 m and 100 m. The last versions support ranges between 40 and 400 m.

Zephyr Bioharness 3BT uses the Bluetooth 1.2+ and the main enhancements on behalf of the other versions are: improved connectivity; better resistance to radio frequency interference; up to 721 kbit/s transmission speed; improved voice quality of audio links by allowing retransmissions of corrupted packets; better concurrent data transfer; operation with three-wire Universal Asynchronous Receiver-Transmitter (UART); flow control and retransmission modes for logical link control and adaptation protocol (L2CAP).

4G/3G Connection

The information that was gathered from the sensors is transferred to the local switch (server) through the network operator and then to the cloud. It is done after identification of the destination folder. The testing environment is based on the known technologies and use-cases. The review of the six of the most commonly used telemedicine sensors is done, i.e. Isansys, Angel health sensor, Biosignalplux, Opensignal - BITalino, Biovotion, e-Health Sensor Platform V2.0 for Arduino and Raspberry Pi. The comparison is based on the type, specifications, certification as a medical device, use of SDK and API, presence of Bluetooth communication or 3G/4G, type of measured vital signs, existence of a cloud and application (Table 1).

Table 1. Review of the market available sensors and their options

Sensor	Options										
	Certified medical device	API SDK	User interface, Mob.app.	ECG	Heart rate	Pulse	Blood pressure	Temp. sensor	BT	Cloud	Extra sensors
Isansys	+	+	+	+	+	+	+	–	+	+	–
Angel health	–	+	+	–	+	+	+	+	+	+	–
Biosignal plux	No data	+	+	+	+	+	+	+	+	+	+
Biovotion	No data	+	+	–	+	+	+	+	+	+	+
e-Health	No data	–	+	+	+	+	+	–	+	+	–

However, abovementioned sensors were not appropriate for ambient living environment. The most convenient biosensor on the market was BioHarness™ 3 (Fig. 2a). It also could be used in different activities (sport, military exercises, everyday activity).

The BioHarness™ 3 captures and transmits comprehensive physiological data from the wearer to mobile and fixed data networks enabling genuine remote monitoring of human performance and condition in the real world.

Concerning experiment in the lab, the following physiological data can be measured: heart rate, respiratory rate, interbeat (R-R) interval, breathing rate, ECG, posture, activity level, peak acceleration. In terms of communication, the connection between BioHarness™ 3 and DellLatitude 3340 Notebook Laptop Computer is established via Bluetooth communication protocol. Also, the communication between Laptop Computer and Samsung Galaxy S7 is established by Samsung OEM Micro USB 2.0 Charging Cable.

Next, Zephyr API for Android operating system is provided by the manufacturer for collecting physiological data (Fig. 2b). Also, regarding Android based API it does not include support for the ECG in the interface.

Communication protocol for transferring physiological data is Bluetooth 2.0 which supports data transfer of up to 3 Mbit/sec.

The above-mentioned laboratory setup is standardized for Android-based application development.

Because there is no function for storing data from sensor the API is upgraded with additional functionalities such as storing data in CSV file. The physiological data are collected in the following order: heart rate, respiratory rate and peak acceleration. Next, the interface is inflated with three additional buttons: “Save Data”, “Weight Chart” and “Read Data” (Fig. 2c).

The “Save Data” button is used to store the data in CSV file (Fig. 2d). It should be stressed that additional methods and variables are added in the class MainActivity.java. Also, AndroidManifest.xml file from API is upgraded with permission for writing data by the following line:

```
<uses-permission        android:name="android.permis-
sion.WRITE_EXTERNAL_STORAGE"/>
```

Another two buttons are mock-up buttons and are planned to gain functionalities in further phase of the system development.

4 Experimental Design

4.1 Description

In addition to laboratory experiment, the field experiment is done. Android J1 PacKage (APK) file is exploited to store physiological data in CSV file. During the experiment, three physiological parameters are collected: heart rate, respiratory rate, and peak acceleration. The case study is created to support field experiment of established communication between a biosensor and a smart device. Also, a new software module is implemented in Zephyr API for storing data into CSV file during testing.

The case study is done in group of two persons (one male and one female) in different activity. The activities are in the following order: calm, office, and sport's activity. The persons are on age of 36 (female) and 40 (male). Next, the time for conducting measurements is: calm activity – 60 min (male), office activity – 60 min (female) and sport's activity 30 min (male).

The photos from the field experiment are in Fig. 3. The Fig. 3a presents the environment where the female is working on daily basis wearing Zephyr Bioharnes 3. The Fig. 3b presents the male in sport's activity equipped with biosensor which is connected to the smart device.

Every activity is stored by the developed application in separate CSV file. The files, which are generated by application during different activities have the following sizes: calm activity – 83 KB; sport's activity – 27 KB; and office activity – 67 KB.

The sport's activity measured interval is 30 min (from 08:56 until 09:26 on July 27, 2017). There are 1913 samples recorded in the CSV file.

The obtained records from each activity are plotted in Fig. 4.

4.2 Methods

Correlation coefficient technique is used to work up the strength of the relationships and the level of dependence between measured data. The scale applied for the relationship between variable starts with perfect, goes through strong and moderate and ends with weak (Fig. 5).

The r value describes the relation with a number, i.e. it compares things whether they are weak (d), strong (b), moderate (c) or perfect (Fig. 5).

When $\boldsymbol{r} = 1$ it is a perfect relationship. When r is between 0,75 and 0,5 it is a very strong relationship. When there is a moderate relationship the value of r is between 0,5 and 0,75. When r is between 0,25 and 0,5 it is a weak relationship.

There is a negative correlation when a perfect relationship is present but goes down the hill in the negative direction (Fig. 6).

For the correlations in Fig. 7 the value of r is going to be negative. For example when $\boldsymbol{r} = -1$ it is a perfect relationship.

The difference between positive and negative correlations is that in the positive correlations the values of the independent (x) and the values of the dependent (y) increases, whereas in the negative correlations the values of the independent (x) increases and the value of dependent (y) decreases. Therefore, the value of r is between $\{-1; 1\}$.

Additional analysis has been done in order to measure the strength of linear association between two variables. In this test, the Pearson Correlation Coefficient (R) is exploited and the focus is on sport's activity because there have been many variations in variables.

Fig. 3. (a) Activity in office environment; (b) Activity in sport's environment

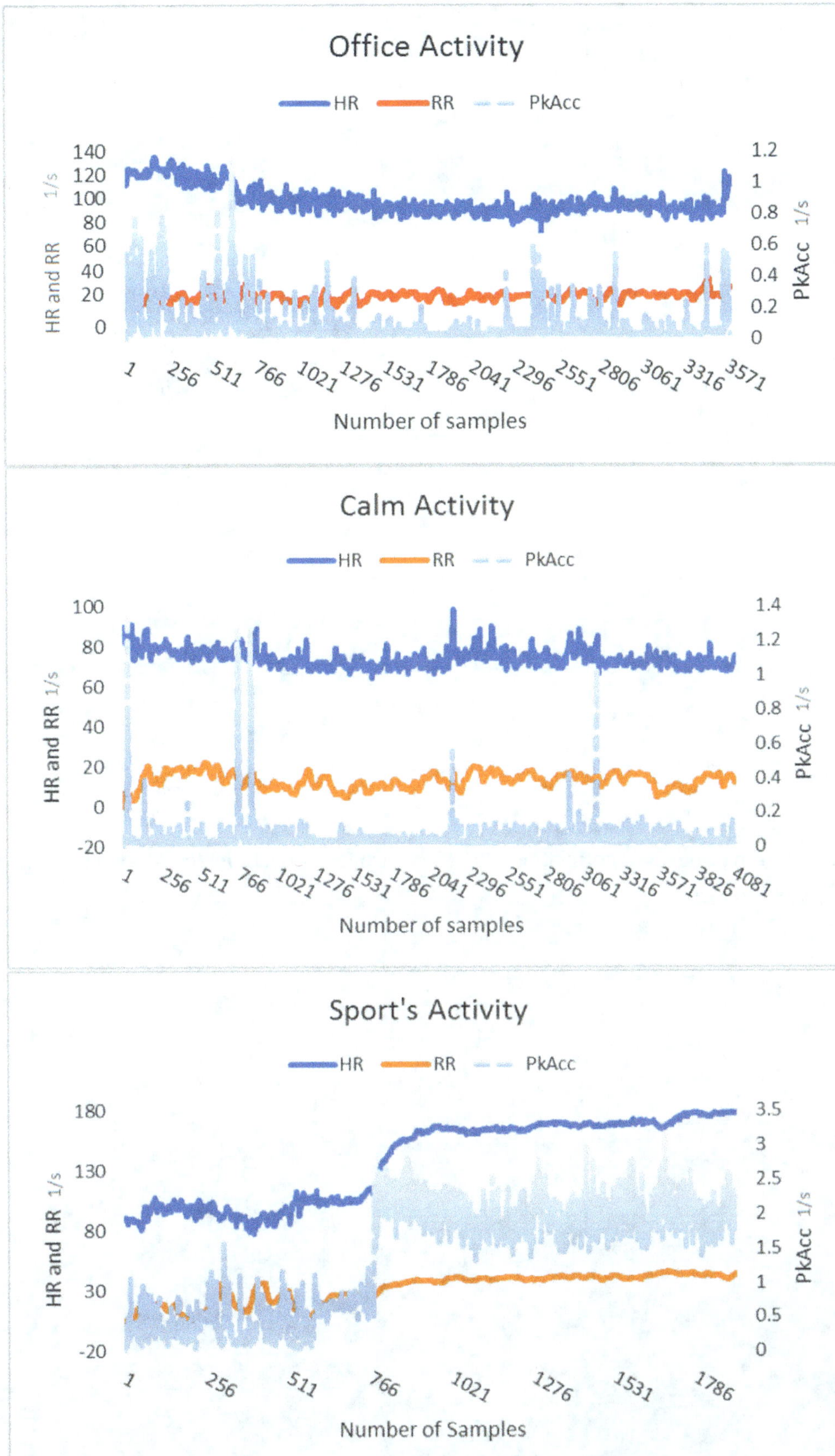

Fig. 4. (a) Office activity; (b) Calm activity; (c) Sport's activity

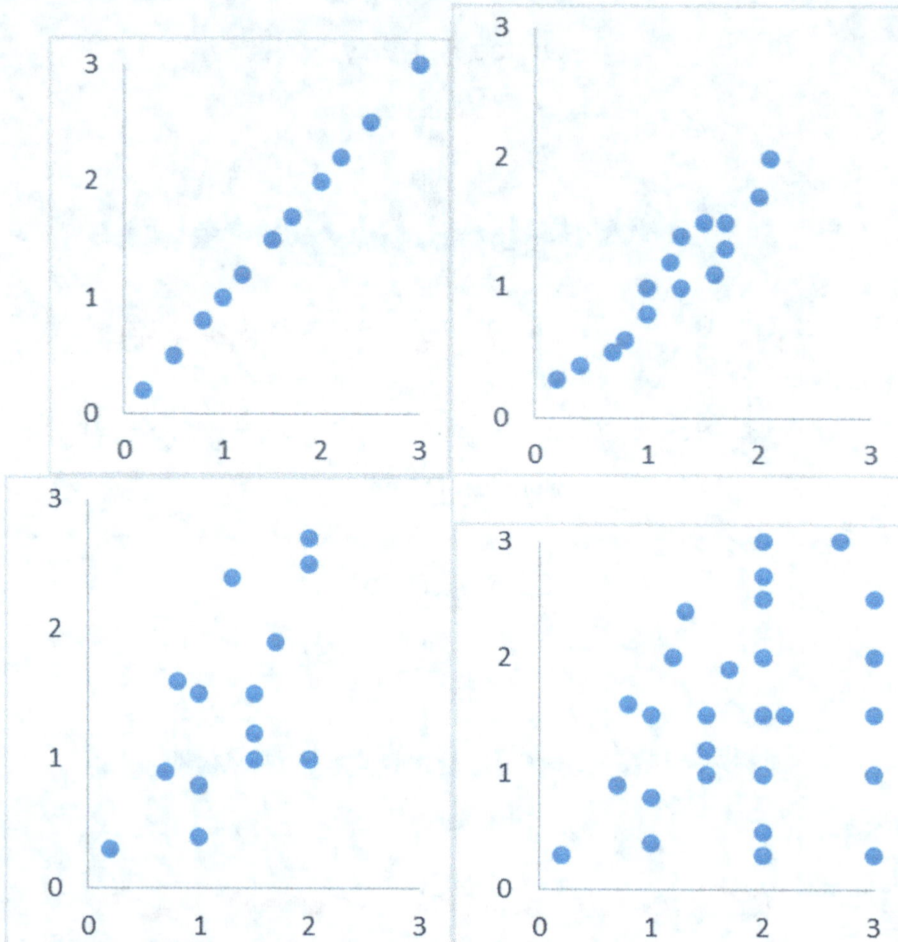

Fig. 5. (a) Perfect positive correlation; (b) Very strong correlation; (c) Moderate correlation; (d) Weak correlation

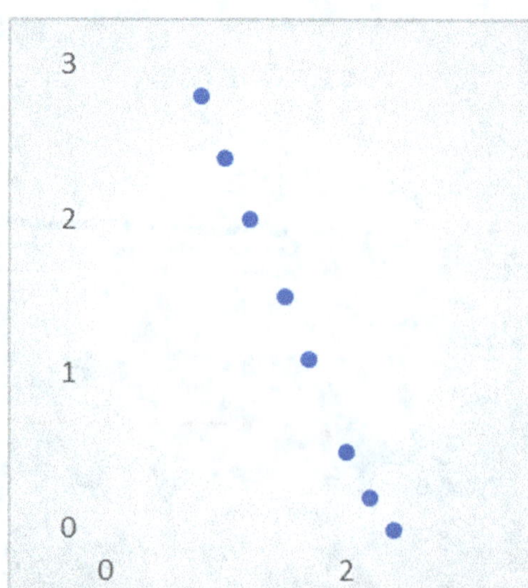

Fig. 6. Perfect negative correlation

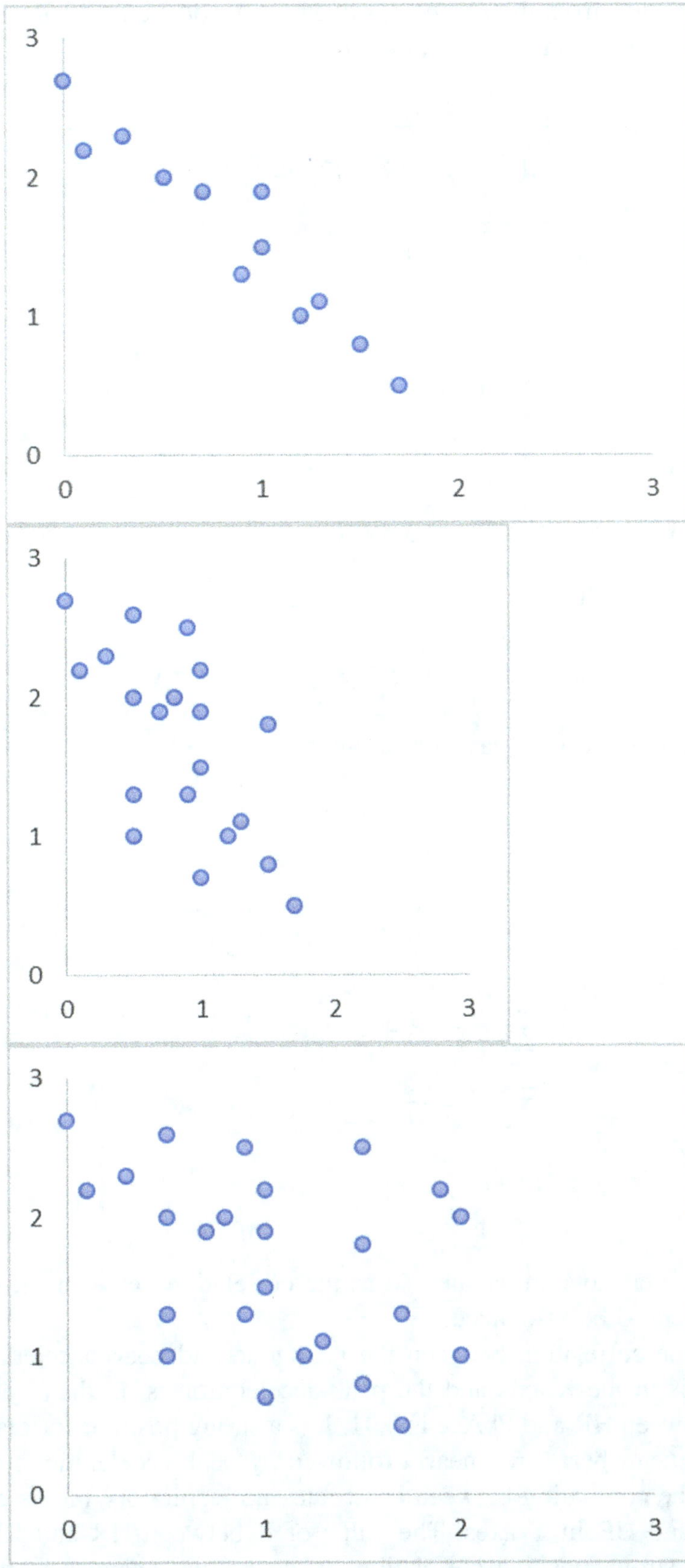

Fig. 7. (a) Very strong correlation; (b) Moderate correlation; (c) Weak correlation

Firstly, the values from the sensor has been taken for the HR, RR and PkAcc. The correlations between x and y is explained by:

$$r = \frac{n(\sum xy) - (\sum x) \times (\sum y)}{\sqrt{\left[n(\sum x^2) - (\sum y)^2\right]\left[n(\sum y^2) - (\sum y)^2\right]}} \quad (1)$$

The sum of the values for (x, y) is:

$$\sum x = x_1 + x_2 + x_3 + \ldots + x_n \quad (2)$$

$$\sum y = y_1 + y_2 + y_3 + \ldots + y_n \quad (3)$$

Multiplications are:

$$xy_1 = x_1 \times y_1; xy_2 = x_2 y_2; xy_3 = x_3 \times y_3 \ldots xy_n = x_n \times y_n \quad (4)$$

And sum of the values for $xy_1, xy_2 \ldots xy_n$ is:

$$\sum xy_n = xy_1 + xy_2 + xy_3 + \ldots + xy_n \quad (5)$$

The following expression has to be found:

$$x_1^2 + x_2^2 + x_3^2 + \ldots + x_n^2 \quad (6)$$

And

$$y_1^2 + y_2^2 + y_3^2 + \ldots + y_n^2 \quad (7)$$

$$\sum x^2 = x_1^2 + x_2^2 + x_3^2 + \ldots + x_n^2 \quad (8)$$

$$\sum y^2 = y_1^2 + y_2^2 + y_3^2 + \ldots + y_n^2 \quad (9)$$

4.3 Results

In Fig. 8 the scatter plots are created so as the correlation between measured physiological parameters to be visualized.

In Fig. 8a the correlation between the heart rate and peak acceleration is shown where the HR is in the X axis and the peak acceleration is on the Y axes. The ratio (value of R) between HR and PkAcc is 0.91. It is a strong positive correlation. It means that changes in heart beats are linearly followed by peak acceleration.

In Fig. 8b the correlation between heart rate and respiratory rate is presented with RR in X axis and HR in Y axes. The value of R between HR and RR is 0.88 and demonstrates a strong positive correlation. It means that changes in heart beats are linearly followed by respiratory rate.

Fig. 8. (a) Correlation between HR and PkAcc; (b) Correlation between HR and RR; (c) Correlation between RR and PkAcc

In Fig. 8c there is a correlation between RR and Pkacc where RR is in X axis and PKAcc in Y axes. The value of R between RR and PkAcc is 0.84 showing a strong positive correlation. It means that changes in respiratory rate are linearly followed by peak acceleration.

5 Conclusion

The obtained results about correlation of psychophysiological parameters are very strong. It means that changes in heart beats are linearly followed by peak acceleration and respiratory rate. The tests need to be performed also by different groups of older adults looking for the changes in correlation results related to the age and disease.

The system will be extended with two new modules in the developed Android application adding a fuzzy logic algorithm as a decision instrument to raise an alert. In addition, the collected data is going to be visualized using the CSV file, monitoring center, live streaming module and cloud services.

Acknowledgement. Our thanks to COST Action IC1303: Algorithms, Architectures and Platforms for Enhanced Living Environments (AAPELE).

References

1. Johnstone, J.A., et al.: BioHarness™ multivariable monitoring device: part. I: validity. J. Sport. Sci. Med. **11**(3), 400 (2012)
2. Hailstone, J., Kilding, A.E.: Reliability and validity of the Zephyr™ BioHarness™ to measure respiratory responses to exercise. Meas. Phys. Educ. Exerc. Sci. **15**(4), 293–300 (2011)
3. Kim, J.-H., et al.: Measurement accuracy of heart rate and respiratory rate during graded exercise and sustained exercise in the heat using the Zephyr BioHarness™. Int. J. Sports Med. **34**(06), 497–501 (2013)
4. Boudet, G., Chamoux, A.: Heart rate monitors and abnormal heart rhythm detection. Arch. Physiol. Biochem. **108**(4), 371–379 (2000)
5. Jovanov, E.: Preliminary analysis of the use of smartwatches for longitudinal health monitoring. In: 2015 37th Annual International Conference of the IEEE Engineering in Medicine and Biology Society (EMBC). IEEE (2015)
6. Markova, V., Ganchev, T.: Technological support to stress-level monitoring. In: Enhanced Living Environments: From Models to Technologies (Healthcare Technologies 2017), Chap. 6, pp. 133–160. IET Digital Library (2017). https://doi.org/10.1049/pbhe010e_ch6
7. Ruskova, I.N., Gieva, E.E.: Sensors for wireless body area networks. In: Enhanced Living Environments: From Models to Technologies (Healthcare Technologies 2017), Chap. 8, pp. 183–205. IET Digital Library (2017). https://doi.org/10.1049/pbhe010e_ch8
8. Lemay, M., et al.: Application of optical heart rate monitoring. In: Wearable Sensors: Fundamentals, Implementation and Applications, pp. 105–129. Elsevier (2014)
9. Liu, Y., et al.: Validity and reliability of multiparameter physiological measurements recorded by the Equivital LifeMonitor during activities of various intensities. J. Occup. Environ. Hyg. **10**(2), 78–85 (2013)

10. Johnstone, J.A., et al.: Bioharness™ multivariable monitoring device: part. II: reliability. J. Sport. Sci. Med. **11**(3), 409 (2012)
11. Castillejo, P., et al.: Integration of wearable devices in a wireless sensor network for an E-health application. IEEE Wirel. Commun. **20**(4), 38–49 (2013)
12. Ehmen, H., et al.: Comparison of four different mobile devices for measuring heart rate and ECG with respect to aspects of usability and acceptance by older people. Appl. Ergon. **43**(3), 582–587 (2012)
13. Redondi, A., et al.: An integrated system based on wireless sensor networks for patient monitoring, localization and tracking. Ad Hoc Netw. **11**(1), 39–53 (2013)
14. Pires, I.M., Garcia, N.M., Pombo, N., Flórez-Revuelta, F., Spinsante, S., Teixeira, M.C.: Identification of activities of daily living through data fusion on motion and magnetic sensors embedded on mobile devices. Pervasive Mob. Comput. **47**, 78–93 (2018). https://doi.org/10.1016/j.pmcj.2018.05.005. ISSN 1574-1192
15. Jovanov, E., Milosevic, M., Milenković, A.: A mobile system for assessment of physiological response to posture transitions. In: 2013 35th Annual International Conference of the IEEE Engineering in Medicine and Biology Society (EMBC). IEEE (2013)
16. Borodin, A., et al.: Architectural approach to the multisource health monitoring application design. In: 2015 17th Conference of Open Innovations Association (FRUCT). IEEE (2015)
17. Siebig, S., Kuhls, S., Imhoff, M., Gather, U., Schölmerich, J., Wrede, C.E.: Intensive care unit alarms—how many do we need? Crit. Care Med. **38**(2), 451–456 (2010)
18. Burykin, A., Peck, T., Buchman, T.G.: Using "off-the-shelf" tools for terabyte-scale waveform recording in intensive care: computer system design, database description and lessons learned. Comput. Methods Programs Biomed. **103**(3), 151–160 (2011)
19. Kowitlawakul, Y.: The technology acceptance model: predicting nurses' intention to use telemedicine technology (eICU). CIN: Comput. Inform. Nurs. **29**(7), 411–418 (2011)
20. Williams, L.M., Hubbard, K.E., Daye, O., Barden, C.: Telenursing in the intensive care unit: transforming nursing practice. Crit. Care Med. **32**(6), 62–69 (2012)
21. Dobre, C., Garcia, N., Goleva, R.I., Mastorakis, G.: Ambient Assisted Living and Enhanced Living Environments: Principles, Technologies and Control. Butterworth-Heinemann, Amsterdam (2016)

Healthcare Sensing and Monitoring

George Vasilev Angelov[1(✉)], Dimitar Petrov Nikolakov[2], Ivelina Nikolaeva Ruskova[1], Elitsa Emilova Gieva[1], and Maria Liubomirova Spasova[1]

[1] Technical University of Sofia, 1000 Sofia, Bulgaria
{angelov, ruskova}@ecad.tu-sofia.bg
[2] St. Anna Hospital, 1000 Sofia, Bulgaria

Abstract. This chapter presents an overview of many wearable devices of different types that have been proven in medical and home environments as being helpful in Quality of Life enhancement of elder adults. The recent advances in electronics and microelectronics allow the development of low-cost devices that are widely used by many people as monitoring tools for well-being or preventive purposes. Remote healthcare monitoring, which is based on non-invasive and wearable sensors, actuators and modern communication and information technologies offers efficient solutions that allows people to live in their comfortable home environment, being somehow protected. Furthermore, the expensive healthcare facilities are getting free to be used for intensive care patients as the preventive measures are getting at home. The remote systems can monitor very important physiological parameters of the patients in real time, observe health conditions, assessing them, and most important, provide feedback. Sensors are used in electronics medical and non-medical equipment and convert various forms of vital signs into electrical signals. Sensors can be used for life-supporting implants, preventive measures, long-term monitoring of disabled or ill patients. Healthcare organizations like insurance companies need real-time, reliable, and accurate diagnostic results provided by sensor systems that can be monitored remotely, whether the patient is in a hospital, clinic, or at home.

Keywords: Healthcare · Sensors · Monitoring · Sensing technologies

1 Introduction

Quality of life in most countries has been increasing a lot over the several few decades due to significant improvements in medicine and public healthcare. Consequently, there is a huge demand for the development of cost-effective remote health monitoring, which could be easy to use for elderly people. The remote health-care monitoring includes sensors, actuators, advanced communication technologies and gives the opportunity for the patient to stay at his/her comfortable home instead in expensive health-care facilities. These systems monitor the physiological signs of the patients in real time, can assess some health-conditions and gives the feedback to the doctors. Why these systems are so comfortable and necessary to use? The first reason is that they are portable, easy to use, with small sizes and light weight. A typical example is a

I. Ganchev et al. (Eds.): Enhanced Living Environments, LNCS 11369, pp. 226–262, 2019.
https://doi.org/10.1007/978-3-030-10752-9_10

Health-care Monitoring System (HMS) that mostly uses a microcontroller, which tracks and processes health data and sends an SMS to a doctor's mobile phone or any family member who could provide emergency aid (Fig. 1). The main advantage of this system is that a person could carry it everywhere because the device is small, light and wireless. Another advantage of these systems is that they can monitor health conditions in real time and all the time. People use HMSs in hospitals, for home care, and to track the vitals of athletes (heart rate, blood pressure, and body temperature). All this data can be processed by various sensors integrated into the systems.

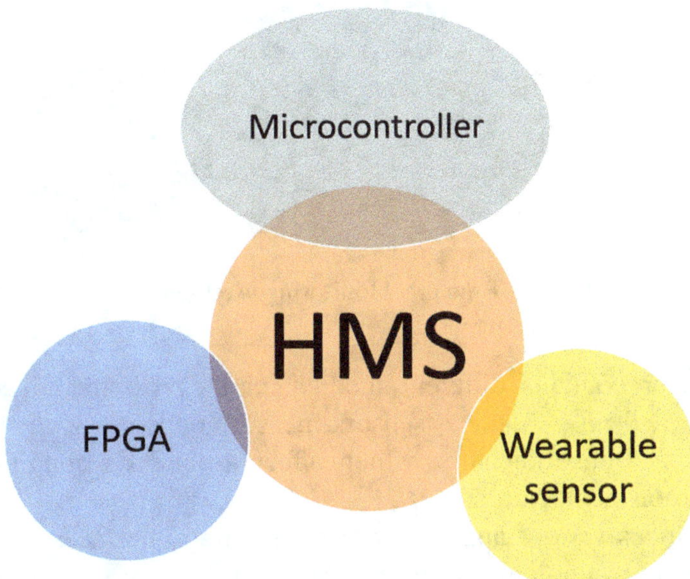

Fig. 1. Block diagram of Health-care Monitoring System (HMS).

Health monitoring systems can use microcontroller, wearable sensors or FPGA.

A transmitter receives physical signals of the heartbeat, processes the data and sends through Wi-Fi to the ZigBee. Then the data is transferred by the receiver to the computer. The transmitter uses a microcontroller which detects the patient's pulse and converts it to a voltage signal and then displayed. The idea is the same with HMS with wearable sensors, the difference comes in the fact that here the sensors which detect body temperature, blood pressure or a heartbeat rate are located on patient's body with no wires. For wireless data transmission in short distances protocols such as Bluetooth or ZigBee are used. The wireless sensor device contains respiration sensor, electro dermal activity sensor (EDA sensor) and electromyography sensor (EMG sensor). FPGA means field-programmable gate array, which could be programmed after production through HDL (hardware description language). A Health-care monitoring system using this technology contains a low-cost, analogue-to-digital converter. Digitization allows users to connect the FPGA to the entire system.

E-health Monitoring Architecture can be divided into three main layers as shown in Fig. 2.

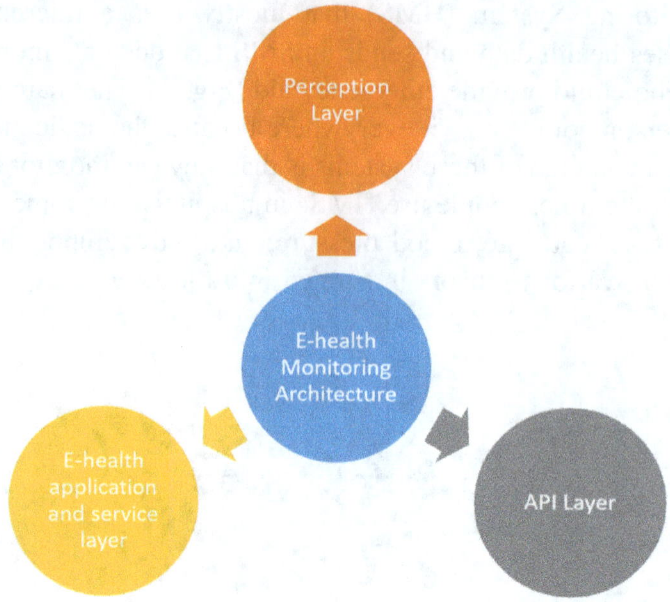

Fig. 2. E-health Monitoring Architecture.

Perception layer contains different medical and environmental sensors that are collecting data in real-time. Medical sensors measure patient's vital signs while environmental one's measure indicators, which affect a patient's condition, such as the oxygen level or room temperature.

API layer includes various application programming interfaces (APIs). The data is stored through cloud technologies providing access to patient's health data and current health records. The API layer is a layer that stores new patient health information by generating a profile using one API, and displays existing medical information for a previously registered patient data using another API.

Service layer contains an e-health application, which analyses the received data and suggests methods to improve patient's condition or give a prescription. The data is analysed by integrated algorithm and can be compared to other patient's experiences or previous health status of the same patient. This layer is responsible for alarming the medical staff in case of emergency.

HMS is an efficient instrument that can save human lives. It is compatible and can be configured depending on patient's needs, which make it cost-effective and useful not only for hospitals but also for home use.

2 Identification and Sensing Technologies

The evolution of semiconductor VSLI technologies has led to the appearance of low-power processors and sensors as well as intelligent wireless networks coupled with Big Data analytics. These are the basic building blocks of the prosperous notion of Internet of Things (IoT) in which context arises the development of identification and sensing technologies. At its core, Internet of Things is about connecting devices (things) and letting them communicate with other devices and applications. Hence, the IoT paradigm requires for networking and sensing capabilities.

At present, the objective is to transduce (sense), acquire (collect), and analyze (process) information from various objects around us in order to ensure optimal resource consumption. The solution to this request is the Internet of Things which represents the capability of connecting every applicable device to the Internet. The huge amount of generated data could be processed by using cloud services, i.e. effective and accessible data frameworks that are able to provide computing as a service.

In the last two decades networking has been well developed and widely spread as a solution to dealing with information of any kind. In brief, the objectives of information technology are to make not just information machines, but information environments that are allowing the access to information from everywhere. The combination of semiconductor and information technologies enabled the use of huge amounts of sensors to be deployed anywhere, not just where electronics and power infrastructure exists, but anywhere valuable information is gathered regarding variety of characteristics a given object or thing.

The notion of controlling things such as rail cars, machines, pumps, pipelines with sensors and SCADA systems is well-known to the industrial world for a century. Dedicated sensors and networks are already deployed in industrial setups ranging from oil refineries to manufacturing lines. But historically these networked sensor control systems have operated as separate networks with their high-level reliability and security.

Contemporary technology advancements, including electronics, digital embedded systems, wireless communications, and signal processing, have made it possible to develop sensor nodes with sensing, control, data processing, and networking features. Connecting these sensor nodes in networks enables the backbone for the Internet of Things and Big Data era.

Smart Sensors

Sensors' importance is constantly growing as a component of overall solutions for environment monitoring and assessment, eHealth (digital healthcare) and Internet of Things (IoT). Besides, there are plenty of appearing sensor applications to spread across large areas while retaining flexibility and comfortability. The sensor market will exceed trillion sensors per year soon. Therefore, for smart sensor development, the manufacturing should be low cost, high output and with short fabrication cycles [1].

Smart sensor is a device that samples signals taken from the physical environment and processes them with its built-in computing resources before passing them to a centralized sensor hub. Smart sensors are key integral elements of the IoT notion. One implementation of smart sensors is as components of wireless sensor networks (WSNs) whose nodes can number in thousands, each of which is connected with other sensors and with the centralized hubs.

Smart sensors have numerous applications including scientific, military, civil, and home applications.

Gas Sensors

Gas sensors are a class of chemical sensors. Gas sensors determine the concentration of gas in its neighborhood. Gas sensing systems are increasingly investigated for applications in environmental monitoring (air quality control, fire detection), automotive industry (fuel combustion monitoring and polluting gases of automobiles), industrial production (process control automation, detection of gases in mines, detection of gas leakages in power stations), medical applications (e.g., electronic noses, alcohol breath tests), boiler control, home safety, etc [2].

Different types of gas sensors exist such as optical, surface acoustic wave (SAW), electrochemical, capacitive, catalytic, and semiconductor gas sensors. Gas sensing methods can be split into two categories: based on variation of electrical properties and based on variation of other properties [3].

The electrical variation methods rely on the following substances as a sensing material: metal-oxide-semiconductor (MOS) stacks, polymers, moisture absorbing materials, and carbon nanotubes. MOS-based sensors are detecting gases via redox reactions between the target gas(es) and the oxide surface; the variation of the oxide surface is transformed into a change of the sensor's electrical resistance [4]. MOS based sensors have been widely utilized as they are low cost and have high sensitivity. However, some MOS sensors need high operating temperature, which restricts their application. The problem is solved by implementing microsensor components with microheaters produced by VLSI CMOS technology [5]. Another issue is the relatively lengthy time needed for the gas sensor to recover after each gas exposure, which is impractical for applications where gas concentration changes quickly. Studies of MOS nanodimension structures (e.g. nanowires and nanotubes) have shown that they could provide a solution to overcome these disadvantages [6].

Polymer-based sensors are detecting gases using a polymer layer that is changing its physical properties (mass, dielectric properties) upon gas absorption. Polymer sensors detect volatile organic compounds such as alcohols, formaldehyde, aromatic compounds or halogenated compounds. The detection process is occurring at room temperature (as opposed to MOS sensors). Polymer gas sensors possess benefits such as high sensitivities and short response times. Their shortcomings include lack of long-term stability, reversibility and reduced selectivity [3].

Carbon nanotube sensors overcome the problem of insufficient sensitivity at room temperature observed at MOS sensors. The properties of carbon nanotubes (CNTs) allow the development of high-sensitive gas sensors. CNT sensors demonstrate ppm-levels response for a range of gases at room temperature, which makes them perfect for low power applications. Their electrical properties carry high sensitivity to very small quantities of gases such as carbon dioxide, nitrogen, ammonia, oxide, and alcohol at room temperature (unlike MOS sensors, which should be heated by a supplementary heater in order to operate normally) [7]. CNTs could be categorized in two: single-walled carbon nanotubes (SWCNTs) and multiwall carbon nanotubes (MWCNTs). Single-walled CNTs are mainly used in RFID tag antennas for toxic gas detection [8]. Multiwall CNTs have been employed for remote sensing of carbon dioxide (CO_2), ammonia (NH_3), and oxygen (O_2) [9]. To enhance selectivity and sensitivity of sensing, CNTs are often combined with other materials.

Moisture absorbing materials could be embedded with RFID tags for detection of moisture, because their dielectric constant might be altered by the water content in the environment. They can be used also as a substrate of the RFID tag antenna because the dielectric constant of moisture absorbing materials could be regulated by the moisture of the neighboring air. The tags enveloped by moisture absorbing material are appropriate for mass production and low cost [3].

The methods for gas sensing that are based on variation of non-electrical properties include optical, calorimetric, gas chromatograph, and acoustic sensing. Optical sensors rely on spectroscopy, which uses emission spectrometry and absorption. The principle of absorption spectrometry is based on absorption of the photons at specific gas wavelengths; the absorption depends on the concentration of photons. Infrared gas sensors operate on the principle of molecular absorption spectrometry; each gas has its own particular absorption properties to infrared radiation with different wavelengths. In general, optical sensors could attain better selectivity, sensitivity, and stability in comparison to non-optical methods. Still, their applications are limited due to their relatively high cost and the need for micro sizes [10].

Calorimetric sensors are solid-state devices. The sensitive elements consist of small ceramic "pellets" with varying resistance depending on the existence of target gases. They are detecting gases with a substantial variation of thermal conductivity with reference to the thermal conductivity of air (e.g. combustible gases).

Gas chromatograph is a classic analytical method with exceptional capabilities for separation as well as high selectivity and sensitivity [11]. However, gas chromatograph sensors are expensive and their miniaturization still requires technology advancement.

Ultrasonic based acoustic sensors are principally classified as (1) ultrasonic, (2) attenuation, and (3) acoustic impedance. Best studied is the ultrasonic category, i.e. the measurement of sound speed. The major method for detection of sound velocity is to determine the time-of-flight that measures the travel time of ultrasonic waves at a known distance to calculate their speed of propagation. The measured gas speed is used for (1) identification of gases by determining gas properties such as gas concentration, which is related to the difference of sound propagation time, and for (2) determining the components or the molar weight of various gases in mixtures proceeding from thermodynamic considerations [12]. Generally, ultrasonic sensors can overcome some shortcomings of gas sensors such as short lifetime and secondary pollution.

Attenuation is the energy loss due to thermal losses and scattering when an acoustic wave propagates through a medium. Each gas demonstrates particular attenuation, which is giving the means to determine target gases. Gas attenuation can be utilized together with sound velocity to find gas properties [13]. However, the attenuation method is not so reliable as the method of sound speed because it is prone to the presence of particles and droplets or the turbulence in the gas.

Acoustic impedance is typically employed for assessment of gas density. Therefore, by the quantified acoustic impedance and speed of sound, the density of a gas could be found out. In any case, the quantification of the acoustic impedance of gases is remarkably troublesome, particularly in a process environment and consequently it is rarely used in practice.

Biochemical Sensors

Biochemical sensors can convert a biological or chemical amount into an electrical signal. The biosensor includes a receptor (usually a biocomponent such as analyte molecule which performs the actual molecular detection of the targeted element), chemically sensitive layer, transducer and electronic signal processor.

We may categorize biochemical sensors in several aspects. Considering the observed parameter, sensors can be categorized as chemical or biochemical, taking into account their structure they can be disposable, reversible, irreversible, or re-usable. With respect to their external form, they can be classified as planar or flow cells. Biochemical sensors intended for detection of electrical signal either directly sense the electric charges (amperometric sensors) or they sense the electric field induced by electric charges (potentiometric sensors) [14].

System-on-chip (SoC) biosensors are integrated on-chip and connected the active circuitry. SoC biosensors have numerous improvements with respect to sensors based on principles such as mechanical, optical and other methods. A major advantage is the ease of integration in CMOS integrated circuits that provides compact size, immunity to noise, potential to multiple detection of the biomolecules, etc. For cost-efficient commercialization of SoC sensors, it is crucial that all manufacturing processes are completely compatible with CMOS technologies [15].

Planar semiconductor (CMOS technology) devices can be used as the foundation for biological and chemical sensors where sensing can occur optically or electrically. Planar Field Effect Transistors (FETs) can be converted to chemically sensitive sensors by adjusting their gate oxide with membranes or molecular receptors to sense an analyte of interest. Fundamental rule of the molecular detecting is the selective attraction between the test molecules and the target molecules. As the target molecules have electrical charges in the electrolyte solution, the nearby channel conductance is affected by these electric charges via the field effect. The electric charges have dissimilar shape depending on the biochemical reactions associated with the particular detection. Interaction of a charged probe will result in accumulation or depletion of carriers within the transistor structure, which can be electrically detected by observing a direct variation in conductance or related electrical property [16].

Most of the electrical biosensor chips are based on CMOS and MEMS technology. MEMS systems are a combination of electronics and mechanical structures at a micro- and nanometer scale. The reason for using these technologies is the ease of integration onto a CMOS chip in which the electrical signals are processed. Typical applications include poly-silicon nanowire-based DNA or protein sensors, cantilever-based DNA sensors, pH sensors based on Ion-Sensitive-FET, glucose sensors, temperature sensors, etc.

Generally, the characteristics of a sensor include sensitivity, detection limit, and noise. The limit of detection is characterized as the minimum concentration of the target molecules to be detected by the sensor. Noise can originate from non-selective tying between the noise molecules and the test molecules because in practice, the noise molecules are significantly more in number than the target molecules so that the avoidance of the non-selective tying is crucial for biosensor operation [17].

Another class of biochemical sensors transduce the chemical tying into mechanical deformation. Chemical reactions provoke mechanical deformation adherent to the nature of nanotechnology, e.g. the ion channels in a cell membrane are proteins that control ionic permeability on lipid bilayer film and the activity of this protein is managed by the mechanical surface stress induced by chemical reaction [18].

One approach to utilize chemical-mechanical transformation is to use micro or nanometer scale cantilevers. Micro and nanocantilevers exhibit change of surface stress caused by a particular biomolecular interaction, for example, self-assembled monolayer arrangement, hybridization of DNA, cellular and antigen-antibody binding. These methods are barely accomplished into a compact gadget because of the massive optical detection equipment and poor selectivity performance [18].

Implementation of membrane technology is an alternative surface stress sensing mechanism. Polymer transducers with thin membrane are capable to exhibit of biomolecular sensing. The variation of adsorption quantity on the resonator is determined by detection of resonance frequency detection. Thin membrane transducers have a couple of valuable characteristics: (1) they are stronger and more solid than cantilever beams and they are very responsive to surface reaction, which allows easy functionalization by using mainstream printing techniques, and (2) the sensing surface is physically separated from the electrical detection surface, which is suitable for accurate low-noise measurements of capacitance [19].

In addition to the conventional field effect transistor CMOS technology, printed thin-film transistor (TFT) technology could be used for sensor development as well. In contrast to the silicon SMOS technology where MOSFETs are made on silicon substrate, TFTs could be fabricated on substrates such as plastic, glass, paper, etc. With printable TFT innovation, it is possible to incorporate an extensive variety of organic, inorganic, nanostructure functional materials for electronics, batteries, energy harvesting and sensor and display devices through coating or printing processes. This enables a new generation of low-cost, large-area flexible electronics generally unachievable with conventional silicon IC technologies. Nevertheless, there is an extensive trade-off in the device performance and integration density if using TFT technology compared to traditional Si-microelectronics [20].

Different selections of solution processable semiconductor materials are existing for TFTs: metal oxide, organic semiconductors, carbon nanotubes. The quick advances in materials widens the opportunities for manufacturing organic transistors and circuits using printing processes. Of all these, the organic semiconductors are distinguished for its mechanical flexibility, fast processing at low temperatures, and great potential for further performance improvement [21].

For practical sensor development, a hybrid integration of transducer circuits composed of printed transistors and a common read-out and signal processing chip might be employed. Various sensing materials together with an antenna can be incorporated into the transducer in the printing processes [22].

Wireless Sensor Networks

Current developments of Micro Electro Mechanical Systems (MEMS) technology and communications allowed for the advent of low-cost, low-power sensor nodes having multiple functions in a compact formfactor. They are the basis of wireless sensor networks.

Wireless Sensor Networks (WSNs) comprises huge number of sensor nodes (also called motes) that are spatially distributed autonomous devices that can accept input information from the connected sensor(s), process the information and transmit the output to other devices via a wireless network. WSNs were driven initially by military applications (e.g. battlefield surveillance), but now they are transformed in civil applications inspired by the IoT notion, such as home and building automation, traffic control, transport and logistics, industrial automation, environment monitoring, health monitoring, agricultural and animal monitoring, etc [23].

Nowadays, wireless sensor networks are allowing a level of integration between computers and the physical world that has been unthinkable before. Advances in microelectronics and communications industries have been a key enabler of the development of huge networks of sensors. Nevertheless, wireless connectivity of sensors might be considered an application facilitator rather than a feature of the sensors [24]. This is due to the fact that wired sensor networks on the scale that is required would be too expensive to set up and maintain, which means they are unusable for applications such as monitoring of the environment, health, military, etc [25].

Typically, a WSN node contains one or more sensors attached, embedded microprocessor with limited computational ability and memory, transceiver unit, and power unit [26]. These units allow each node to communicate with the network. Communication between the nodes is centralized – it can be a networking platform of dedicated servers or remote (cloud) servers. This network architecture corresponds to the core of the IoT, that is to provide immediate access to information at any time and any place.

The sensor is sampling the physical measure of interest into a signal that is processed by the subsequent microcontroller giving analogue to digital conversion as well as computational capability and storage. Next, the result is passed to the wireless transceiver unit for connecting to the network [27].

The sensor transducer converts physical quantities into electrical signals. Sensor output signals may be either digital or analogue which requires for the latter case to have an Analog to Digital Converter (ADC) included (either built-in or attached to the sensor) in order to digitalize the information to let the CPU to process it. The microprocessor unit consists of an embedded CPU and memory; the latter includes program memory, RAM and optionally non-volatile data memory. A distinctive characteristic of processors in motes is that they have several modes of operation – typically active, idle, and sleep. The purpose is to preserve power without obstructing the CPU operation when it is required. The transceiver unit allows the communication between the sensor nodes and the communication with a centralized hub. The WSN communication standards include Bluetooth, ZigBee, and 6LoWPAN but the use of infrared, ultrasound and inductive communication has also been studied. The power unit consists of an energy source for supplying power to the mote. The energy source is usually an electrochemical battery but an energy harvester can also be implemented to convert external energy (such as kinetic, wind, thermal, solar, electromagnetic energy) into electrical energy for recharging the battery; an external power generator may also be used for recharging [25].

Depending on the actual implementation, motes typically (1) realize data-logging, processing, and transmitting sensor information or (2) they are operating as a gateway in the wireless network composed of all the sensors that are sending data to a hub point.

Sensor nodes are described by several parameters ranging from physical weight, size, and battery life to electrical characteristics for the embedded CPU and transceiver unit in the respective node architecture. The parameters being monitored by the motes' sensors include temperature, sound, vibration, light, pressure, pollutants, etc., which means different sensors, should be implemented: thermal, acoustic, vibration, optical, pressure, etc [28].

One approach for handling the data generated by the networks of sensors is to use a platform of dedicated servers for collecting and processing information originating from the sensors. Another approach is to rely on cloud computing service. Typically, general purpose IoT applications rely on cloud computing which inherently provides remote access via Internet [23].

The most popular communication standard is the IEEE 802.15.4 standard (ZigBee and 6LoWPAN). The protocol stack for WSN integrates power with routing aspects. It is composed of 5 layers (physical, data link, network, transport, application) and 3 planes (power management, mobility management, task management) to ensure reliable and power efficient data transmission through the wireless medium [27, 29].

WSNs usually operate in various environments, which make them significantly different from other wireless networks such as cellular mobile networks or ad hoc networks, etc. In addition, WSNs normally have strict requirements for power, computation, and memory. All these constraints predetermine the cost of sensor devices and network topology and pose specific WSN design challenges. The most important design factors include reliability (fault tolerance), density of nodes (network size), network topology and scalability, power consumption, hardware specifications, quality of service, security of communications [30].

Foremost among all is the factor of security. Many WSNs are intended to collect sensitive data (e.g. personal health, confidential manufacturing data of a company, etc.). The wireless character of the sensor networks greatly complicates detecting and avoiding of snooping on the data. Best choice for ensuring WSN security is to implement hardware-based encryption rather than software encryption, which is advantageous in terms of speed and memory handling for network nodes [25].

RFID

Radio Frequency IDentification (RFID) is a notably evolving technology for automated identification based on near-field electromagnetic tagging. It is a wireless method for sending and receiving data for various identification applications. Compared to other identification systems (e.g. smart cards, biometrics, optical character recognition systems, barcode systems, etc.) RFID has many advantages since it is cost and power efficient, withstands severe physical environments, permits concurrent identification, and does not require line-of-sight (LoS) for communication. A RFID can turn common daily objects into mobile network nodes that might be followed and monitored, and can respond to action requests. All these perfectly fit the notion of Internet of Things.

A RFID system typically consists of 3 major components: (1) an application host, which provides the interface to encode and decode the ID data from data reader into a personal computer or a mainframe, (2) an RFID tag, which stores the identification information or code, and (3) a tag reader or tag integrator, which sends polling signals to an RFID transponder (transmitter-responder) or to a tag that should be identified [31].

A tag (analogous to a barcode) is a unique entity that can be attached to an object or a person and thereby enables information environments to remotely distinguish objects and individuals, track their position, detect their status, etc. The RFID tag is a microchip with programmed identification plus an antenna. The distance between the tag and the tag reader (in fact the reader is the base station) should be short enough so that the signal could be coupled. In reality, there is no true antenna because no far-field transmission is employed. The tag communicates with the tag reader by electromagnetic coupling via radio frequencies. Parts of the tag and parts of the reader are coupled together in a way that is analogous to the transformer windings (inductive coupling) or as opposing plates in a capacitor (capacitive coupling). Generally, the information acquired by the tag is further processed by a more complex computer equipment. In fact, the tag is a kind of low-level network, which enables the transmission of sensor data.

The principle of operation is so that the tag behaves as an electrical load on the tag reader. Hence, the tag can transfer information to the reader by altering its own impedance. The RFID tag changes the value of the impedance via an electronic chip that is effectively an active switch. In result, the tag is not required to create a transmitted signal, and the impedance switching sample is utilized to encode the data in the tag. At any random moment, a tag reader can just read one tag in its locality and a tag must be read by one tag reader [32].

Tags might be either active or passive. Active tags have a dedicated power supply (a battery). They possess extended processing functionalities and have some capabilities for pressure or temperature sensing. Active tags are characterized with an operating perimeter of hundred meters and a relatively lower error rate.

On the contrary, passive tags have a limited operating perimeter of up to several meters and they are characterized with a pretty high error rate. Passive tags are cheaper and that is why they are most common in the RFID marketplace. They have no physical power source as they are powered by the near-field coupling between the reader (the radio waves caused by the reader) and the RFID tag. Passive tags have limited processing and communication capabilities but have no sensing capabilities for the information-carrying medium [33].

RFID technology has numerous applications such as tracking of assets and people, healthcare, agriculture, environment monitoring, etc. Many tracking RFID applications are based on the universal communication and computing technologies available [34–37].

A prospective area for development of applications is the integration of RFID systems and wireless sensor networks (WSNs). So far these are relatively separate areas of research and development. The combination of RFID and WSNs would open new scientific and industrial fields by utilizing the benefits of these technologies.

RFID systems are primarily used for identification of objects or tracking their location without delivering information about the object and its physical condition. In numerous applications the location or the identity of an object is not enough and extra information is needed – it can be extracted from other parameters characterizing the environmental conditions. Sensor networks could help in such cases. WSNs are systems consisting of small sensor nodes that can collect and deliver information by detecting environmental conditions, for example, temperature, humidity, light, sound, pressure, vibration, etc [38]. Nevertheless, the identity and location of an object is still vital information and it can be extracted by RFID techniques. In these situations, the ideal arrangement is to combine both technologies in order to ensure extended capabilities, portability, and scalability [39].

Sensors with integrated RFID tags can be classified in two categories: (1) tags communicating with RFID readers only and (2) tags communicating with each other and creating an ad hoc network [38]. RFID systems can be combined with wireless sensor networks by integrating the sensor nodes with RFID readers [40]. Another option for integration is the so-called mixed architecture where the sensor nodes and the RFID tags remain physically separate but they exist together and they operate separately in an integrated network. Accordingly, it is not necessary to design a separate hardware device in order to integrate the benefits of both technologies.

3 Monitoring and Assisted Living Systems for Elderly and Disabled People

Trend of the European Population

The proportion of the adult-population in the European Union is in a phase of rapid increase. The aging of the population is accompanied by increased occurrence and spread of chronic diseases, and hence a significant increase in healthcare costs. Staying at their own homes, or at places freely chosen by the elderly people, is one of the approaches already taken improve the quality of life and to reduce healthcare costs of the aging population.

The idea is to support elderly people to improve their quality of life and to create better conditions for their stay in the environment of their choice. To do this, it is necessary to develop modern equipment and systems for health status monitoring and to introduce comprehensive eHealth technologies. The use of such technologies at home or at home-like setting is still in its infancy, but this method is one of the most promising approaches to facilitate the independent living of the elderly people.

Combining health monitoring systems with smart home technologies (Fig. 3) makes it much easier for elderly people to access medical care without the need to leave their homes.

Contactless sensor systems provide 24-h surveillance of the elderly in their homes by collecting data from different sensors and fusing them from the so- "Data aggregators". Data aggregators can be devices that provide only simple offline storage and analysis features. However, in modern monitoring systems, they typically perform preprocessing and retransmission of online analysis data to systems of higher hierarchical level.

In addition to monitoring some medical-specific indicators, the main groups of indicators that can be monitored (Fig. 4) are related to:

- Activities of everyday life
- Safety
- Location - Position system
- Characteristics and speed of gait.

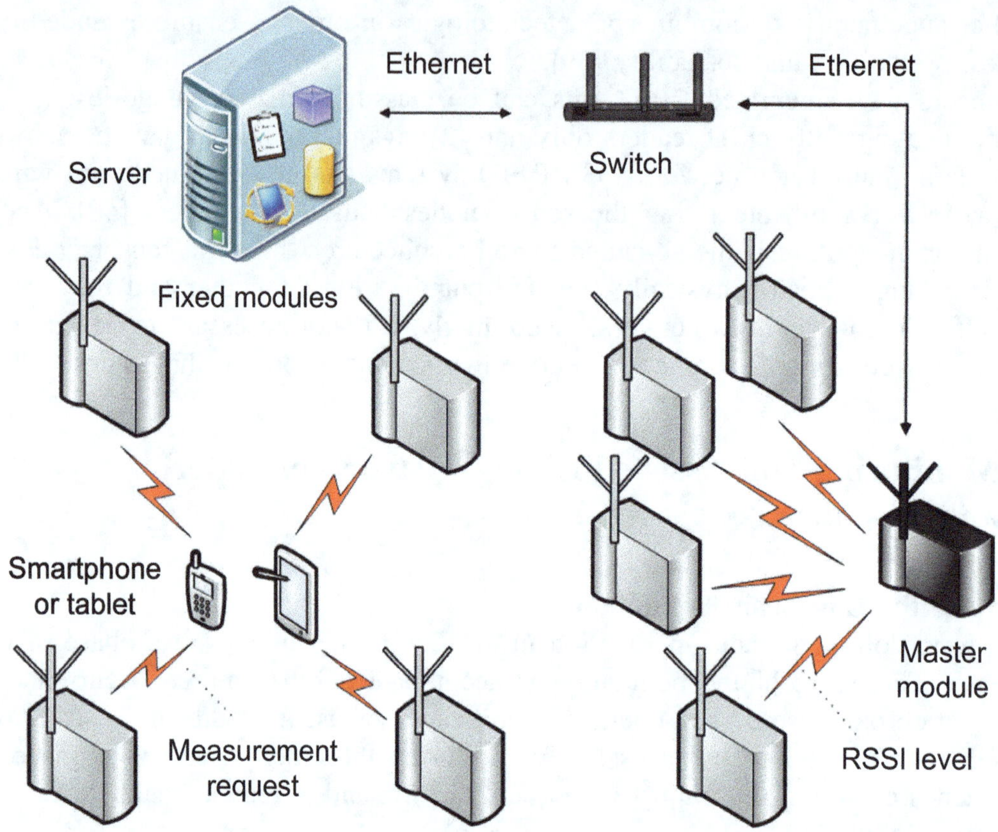

Fig. 3. Combining health monitoring systems

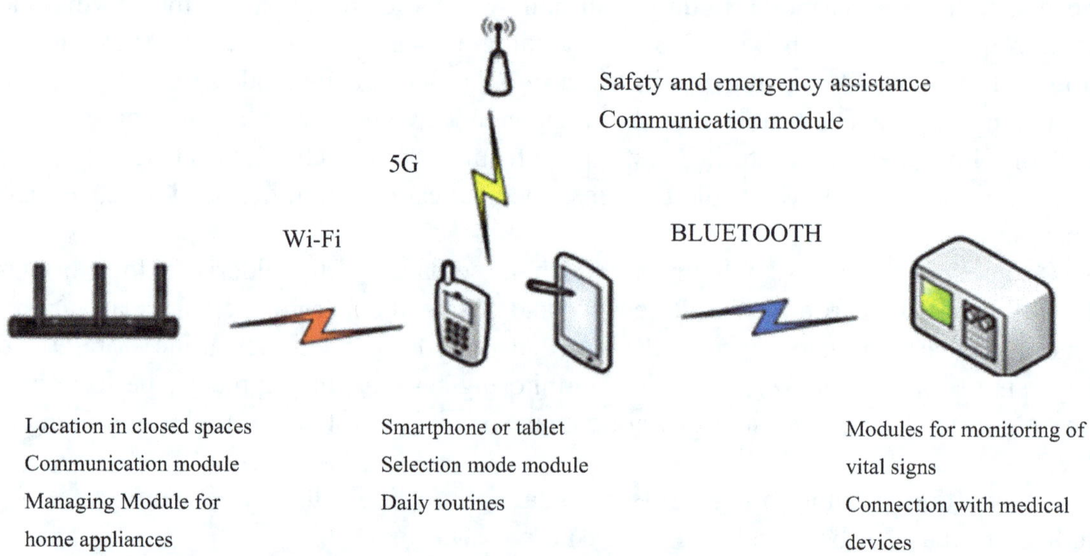

Fig. 4. Main groups of indicators.

Since the end of the last century, global trends have seen a rapid increase in the share of elderly people. In 2035, one-third of the Europeans will be over the age of 65 [41]; for the USA this figure is expected to rise to 70 million in year 2030. This estimated figure is double than the one counted in 2000. In 2009 the average age, which allows daily activities can be carried out without difficulty, was about 67 for women and 63 for men.

The most developed countries are concerned about the aging of their population [42]. Quality of life is deteriorating with aging, which leads to worsening the skills and abilities of the people [43]. Statistics show that 30% of adults fall at least once per year and 75% of these events can even cause death. Much of the elderly people suffer from chronic illnesses that require medical treatment or periodic reviews.

Various initiatives have been taken to handle these issues. One approach is the called Assisted Living Systems (ALS). It acquires immense importance in helping elderly people who live alone in their own homes and need care [44]. The proposed assistance aims at increasing the autonomy and quality of life of the consumer and contributing to its social consolidation. The results in this area have a direct public impact. Many authors have discussed the requirements and engineering aspects of ALS.

Development of technology and research are directed towards systems for fall detection, detection of pressure to a chair or bed, video monitoring, motion and tilt sensors and devices, accelerometers, smart clock with gyroscopes or worn on the belt [45].

A European Union initiative [46] is being undertaken to increase the care of the aging through the penetration and use an information and technologies of communication. It aims to help elderly people to carry out their daily activities, thereby increasing their autonomy [47].

Assistive Systems: State-of-the-Art [47]

Ambient Assisted Living (AAL) includes concepts, devices, systems, methods, and services that ensure constant support without intruding user's system. Assisting everyday life depends specifically on the situation of the user. The technologies that are used in AAL are user-centric, that is, oriented to the potential needs of the particular consumer and integrated into the user's immediate personal environment. As a result, the technology adapts to the user, not vice versa. Internal and external monitoring is necessary especially for elderly people or people with disabilities (heavy hearing, deafness, limited mobility, etc.) The use of intelligent sensors is a desirable service that can potentially increase consumer autonomy and independence, while reducing the risk of life alone.

The services and systems developed aim being tailored to elderly people and their cognitive problems. By default, it is expected that the systems are able to integrate several subsystems that have been developed by different manufacturers [48]. Also, it is expected that every user could to adapt quickly and easily so that no constraints and difficulties arise. However, the real implementations are still fragmented and isolated.

One of the major projects in the field is Intel's fashionable smart home [43]. The aim is to help elderly people by making use of four technologies: sensors, networks, monitoring daily activities and environment visualizing. Sensors determine the location of people and objects. The networks integrate motion sensors, cameras and switches that define the activity and visualize the environment.

The idea of automating and introducing technology into people's homes is to build a positive home atmosphere. Numerous authors make analyses of experimental data from sensor systems used to monitor and demonstrate the functional capabilities of elderly people and analyze and produce statistics on how they change over time. The built-in system includes sensors in all rooms: kitchen, living room, vestibule, bedroom, bathroom, etc. There are high requirements for data visualization displays as it reflects to the end-user perception of the service [47].

The Intelligent Home Monitoring System at the University of Virginia [49] focuses on collecting data using a set of cheap, unobtrusive sensors. The information was recorded and analyzed in an integrated data system. It is managed through the Internet and collects the information in a passive way respecting the privacy of the older adults.

The Rochester University [50] developed a prototype smart medical home, consisting of computers, infrared sensors, video cameras and biosensors. The main service is used for a medical consultation through a conversation between the medical person and the patient. The activities and movements of the users are also monitored. The process supports decision making for the patient and caring personnel.

Hong Sun and others [51] show arguments that most of AAL's ongoing efforts to tackle older people's problems do not fully reflect the importance of social activities. Intelligent sensors and devices use has preference in comparison to the more important than human interaction. The AAL's assume that the older adults are passive and weak by default and it is not true in all cases as some people desire to support monitoring.

The SOPRANO Integrated Project [52] aims to extend the time that people can spend living alone in their own homes being independent in their activities and feeling safer. Required technologies include products and services that allow people to perform their everyday tasks.

Aviles-Lopez et al. [53] tested a lab platform for deployment at home for the older adults. This research aimed at helping people with physical and psychological abnormalities such as arthritis, Alzheimer's disease, diabetes, senile dementia, and cardiovascular diseases coming from the aging process. It is achieved by maintaining a certain degree of independence using new types of mobile embedded computing devices, wireless intelligent sensors and so on. The platform is contextual, mobile, invisible, and adaptable supposing that the users are traced and identified in space thanks for the wearable device as watch, bag, cups or other embedded accessory in clothing. If the older user has suffered a fall or an unpleasant event, the system should alert caring personnel without any interference. The communication way to the end-user and data on blood pressure, sugar levels, etc. have to be acquired, extracted and transmitted in a reliable and way.

Drug management applications have a special place in the daily schedule. customized approach towards this problem is presented in [47].

In this way, the supervising medical consultant could do a medical examination remotely and change the dose of any drug. Other components of the supervision include cameras and sensors with a built-in accelerometer. This provides an opportunity to track the motion of users and instantly record an event such as a fall. Patients who use electrically powered wheelchairs can move freely. However, very often they need help in opening or closing doors.

Various studies have found that large TVs and monitors are not the most appropriate means of monitoring. The whole system should be easy to use by the elderly. They find it difficult to adopt new technologies that they cannot understand. Homes are equipped with sensors that measure the state of the users and maintain communication with their friends and relatives.

Holtzinger and others [44] assessed the wrist unit that is well received by users. It is designed to monitor the vital signs and detect different situations such as loss of consciousness, detection of falling, etc. Healey and others [54] presented a monitoring prototype system that can record, transmit and analyze permanent echocardiogram data. The system is also designed to have the ability to record events, activities, and various medical symptoms.

Different researchers do experiments using systems to monitor daily activities, activity, exercises and medical tests. Madeira et al. [55] looked at the possible enhancement of the quality of life of the elderly people through telemedicine. The proposed system combines intelligent items such as wheelchairs and walkers with corresponding built-in sensors for remote measurement of mechanical and physiological parameters. In this way, the elderly will be monitored in different situations.

Some studies [56–58] focus on the development of a smart home where the elderly and disabled people can enjoy quality of life and greater independence. Smart monitors can constantly monitor patients and their vital parameters. Technologies that can track changes in activities and alert the care provider are: a smoke detector; flood detector; temperature sensor; gas detector; occupancy sensor for bed; occupancy sensor for the chair; a fall detector; hanging around the neck, on the wrist, or clinging to clothing; an epilepsy sensor located under the bed and more.

The publication of Wang et al. [59] describes the prototype of the so-called I-Living Assisted Living architecture, which includes various built-in devices such as sensors, actuators, displays, and Bluetooth-enabled medical device. This device may be a dedicated computer or black box equipped with one or more wireless interface cards. Independent devices can communicate with the appropriate server over the Internet that provides web-based interfaces to allow cares, healthcare providers and healthcare professionals to monitor the environment and analyze measured data.

De Florio and Blondia [60] do not believe that the expansion of the traditional approaches to social organization might be enough to provide effective support for the elderly [47].

All listed and described projects are only part of the AAL activities collected. Analyzing the results and new opportunities and trends shows that the topics discussed are up-to-date and will continue to develop significantly in the coming years. Various projects are aimed at solving many problems of some groups (adults, adults with special needs and people with diseases). Applied approaches and applications are specific, which limits the dissemination of results.

Flexibility of systems is a prerequisite for universality, as far as possible, of hardware that would lead to rapid production of the product at a reduced price. Similar to telemetric monitoring systems for high-risk patients, relatively simple AAL systems can perform two main tasks:

- Warning about life-threatening situations
- Minimize false signals, which are the common cause of system compromises.

In addition to the constantly available communication interface between the observer and the user, it is also possible to automatically detect falls as well as momentary observation of many vital parameters.

4 Risks and Accidents Detection for Elderly Care

In order to improve people's lives, it is very important to reduce threats when people get older, such as detect and prevent falls. The research areas as fall detection (FD) and fall prevention (FP) have been developed for over a decade trying to improve people's lives through the use of pervasive sensing and computing. The most common reasons that can cause falling are obstacles at home and the aging. Getting older, people's bodies pass through some physical changes making them more fragile, and more prone to falls.

Why is so important to detect falls? Falls can result in critical injuries, especially for the elderly. The longer someone stays unassisted, the less chance he/she has to make a full recovery. Unfortunately, a fall detection system does not detect all fall cases. The most common injuries are to the head and lips which results in long-term complications. So, the faster help is very important in these cases [61].

Fall sensors use advanced technology to detect your movements and the position of human's body. They are able to give the difference between an emergency case and everyday movements, for example, can detect if the person is just laying down or there is a sudden change in the position, which means a fall.

Most falls happen at home because there are a lot of hazards there, such as slippery floors, clutter, poor lighting, unstable furniture, obstructed ways and pets, etc [61].

The first measure to be taken into account is to conduct a detailed analysis of the house and to identify the possible reasons which may lead to injuries. Then a preventive checklist can be developed to minimize the risk of fall.

Figure 5 demonstrates an example of a wearable elderly care system. The technologies are used for detection of accurate positioning, tracking the physical activity and monitoring the body signs data.

In order to track precisely the position of elderly people, a precise positioning sensor network should be developed in real time. Also, a software system should be designed with modules for data processing, data extraction, vital signs detection to support human activity recognition (Fig. 6). Biomechanical sensors are needed to monitor the physical state of elderly care which in essence are multiple sensors incorporated into the clothing, for example.

Overall, a wearable system consists of interconnected modules that can be placed at different body areas. Each module consists of sensors, Analog to Digital Converter (ADC), Radio Frequency, computing elements, circuitry and hybrid power supplies. When designing such systems, it should be taken into account the so called "wearability", which means weight, form, heat generation, flexibility and other properties. In technical point of view, the main considerations include the power consumption and overall system size in order to achieve good "wearability" [62].

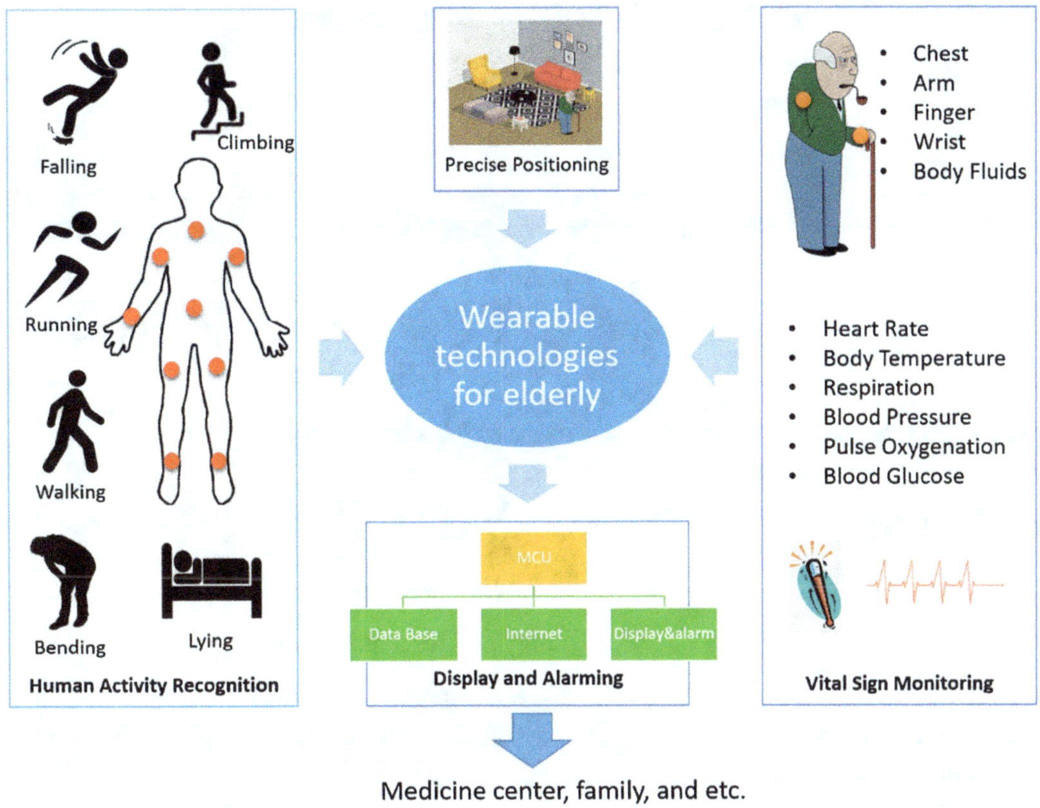

Fig. 5. Wearable elderly system

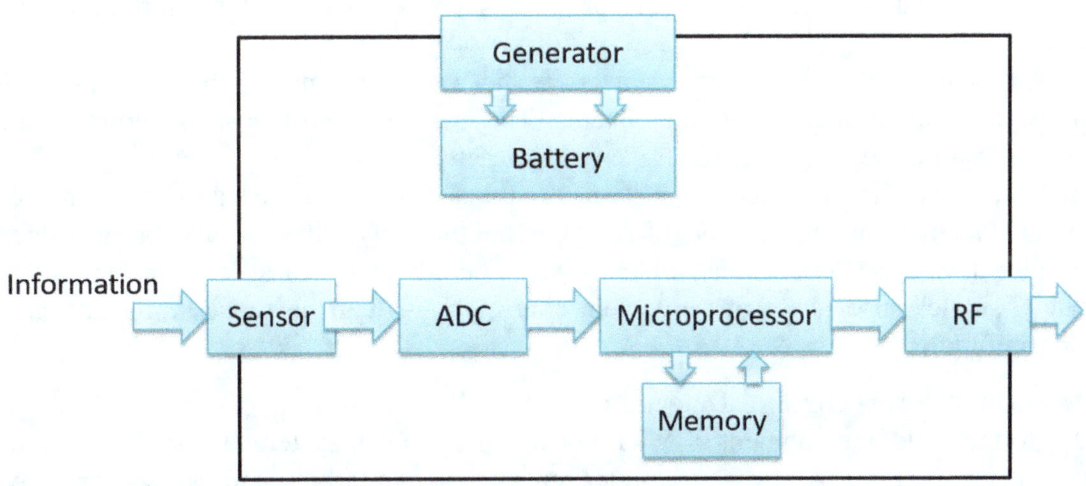

Fig. 6. Monitoring system for data processing

One fall detection (Fig. 7) and prevention systems consist of either external sensors or wearable sensors. External sensors depend on subject of interest (SOI), and wearable sensors are attached to the SOI.

The most common types of external sensors are the camera sensors. They are placed in fixed locations where the person daily activities will be performed. The main

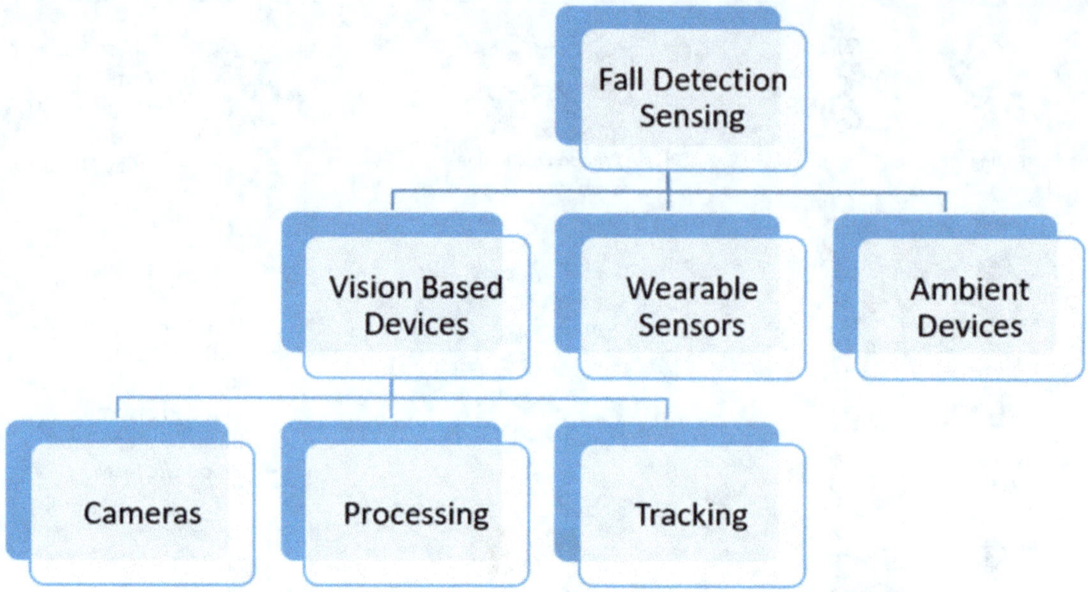

Fig. 7. Fall detecting sensing components

disadvantage of these sensors is that the person can fall out of the visibility area and the system can be unable to track the user.

Another type of external sensors is the proximity sensors, which are used in fall detection systems. They are commonly attached to walking-aid devices (cane, walker, etc.). When the user suddenly falls, the sensor detects the change of the position of the SOI. The disadvantages involve the price of such sensors and the short proximity range.

An alternative to the external sensors is the wearable sensor, which is employed into fall detection and prevention systems. They are attached to user's body and are cheaper than the external sensors.

Widely used in fall detection systems are the accelerometers because of their price and the fact that can be placed on different parts of the body. They can also be embedded in other devices as shoes, belts, watches, etc. The advantage of accelerometers is that with a single sensor a lot of movement characteristics can be successfully detected, especially falls.

Wearable Sensors for Fall Detection

Due to the rapid development of Micro-electro-mechanical systems technologies, such as accelerators, gyroscopes, magnetic sensors, particularly wearable sensor-based human activity recognition technologies, such devices become more and more attractive for use in ambient assisted living systems, especially in monitoring elderly people. Because of the advances in these technologies, MEMS sensors become cheaper, lighter and small enough to carry. These systems do not require the use of base station, as cameras which have to be installed on particular area. These systems collect the data in passive mode and do not create electromagnetic pollution. Accelerometers and gyroscopes are easy to wear but also have less power consumption and also less sensitivity to body movements, which may cause false alarms. But from a commercial point of view, this technology is the most utilized one for commercial devices and can take the form of a belt or watch, for example. In order to minimize false alarms using such kind of sensors, researchers propose different methods, such as placing the sensor into human's head or ear [63–65].

The advanced wearable sensors incorporated multiple sensor technologies, for example in [66] proposed a system of gyroscopes and accelerometers, another approach has barometric sensors in additions for high variations sensors.

Interesting solutions for fall detections and prevention away from home became attractive after phone technology developments. In [67] a very promising solution is proposed that reports 100% fall detection prevention. The system is based on accelerometers which are used in mobile phones.

There are also systems that can not only detect a fall but also can specify the fall type. Such systems are proposed from [68, 69] and incorporate a tri-axis accelerometer, gyroscope and magnetometer, as well as the data processing, fall detection and messaging.

Ambient Devices for Fall Detection

Ambient devices detect the environment of a person under protection. The technologies are used in commercial fall detection devices and the most common one is the infra-red technology, but there is also vibration sensing, noise sensing, etc. In order to cover the whole area, the system has to be installed in all needed rooms which is one of the drawbacks of such systems.

One example of infrared ceiling sensor network (Fig. 8) is proposed by [70]. They are using the "values of pixels" as features, 8 activities recognition, which are performed by 5 subjects at an average recognition rate of 80.65%. They have obtained a performance of 95.14%, the false alarm recognition of 7.5% and the FRR of 2.0%. This accuracy is not sufficient in general but high according to with such low-level information.

It is explained that such system has the potential to be used at home providing personalized services and detecting abnormalities of elders who live alone.

Another way for fall detection is through vibration sensors, which are incorporated into the flooring. In source [71] a system with 100% success is reported, which detects movement through vibrations. Electromagnetic sensors are present [72] which are again incorporated into the flooring, which can generate images of objects touched to the floor.

There are systems for fall detection based on lasers. A laser is used which interacts with light-sensitive device, which generate together a network of theoretical cross-sections, which detect stable objects [73].

Vision Based Devices for Fall Detection

Systems based on object monitoring have the same disadvantage as ambient devices and must be installed in all necessary rooms in order to cover the required range. Another issue is privacy, working with photo material from everyday life. There are cases in which pictures are sent only when a fall is detected. It is also easy to process these photos; the person's face can be faded.

Camera-based monitor the posture and shape of the subject during and after a fall, which happens in fractions of seconds.

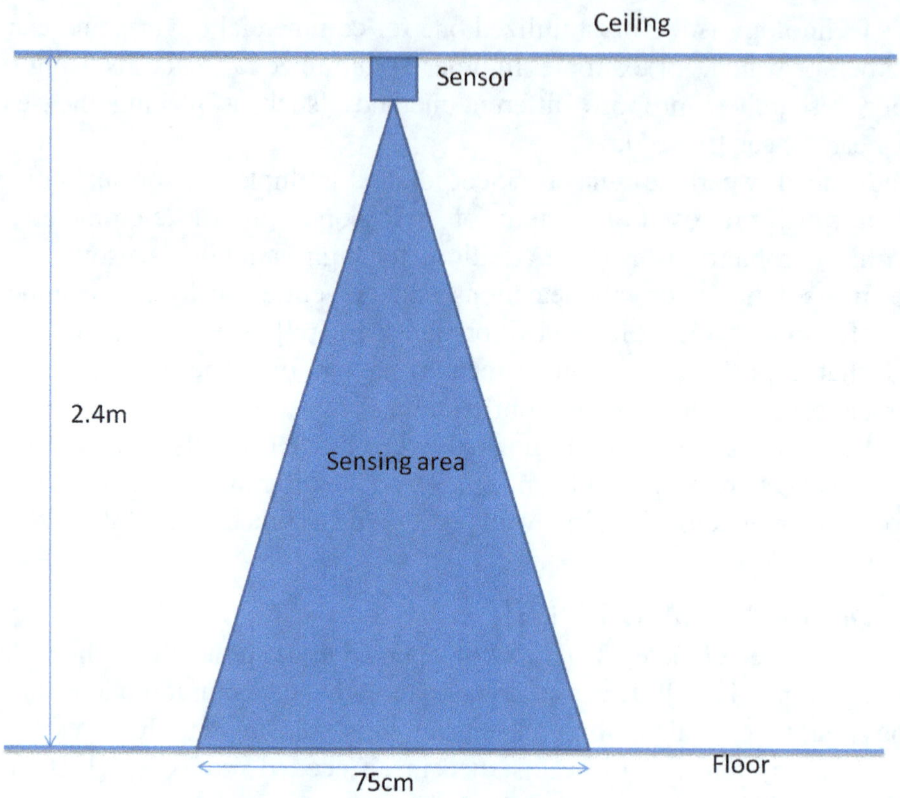

Fig. 8. Example of infrared ceiling sensor network

A considerable amount of processing power is consumed by the image dealing. To compensate the computational cost, images are usually compacted and with smaller pixels in a pre-processing stage.

In camera-based sensing systems there are different ways in detecting falls. Some systems are based on human skeleton, but their computational cost is not valuable for real time situations. Other types calculate and transform some parameters, as falling angle, vertical projection histogram etc., but their disadvantage is the false alarm rates.

Nevertheless, regardless of the number of cameras installed, continuous monitoring is still restricted to the camera locations. Another disadvantage is that such systems are influenced by light variability, which leads to lower recognition from laboratory environment to outdoor environment. Due to such limitations, vision-based human activity recognition systems are not so well suited to most elderly care applications.

A system architecture (Fig. 9), for example, includes a wearable device which is placed on human's waist [74]. The system uses acceleration analysis for fall detection. Then it gets the geographic position of the SOI and send short message for fall alarm.

The system has low power consumed hardware design and highly efficient algorithm which could extend the service time of the wearable device.

Overall, a wearable system is comprised of interconnected modules, which can be installed at different parts of the body. Each module consists of sensors, Analog to Digital Converter, computing elements, RF circuitry and hybrid power supplies (batteries and energy scavenging generator).

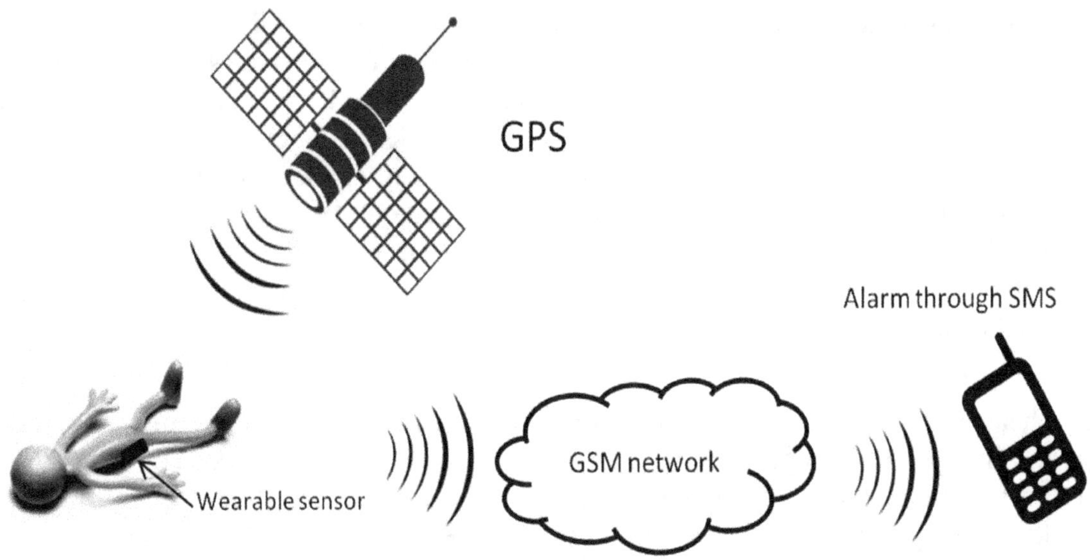

Fig. 9. Example of system architecture for fall detection with wearable sensors

Vital Signs Monitoring

Most elderly people suffer from age-related diseases, as diabetes, hypertension, hypertension, etc. So, it is of great importance to design reliable real-time health monitoring system for elderly care. Most common used are wearable and non-invasive biosensors, which can be put on the body or near the body which can successfully measure a variety of vital signs. In Table 1 a summary of several vital signs is presented.

Table 1. Summarize of most common vital signs.

Parameter	Range	Technology
Rate of the heart	0.5 ÷ 4.0 mV	Skin electrode Optical MI sensor
Body temperature	32.0 ÷ 45.0 °C	Thermistors Optical means Thermoelectric effects
Blood pressure	10.0 ÷ 400.0 mm Hg	Capacitive strain sensors Piezoelectric capacitors
Respiration rate	2.0 ÷ 50.0 breaths/min	Strain gauge/Impedance
Glucose in blood	0.5 ÷ 1.0 mM (millimoles per liter)	Electrochemical
Pulse oxygenation	80% ÷ 100%	Optical means

Body Temperature

One of the most important vital signs to be monitored is the body temperature. Another important issue that should be taken into account is the location at which the temperature will be measured because it is different at the different locations. There are several means that can be used for measurements, such as thermistors, thermoelectric effect, optical means, etc. The most common technique for non-invasive measurement using wearable sensors is the thermistor. There are methods proposed in [75], where negative temperature coefficient resistors a temperature sensing element is used and the textile wires incorporated into the sensor element are integrated into wearable system for monitoring, in this case baby jacket. Other methods propose textile-based temperature sensor which is incorporated into knitted structure [76]. There are a lot of wearable temperature sensors available at the market that can be directly attached to the skin, as LM35 [77].

Heart Rate

The heart rate is one of the most important signs, especially when we talk for elderly care, which should be precisely monitored. The heart should be in perfect working condition in order to consider that the patient is healthy. The heart rate of a healthy adult in resting position ranges from 60 to 100 beats per minute. Nevertheless, depending on person's activity and physiological state, these values can vary. During the night, a healthy person's heartbeat may vary from 40 to 50 beats per minute, which also should be considered. This parameter can be used in order to diagnose a lot of cardiovascular diseases. Heart rate can be measured through various technologies, as electrical, optical or strain sensors. The electrical measurements include electrocardiography through electrodes. There are some methods for such measurements proposed, for example in [78] chest electrodes are investigated which are silver coated, without the need to use gel or paste during the measurements. Other approaches use soft micro fluidics and adhesive surfaces to achieve highly stretchable state-of-the art systems [79]. Other researches describe magnetic sensitive sensors which are able to measure quasi noncontact pulse rate. These sensors can measure magneto-cardiogram in non-shielded conditions [80, 81].

Respiration Rate

Respiration rate is very indicative parameter for distinguishing diseases as asthma, sleeping apnea, anemia, etc. A healthy resting person respiration rate is typically one breath in every 6.4 s, the amount of inhaled air is approximately 500 mL [77]. Elderly people often have difficulties in breathing normal because the lungs expansion and contraction rates decreases. The methods for respiration rate measurement can be divided into two types, the first one detects directly the airflow during the breathing, the second one measure indirectly responding to chest and its expansion and contraction. For directly measurements sensors can be placed near the nose or mouth and respond to changes in the temperature of the air, the pressure, humidity, the concentration of carbon dioxide, etc [82]. The indirect measures involve physical parameters that need to be monitored, as changes in the lung volume and movement. With the advanced developed textile-based technologies nowadays, there are a lot of sensors available, which can be directly incorporated into the clothing which accurately detect the breath levels without interfering person's comfort. In [83] a garment-based sensing system with piezoresistive sensor is represented, which is able to determine a 10 s pause in breathing.

Blood Pressure

The blood pressure gives the force inside an artery and is typically 120/80 mm of mercury for healthy persons, the systole is 120 mm Hg (maxima) and the diastole is 80 mm Hg (minima) [77]. Blood pressure is typically detected using sphygmomanometers, but they need stationary setup, not cost effective and do not have the possibility of monitoring. Nowadays the state-of-the-art sensors are capacitive sensitive strain sensors [84], which are compressible and piezoelectric. The difference between both of them is that compressible capacitive strain sensors are composed of elastic dielectric, while the piezoresistive sensors are composed of robust dielectric placed between 2 flexible electrodes. When an external pressure is applied to the dielectric, it will lead to change in the capacitance of the device. In the same way, if the piezoelectric material is strained, this will generate an induced voltage in the device. For example, in [85] a conformable lead zirconate titanate sensors are presented, which have piezoelectric response. It is reported that these sensors have 0.005 Pa sensitivity and 0.1 ms response time. Such kind of performance ensures that the sensor can be used for blood pressure measurements. Another approach that can be used for blood pressure measurements is the RFID (radio-frequency identification) technique, but such device require implantation under skin, such as presented in [86].

Pulse Oxygenation

Oxygenation is the oxygen saturated hemoglobin compared to total hemoglobin in the blood, which is saturated and unsaturated. The normal state for the human organism is considered as 95% to 100% blood oxygen level. When this level is below 90% it can cause hypoxemia (more particularly tissue hypoxemia). The oxygenation may be separated into three groups: tissue, venous and peripheral oxygenation. The measurement technique is non-invasive in fresh pulsatile arterial blood. The most common method for measurements is using optic-based device, such as a pulse oximeter. The working principle is based on generated light by light emitting diodes through parts of the body as earlobe, forehead, wrist, fingertips, etc. Nowadays with the advances in organic electronics, the production of OLED (organic light emitting diode) and organic photo-detectors became prime devices for use in pulse oxygenation measurement due to their comfort in use [77]. Such sensors are described in details in [87].

Blood Glucose

The measurements for blood glucose involve the glucose amount in human blood which concentration is usually lower in the morning and increases after every meal. If the blood glucose is out of its normal range, this may indicate health problems as hyperglycemia (low levels) or diabetes (high levels). In recent years, the number of people with diabetes has increased. The World Health Organization reports that 9% of adults worldwide suffer from diabetes [77]. It has been found that frequent (possibly continuous) measurement of blood glucose levels is essential for conducting insulin therapy and minimizing the harmful effects on the body. Modern methods of testing include periodic tests in specialized laboratories or analysis of daily profiles (periodically over several hours), using a portable blood analyzer at home. For this purpose, after a pinch, usually on the fingertip, a certain amount (drop) of blood is delivered to a special test strip which is placed in the analyzer and within a few seconds the current blood glucose level is indicated. These persistent pricks cause discomfort, especially in young children, and rarely can lead to infections. New developments in the art are directed to alternative methods for measuring glucose concentration, e.g. bloodless, by measuring glucose levels in body fluids (sweat, tears, urine) as indicated in [88]. Saliva nano-bio-sensor is presented there for noninvasive glucose monitoring which provide low-cost, accurate and disposable bio-sensor. Another method for non-invasive method is proposed in [89]. The described methods are still not applicable in mass practice. Another part of the research is directed to the development of invasive methods for the delivery and analysis of blood micro-bleeds. At this stage, there are no data on the implementation and applications in the mass practice of nanobiobs for determining blood glucose levels by analyzing blood micro beats in the absence of pain sensations for the patient.

5 Activity Recognition for Sports

Research of human activity is becoming a most popular and relevant topic for multiple scientific areas. Human activity recognition includes mobile computing [90], surveillance-based security [91], context-aware computing [92] and ambient assistive living [93]. The sensor technologies and data processing techniques have achieved much progress. Work on these supporting technologies has led to developments in the area of data collection and transfer and information integration. Many of the solutions to real problems related to human life are increasingly dependent on the human activity recognition. Recognizing human activity as a topic of work can contribute to many important activities related to security and monitoring, preservation of the environment, help in maintaining independent living and aging, etc. To develop such a system, it is crucial to work on four main tasks. The tasks include selection and deployment of sensors designed to collect information about and capture a specific user's behaviour while simultaneously monitoring respective changes within the environment. Another task is related to the application data analysis techniques which are used for/while processing and storing the accumulated information, to create computational activity models which, when incorporated within complicated software (packages/products), are designed to select algorithms to provoke responsive activities from sensor data through reasoning and manipulation. There is a variety of tools, methods and technologies available to implement each task.

Sensor-based activity is used for activity monitoring. The approaches involve computer surveillance, structural modelling, characteristic elements extraction, action extraction and movement tracking with the main purpose being to make analysis aiming to recognize certain pattern based on collected visual information. Another category is based on the application of recently developed sensor network technologies for activity monitoring [94].

Sensors are attached to the monitored person. This approach is applicable in order to follow physical movements such as workouts. There are multiple types of sensors available for activity monitoring (contact sensors, accelerometers, audio and motion detectors etc.). The sensors are divided according to their purpose – there are different types based on particular output signals, involving theoretical principles and defined by technical infrastructure. They are represented within two basic categories according to the way they are positioned during the activity monitoring process. Activity monitoring based on Wearable sensor. This type of sensor is attached directly or indirectly to the observed person. While the monitored object performs any type of action, the sensors generate signals. In this way we are able to monitor features which describe the human state of mind and respective motion patterns. The sensors can be put into clothing, in shoe soles or heels, inside cell phones, watches and other mobile devices etc. They can be located directly on the body as well. From them we get the necessary indicators about the position and movement of the test object at a given moment, the pulse, temperature, and so on. There are different types of relevant sensor information applicable for various types of activities. Accelerometer sensors are sensors for activity monitoring. They are used to monitor actions such as body movements such as walking, running, jumping and more. In a paper [95] a network of three-axis accelerometers has been reported. These accelerometers are fixed on different parts of the object's body and provide movement and orientation data for the part of the body that is selected. In [96] are used body worn microphones and accelerometers to measure acceleration and angular velocity through accelerometers and gyroscopes. In the paper [97] provides a method for determining the user's location. With this method, the behavior of sitting, standing and walking can be recognized. Another used wearable sensor are GPS sensors. These types of sensors are mostly applied when monitoring activities involving location changes or open air and mobile environments [98].

The state of the art can be divided into two sub-topics, the recognition of human activity and Human Activity Prediction. Activity recognition is a complex process. The basic tasks include:

- selecting and using appropriate sensors to objects and environments. The main purpose is to observe and capture the user's behavior.
- collection, storage and processing of the information received. This task is performed through data analysis techniques.
- Creating computing models so that software systems generate reasoning and manipulation.
- selecting or developing reasoning algorithms, to derive activities from sensor data.
- Depending on the type of sensor, there are two categories of activity recognition sensors.

The first one is based on surveillance tools, such as video cameras to monitor the object's behaviour and environmental fluctuations. The provided data can be a series of video or digitally presented visual image. Common are computer vision techniques for action extraction, feature extraction, structural modelling, motion detection, and motion tracking to specify pattern recognition.

The second one is based on sensor-based activity recognition using the newly developed sensor network systems for motion monitoring. The acquired sensor data is presented as time series of state changes. They can be used as parameters for data integration, probabilistic or statistical analysis. Beside the already described attachment techniques, the sensors can be also placed within the object's environment as long as the position allows the tracking activity. These types of sensors use inertial measurement units to capture the object's behavior. This method is used for registering motion. The use of multiple multi-modal miniature sensors enables a robust capture of activities to be accomplished by monitoring interactions between a person and an object. The activity information can be acquired through motion monitoring models. The motion monitoring models can be built to recognize activity models from previous experiments including rich database about monitored persons' behaviors. For this purpose, they can be used data mining and machine learning techniques through creation of statistical activity models. This method is based on data. The actions that follow are based on probabilistic or statistical classification. This approach has its advantages as handling uncertainty and timing information. On the other hand, requires large datasets for training and learning, and also suffers from the problems of scalability and re-usability. Another method involves the use of predefined models with a large database and research results directly using knowledge engineering and management technologies. The models in this method are used for activity recognition or prediction through logical reasoning. Knowledge-driven approaches are semantically clear and easy to get started. The drawback of this method comes from handling uncertainty and temporal information.

The field of vision-based activity recognition is focused on surveillance, improvement of robots and counter-terrorism, and this field includes a wide variety of options.

Human body structure extraction data from images, action recognition and tracking across frames [99], survey on the approaches based on the movement recognition as opposed to structured approaches [100], research focused on monitoring human movement using 2D or 3D models and the other recognition techniques [101] etc.

In the 2000s, a new approach based on sensors utilizing other sensors fixed to objects was development. This approach has been named "dense sensing" approach with the main purpose of performing activity recognition through user-object interactions. Over the past few years, there have been numerous impressive developments in sensor-based activity recognition [95].

There are two approaches:

- Wearable sensors focus mainly on mobile computing.
- Dense sensing-based activity recognition is predominantly driven by smart environment applications such as ambient assisted living. The application smart sensors and sensor fusion directed to biomedical applications and the different types of sport are an interesting topic. There is an ever-growing demand in the field of systems for monitoring with local processing or a network of sensors. We will classify the following activities and will explore how these technologies are implemented in several fields, such as:
- Biomedicine: monitoring biological functions of human;
- Bio signal interfaces: using bio signals for performing activities;
- Physical therapy and sports – this science studies sports and human achievements in this field;

Smart sensors are devices able to acquire, process and display data to users. The interconnection between two or more sensors present in the same system is called sensor fusion. This provides a more complex analysis which is not achievable using a single or multiple separate sensor. Sensor fusion combines this data with strategies to provide consistent and effective responses.

In the sensor fusion, two cases are possible. In the first case, sensors with different signals are merged, while in the second case, data is merged from sensors operating in different situations. The sensor fusion has three levels: acquisition and data merger, fusion of characteristics, and merger of decisions.

Figure 10 shows the three levels of a sensor fusion system. Signal types can be physical, chemical or biological quantities or images. Below is description of processing obtained signals. Smart sensors are used when the accuracy of signal processing complexity is not as significant, but different points should be interconnected. The smart sensors must contain a discrete communication system. In this way the sensors are integrated into a sensor network [102].

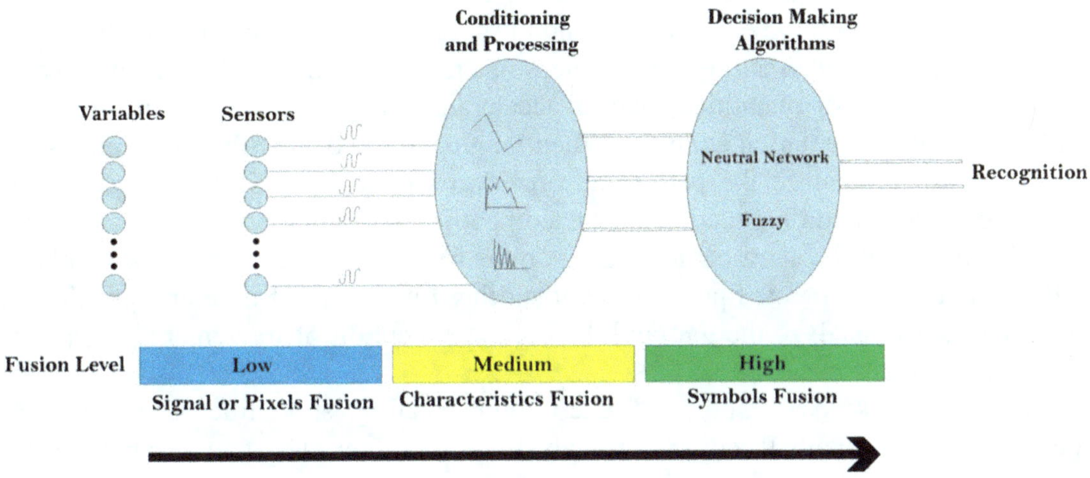

Fig. 10. Sensor fusion system [102].

In Fig. 11 a single module which includes the acquisition of all physical quantities by the sensor(s) is presented. Generated signals are electronically conditioned by filters, A/D converters, etc., and then they are processed by microcontrollers and/or microprocessors. The stage of communication, using different means in a system with other sensors for post processing elements and analysis of data is followed. The full system can be configured remotely or on the device itself.

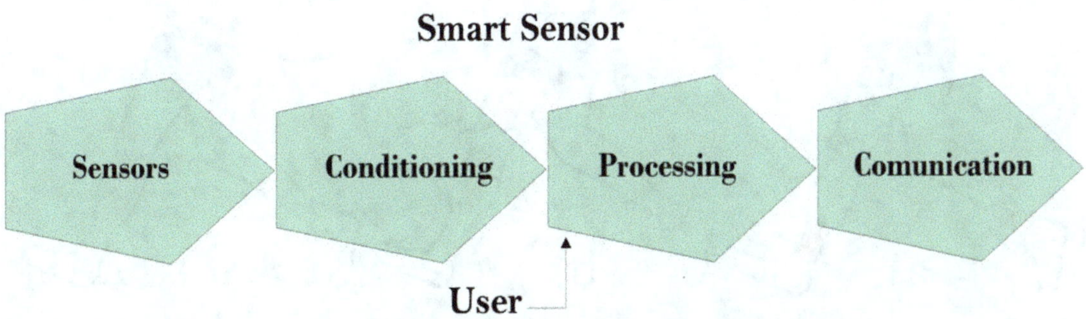

Fig. 11. Flowchart of a smart sensor [102]

There is a great interaction between biomedical and sports applications. The physiological, physical and technical types of data can be analyzed in the development of athletes in sport. The physiological variables can be described as power, oxygen consumption, and others, to the physical variables: detach speed, acceleration, and fatigue index, and technical variables: starting time, correct execution of movements, correct gait, posture, etc.

Sensor fusion contains the following sensors: Accelerometer, Gyroscope and Magnetometer. The concepts of sensor fusion and smart sensor can be used in combination.

Athletics is the basis of many sports. For many types of sports, the main thing is running, jumping and throwing. The main thing is to perform an analysis during training and to have an interaction between the trainer and the sportsperson thus giving more help in a competitive environment and in sport. Inertial sensors are widely used in athletics. This category includes an accelerometer, a gyroscope and a magnetometer. They provide data for quantities such as acceleration, angular velocity and magnetic field and provide orientation analysis. When we fusion the data with video signals, we can compare and analyze the performance of two athletes. In order for the coach to provide corrections and instructions to the competitor, it is important to investigate the inertial behavior of the sensors, depending on the time of displacement of two athletes. In this way can be corrected positioning at starting time, starting time and others. It is also important to analyze the gait and the correct execution of movements in training and racing in real time.

In almost all kinds of sport (athletics, figure skating, short track speed skating, hockey, soccer, basketball, etc.), gait analysis is important. The gait depends on the correct position and movement. This analysis can be done by means of sensors for force and inertia in the athlete's footwear. In order to achieve the necessary analysis of the athlete's pace, three sensors measure force, acceleration and angular velocity.

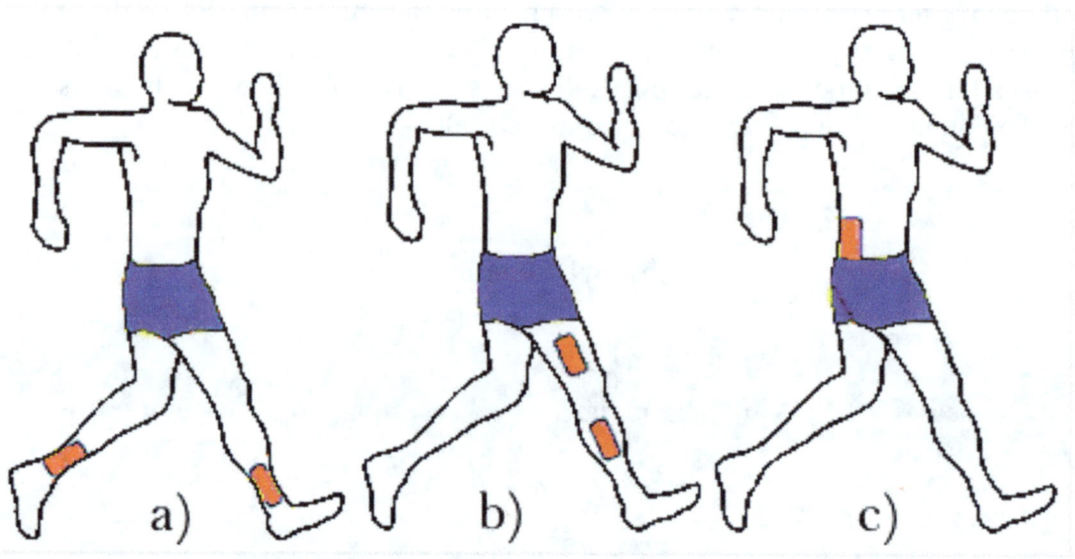

Fig. 12. Smart sensors body placement: (a) ankle; (b) thigh and tibia; and (c) lumbar [102].

In Fig. 12 some examples of area to attached smart sensors are shown: (a) sensor on each ankle, (b) two sensors that are positioned on the thigh and tibia and (c) a sensor placed in the lumbar. Below we will describe the application of the types of sensors in different sports [102].

In the different swimming styles, the turn type and speed and resistance are measured. Two variables in the development of the sport person are important, the resistance and propulsion of the body in water, and also the efficiency of the arms during the movement. Based on these results, an analysis of the style of swimming and assessment of the necessary adjustments is made. In team sports (hockey and football), protection of the athlete is required [103]. Using the same type of sensor application, an analysis of the impacts experienced by the athlete can be made. In [103, 104] concussions and other injuries in the head area caused by impacts, especially in hockey and football are described. The impact monitoring system is built of smart inertial sensors. The sensors transmit impact acceleration, impact time, impact locale, impact direction, and the amount of impacts in sequence. A research impact on the head is important, such as the protective equipment is the helmet. The vest can also be instrumented. There are smart sensors in the hockey stick as well. These sensors analyze athlete movements, force and position of the hands. To analyze the stick movement in the hands during movement, the fusion of three sensors installed on the stick can be used. Inertial sensors at the top of the stick analyze the movements of the stick in the hands and linear potentiometers can be used to analyze the position of the hands on the stick and deflection of the stick at the time of the strike [102].

Figure skating (Fig. 13) is an individual's, duos, or groups sport. The skaters perform on figure skates on ice. This sport includes the disciplines men's singles, ladies' singles, pair skating, and ice dancing. UD biomechanics analysis is used to improve the potential in figure skaters. A behavioral analysis of 60 figure skaters was made. Richards and his research team used an array of 10 cameras that capture data from reflective markers. The markers are placed on the skaters. The cameras capture their precise positions, the speed of their rotation, and their time in the air. The movement in the air are monitored. The figure skaters have to get into their tightest position within a specific time period [105].

Figure skating is an extremely precise sport. Improving each jump requires a lot of work and hours on ice. Minimal displacement of a part of the body is sufficient for an inaccuracy in the performance of the jump and can cause the competitor to fall. Working in this area saves the contestants a lot of falls and makes it possible to see the error and adjust it in time, also to improve and reach a level of triple and quadruple jumps in combinations.

Additional comparison parameters for different environments could be found in [106]. The sensor use in the AAL/ELE platform is shown also in [107] and the position in the use-case scenarios is demonstrated in [108].

Fig. 13. Position: preparation of the competitor for the Lutz

6 Conclusion

The integration of RFID and WSNs will bring a higher level of synergy and more technological advances. These integrated networks will extend traditional RFID and sensor systems giving an advantage to control the environment.

An important step toward the wider adoption of identification and sensing technologies would be the implementation of techniques, methodologies, and approaches that are mature enough to be used in a wide range of applications. Nevertheless, it is important to take into account the restrictions posed by the available resources when deploying these tools methods and standards. In addition, it is desirable that the developed solutions would allow their evolvement into technical standards and future integrated platforms.

Acknowledgement. Our thanks to ICT COST Action IC1303: Algorithms, Architectures and Platforms for Enhanced Living Environments (AAPELE).

References

1. Bogue, R.: Towards the trillion sensors market. Sens Rev. **34**, 137–142 (2014)
2. Lin, Y.-L., Kyung, C.-M., Yasuura, H., Liu, Y.: Smart Sensors and Systems. Springer, Cham (2015). https://doi.org/10.1007/978-3-319-14711-6
3. Liu, X., Cheng, S., Liu, H., Hu, S., Zhang, D., Liu, H.N.: A survey on gas sensing technology. Sensors **12**(7), 9635–9665 (2012)
4. Yamazoe, N., Shimanoe, K.: Theory of power laws for semiconductor gas sensors. Sens. Actuators B **128**, 566–573 (2002)
5. Lee, D.D., Chung, W.Y., Choi, M.S., Baek, J.M.: Low-power micro gas sensor. Sens. Actuators B **33**, 147–150 (1996)
6. Comini, E.: Metal oxide nano-crystals for gas sensing. Analytica Chimica Acta **568**, 28–40 (2005)

7. Thai, T.T., Yang, Y., DeJean, G.R., Tentzeris, M.M.: Nanotechnology enables wireless gas sensing. IEEE Microwave Mag. **12**, 84–95 (2011)
8. Yang, L., Rongwei, D., Staiculescu, D., Wong, C.P., Tentzeris, M.M.: A novel conformal RFID-enabled module utilizing inkjet-printed antennas and carbon nanotubes for gas-detection applications. IEEE Antennas Wirel. Propag. Lett. **8**, 653–656 (2009)
9. Keat, G.O., Kefeng, C.A., Grimes, C.A.: A wireless, passive carbon nanotube-based gas sensor. IEEE Sens. J. **2**, 82–88 (2002)
10. Haiming, Z.: Experiment study of continuous emission monitoring system based on differential optical absorption spectroscopy. In: Proceedings of 2008 International Workshop on Education Technology and Training and Geoscience and Remote Sensing (ETT and GRS), Shanghai, China (2008)
11. van Ruth, S.M.: Evaluation of two gas chromatography-olfactometry methods: the detection frequency and perceived intensity method. J. Chromatogr. A **1054**, 33–37 (2004)
12. Shan, M., Li, X., Zhu, C., Zhang, J.: Gas concentration detection using ultrasonic based on wireless sensor networks. In: Proceedings of 2nd International Conference on Information Science and Engineering (ICISE 2010), Hangzhou, China (2010)
13. Petculescu, A., Hall, B., Fraenzle, R., Phillips, S., Lueptow, R.M.: A prototype acoustic gas sensor based on attenuation. J. Acoust. Soc. Am. **120**, 1779–1782 (2006)
14. de la Guardia, M.: Biochemical sensors: the state of the art. Microchimica Acta **120**, 243–255 (1995)
15. Lu, S.-S., Chen, H.-C.: Wireless CMOS bio-medical SoCs for DNA/protein/glucose sensing. In: Lin, Y.L., Kyung, C.M., Yasuura, H., Liu, Y. (eds.) Smart Sensors and Systems, pp. 303–358. Springer, Cham (2015). https://doi.org/10.1007/978-3-319-14711-6_13
16. Cui, Y., Wei, Q., Park, H., Lieber, C.M.: Nanowire nanosensors for highly sensitive and selective detection of biological and chemical species. Science **293**, 1289–1292 (2001)
17. Park, Y.J., Ahn, J., Lim, J., Kim, S.H.: "C-chip" platform for electrical biomolecular sensors. In: Lin, Y.L., Kyung, C.M., Yasuura, H., Liu, Y. (eds.) Smart Sensors and Systems, pp. 3–24. Springer, Cham (2015). https://doi.org/10.1007/978-3-319-14711-6_1
18. Fritz, J., et al.: Translating biomolecular recognition into nanomechanics. Science **288**, 316–318 (2000)
19. Datar, R., et al.: Cantilever sensors: nanomechanical tools for diagnostics. MRS Bull. **34**, 449–454 (2009)
20. Klauk, H.: Organic Electronics: Materials, Manufacturing and Applications. Wiley, Hoboken (2006)
21. Arias, A.C., MacKenzie, J.D., McCulloch, I., Rivnay, J., Salleo, A.: Materials and applications for large area electronics: solution-based approaches. Chem. Rev. **110**, 3–24 (2010)
22. Guo, X., Feng, L., Tang, W., Jiang, C., Zhao, J., Wenjiang, L.: Fully printable organic thin-film transistor technology for sensor transducer. In: Lin, Y.L., Kyung, C.M., Yasuura, H., Liu, Y. (eds.) Smart Sensors and Systems, pp. 47–62. Springer, Cham (2015). https://doi.org/10.1007/978-3-319-14711-6_3
23. Flammini, A., Sisinni, E.: Wireless sensor networking in the internet of things and cloud computing era. Procedia Eng. **87**, 672–679 (2014)
24. Part 15.4: Wireless Medium Access Control (MAC) and Physical Layer (PHY) Specifications for Low-Rate Wireless Personal Area Networks (WPANs), New York, USA (2006)
25. Mukhopadhyay, S.C., Gupta, G.S.: Smart Sensors and Sensing Technology. Springer, Berlin (2008). https://doi.org/10.1007/978-3-540-79590-2
26. Healy, M., Newe, T., Lewis, E.: Wireless sensor node hardware: a review. In: 7th IEEE Conference on Sensors (IEEE Sensors 2008), Lecce, Italy (2008)

27. Akyildiz, I.F., Sankarasubramaniam, W.S.Y., Cayirci, E.: A survey on sensor networks. IEEE Commun. Mag. **40**, 102–114 (2002)
28. Johnson, M., et al.: A comparative review of wireless sensor network mote technologies. In: 8th IEEE Conference on Sensors (IEEE SENSORS 2009), Christchurch, New Zealand (2009)
29. Ramesh, S.: A protocol architecture for wireless sensor networks. School of Computing, University of Utah (2008)
30. Kocakulak, M., Butun, I.: Overview of wireless sensor networks towards IoT. In: IEEE 7th Annual Computing and Communication Workshop and Conference (CCWC) (2017)
31. Karmakar, N.C., Roy, S.M., Ikram, M.S.: Development of a low cost compact low profile phase array antenna for RFID applications. In: Mukhopadhyay, S.C., Gupta, G.S. (eds.) Smart Sensors and Sensing Technology, pp. 333–342. Springer, Berlin (2008). https://doi.org/10.1007/978-3-540-79590-2_22
32. Fletcher, R.R.: A low-cost electromagnetic tagging technology for wireless identification, sensing, and tracking of objects. Thesis (M.S.) - Massachusetts Institute of Technology, Program in Media Arts & Sciences (1997)
33. Zhang, Y., Yang, L.T., Chen, J.: RFID and Sensor Networks: Architectures, Protocols, Security, and Integrations. CRC Press, Taylor & Francis Group, Boca Raton (2010)
34. Poon, T.C., Choy, K.L., Chow, H.K., Lau, H.C., Chan, F.T., Ho, K.C.: A RFID case-based logistics resource management system for managing order-picking operations in warehouses. Expert Syst. Appl. **36**(4), 8277–8301 (2009)
35. Kiritsis, D.: Ubiquitous product life-cycle management using product embedded information services. In: Proceedings of International Conference in Intelligent Maintenance Systems (IMS 2004), Arles, France (2004)
36. Jackson, J.: Ready, aim, record: army's prototype system uses RFID tags to track weapons use. GCN Government Computer News (2008)
37. Kim, S.-J., et al.: Smart blood bag management system in a hospital environment. In: Cuenca, P., Orozco-Barbosa, L. (eds.) PWC 2006. LNCS, vol. 4217, pp. 506–517. Springer, Heidelberg (2006). https://doi.org/10.1007/11872153_44
38. Mitrokotsa, A., Douligeris, C.: Integrated RFID and sensor networks: architectures and applications. In: RFID and Sensor Networks: Architectures, Protocols, Security, and Integrations, pp. 511–536. CRC Press, Taylor & Francis Group, Boca Raton (2010)
39. Mason, A., Shaw, A., Al-Shamma'a, A.I., Welsby, T.: RFID and wireless sensor integration for intelligent tracking systems. In: Proceedings of 2nd GERI Annual Research Symposium GARS, Liverpool, U.K. (2006)
40. Zhang, L., Wang, Z.: Integration of RFID into wireless sensor networks: architectures, opportunities. In: Proceedings of the Fifth International Conference on Grid and Cooperative Computing Workshops (GCCW 2006), Changsha, China (2006)
41. Bravo, J., et al.: Enabling NFC technology for supporting chronic diseases: a proposal for alzheimer caregivers. In: Aarts, E., et al. (eds.) AmI 2008. LNCS, vol. 5355, pp. 109–125. Springer, Heidelberg (2008). https://doi.org/10.1007/978-3-540-89617-3_8
42. International Newsletter on Micro-nano Integration: Ambient Assisted Living. http://mstnews.de. Accessed 6 July 2007
43. Intel Corporation: Age-in-Place. http://www.intel.com/research/prohealth/cs-aging.place.htm, 2011
44. Holzinger, A., et al.: Perceived usefulness among elderly people: experiences and lessons learned during the evaluation of a wrist device. In: International Conference on Pervasive Computing Technologies for Healthcare, in Technische Universitat Munchen, Germany, pp. 1–5. IEEE (2010)

45. Iliev, I.: Ultra low-power acoustic detector applicable in ambient assistive living systems. Bioautomation **13/4**(1314-1902), 72–78 (2009)
46. Holzinger, A., Ziefle, M., Röcker, C.: Human-computer interaction and usability engineering for elderly (HCI4AGING): introduction to the special thematic session. In: Miesenberger, K., Klaus, J., Zagler, W., Karshmer, A. (eds.) ICCHP 2010. LNCS, vol. 6180, pp. 556–559. Springer, Heidelberg (2010). https://doi.org/10.1007/978-3-642-14100-3_83
47. Iliev, I., Dotsinsky, I.: Assisted living systems for elderly and disabled people: short review. Bioautomation **15/2**(1314-1902), 131–139 (2011)
48. Kleinberger, T., Becker, M., Ras, E., Holzinger, A., Müller, P.: Ambient intelligence in assisted living: enable elderly people to handle future interfaces. In: Stephanidis, C. (ed.) UAHCI 2007. LNCS, vol. 4555, pp. 103–112. Springer, Heidelberg (2007). https://doi.org/10.1007/978-3-540-73281-5_11
49. University of Virginia: Smart In-Home Monitoring System (2011). http://marc.med.virginia.edu/projectssmarthomemonitor.html
50. University of Rochester: Center of Future Health (2011). http://www.futurehealth.rochester.edu/news/
51. Sun, H., De Florio, V., Gui, N., Blondia, C.: Promises and challenges of ambient assisted living systems. In: Proceedings of the 6th International Conference on Information Technology: New Generations, pp. 1201–1207. IEEE Computer Society Washington, DC (2009). https://doi.org/10.1109/itng.2009.169
52. Integrated Project Service Oriented Programmable Smart Environments for Older Europeans SOPRANO. Review State-of-the-art and Market Analysis, Version 1.1 (2001). http://www.brainable.org/en/Dissemination/PublicDeliverables/Documents/D5.1
53. Aviles-Lopez, E., Macias, J.A.G., Villanueva-Miranda, I.: Developing ambient intelligence applications for the assisted living of the elderly. In: International Conference on Ambient Systems, Networks and Technologies – ANT, Paris, France (2010)
54. Healey, J., Logan, B.: Wearable Wellness Monitoring using ECG and Accelerometer Data (2005). http://www.hpl.hp.com/techreports/2005/HPL-2005-134.pdf
55. Madeira, R.N., Postolache, O., Correia, N., Girao, P.S.: Designing a pervasive healthcare assistive environment for the elderly. In: 5th International Workshop on Ubiquitous Health and Wellness part of UbiComp, Copenhagen, Denmark (2010)
56. Spasova, V., Iliev, I.: Computer vision and wireless sensor networks in ambient assisted living: state of the art and challenges. J. Emerg. Trends Comput. Inf. Sci. **3**(2079–8407), 585–595 (2012)
57. Iliev, I., Tabakov, S., Spasova, V.: Multipoint video control and fall detection system applicable in assistance of the elderly and people with disabilities. Int. J. Reason.-Based Intell. Syst. **6**(1/2), 34–39 (2014)
58. Marinov, M., Nikolov, G., Ganev, B.: Wireless sensor network - based illumination control. Annu. J. Electron. **1**(1314–0078), 155–158 (2015)
59. Qixin, W., et al.: I-living: an open system architecture for assisted living. In: Proceedings of IEEE International Conference on Systems, Man, and Cybernetics (ICSMC 2006) (2006)
60. De Florio, V., Blondia, C.: Service-oriented communities: visions and contributions towards social organizations. In: Meersman, R., Dillon, T., Herrero, P. (eds.) OTM 2010. LNCS, vol. 6428, pp. 319–328. Springer, Heidelberg (2010). https://doi.org/10.1007/978-3-642-16961-8_51
61. Pasi, A.: The brave new world of ambient intelligence. In: Wright, D., Gutwirth, S., Friedewald, M., Vildjiounaite, E., Punie, Y. (eds.) Safeguards in a World of Ambient Intelligence, pp. 11–32. Springer, Dordrecht (2010). https://doi.org/10.1007/978-1-4020-6662-7_2

62. Bharatula, N.B., Lukowicz, P., Tröster, G.: Functionality-power-packaging considerations in context aware wearable systems. Pers. Ubiquit. Comput. **12**(2), 123–141 (2008). Special Issue: Selected Papers of the ARCS06 Conference
63. Wang, C.-Y., et al.: Development of a fall detecting system for the elderly residents. In: 2nd International Conference on Bioinformatics and Biomedical Engineering, Shanghai, China (2008)
64. Lindemann, U., Hock, A., Stuber, M., Becker, C.: Evaluation of a fall detector based on accelerometers: a pilot study. Med. Biol. Eng. Comput. **43**(5), 548–551 (2005)
65. Tzanova, S., Codreanu, N.: Training microsystems technologies in an european eLearning environment. In: 2010 IEEE Education Engineering Conference, EDUCON 2010, Madrid, Spain (2010)
66. Mathie, M.J., Coster, A.C., Lovell, N.H., Celler, B.G.: Accelerometry: providing an integrated, practical method for long-term, ambulatory monitoring of human movement. Physiol. Meas. **25**(2), 1–20 (2004)
67. Abbate, S., Avvenuti, M., Bonatesta, F., Cola, G., Corsini, P., Vecchio, A.: A smartphone-based fall detection system. Pervasive Mob. Comput. **8**(6), 883–899 (2012)
68. Mao, A., Ma, X., He, Y., Luo, J.: Highly portable, sensor-based system for human fall monitoring. Sensors **17**(9), 1–15 (2017)
69. Albert, M.V., Kording, K., Herrmann, M., Jayaraman, A.: Fall classification by machine learning using mobile phones. PLoS ONE **7**(5), e36556 (2012)
70. Tao, S., Kudo, M., Nonaka, H.: Privacy-preserved behavior analysis and fall detection by an infrared ceiling sensor network. Sensors **12**(12), 16920–16936 (2012)
71. Alwan, M., et al.: A smart and passive floor-vibration based fall detector for elderly. In: Information and Communication Technologies, Damascus, Syria (2006)
72. Rimminen, H., Lindström, J., Linnavuo, M., Sepponen, R.: Detection of falls among the elderly by a floor sensor using the electric near field. IEEE Trans. Inf. Technol. Biomed. **14**(6), 1475–1476 (2010)
73. Cheng, A.L., Georgoulas, C., Bock, T.: Fall detection and intervention based on wireless sensor network technologies. Autom. Constr. **71**(Part 1), 116–136 (2016)
74. Wu, F., Zhao, H., Zhao, Y., Zhong, H.: Development of a wearable-sensor-based fall detection system. Int. J. Telemed. Appl. **2015**(2015), 1–11 (2015)
75. Chen, W., Dols, S., Bambang-Oetomo, S., Feijs, L.M.G.: Monitoring body temperature of newborn infants at neonatal intensive care units using wearable sensors. In: BODYNETS, Corfu Island, Greece (2010)
76. Husain, M.D., Kennon, R.: Preliminary investigations into the development of textile based temperature sensor for healthcare applications. Fibers **1**(1), 2–10 (2013)
77. Wang, Z., Yang, Z., Dong, T.: A review of wearable technologies for elderly care that can accurately track indoor position, recognize physical activities and monitor vital signs in real time. Sensors **17**(2), 1–36 (2017)
78. Anliker, U., et al.: AMON: a wearable multiparameter medical monitoring and alert system. IEEE Trans. Inf Technol. Biomed. **8**(4), 415–427 (2004)
79. Xu, S., et al.: Soft microfluidic assemblies of sensors, circuits, and radios for the skin. Science **344**(6179), 70–74 (2014)
80. Uchiyama, T., Nakayama, S.: Magnetic sensors using amorphous metal materials: detection of premature ventricular magnetic waves. Physiol. Rep. **1**(2), 1–6 (2013)
81. Wang, Z., Xu, M., Xu, X., Zhou, Z.: Bio-magnetic sensor circuit design based on giant magneto-impedance effect. In: 2016 IEEE International Conference on Mechatronics and Automation (ICMA 2016), Harbin, China (2016)
82. Folke, M., Cernerud, L., Hök, B.: Critical review of non-invasive respiratory monitoring in medical care. Med. Biol. Eng. Comput. **41**(4), 377–383 (2003)

83. Guo, L., Berglin, L., Wiklund, U., Mattila, H.: Design of a garment-based sensing system for breathing monitoring. Text. Res. J. **83**(5), 499–509 (2012)
84. Schwartz, G., et al.: Flexible polymer transistors with high pressure sensitivity for application in electronic skin and health monitoring. Nat. Commun. **4**, 1–8 (2013)
85. Dagdeviren, C., et al.: Conformable amplified lead zirconate titanate sensors with enhanced piezoelectric response for cutaneous pressure monitoring. Nat. Commun. **5**, 1–10 (2014)
86. Shin, K.-H., Moon, C.-R., Lee, T.-H., Lim, C.-H., Kim, Y.-J.: Flexible wireless pressure sensor module. Sens. Actuators A **123–124**, 30–35 (2005)
87. Lochner, C.M., Khan, Y., Pierre, A., Arias, A.C.: All-organic optoelectronic sensor for pulse oximetry. Nat. Commun. **5**, 1–7 (2014)
88. Zhang, W., Du, Y., Wangab, M.L.: Noninvasive glucose monitoring using saliva nano-biosensor. Sens. Bio-Sens. Res. **4**, 23–29 (2015)
89. American Chemistry: ACS Chemistry for life. American Chemical Society, 03 March 2015. https://www.acs.org/content/acs/en/pressroom/presspacs/2015/acs-presspac-january-14-2015/tattoo-like-sensor-can-detect-glucose-levels-without-a-painful-finger-prick.html. Accessed 2018
90. Choudhury, T., Consolvo, S., Harrison, B.: The mobile sensing platform: an embedded activity recognition system. IEEE Pervasive Comput. **7**, 32–41 (2008)
91. Weinland, D., Ronfard, R., Boyer, E.: A survey of vision-based methods for action representation, segmentation and recognition. CVIU J. **115**, 224–241 (2011)
92. Wren, C., Tapia, E.: Toward scalable activity recognition for sensor networks. In: Proceedings of the Second International Workshop in Location and Context-Awareness, pp. 168–185 (2006)
93. Cooc, D., Schmitter-Edgecombe, M.: Assessing the quality of activities in a smart environment. Methods Inf. Med. **48**, 480–485 (2009)
94. Chen, L., Hoey, J., Nugent, C., Cook, D., Yu, Z.: Sensor-based activity recognition. In: IEEE SMC-C Trans (2012)
95. Kern, N., Schiele, B., Junker, H., Lukowicz, P., Troster, G.: Werable sensing to annotate meeting recordings. Pers. Ubiquit. Comput. **7**, 263–274 (2003)
96. Lukowicz, P., Ward, J., Junker, H., Starner, T.: Recognizing workshop activity using body worn microphones and accelerometers. In: Proceedings of Pervasive Computing, pp. 18–23 (2004)
97. Lee, S., Mase, K.: Activity and location recognition using wearable sensors. IEEE Pervasive Comput. **1**, 24–32 (2002)
98. Ashbrook, D., Starner, T.: Using GPS to learn significant locations and predict movement across multiple users. Pers. Ubiquit. Comput. **7**, 275–286 (2003)
99. Aggarwal, J., Cai, Q.: Human motion analysis: a review. Comput. Vis. Image Underst. **73**, 428–440 (1999)
100. Cedras, C., Shah, M.: Motion-based recognition: a survey. Image Vis. Comput. **73**, 129–155 (1995)
101. Gavrila, D.: The visual analysis of human movement: a survey. Comput. Vis. Image Underst. **73**, 82–98 (1999)
102. Mendes Jr., J.J., Vieira, M.E., Pires, M.B., Stevan Jr., S.L.: Sensor fusion and smart sensor in sports and biomedical applications. Sensors **16**(10), 1–31 (2016)
103. Mihalik, J.P., Guskiewicz, K.M., Marshall, S.W., Blackburn, J.T., Cantu, R.C., Greenwald, R.W.: Head impact biomechanics in youth hockey: comparisons across playing position, event types, and impact locations. Ann. Biomed. Eng **40**, 141–149 (2012)
104. Crisco, J.J., et al.: Head impact exposure in collegiate football players. J. Biomech. **44**, 2673–2678 (2011)

105. Miller, B., LaPenta, D.: Sharpening that competitive edge. University of Delaware, 11 December 2017. http://www.udel.edu/udaily/2017/december/figure-skating-biomechanics-olympics/. Accessed 28 Mar 2018
106. Ruskova, I.N., Gieva, E.E.: Sensors for wireless body area networks (Healthcare Technologies, 2017) (Chap. 8). In: Enhanced Living Environments: From Models to Technologies, pp. 183–205. IET Digital Library. https://doi.org/10.1049/pbhe010e_ch8. http://digital-library.theiet.org/content/books/10.1049/pbhe010e_ch8
107. Goleva, R., et al.: AALaaS/ELEaaS platforms (Healthcare Technologies, 2017) (Chap. 9), In: Enhanced Living Environments: From Models to Technologies, pp. 207–234. IET Digital Library. https://doi.org/10.1049/pbhe010e_ch9. http://digital-library.theiet.org/content/books/10.1049/pbhe010e_ch9
108. Autexier, S., et al.: End-users' AAL and ELE service scenarios in smart personal environments (Healthcare Technologies, 2017) (Chap. 5). In: Enhanced Living Environments: From Models to Technologies, pp. 101–131. IET Digital Library. https://doi.org/10.1049/pbhe010e_ch5. http://digital-library.theiet.org/content/books/10.1049/pbhe010e_ch5

Semantic Middleware Architectures for IoT Healthcare Applications

Rita Zgheib[1(✉)], Emmanuel Conchon[2(✉)], and Rémi Bastide[3(✉)]

[1] Université de Pau & Pays Adour, E2S-UPPA, LIUPPA, 64600 Anglet, France
rzgheib@iutbayonne.univ-pau.fr

[2] Université de Limoges, XLIM UMR CNRS 7252, 87060 Limoges Cedex, France
emmanuel.conchon@xlim.fr

[3] Université de Toulouse, ISIS-IRIT, Campus Universitaire, 81104 Castres, France
remi.bastide@irit.fr

Abstract. The adoption of the Internet of Things (IoT) in healthcare has received considerable interest in the past decade. Indeed, IoT-based solutions are poised to transform how we keep people safe and healthy especially as the demand for solutions to lower healthcare costs increases in the coming years. However, the heterogeneity of the *things* that can be connected in such environments makes interoperability among them a challenging problem. Moreover, the observations produced by these things are made available with various vocabularies and data formats. This heterogeneity prevents generic solutions from being adopted on a global scale and makes difficult to share and reuse data for other purposes than those for which they were initially set up. In this book chapter, we provide an overview of the different solutions from both technical and semantic perspectives that have been used recently to tackle the interoperability issue in such IoT environments and especially in healthcare domain. We also present an overview of semantic middleware solutions that have combined the technical and semantic techniques for a complete interoperable solution.

Keywords: Semantic architecture · Ontology · Middleware
Internet of Things

1 Introduction

With the evolution of smart connected devices in the last decades, the world keeps asking "How smart will the Internet of Things be?". We all know that sensors are already embedded in all sorts of objects, machines, and things and that many of those sensors are communicating with other machines over the Internet. IoT is a reality today, and its power on improving the quality of life and business is quite remarkable. In this context, building IoT-based healthcare applications provides the possibility to improve people lives. However, IoT in

This chapter is an extended version of Chap. 2 of Rita Zgheib's Ph.D.

I. Ganchev et al. (Eds.): Enhanced Living Environments, LNCS 11369, pp. 263–294, 2019.
https://doi.org/10.1007/978-3-030-10752-9_11

healthcare domain presents several challenges related to the fact that almost every week a significant vendor announces a new IoT strategy or division. The proliferation of ad-hoc and specific healthcare products, sensors and applications pose significant challenges about the complexity of designing and managing such systems, to the heterogeneity of the generated data, to the scalability, and the flexibility of the system to support the integration of highly distributed and heterogeneous data and knowledge sources.

In the research area, several Middleware architectures have been proposed in order to manage IoT system components and mediate between sensors and IoT applications. From the other side and beyond traditional management of sensors, some projects have addressed interoperability and scalability challenges in IoT from a semantic perspective. In this trend, ontologies [101] for describing sensors data and metadata as well as describing domain description, have been widely used and found as a reliable technique due to its significant efficiency in ensuring interoperability and clarification of knowledge structure. Middleware and ontologies have mostly been proposed individually. However, IoT environments are evolving rapidly, and the needs for a complete semantic middleware architecture is becoming an essential requirement in IoT environments. Especially in healthcare where the technical with the semantic interoperability promote the reduction of the number of sensors in the person's environment and the development of smarter applications by exchanging analyzed and processed data between all components.

Recently, some projects have tried to combine middleware solutions with semantic techniques in order to have a complete interoperable IoT architecture. Few developers and researchers rely on this combination due to the complexity of designing and integrating their concepts. Our objective is to promote research in combining semantic and middleware solutions while most researches focus on advancing one topic. For that aim, we provide in this chapter an overview of several middleware approaches in Sect. 2. Then, we outline in Sect. 3 the ontologies used to describe sensors and the domain knowledge in IoT. In Sect. 4, we study projects that have combined both approaches in their proposals, we show their characteristics and their advantage regarding traditional architectures for IoT management. Finally, we present the ongoing challenges in providing the most relevant semantic middleware for IoT healthcare applications.

2 Middleware Architectures for IoT Systems

Middleware [11] solutions provide a technical infrastructure that mediates between two or more systems. Their historical role is to ensure the transport of a message from one subsystem to another with a more or less important level of coupling. Researchers find middleware as a suitable solution to fill the gap of heterogeneity and manageability of sensors because it provides an abstract layer positioned between the network layer and the application layer as it is shown in Fig. 1. Moreover, It aims to hide the technological details of communication technologies to enable the application developers to focus on the development of the IoT applications.

2.1 Middleware Challenges

Several middleware architectures have been proposed in the literature trying to address the infrastructure challenges and the applications challenges in IoT. They are regarded as essential problems to be solved before presenting an approach as a final solution.

The infrastructure challenges refer to (1) the **interoperability** issue as heterogeneous devices will communicate and exchange information together; (2) the **scalability** issue since a large number of devices are expected to be supported by IoT application; (3) the **spontaneous interactions** of objects and devices; (4) the **diversity of infrastructure** since IoT devices have a specific infrastructure (mobile, wirelessly connected, etc.), and resource constrained which gives the IoT network a **dynamic behavior**; and (5) the need for **abstraction** at many levels such as the physical layer, interfaces, data stream, and development process.

The application challenges consist of guaranteeing (1) the **availability** of services and information at all time; (2) a high level of system **reliability** that should remain operational even in the presence of failures; (3) a **real-time** information delivery especially for critical domain such as healthcare; (4) and finally the **security and privacy** as much information is shared between IoT components. This information can be private and even personal such as with information about daily life.

The common goal of all these middleware development initiatives is to develop a framework which can enable an adaptation layer in a plug-n-play mode. Despite that, each middleware architecture [94] focuses on some of the challenges cited before and takes into account some application's requirements which differ from each other's regards to IoT domains they target. In light of the presented challenges, we provide an overview of these approaches emphasizing their characteristics.

2.2 Overview of Middleware Approaches for IoT

Several studies on middleware approaches for IoT have been proposed like the classifications presented in [92,93]. A specific study is presented by Razzaque et al. in [94]. In this paper, authors have analyzed in depth several existing solutions and have presented a recent overview of the different kinds of middleware architecture. Thanks to this study, we have identified the different types of middleware (see Fig. 1) for intelligent environments that have been classified as follows: Application-specific, Agent-based, VM-based, tuple-spaces, database-oriented, Service-oriented architecture and Message-oriented Middleware.

Application-Specific: This approach is based on the needs of a specific application and focuses on resource management. Thus, a strong coupling exists between application and data providers which leads to specialized middleware.

MidFusion [8] represents an example of this middleware approach. It discovers and selects the best set of sensors or sensor agents on behalf of applications.

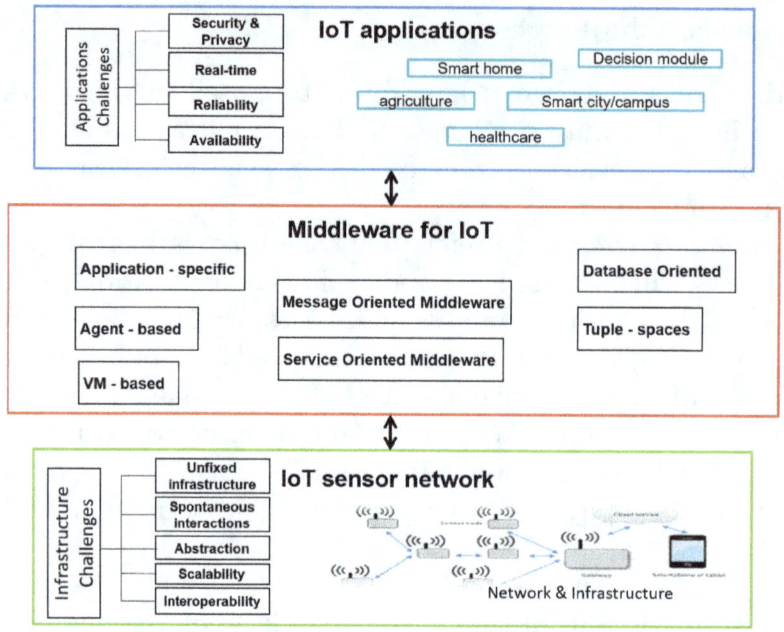

Fig. 1. The Relationship between IoT Data sources and IoT applications via the middleware mediator

It provides a sensor selection algorithm to select the best set of sensors using the principles of Bayesian and Decision theories. Its limitation is that it provides a (Quality of Service (QoS) support only for networks based on Bayesian algorithms. Other middleware in the same category can be found in [60] which focuses on applications in smart homes. It uses application-specific functions to choose a specific context. Given multiple alternatives, one alternative at any time provides the context for all applications, whilst maximizing the applications total satisfaction with the quality of context from the chosen provider. In [55], authors propose MiLAN, a middleware based on tight coupling between the components. It allows applications to specify a policy for managing network and sensors. They argued that the needs of the application should be integrated with the management of the network into a single unified middleware system.

This kind of architecture does not satisfy all IoT middleware requirements due to its tight coupling nature between applications and data providers. It does not address the heterogeneity characteristic of the IoT environment.

Agent-Based: Agent or modular based approach [73] consists in applications division into modular programs to promote distribution and injection through the network using mobile agents. Impala [71], Smarty messages [66] and Agilla [46] are examples of this approach. They can be highlighted by providing decentralized systems capable of tackling the availability, reliability, and resource management requirements of middleware. This approach can reduce the complexity of a middleware architecture. However, it presents some limitations related to its inability to perform code management tasks and the unpredictability of agents in the system at runtime.

VM-Based: This approach is flexible and contains virtual machines (VMs), interpreters, and mobile agents. The middleware is then composed of two layers. Each physical device is deployed as a VM in the first layer of the middleware. In the second layer, a general VM interprets the modules and delivers data to the application that expresses its needs with a query. This approach addresses architectural requirements such as high-level programming abstractions, self-management, and adaptivity while supporting transparency in distributed heterogeneous IoT infrastructures [58,74]. However, this approach suffers from the overhead that the exchanged instructions introduce.

Tuple-Spaces: A tuple space [82] is a data repository that can be accessed concurrently. Each device from the physical layer is represented as a tuple-space in the middleware. All tuple-spaces form a federated tuple space on the gateway. This approach suits mobile devices in an IoT infrastructure as they can transiently share data within gateway connectivity constraints. TinyLime [34] and TeenyLIME [33] are tuple-space middleware solutions for mobile ad hoc networks and sensor networks. Although they have a flexible architecture that allows middleware to be used in different environments, they address frequent disconnections and asynchronous communications problems. However, they offer limitations in resource management, scalability, security, and privacy.

Database-Oriented: This middleware approach considers the whole sensor network as a distributed and virtual database. It uses SQL like queries to collect data over the network. GSN [4] is a database-oriented middleware that has been integrated into other projects such as OpenIoT [68]. While this approach offers good programming abstraction and proper data management support, the remaining IoT requirements are not necessarily addressed like scalability, real-time and spontaneous interactions. Moreover, its centralized nature makes it difficult to handle dynamic and heterogeneity characteristics of the IoT network.

The architectures as mentioned above have been used in many specific IoT projects and research area. However, the important use of Service Oriented Architecture (SOA) and Message Oriented Middleware (MoM) solutions is remarkable in IoT projects in the past decade.

Service-Oriented Architecture (SOA): Two major trends in the world of IoT have been witnessed in the past years [49]. First, the hardware is becoming smaller, cheaper and more powerful. Second, the software industry is moving towards service-oriented integration technologies. Service-Oriented Architecture (SOA) is a way of thinking and designing the Information System and has been traditionally used in corporate IT systems. The key concept of SOA is the service which is a distributed software invocable that can that can be quickly modified or redeployed in new contexts, allowing applications to respond to changing consumer needs quickly. In IoT approaches based on SOA, intelligent sensors are depicted as services for consumer applications. The key point with these services is their encapsulated nature (i.e., the service interface is independent of the implementation). Service providers describe their services (sensors characteristics) and expose them to consumers. Web Services Description Language (WSDL) is the standard used for such a description [38].

A state of the art of SOA-based middleware solutions for wireless sensor network can be found in [81]. It refers to *SStreaMWare*, *USEME*, *SensorWeb 2.0*, *OASiS*, *B-VIS*, *MiSense*, *SOMDM (SI)*, *SOA-MM* as middleware proposals for wireless sensor networks. Their main features are supporting real-time monitoring, management of heterogeneous devices, data collection and filtering. However, the survey demonstrates that none of these solutions covers all the requirements of the management of sensors network in intelligent environments.

More recent approaches have tried to enhance the SOA features and adapted it to IoT. For example, SenseWrap [45] provides a standardized communication interface to hide the sensor-specific details from applications. It introduces the concept of the virtual sensor to offer transparent discovery of sensors. However, virtualization is applied only to sensors and not to actuators or computing resources which makes it not fully suitable for IoT environments. TinySOA [10] uses simple and deterministic mechanisms for WSN resource (e.g., sensor nodes) registration and discovery. It supports only a few basic functional requirements (e.g., abstraction, resource discovery, and management). SensorsMW [9] has been found as an adaptable and flexible middleware for sensors management. It allows easy and efficient configuration of wireless sensor networks for information gathering. However, the reconfiguration may fail in critical applications as they define strict QoS rules. MOSDEN [87] supports sensing as a service model built on top of GSN. It is based on a plugin architecture which improves the scalability and user-friendliness. However, the predefined resource/service discovery and service composition mechanisms features presented in this approach may be challenging in a dynamic IoT environment.

Message Oriented Middleware (MoM): A Message Oriented Middleware has been used for a long time in network communications especially in industrial networks such as integrated manufacturing systems [13,36]. It offers an event-based architecture and a publish/subscribe communication model. In event-based architecture, components, applications, and all other participants interact through events. Events are propagated from the sending application components to the receiving application components following the publish/subscribe paradigm. The publish/subscribe model is an interaction model that consists both of publishers and subscribers. Data sources (publishers) and destinations (subscribers) are decoupled from each other and data objects (messages) are filtered and delivered to destinations based on predefined topics expressed as subscriptions thanks to a dedicated component called the message broker as depicted in Fig. 2. The broker can be seen as a mediator responsible for the management of the distribution of messages to serve the right information to the right consumer. The strength of this middleware mainly lies in its support for asynchronous communication allowing a loose coupling between the sender and the receiver.

Since the apparition of the Internet of Things, the publish/subscribe mechanism has been put into the light for its effectiveness in offering loose coupling.

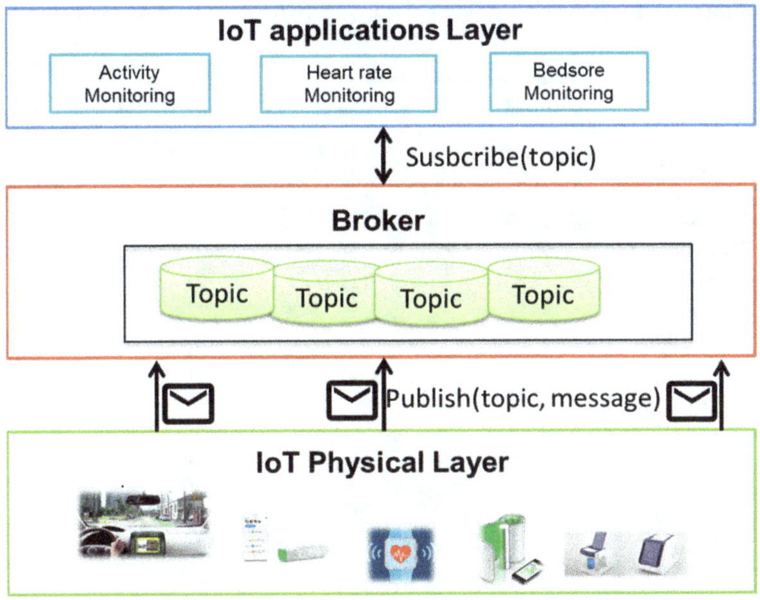

Fig. 2. General design model for an event-based middleware.

Compared to the SOA architecture which is also widely proposed for IoT solutions, a MOM follows a message-based distribution model focusing on the information. It differs from the classical client/server paradigm in that neither the source nor the destination of the message has to be known from each other before communication.

Few IoT projects have proposed publish/subscribe solutions in the literature. For instance, CenceMe project [78] aims to automatically infer people's activity (e.g. dancing in the party) based on a sensor-enabled smartphone in order to share this activity through social media like Facebook. Another example supporting easy access to sensor data on mobile phones is Pogo [21], a publish/subscribe middleware infrastructure for mobile phone sensing. It uses simple topic-based subscriptions to manage access to sensor data and reports significant energy gains due to topic-based filtering of sensed data on mobile devices.

On the other hand, a number of Cloud-based services dedicated to storing sensor-based data are nowadays available. Few examples that could be mentioned are Xively [3], ThingSpeak [2] and iDigi [1] which support connections using MQTT (Message Queuing Telemetry Transport) protocol. They represent a scalable infrastructure that enables users to build IoT products and services and to store, share and discover real-time sensor. To sum up, a comparative table is presented in Table 1. In the following section, we outline middleware solutions developed in the healthcare context.

2.3 Middleware Solutions in Healthcare

Healthcare is an active research topic in IoT where applications can be classified into Medical applications and Ambient Assisted Living (AAL) applications.

Table 1. Comparative table of Middleware approaches

IoT challenges		Middleware approaches						
		Application-specific	Agent-based	VM-based	Tuples-spaces	Database-oriented	SOA	MoM
Infrastructure challenges	Technical interoperability		X	X			X	X
	Scalability							X
	Spontaneous interactions			X	X			X
	Unfixed infrastructure		X	X	X		X	X
	Abstraction	X	X	X	X	X	X	X
Application challenges	Availability	X	X	X	X	X	X	X
	Reliability		X	X		X	X	X
	Real-time						X	X
	Privacy & security							

Medical applications are mainly installed at hospitals and retirement homes to prevent, detect diseases or even monitor patients health condition. AAL applications are mainly installed at a patient's home to monitor and follow his/her health and activity at home. In this context, middleware solutions have been proposed to fulfill the requirement of IoT and healthcare domains.

- **Middleware for Medical applications:** In this strand we find the *Sphere* project [120] that follows a clustered-sensor approach. It aims to build a generic platform that fuses corresponding sensor data to generate rich datasets that support the detection and management of various health conditions. LinkSmart [85] within the REACTION European project is another SOA-based middleware with the aim of monitoring and managing the diabetes of patients as well as their therapy in operational healthcare environments. It has also been used recently for a smart home application [107]. A middleware for bedsore detection can be found in [86] where authors defined a SOA architecture for bedsores detection and sleep monitoring. The main contribution of this work is about collecting information from wireless and wearable sensors. Other monitoring system proposal can be found in [77] where body sensors are connected to a smartphone via Bluetooth to get information like heart rate and body temperature. MyHealthAssistant [103] is an Event-driven Middleware for Multiple Medical Applications. Its objective is to merge information from several wireless sensors on a Smartphone-mediated Body Sensor Network.
  Uranus [31] is a SOA-based middleware architecture for dependable AAL and vital signs monitoring applications. It provides a rapid-prototype for monitoring the level of oxygen in the blood of a chronically ill patient. It also describes another prototype for monitoring patients in the context of a smart hospital. MyHealthAssistant [103] presents an event-driven middleware targeted for medical applications on a smartphone to enable flexible coupling

with changing sets of wireless sensor units. Waluyo et al. [114] propose a middleware for medical Body sensor network that supports multiple sensors and applications, plug and play features, and resource management. In that project, however, parts of the middleware and the applications are hosted on a single PC.

- **Middleware for AAL applications:** SM4ALL [115] has been developed and build on top of the OSGi/UPnP standards for building smart homes in the context of European Framework 7 project and Smart Homes for All (SM4ALL) project. It targets Ambient Assisted Living (AAL) environments to monitor disabled elders. VIRTUS [12] is an event-driven middleware based on the standard XMPP (eXtensible Messaging and Presence Protocol). It guarantees a (near) real-time, secure and reliable communication channel among heterogeneous devices. In [43, 54], the authors present a platform based on cloud computing to manage mobile and wearable healthcare sensors that demonstrates that the IoT paradigm can be applied to pervasive healthcare. In [30], a SOA based solution offering a distributed telemonitoring system that aims at improving healthcare and assistance for dependent people in their homes. In [110], authors present a pervasive health system integrating patient monitoring, status logging, and social sharing enabling self-management of chronic patients in their environment. Junnila et al. propose in [64] in-Home health monitoring platform with a *common sensor interface* architecture that supports a large number of Zigbee sensors. The platform is tested with two health related case studies: one with an senior woman living in sheltered housing and the other with a hip-surgery patient during his rehabilitation phase.

2.4 Discussion

Middleware proposals based on Application-specific, Agent-based, VM-based, tuple-spaces and database-oriented, have tried to tackle the requirements of manageability and heterogeneity of IoT environments. These approaches have been used in specific IoT applications, and their limitations stated in each case make them not so popular in this environment. Moreover, it is clear that the most used approach in the IoT world is SOA-based architecture, in particular, most healthcare solutions rely on SOA-based middleware. However, we recognized that even if SOA presents a good solution for IoT healthcare applications, it can not meet all IoT requirements especially related to heterogeneity, scalability, real-time processing and flexibility. From the other side, we recognized that although a few recent studies have considered the MoM approach, it has been recognized as a flexible and suitable communication model in IoT. Based on the before mentioned middleware solutions, a comparison between SOA and MoM shows that:

- In regards to SOA architecture, MoM follows a message-based model focusing on the information itself and supports sending and receiving of messages between distributed systems. While in the SOA approach, data providers and data consumers agree on a service contract before data flow sharing as it is evident in Fig. 3, this approach makes the communication not completely decoupled between system components.

- Despite its historical role in sensors management and its potential benefits in IoT middleware solutions, SOA-based solutions focusing on services provided by the system do not scale well in ultra large and dynamic IoT environments. While on the other side, publish-subscribe approaches are gaining more momentum due to their ability to promote scalable, flexible and fully decoupled communication in intelligent environments. As a result, we believe that a MoM with the publish/subscribe paradigm is the most suitable middleware solution for IoT healthcare applications.

To sum up, middleware solutions have been found to address technical interoperability issues and communication requirements in an IoT environment. However, the heterogeneity of connected devices and the variety of data sent over the network introduce the requirement of providing a unified and coherent manner of representing data among system components. Moreover, in healthcare, it is necessary to take into account the patient comfort by reducing the number of sensor around him. This can be done by improving data sharing between IoT application. Although the benefits of middleware solutions in virtualizing the technological details and infrastructure, providing a semantic description would enhance the interoperability and provide a full abstraction of the technical level. In the following section, we present how semantic technologies have been integrated into IoT.

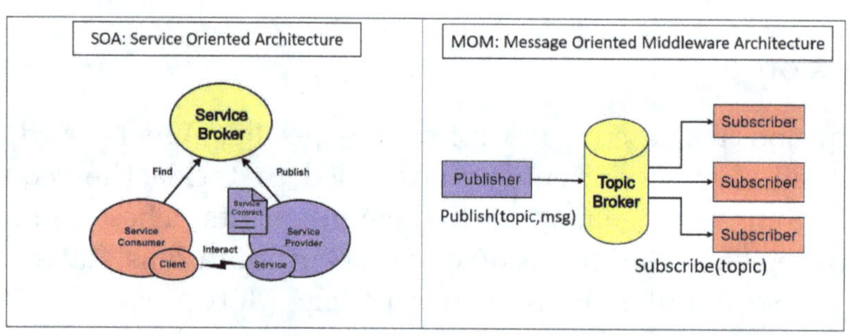

Fig. 3. Service Oriented Architecture vs Message Oriented Middleware Architecture

3 Semantic Description in IoT

Different data providers send sensor data in IoT environments and received by many data consumers. Querying sensors and information sharing present a challenge for IoT applications due to the massive number of heterogeneous sensors with specific characteristics. To address this issue, research initiatives and standardization activities have mainly focused on modeling sensors observations and on sending the semantic observations over the network. In [35], different data models have been presented as a coherent and reliable way to share information across an IoT system: XML, Web Service Definition Language (WSDL), JavaScript Object Notation (JSON), Resource Description Framework (RDF) and Web Ontology Language (OWL). RDF and its new version, the OWL format, has become the most used technique for sensor data description due to their ability to ease both reasoning over sensor data and semantic interoperability among devices [51,109].

The Web Ontology Language (OWL) built upon a W3C XML standard is a Semantic Web language designed to represent rich and complex knowledge about things, groups of things, and relations between things. It can easily be integrated with many programming languages like Java through APIs (Jena or OWL-API). Ontologies in IoT have an essential role in representing sensors networks (physical aspect and infrastructure) and also in describing complex domain knowledge and concepts. Furthermore, the main advantage of using ontologies is the possibility to generate OWL representations which provide the opportunity to exchange formal messages at the technical layer in OWL format. Describing data in a formal language such as OWL guarantees the reliability of information and improves the interoperability of the system. Finally, it fills the need to fuse heterogeneous sensor data and potentially inaccurate data. In this section, we present an overview of the several ontologies used to describe sensors in IoT, and we also outline ontologies that describe the healthcare domain.

3.1 Sensors Modeling and Description

Sensors description has been proposed from one hand to promote reusability and integration of sensors and from the other hand to help to solve the difficulties of installing, querying [7] and maintaining complex, heterogeneous sensor networks. In this field, XML schema has been used for sensors description such as in sensor model language (SensorML) [18] that provides metadata model to describe sensor capabilities and measurement process. They are also used by SOA-based middleware solutions to describe sensors characteristics as a service contract to data consumers. Also, ontologies [101] for sensors description have been widely used as a reliable technique due to their efficiency in ensuring both interoperability and clarification of knowledge structure.

The main advantage of ontologies is their ability to describe three perspectives of a sensor [5]. First, it describes sensors metadata, sensor type, components, configuration, process, and properties. Second, it allows to describe what a sensor can measure after a stimulus is detected or to describe the observation of the sensor in term of frequency, accuracy and measurement capabilities. Third, it provides the concepts to describe data stream and the observation result, allowing semantic reasoning, generating new knowledge and detecting inconsistency in IoT environments.

Key standardization efforts that have sought to establish sensor data models for sensors to be accessible and controllable via the Web include the OGC Sensor Web Enablement (SWE). The SWE efforts established by the Open Geospatial

Consortium include the following essential specifications: Observation & Measurement (O&M), Sensor Model Language (SensorML) and Sensor Observation Service (SOS) [19]. The O&M and SensorML contain standard model and XML schema for observations/measurements and sensors/processes respectively. The SOS is a standard service model, which provides a mechanism for querying observation and sensor metadata. Based on these standards, several ontology approaches have been developed to describe sensors. Compton et al. [29] and Bendadouche et al. [15] have surveyed the different attempts aiming at establishing a sensor ontology covering the description of all sensor topics.

In 2008, four potential ontologies have been proposed CESN, SWAMO, A3ME, and ISTAR. The Coastal Environmental Sensing Networks (CESN) [22] project for sensor networks for coastal observing has built an ontology to describe relationships between sensors and their measurements. It also provides logic programming rules reasoner to validate sensor observation and to test anomalous sensor observation by a decision maker. SWAMO [116] describes physical devices and process models and tasks in distributed and intelligent software agents environment. Also, A3ME ontology [57] was developed to classify devices and their capabilities in a heterogeneous network. The ISTAR [47] ontology was developed as part of a system to automatically select sensors for tasks based on their fitness for the task description.

In 2009, OOSTETHYS [16], MMI [100] and CSIRO [84] ontologies were proposed. The OOSTETHYS ontology has been designed to describe sensors and get observation and capabilities for oceanographic observing. Likewise, The Marine Metadata Interoperability (MMI) Device Ontologies Working Group has developed the MMI ontology of oceanographic devices, sensors and samplers. The CSIRO ontology is a generic ontology for describing sensors and deployments. It is intended to be used in data integration, searches, and classification features. It can express complex compositions and finds details of the function and results of sensors and processes. The ontology can also encode much of the information in SensorML documents.

Ontologies developed until 2009 are either specific to a domain (oceanographic, ecology, etc.) or discontinued. Therefore these efforts did not lead to a mature and general solution applied for ongoing projects. None of the ontologies can express all the properties required for a full description of sensors, and a standard is still not available until 2011.

In 2011, the W3C organism proposed SSN, the Semantic Sensor Network Ontology [28]. It has been initiated by the CSIRO, Wright State University, and the OGC as a forum for the development of an OWL ontology for sensors and to further investigate annotation of existing concepts, and links to existing standards. SSN has been designed as a generic ontology which has become one of the most popular and efficient ontology to describe sensors and observations. It has been conceived as a domain-independent ontology where extensions can be made to add domain-specific knowledge.

Extensions of SSN have been developed in the last years by adding concepts related to time, space, communication and concepts related to domain characteristics. We review in this section a broad range of these solutions considering that the presented ontologies are just a small example of existing ontologies that are built on top of SSN. It helps to show the impact of SSN on the semantic description of sensors over the years.

BFO [61] is a spatio-temporal extension that make a distinction between describing identities that happen at a finite time and events like storm and routing. It is a hierarchical system approach where sensors collect data from the real world and send it to clusterhead-node.

In Bandadouche et al. in [15], authors present the limitation of SSN in describing the communication process of a wireless sensor network. They propose a new ontology design pattern Stimulus-WSNnode-Communication, an extension of SSN, that addresses the communication limitation by integrating new concepts that describe the communication process of a wireless sensor network. Another extension for SSN based on fuzzy logic is proposed in [14] to support fault tolerance and for large-scale Wireless Sensor Network. It is a service-oriented approach to build diagnosis and test services for wireless sensors.

Authors in [96] present another SSN extension ontology for WSN, and it is presented as an alignment of many ontologies SSN, SWRLTO, TAO, and DOLCE. This solution aims to improve time descriptions limitation in SSN by representing temporal abstraction to analyze data in real time. SSN is used for sensors measurements; SWRLTO is used for temporal modeling and reasoning; and TAO designed by the authors of this paper to capture the semantic TA (Temporal Abstractions). This framework uses temporal reasoning to search and classify temporal patterns that help to infer the processed data. For the alignment of the three ontologies, the authors use DOLCE, a known upper ontology.

Recently, in [104], authors have analyzed general IoT ontologies: SSN, Smart Appliance REFerence (SAREF)[1], IoT-ontology[2], IoT-lite[3], Spitfire[4], IoT-S[5], SA[6] and the oneM2M ontology[7]. They did not consider specific domains impacted by IoT (domotics, agriculture, smart cities...) but they studied ontologies that they found on the web. Based on their comparative study, none of the presented ontologies can describe actuators. Actuators are devices that transform an input signal into a physical output, making them the exact opposite of sensors. They have proposed the IoT-O ontology in order to describe actuators, services and energy consumption.

In October 2017, the last version of SSN ontology was recommended by the World Wide Web Consortium (W3C). The main innovation of this version of SSN has been the introduction of the Sensor, Observation, Sample, and Actuator (SOSA) ontology, which provides a lightweight core for SSN. SOSA aims

[1] http://sites.google.com/site/smartappliancesproject/ontologies.
[2] http://ai-group.ds.unipi.gr/kotis/ontologies/IoT-ontology.
[3] http://iot.ee.surrey.ac.uk/fiware/ontologies/iot-lite.
[4] http://sensormeasurement.appspot.com/ont/sensor/spitfire.owl.
[5] http://personal.ee.surrey.ac.uk/Personal/P.Barnaghi/ontology/OWL-IoT-S.owl.
[6] http://sensormeasurement.appspot.com/ont/sensor/hachemonto.owl.
[7] http://www.onem2m.org/ontology/BaseOntology/.

at broadening the target audience and application areas that can make use of Semantic Web ontologies. With the new version of SSN, actuators and virtual sensors can be easily described which was not possible with the last version.

SSN is commonly used by many projects and is still the most appropriate ontology that can describe an IoT sensor system. Describing physical sensors with SSN promotes the reusability of sensors and makes IoT systems sustainable. Furthermore, the new SOSA ontology integrated with SSN allows having a complete description of physical and virtual sensors that can be deployed in an IoT environment. We recognize virtual sensors as any application that generates information that can not be gathered from the physical world. For example, an application that uses a motion sensor in a living room data and outputs the presence of the person can be seen as a virtual sensor in the IoT world (Fig. 4).

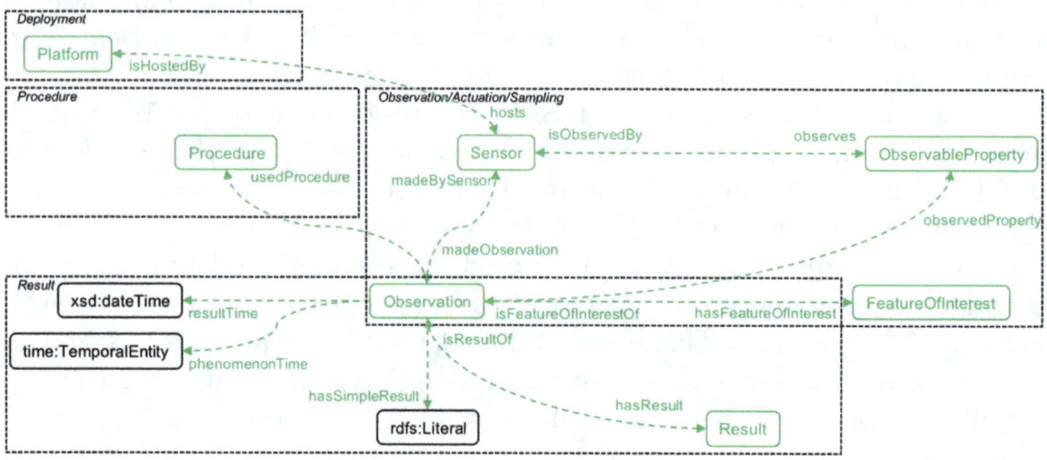

Fig. 4. Overview of the SOSA ODP

3.2 Ontologies for Healthcare Description

Domain-specific IoT applications are becoming increasingly popular and, domain knowledge description is gaining even more popularity. Domain knowledge is already defined in more than 200 ontologies and sensor-based projects [52]. These ontologies provide expert knowledge description as well as the conceptualization of the different domains like transportation or diseases. Specifically, domain applications use ontologies and semantic description as a way to define types, properties, and interrelationships of the entities that exist for a specific domain.

As an example, authors in [56] have proposed an ontology to define logistic terminologies. It is intended to assist a logistics expert in identifying and precisely specifying the logistic problem for solving a passenger train optimization problem. In the same context, in [44], an ontology is proposed for monitoring and improving public transportation. Another example of ontologies domain is related to energy concepts as presented in [102] where authors created ontologies to describe energy sources: wind power, biomass, and fossil fuels. Further domains have relied on ontologies to describe concepts and relations that constitute their particular fields. In agriculture, we distinguish AgroPortal ontology for agriculture and nutrition data [63].

In healthcare, many ontologies have been developed to describe both medical and AAL applications.

- **Ontologies for Medical applications:** the **Disease Ontology** (DO) [67] represents human diseases for linking biomedical knowledge through disease data. Also, the well known **SNOMED-CT** [42] represents an advanced terminology and coding system for eHealth. In the same context, authors in [70] proposed an ontology to describe the **patients vital signs**. The ontology aims to create a profile for each patient containing the several medical control information. Moreover, authors in [23] present an example of **food ontology** for diabetes control. The **HL7** Security and Privacy Ontology is another example that serves to name, define, formally describe, and interrelate key concepts within the scope of Healthcare Information Technology. Kim et al. [69] proposed an Ontology-driven Interactive Healthcare with Wearable Sensors **(OdIH_WS)** to achieve customized healthcare service. It aims to acquire context information at real-time using ontological methods by integrating external data such as a meteorological website in order to prevent disease. **ContoExam** [20] is an ontology developed to address the interoperability problem of sensor networks in the context of e-health domain applications. It contains specific expressions and specifications for medical use as examination vocabulary and expressions.
- **Ontologies for AAL applications:** In this context, Activities for Daily Living (ADL) is a contemporary topic. Researchers are working in improving the quality of life of elderly at home by providing monitoring systems. In this strand, Ontologies-based solutions have been proposed to describe human activities and behavior like in [76]. These ontologies propose a description of a set of actions and activities of daily life where the activity is inferred from several actions [26,27]. For example, going to the kitchen, taking a cup, and adding water are single actions and drinking is an activity. The CoDAMoS [37] ontology focuses on modeling roles, hardware, and software services around four main core entities: user, environment, platform, and service. A more in-depth survey of ontologies for human behavior representation can be found in [98].

  Other researchers have illustrated the limitations of ontology-based solutions in describing uncertainty. For instance, Authors in [41,97] rely on fuzzy concepts to describe real-world context and uncertainty in activities where several solutions can be deduced based on the same sensors data. In the same context, an ontology for gym addict and lifestyle profiling is presented in [40].

  From the other side, there is a set of ontologies that try to tack the concurrent activities. For example, the Knowledge-driven approach for Concurrent Activity Recognition (KCAR) [118] consists on segmentation of sensors data into fragments, each of which corresponds to one ongoing activity.

With respect to other solutions, knowledge-based methods are semantically clear in modeling and representation and highly effective in inference and reasoning. They create a completely accurate model of ADL [95] that enhances the semantic interoperability of an IoT system without a prior learning phase. However, there are still some issues and challenges to tackle in this field such as defining an ontology that take into account the description of actions, activities with uncertainty, concurrent and overlapping activities that have been identified in [59].

3.3 Discussion

In this section, we have discussed the several perspectives of using the semantic description in IoT. We have found that ontologies are the most common semantic technology that describes the three main concepts: sensors, data, and domain.

A well designed ontology enhances IoT environments and architectures by ensuring some features like abstraction, scalability, integration, smart reasoning and interoperability as summarized in Fig. 5. Moreover, an IoT ontology model relies on several design principles: it should be modular to facilitate its evolution, extension and integration with external ontologies; and it should be lightweight to be widely adopted and reusable. Furthermore, an ontology should be a complete reflection of a full description of an IoT environment which reduces the need to import other ontologies. The compatibility principle is related to the needs to be consistent with existing ontologies.

We have shown that SSN is a suitable ontology for sensors description in IoT and is able to generate data in RDF/OWL format. Presenting data in a formal way using RDF/OWL enhances the interoperability and homogeneity of information between IoT systems. In the context of healthcare application, several ontologies have been proposed to describe diseases and activities of daily living. We also found that requirements and challenges are still ongoing in this field as it is an active and recent topic. Moreover, the alignment of sensors ontologies and domain ontologies could be a research aspect of improving.

As we discussed before, integrating middleware approaches with semantic technologies creates a suitable platform and environment for IoT applications. It provides manageability and technical and semantic interoperability in the overall system. For that, it was cumbersome to state the several projects that used these two paradigms.

4 Semantic Middleware Approaches

4.1 Overview on Existing Semantic Middleware Architectures

Existing approaches have considered semantic description in proposing a middleware architecture for IoT applications. SOA and MoM approaches are prominent IoT architectures where semantic enhancements have been added.

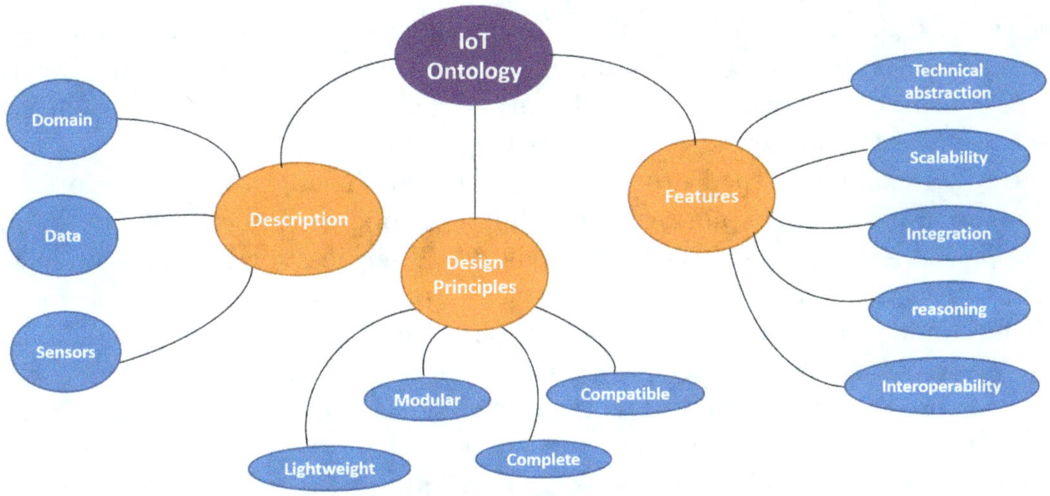

Fig. 5. Main characteristics of an IoT Ontology

Semantic SOA-Based Architecture: Authors in [106] propose an application layer solution for interoperability for IoT aiming to resolve the interoperability issue between different kinds of protocols (Bluetooth and UPnP). The key idea is to use device semantics provided by existing specifications and dynamically wrap them in their SOA middleware into semantic services.

SENSEI [111] is a SOA middleware for IoT. It includes a context model, context services, actuation tasks, and dynamic service composition of services. The main component of this middleware is the resource layer, which stands between the application layer and communication services layer. Resources in SENSEI use ontologies for their semantic modeling.

ubiSOAP [24] is a lightweight service oriented middleware that offers resource management and network level interoperability by supporting heterogeneous networking devices and technologies. Dynamic composition and instantiation of new services are facilitated by the semantically rich models and XML descriptions of sensors, actuators, and processing elements. The lack of context-awareness in ubiSOAP could be an issue, as this is key in the adaptive and autonomous behavior of the things.

SMArc [99] is an acronym for Semantic Middleware Architecture based on SOA. It focuses on smart city energy management for smart grid environments. A light ontology and a data representation under a specific format have been used in the implementation in order to guarantee that the interchanged data uses a representation format which will be common in the system, and therefore information will be easier to extract.

OM2M [6] is an advanced semantic middleware based on SOA architecture. It is a Machine-to-Machine service based on autonomic computing and semantic annotation to provide an inter-operable system to connect billions of devices, but they do not consider real-time analysis and full loosely coupled architecture. Authors proposed the IoT Ontology (IoT-O) [104] for the autonomic management of M2M systems. They extended SSN with four main modules: Acting module to describe actuators, Lifecycle module to model state machines, Service module to describe services and finally the Energy module to represent the power consumption for appliances. However, this ontology does not consider the description of virtual sensors and cognitive processing of information.

Another example is the European project OpenIoT [68] that has developed an open-source middleware platform providing a "cloud-of-things". OpenIoT aims to propose on-demand access to cloud-based IoT services for Internet-connected objects. Trying to use sensing as a service, OpenIoT architecture embeds the CUPUS middleware as a cloud-Based publish/subscribe processing engine and relies on SSN for sensors description. The observed data is stored as linked data and processed based on SPARQL queries which are continuously executed as data arrive. It can be viewed as a federation of several middleware projects interconnected with each other targeting applications for smart cities or campus and agriculture domain. OpenIoT could have been a good candidate to target IoT health applications, but its complexity due to the variety of middleware solutions under use can be a major drawback for the programmer.

The aforementioned middleware projects seek to tackle general IoT requirements without taking into account specific IoT application domains. They evaluated their proposals by deploying IoT sensors and testing the performance in some context however, they present their work as general and applicable to IoT applications. From the other side, Semantic middleware approaches have been proposed in a specific domain such as **healthcare**.

In this context LinkSmart and KASOM are SOA-based middleware for **medical applications**. LinkSmart is SOA middleware [108] developed for diabetes monitoring and therapy in the REACTION project. IT relies on a semantic model-driven architecture and enables the use of devices as services. The semantic description of devices is based on ontologies. KASOM [32] is a knowledge-Aware Service Oriented Middleware proposal for pervasive environments. Its architecture consists of offering services through registration, discovery, composition, and orchestration of services. Most of these services are established on complex reasoning mechanisms and protocols based on a contextual model, which represents a semantic description of low- and high-level resources of the WSN. Real-life implementations in hospital and health management show its potential in terms of response time, efficiency, and reliability. However, KASOM does not provide dynamic service composition in mobile and resource constrained IoT infrastructures because of predefined service composition rules provided by in-network agents.

From **AAL applications** perspective, openAAL [117] is an open source middleware for AAL applications, it relies on SOA architecture as a communication paradigm and on ontology description enabling service discovery. It defines a framework on top of the OSGi specification to facilitate integration and communication among services, including the context manager, procedural manager, and composer. CHOReOS [53] enables large scale choreographies or compositions of adaptable, QoS-aware, and heterogeneous services in IoT. It provides a scalable probabilistic thing-based service registration and discovery to address scalability, interoperability, mobility, and adaptability. It uses ontologies for semantic enrichment over the architecture. The semantic thing based service compositions are transparently and automatically executable with no involvement from end-users, which is highly desirable in IoT, especially in M2M communications.

Semantic MoM-Based Architecture: Semantic MoM-based proposals have not been widely discussed in the literature regarding SOA-based proposals. However, new solutions have considered MoM and semantic description in their research work. Namely, SITRUS, EnTimid and xAAL middleware proposals. Bispo et al. propose SITRUS (Semantic Infrastructure for Wireless Sensor Networks) in [17]. Beside a MOM communication model, authors rely on ontology as semantic description processing module whose purpose is to generate a semantic database that provides the basis to decide whether a WSN node needs to be reconfigured or not.

EnTimid and xAAL have been proposed for **AAL applications**. EnTimid [83] is a MOM middleware for smart home monitoring. It relies on a component model for sensors description but it does not address messages or domain description in this contribution. xAAL [72] is another example of MOM middleware, it has been designed in the context of the PRECIOUS[8] European project for AAL. Sensors schema model has been proposed in this work for sensors description and system components exchange Json messages between them.

4.2 Overview on Existing Semantic Middleware Platforms

The previously mentioned approaches have been presented in the literature as semantic middleware solutions. However, other middleware solutions have been introduced through IoT platforms. In [75,79,80] for instance, authors present a large review of 38 contemporary IoT platforms. They described each platform and classified them based on seven characteristics: support of heterogeneous devices, type of the platform, architecture's design, proprietary or open source, support of REST, data access control and service discovery.

As presented in Table 2, the second column shows if the platform supports heterogeneous devices or otherwise what kind of sensors it handles. We can see that most of the described projects support heterogeneous devices. Some solutions like Everyware needs a gateway to manage devices and there are solutions that support only one kind of sensors like Fosstrack that supports only RFID sensors.

We also deduce that in most cases, the platforms are provisioned from a cloud, either in the form of a Platform-as-a-Service (PaaS) or a Software-as-a-Service (SaaS). This type of platforms provides storage facilities, devices management, device connectivity, backup mechanisms or online support.

Table 2 also includes information about the openness of the platforms. Open-source platforms are considered more promising compared with the proprietary

[8] http://www.thepreciousproject.eu/.

Table 2. Comparative table (Recap) of IoT Platforms [80]

Platforms	Support of heterogeneous devices	Type	Architecture	Open source	REST	Data access control	Service discovery	**Data description**
AirVantage	Needs gateway	M2M PaaS	Cloud-based	Libraries only (Apache v2, MIT and Eclipse v1.0)	Yes	OAuth2	No	**n.a.**
Arkessa	Yes	M2M PaaS	Cloud-based	No	n.a.	Facebook like privacy settings	No	**n.a.**
ARM mbed	Embedded devices	M2M PaaS	Centralized/ Cloud-based	No	CoAP	User's choice	No	**n.a.**
Carriots	Yes	PaaS	Cloud-based	No	Yes	Secured access	No	**JSON, XML**
DeviceCloud	Yes	PaaS	Cloud-based	No	Yes	n.a.	No	**n.a.**
EveryAware	Yes	Server	Centralized	No	Yes	4 levels	No	**JSON, XML**
Everyware	Needs gateway	Paas	Cloud-based	No	Yes	n.a.	No	**JSON, XML**
EvryThng	Yes	M2M PaaS	Centralized	No	Yes	Fine-grained	No	**n.a.**
Exosite	Yes	Paas	Cloud-based	Libraries only (BSD license)	Yes	n.a.	No	**JSON**
Fosstrack	RFID	Server	Centralized	No	No	Locally stored	No	**n.a.**
GroveStreams	No	PaaS	Cloud-based	No	Yes	Role-based	No	**JSON**
Hub-of-All-Things H.A.T	Home devices	PaaS	Decentralized	Yes	Yes	Locally stored	Yes	**n.a.**
IoT-framework	Yes	Server	Centralized	Apache license 2.0	Yes	Locally stored	Yes	**n.a.**
IFTTT	Yes	SaaS	Centralized	No	No	No storage	Limited	**n.a.**
Kahvihub	Yes	Server	Centralized	Apache license 2.0	Yes	Locally stored	Yes	**n.a.**
LinkSmart	Embedded devices	P2P	Decentralized	LGPLv3	No	Locally stored	Yes	**ontologies to discover devices**
MyRobots	Robots	Robots PaaS	Cloud-based	No	Yes	2 levels	No	**JSON, XML**
Niagara	Yes	M2M SaaS	Distributed	No	n.a.	n.a.	n.a.	**n.a.**
Nimbits	Yes	Server	Centralized/ Cloud-based	Apache license 2.0	Yes	3 levels	No	**JSON**
NinjaPlatform	Needs gateway	PaaS	Cloud-based	Open source hard-ware and Operating System	Yes	OAuth2	No	**JSON**
Node-RED	Yes	Server	Centralized	Apache license 2.0	No	User-based privileges	No	**n.a.**
OpenIoT	Yes	Hub	Decentralized	LGPLv3	No	User-based privileges	Yes	**ontologies to discover devices**
OpenMTC	Yes	M2M client/server	Centralized/ Cloud-based	No	Yes	Secured access	No	**n.a.**
OpenRemote	Home devices	Server	Centralized	Affero GNU Public License	Yes	Locally stored	No	**n.a.**
Open.Sen.se	Ethernet enabled	PaaS / SaaS	Cloud-based	No	Yes	2 levels	Limited	**JSON**
realTime.io	Needs gateway	PaaS	Cloud-based	No	Yes	Secured access	No	**JSON**
SensorCloud	No	PaaS	Cloud-based	No	Yes	n.a.	No	**n.a.**
SkySpark	No	SaaS	Centralized/ Cloud-based	No	Yes	n.a.	No	**n.a.**
Swarm	Yes	PaaS	Cloud-based	Client is open source (unknown license)	Yes	n.a.	n.a.	**JSON**
TempoDB	No	PaaS	Cloud-based	No	Yes	Secured access	No	**n.a.**
TerraSwarm	Yes	OS	Decentralized	n.a.	n.a.	n.a.	Yes	**n.a.**
The thing system	Home devices	Server	Centralized	M.I.T.	Yes	User's choice	No	**n.a.**
Thing Broker	Yes	Server	Centralized	Yes	Yes	Locally stored	No	**n.a.**
ThingSpeak	Yes	Server	Centralized/ Cloud-based	GNU GPLv3	Yes	2 levels	Limited	**JSON, XML**
ThingSquare	Embedded devices	Mesh	Cloud-based	Gateway firmware is open source	Yes	No	No	**n.a.**
ThingWorx	Yes	M2M PaaS	Cloud-based	No	Yes	User-based privileges	Yes	**n.a.**
WoTkit	Yes	PaaS	Cloud-based	No	Yes	Secured access	Yes	**n.a.**
Xively	Yes	PaaS	Cloud-based	Libraries are open source (BSD 3-clause), platform is not	Yes	Secured access	Yes	**JSON, XML**

alternatives because they are expected to enable the faster integration of new IoT solutions across the application domains. Among the platforms presented in the table, only 11 are open-source.

Moreover, it may be deduced from the table that only a few platforms do not have a REST API. This demonstrates that the current IoT services will tend to adopt the web of things paradigm [89]. We also deduce that only a few platforms have integrated some type of service discovery mechanisms. A comprehensive survey on discovery protocols for M2M communications can be found in [113].

The presented solutions have not been studied from a semantic perspective. For that aim, we added the last column in the table to show if a platform integrates semantic description or not. We also present the semantic data format when the semantic description is applied. As it is depicted in the table, few platforms have integrated semantic descriptions in their solution. JSON and XML are predominant used formats in both open and proprietary platforms.

Besides the before mentioned platforms, there are some open source solutions that have been developed in the context of home automation and AAL environments. We have studied these solutions and classified them in Table 2 taking into consideration how the semantic description in each solution is addressed.

- AllJoyn Lambda [112] relies on Bus-D architecture and offers an open source framework for the management of IoT environments. It can be seen as a software solution integrating AllJoyn in the Lambda architecture used for Big Data storage and analytics. This proposal offers a graphical user interface (GUI) for devices discovery and management, secure data transport between communication technologies (Wi-Fi, Bluetooth, etc.), interoperability between different OS and notifications interface that sends/receives human readable messages. A simple smart home case study has been tested using this approach. It consists on turning on/off devices at home. Semantic descriptions have not been considered in this approach.
- Kaa[9] is a server-endpoints platform with the aim to create IoT applications including applications for healthcare, agriculture and smart city. It has been promoted as compatible virtually with any type of connected devices, sensors, and gateways. However, Kaa requires the integration of a specific microchip in the hardware of the IoT device which can be problematic for commercial sensors.
- Mango[10] is a modular web-application framework. The main functionalities offered by this proposal are data collection, real time data monitoring, high performance database, logic and automation, security, cross platform, graphic dashboard and internal performance monitoring. It is based on a list of middleware and on an application that is compiled into a single HTTP server object. The middleware and applications are written in a functional style, which keeps everything modular. Semantic description is not provided.

[9] https://www.kaaproject.org.

[10] https://github.com/paulbellamy/mango.

- Nimbits[11] is an open source PaaS that can be used for hardware and software applications. It can be downloaded on platforms like raspberry PI, Amazon EC2 and Google App Engine. This solution has many key features including geo and time-stamped data processing, event and alerts triggering and offer a build provided for Google App Engine and Linux Systems but it does not offer semantic features.
- OpenRemote [65] is a software integration platform for residential and commercial building automation with the ambition to overcome the challenges of integration between many different protocols and solutions available for home automation. It relies on cloud-based design tools to offer user interface design, installation management and configuration. An Internet connection is only required for communication to systems outside the own network, or during configuration. Complex IoT applications with decision module programming are not supported in this platform neither are semantic descriptions.
- servIoTicy API [88] is an IoT-as-a-Service Data Management Platform. It provides multi-provider data stream processing capabilities on the cloud, a REST API, data analytics, advanced queries and multi-protocol support in a combination of advanced data-centric technologies. This work is still in early stages.
- OpenIoT [68] is a generic and open source middleware platform funded by the European Union. It offers open access to a wide range of technologies for Internet-connected sensors and other objects exposed as services with the ability to support large-scale deployments. It offers a friendly user interface and allows to link together different IoT devices and semantic web services.

Commercial IoT platforms have been put into light by technology companies such as Amazon and Microsoft. We summarize some of the industrial IoT platforms in this section.

- Predix[12] is a PaaS and cloud-based IoT platform made for mainstream sectors like aviation. The main three components are *Predix Machine* responsible for collecting data from industrial assets and pushing it to the *Predix cloud* which is a global, secure cloud infrastructure. *Predix Services* are used by developers to build, test, and run industrial IoT applications.
- IBM Watson[13] for its part, employs speech and visual recognition, analyses the visual content of images and videos to understand their content.
- AWS from Amazon[14] and Azure IoT Suite[15] present successful IoT platforms in industrial domain. In addition to their private philosophy, industrial solutions do not consider semantic description in their proposals.

[11] https://www.nimbits.com/.
[12] https://www.ge.com/digital/predix/industries.
[13] https://www.ibm.com/watson/.
[14] https://aws.amazon.com/.
[15] https://azure.microsoft.com/en-us/suites/iot-suite/.

4.3 Discussion

To sum up, a comparative table is presented in Table 3 with respect to the different perspectives of semantic modeling in IoT: sensors, messages and domain. This table summarizes the open source semantic middleware solutions cited in this section with respect to the two middleware architectures SOA and MOM. Finally, we provide the application domain that each solution has been proposed for.

Table 3. Comparative table (Recap) of Semantic Middleware solutions for IoT

Middleware projects	Architecture type		Semantic description			Application
	SOA	MOM	Sensors	Messages	Domain	
Song et al.	X		X			Sensors as services
OpenAAL	X		X			IT services, Living Lab
Sensei	X		X			IoT applications
LinkSmart	X		X			Diabetes monitoring and therapy
SM4ALL	X		X			AAL (elderly, disabled people)
EnTimid		X				AAL, Home automation
ubiSOAP	X		X			Ubiquitous networking
KASOM	X		X			Ubiquitous environments
CHOReOS	X		X	X		AAL, Home automation
SMArc	X		X	X		Smart city, Smart grid
universAAL	X					AAL, Home automation
SOPRANO	X		X			AAL, Home automation
OM2M	X		X	X		IoT applications
xAAL		X	X	X		AAL, Home automation
XGSN (OpenIoT)	X		X	X		OpenIoT, Smart city, Agriculture
SITRUS		X	X	X		Automatic reconfiguration of WSN
AllJoyn	X		X			AAL, Home automation
Kaa	X		X			AAL (Elderly, Disabled people)
Mango	X		X			Diabetes monitoring and therapy
OpenRemote	X		X			AAL, Home automation
servIoTicy API		X	X	X		AAL, Home automation

As depicted in this table, semantic IoT middleware proposals have been integrated in different domain applications, namely in AAL and home automation, monitoring of elderly and disabled people, smart cities, agriculture, and monitoring of vital and health signs. It is noticeable the predominant choice of SOA architecture as a middleware solution. Moreover, when semantic approaches are proposed they are mainly integrated for semantic descriptions of sensors. But there is no full description including sensors, sensor data and domain.

Moreover, the semantic description in SOA architectures has been proposed in order to describe services which refer to sensors specifications in IoT systems. For example, XML schema has been proposed in SM4ALL [25] for sensors description and used as a contract for applications service description.

Other semantic description techniques can also be noticed like model driven architecture for devices description in [62] and Linksmart[16]. Lately, ontologies have gained sufficient importance for knowledge and sensors description as it is presented in SOPRANO [105], Sensei [91] OpenIoT, SMArc, UBIWARE and OM2M. Another important aspect of this comparison study is the lack of messages and domain description in these propositions, we can see that two ontology-based solutions OM2M and XGSN/OpenIoT have considered OWL format for exchanging messages.

From the other side, only a few attempts address the semantic topic in their proposals and most of these attempts rely on existing SOA-based solutions. So we end up with more semantic SOA-based then MOM-based architectures for IoT. But as previously mentioned, to provide a loose coupling and information centric solution, SOA-based solutions are not so relevant. Therefore, MOM in the past few years has been a topic of interest for IoT researcher and some semantic MOM solutions have been proposed. Entimid, XAAL and SITRUS are MOM-based middleware solutions that have addressed semantic representation in their solution. However, these solutions do not offer a full description model for IoT as it is shown in the table.

5 Conclusion and Ongoing Challenges

IoT has been gradually bringing changes in the healthcare domain. There is innumerable usefulness of IoT applications in enhancing the quality of life of elderly and in helping medical staff. Though IoT has abundant benefits, there are some challenges related to the heterogeneous components in an IoT system that should communicate and exchange data. In this book chapter we have presented several paradigms used to answer these challenges. Some projects have proposed to tackle the interoperability issue from a technological perspective by relying on middleware solutions that promote the interoperability and the manageability of sensors in an IoT system. From a semantic perspective, ontologies have been used to promote the semantic interoperability in IoT systems and to ensure the homogeneity of data formats. The coupling of both technologies has been found as a promising solution for IoT environments. Hence, semantic middleware architectures have been proposed as a complete IoT solution.

Although the existing semantic middleware proposals address many challenges and requirements regarding the interoperability in IoT systems, there are still some open research challenges related to the scalability and real-time reasoning. Using ontologies affects these two requirements as parsing, storing, inferencing and querying of/over OWL/RDF data as well as communicating such data take longer time than working with simple native data. Furthermore, ontologies present a high computational cost and require domain knowledge and expertise leading developers to avoid its use. Furthermore, the complexity related to the diversity of libraries to use and the complexity of the programming environment, make its use more complex. Providing simple software API usable in

[16] http://hydramiddleware.eu/news.php.

various application domains, to alleviate the tasks of software developers who decide to rely on semantic middleware architecture would be an open challenge to investigate. Another challenge that could be addressed in the research area is related to ontologies for sensors and domain description. As pointed out in most projects, these two aspects are described separately. Providing a complete ontology that is able to describe both domain and sensors in IoT is still a challenge to tackle. From the other side, using MoM approaches with semantic description in IoT is still in an early stage. Extensive researches in this context help invention of promising interoperable and scalable IoT architecture that adopt the Web of Things concepts as described in [119].

Web of Thing (WoT) [50] paradigm has been introduced as one of the major solutions for interoperability issue in IoT. It is an improvement of IoT allowing an easier way for IoT applications to build upon smart things. The WoT concept relies on the connectivity service of IoT and easy access to sensors in order to create applications exploiting the IoT data [48]. It can be seen as an evolution of the Internet of things where all components share their information and collaborate to generate advanced knowledge such as wisdom. Moreover, using semantic description allows data contextualization for optimized data stream discovery, indexing and querying. Moreover, new research projects are shifting to the semantic web of things [90] where data can be integrated with data and services available in other information systems. This flexibility eases the production of novel applications and services that are based on the state of the real world. It also supports autonomous semantic reasoning and decision making mechanisms to provide higher-level actionable knowledge from low-level sensor data [39]. Hence, performing semantic reasoning is linked to the ability to define a description model of sensors observations. The WoT is an open research topic to improve and investigate by testing in several IoT environments such as Healthcare.

References

1. iDigi device cloud. https://www.digi.com/
2. Internet of Things thingspeak service. https://thingspeak.com/
3. The pachube feed cloud service. https://www.xively.com/
4. Aberer, K., Hauswirth, M., Salehi, A.: A middleware for fast and flexible sensor network deployment. In: Proceedings of the 32nd International Conference on Very Large Data Bases, pp. 1199–1202. VLDB Endowment (2006)
5. Alam, S., Chowdhury, M.M., Noll, J.: SenaaS: an event-driven sensor virtualization approach for Internet of Things cloud. In: 2010 IEEE International Conference on Networked Embedded Systems for Enterprise Applications (NESEA), pp. 1–6. IEEE (2010)
6. Alaya, M.B., Banouar, Y., Monteil, T., Chassot, C., Drira, K.: OM2M: extensible ETSI-compliant M2M service platform with self-configuration capability. Procedia Comput. Sci. **32**, 1079–1086 (2014). https://doi.org/10.1016/j.procs.2014.05.536
7. Alaya, M.B., Medjiah, S., Monteil, T., Drira, K.: Towards semantic data interoperability in oneM2M standard. IEEE Commun. Mag. **53**(12), 35 (2015)

8. Alex, H., Kumar, M., Shirazi, B.: MidFusion: an adaptive middleware for information fusion in sensor network applications. Inf. Fusion **9**(3), 332–343 (2008)
9. Anastasi, G.F., Bini, E., Romano, A., Lipari, G.: A service-oriented architecture for QoS configuration and management of wireless sensor networks. In: 2010 IEEE Conference on Emerging Technologies and Factory Automation (ETFA), pp. 1–8. IEEE (2010)
10. Avilés-López, E., García-Macías, J.A.: TinySOA: a service-oriented architecture for wireless sensor networks. Serv. Oriented Comput. Appl. **3**(2), 99–108 (2009)
11. Bandyopadhyay, S., Sengupta, M., Maiti, S., Dutta, S.: Role of middleware for Internet of Things: a study. Int. J. Comput. Sci. Eng. Surv. **2**(3), 94–105 (2011)
12. Bazzani, M., Conzon, D., Scalera, A., Spirito, M.A., Trainito, C.I.: Enabling the IoT paradigm in e-health solutions through the virtus middleware. In: 2012 IEEE 11th International Conference on Trust, Security and Privacy in Computing and Communications (TrustCom), pp. 1954–1959. IEEE (2012)
13. Benatallah, B., Motahari Nezhad, H.R.: Service oriented architecture: overview and directions. In: Börger, E., Cisternino, A. (eds.) Advances in Software Engineering. LNCS, vol. 5316, pp. 116–130. Springer, Heidelberg (2008). https://doi.org/10.1007/978-3-540-89762-0_4
14. Benazzouz, Y., Parissis, I., et al.: A fault fuzzy-ontology for large scale fault-tolerant wireless sensor networks. Procedia Comput. Sci. **35**, 203–212 (2014)
15. Bendadouche, R., Roussey, C., Sousa, G.D., Chanet, J.P., Hou, K.M.: Extension of the semantic sensor network ontology for wireless sensor networks: the stimulus-WSNnode-communication pattern. In: 5th International Workshop on Semantic Sensor Networks in Conjunction with the 11th International Semantic Web Conference (ISWC) (November 2012, Boston, US) (2013)
16. Bermudez, L., Delory, E., O'Reilly, T., del Rio Fernandez, J.: Ocean observing systems demystified. In: MTS/IEEE Biloxi-Marine Technology for Our Future: Global and Local Challenges, OCEANS 2009, pp. 1–7. IEEE (2009)
17. Bispo, K.A., Rosa, N.S., Cunha, P.R.: Sitrus: semantic infrastructure for wireless sensor networks. Sensors **15**(11), 27436–27469 (2015)
18. Botts, M.: OGC implementation specification 07–000: OpenGIS sensor model language (SensorML)-open geospatial consortium. Technical report (2007)
19. Botts, M., Percivall, G., Reed, C., Davidson, J.: OGC® sensor web enablement: overview and high level architecture. In: Nittel, S., Labrinidis, A., Stefanidis, A. (eds.) GSN 2006. LNCS, vol. 4540, pp. 175–190. Springer, Heidelberg (2008). https://doi.org/10.1007/978-3-540-79996-2_10
20. Brandt, P., et al.: Semantic interoperability in sensor applications making sense of sensor data. In: 2013 IEEE Symposium on Computational Intelligence in Healthcare and e-health (CICARE), pp. 34–41. IEEE (2013)
21. Brouwers, N., Langendoen, K.: Pogo, a middleware for mobile phone sensing. In: Narasimhan, P., Triantafillou, P. (eds.) Middleware 2012. LNCS, vol. 7662, pp. 21–40. Springer, Heidelberg (2012). https://doi.org/10.1007/978-3-642-35170-9_2
22. Calder, M., Morris, R.A., Peri, F.: Machine reasoning about anomalous sensor data. Ecol. Informat. **5**(1), 9–18 (2008)
23. Cantais, J., Dominguez, D., Gigante, V., Laera, L., Tamma, V.: An example of food ontology for diabetes control. In: Proceedings of the International Semantic Web Conference 2005 Workshop on Ontology Patterns for the Semantic Web, pp. 1–9 (2005)
24. Caporuscio, M., Raverdy, P.G., Issarny, V.: ubiSOAP: a service-oriented middleware for ubiquitous networking. IEEE Trans. Serv. Comput. **5**(1), 86–98 (2012)

25. Catarci, T., et al.: Service composition and advanced user interfaces in the home of tomorrow: the SM4All approach. In: Gabrielli, S., Elias, D., Kahol, K. (eds.) AMBI-SYS 2011. LNICST, vol. 70, pp. 12–19. Springer, Heidelberg (2011). https://doi.org/10.1007/978-3-642-23902-1_2
26. Chen, L., Nugent, C., Okeyo, G.: An ontology-based hybrid approach to activity modeling for smart homes. IEEE Trans. Hum.-Mach. Syst. **44**(1), 92–105 (2014). https://doi.org/10.1109/thms.2013.2293714
27. Chen, L., Nugent, C.D., Wang, H.: A knowledge-driven approach to activity recognition in smart homes. IEEE Trans. Knowl. Data Eng. **24**(6), 961–974 (2012). https://doi.org/10.1109/tkde.2011.51
28. Compton, M., et al.: The SSN ontology of the W3C semantic sensor network incubator group. Web Semant.: Sci. Serv. Agents World Wide Web **17**, 25–32 (2012). https://doi.org/10.1016/j.websem.2012.05.003
29. Compton, M., Henson, C., Lefort, L., Neuhaus, H., Sheth, A.: A survey of the semantic specification of sensors. In: Proceedings of the 2nd International Conference on Semantic Sensor Networks, vol. 522, pp. 17–32. CEUR-WS.org (2009)
30. Corchado, J.M., Bajo, J., Tapia, D.I., Abraham, A.: Using heterogeneous wireless sensor networks in a telemonitoring system for healthcare. IEEE Trans. Inf. Technol. Biomed. **14**(2), 234–240 (2010)
31. Coronato, A.: Uranus: a middleware architecture for dependable AAL and vital signs monitoring applications. Sensors **12**(3), 3145–3161 (2012)
32. Corredor, I., Martínez, J.F., Familiar, M.S., López, L.: Knowledge-aware and service-oriented middleware for deploying pervasive services. J. Netw. Comput. Appl. **35**(2), 562–576 (2012)
33. Costa, P., Mottola, L., Murphy, A.L., Picco, G.P.: TeenyLIME: transiently shared tuple space middleware for wireless sensor networks. In: Proceedings of the International Workshop on Middleware for Sensor Networks, pp. 43–48. ACM (2006)
34. Curino, C., Giani, M., Giorgetta, M., Giusti, A., Murphy, A.L., Picco, G.P.: TinyLIME: bridging mobile and sensor networks through middleware. In: Third IEEE International Conference on Pervasive Computing and Communications, PerCom 2005, pp. 61–72. IEEE (2005)
35. De, S., Barnaghi, P., Bauer, M., Meissner, S.: Service modelling for the Internet of Things. In: 2011 Federated Conference on Computer Science and Information Systems (FedCSIS), pp. 949–955. IEEE (2011)
36. Delamer, I.M., Lastra, J.L.M.: Service-oriented architecture for distributed publish/subscribe middleware in electronics production. IEEE Trans. Ind. Informat. **2**(4), 281–294 (2006)
37. D'Elia, A., Roffia, L., Zamagni, G., Vergari, F., Toninelli, A., Bellavista, P.: Smart applications for the maintenance of large buildings: how to achieve ontology-based interoperability at the information level. In: 2010 IEEE Symposium on Computers and Communications (ISCC), pp. 1–6. IEEE (2010)
38. Delicato, F.C., Pires, P.F., Batista, T.: Middleware Solutions for the Internet of Things. Springer, Heidelberg (2013). https://doi.org/10.1007/978-1-4471-5481-5
39. Desai, P., Sheth, A., Anantharam, P.: Semantic gateway as a service architecture for IoT interoperability. In: Mobile Services (MS), pp. 313–319. IEEE (2015)
40. Díaz-Rodríguez, N., Härmä, A., Helaoui, R., Huitzil, I., Bobillo, F., Straccia, U.: Couch potato or gym addict? Semantic lifestyle profiling with wearables and knowledge graphs. In: Proceedings of the 6th Workshop on Automated Knowledge Base Construction (AKBC 2017), Long Beach (USA) (2017)

41. Díaz-Rodríguez, N., Cadahía, O.L., Cuéllar, M.P., Lilius, J., Calvo-Flores, M.D.: Handling real-world context awareness, uncertainty and vagueness in real-time human activity tracking and recognition with a fuzzy ontology-based hybrid method. Sensors **14**(10), 18131–18171 (2014)
42. Donnelly, K.: SNOMED-CT: the advanced terminology and coding system for e-health. Stud. Health Technol. Informat. **121**, 279 (2006)
43. Doukas, C., Maglogiannis, I.: Bringing IoT and cloud computing towards pervasive healthcare. In: 2012 Sixth International Conference on Innovative Mobile and Internet Services in Ubiquitous Computing (IMIS), pp. 922–926. IEEE (2012)
44. Duarte, P.H., Faina, L.F., Camargos, L.J., de Paula, L.B., Pasquini, R.: An architecture for monitoring and improving public transportation systems. In: 2016 IEEE 30th International Conference on Advanced Information Networking and Applications (AINA), pp. 871–878. IEEE (2016)
45. Evensen, P., Meling, H.: Sensewrap: a service oriented middleware with sensor virtualization and self-configuration. In: 2009 5th International Conference on Intelligent Sensors, Sensor Networks and Information Processing (ISSNIP), pp. 261–266. IEEE (2009)
46. Fok, C.L., Roman, G.C., Lu, C.: Agilla: a mobile agent middleware for self-adaptive wireless sensor networks. ACM Trans. Auton. Adapt. Syst. (TAAS) **4**(3), 16 (2009)
47. Gomez, M., et al.: An ontology-centric approach to sensor-mission assignment. In: Gangemi, A., Euzenat, J. (eds.) EKAW 2008. LNCS (LNAI), vol. 5268, pp. 347–363. Springer, Heidelberg (2008). https://doi.org/10.1007/978-3-540-87696-0_30
48. Guinard, D., Trifa, V.: Towards the web of things: web mashups for embedded devices. In: Proceedings of WWW (International World Wide Web Conferences) Workshop on Mashups, Enterprise Mashups and Lightweight Composition on the Web (MEM 2009), Madrid, Spain, vol. 15 (2009)
49. Guinard, D., Trifa, V., Karnouskos, S., Spiess, P., Savio, D.: Interacting with the SOA-based Internet of Things: discovery, query, selection, and on-demand provisioning of web services. IEEE Trans. Serv. Comput. **3**(3), 223–235 (2010)
50. Guinard, D., Trifa, V., Mattern, F., Wilde, E.: From the Internet of Things to the web of things: resource-oriented architecture and best practices. In: Uckelmann, D., Harrison, M., Michahelles, F. (eds.) Architecting the Internet of Things, pp. 97–129. Springer, Heidelberg (2011). https://doi.org/10.1007/978-3-642-19157-2_5
51. Gyrard, A., Bonnet, C., Boudaoud, K.: Enrich machine-to-machine data with semantic web technologies for cross-domain applications. In: 2014 IEEE World Forum on Internet of Things (WF-IoT), pp. 559–564. IEEE (2014)
52. Gyrard, A., Datta, S.K., Bonnet, C., Boudaoud, K.: Standardizing generic cross-domain applications in Internet of Things. In: Globecom Workshops (GC Wkshps), pp. 589–594. IEEE (2014)
53. Hamida, A.B., et al.: Integrated choreos middleware-enabling large-scale, QoS-aware adaptive choreographies (2013)
54. Hassan, M.M., Albakr, H.S., Al-Dossari, H.: A cloud-assisted Internet of Things framework for pervasive healthcare in smart city environment. In: Proceedings of the 1st International Workshop on Emerging Multimedia Applications and Services for Smart Cities, pp. 9–13. ACM (2014)
55. Heinzelman, W.B., Murphy, A.L., Carvalho, H.S., Perillo, M.A.: Middleware to support sensor network applications. IEEE Netw. **18**(1), 6–14 (2004)

56. Hendi, H.I., Ahmad, A., Bouneffa, M., Fonlupt, C.: Ontology based reasoning for solving passenger train optimization problem. In: Al-Sadeq International Conference on Multidisciplinary in IT and Communication Science and Applications (AIC-MITCSA), pp. 1–6. IEEE (2016)
57. Herzog, A., Jacobi, D., Buchmann, A.: A3ME-an agent-based middleware approach for mixed mode environments. In: The Second International Conference on Mobile Ubiquitous Computing, Systems, Services and Technologies, UBICOMM 2008, pp. 191–196. IEEE (2008)
58. Hong, K., et al.: TinyVM: an energy-efficient execution infrastructure for sensor networks. Softw.: Pract. Exp. **42**(10), 1193–1209 (2012)
59. Hoque, E., Stankovic, J.: AALO: activity recognition in smart homes using active learning in the presence of overlapped activities. In: 2012 6th International Conference on Pervasive Computing Technologies for Healthcare (PervasiveHealth), pp. 139–146. IEEE (2012)
60. Huebscher, M.C., McCann, J.A.: Adaptive middleware for context-aware applications in smart-homes. In: Proceedings of the 2nd Workshop on Middleware for Pervasive and Ad-Hoc Computing, pp. 111–116. ACM (2004)
61. Ibrahim, A., Carrez, F., Moessner, K.: Spatio-temporal model for role assignment in wireless sensor networks. In: Proceedings of the 2013 19th European Wireless Conference (EW), pp. 1–6. VDE (2013)
62. Janse, M.D.: Amigo Final Report, pp. 1–42, September 2008
63. Jonquet, C., et al.: AgroPortal: an open repository of ontologies and vocabularies for agriculture and nutrition data. In: GODAN Summit (2016)
64. Junnila, S., et al.: Wireless, multipurpose in-home health monitoring platform: two case trials. IEEE Trans. Inf. Technol. Biomed. **14**(2), 447–455 (2010)
65. Jyothi, T.: Open source middleware for Internet of Things. Int. J. Innov. Res. Electr. Electron. Instrum. Control Eng. **4**(11), 71–75 (2016). http://www.openremote.com/
66. Kang, P., Borcea, C., Xu, G., Saxena, A., Kremer, U., Iftode, L.: Smart messages: a distributed computing platform for networks of embedded systems. Comput. J. **47**(4), 475–494 (2004)
67. Kibbe, W.A., et al.: Disease ontology 2015 update: an expanded and updated database of human diseases for linking biomedical knowledge through disease data. Nucleic Acids Res. **43**, D1071–D1078 (2014). https://doi.org/10.1093/nar/gku1011
68. Kim, J., Lee, J.W.: OpenIoT: an open service framework for the Internet of Things. In: 2014 IEEE World Forum on Internet of Things (WF-IoT). Institute of Electrical and Electronics Engineers (IEEE), March 2014. https://doi.org/10.1109/wf-iot.2014.6803126
69. Kim, J., Kim, J., Lee, D., Chung, K.Y.: Ontology driven interactive healthcare with wearable sensors. Multimedia Tools Appl. **71**(2), 827–841 (2014)
70. Lasierra, N., Alesanco, A., Guillén, S., García, J.: A three stage ontology-driven solution to provide personalized care to chronic patients at home. J. Biomed. Inform. **46**(3), 516–529 (2013)
71. Liu, T., Martonosi, M.: Impala: a middleware system for managing autonomic, parallel sensor systems. In: ACM SIGPLAN Notices, vol. 38, pp. 107–118. ACM (2003)
72. Lohr, C., Tanguy, P., Kerdreux, J.: xAAL: a distributed infrastructure for heterogeneous ambient devices. J. Intell. Syst. **24**(3) (2015). https://doi.org/10.1515/jisys-2014-0144

73. Mamei, M., Zambonelli, F.: Field-Based Coordination for Pervasive Multiagent Systems. Springer, Heidelberg (2006). https://doi.org/10.1007/3-540-27969-5
74. Marques, I.L., Ronan, J., Rosa, N.S.: TinyReef: a register-based virtual machine for wireless sensor networks. In: Sensors, pp. 1423–1426. IEEE (2009)
75. Mazhelis, O., Tyrvainen, P.: A framework for evaluating Internet-of-Things platforms: application provider viewpoint. In: 2014 IEEE World Forum on Internet of Things (WF-IoT), pp. 147–152. IEEE (2014)
76. Meditskos, G., Dasiopoulou, S., Kompatsiaris, I.: MetaQ: a knowledge-driven framework for context-aware activity recognition combining SPARQL and OWL 2 activity patterns. Pervasive Mob. Comput. **25**, 104–124 (2016). https://doi.org/10.1016/j.pmcj.2015.01.007
77. Megalingam, R.K., Pocklassery, G., Jayakrishnan, V., Mourya, G., Thulasi, A.A.: Smartphone based continuous monitoring system for home-bound elders and patients. In: 2014 International Conference on Communications and Signal Processing (ICCSP), pp. 1173–1177. IEEE (2014)
78. Miluzzo, E., et al.: Sensing meets mobile social networks: the design, implementation and evaluation of the CenceME application. In: Proceedings of the 6th ACM Conference on Embedded Network Sensor Systems, pp. 337–350. ACM (2008)
79. Mineraud, J., Mazhelis, O., Su, X., Tarkoma, S.: Contemporary Internet of Things platforms. arXiv preprint arXiv:1501.07438 (2015)
80. Mineraud, J., Mazhelis, O., Su, X., Tarkoma, S.: A gap analysis of Internet-of-Things platforms. Comput. Commun. **89**, 5–16 (2016)
81. Mohamed, N., Al-Jaroodi, J.: Service-oriented middleware approaches for wireless sensor networks. In: 2011 44th Hawaii International Conference on System Sciences (HICSS), pp. 1–9. IEEE (2011)
82. Mottola, L., Murphy, A.L., Picco, G.P.: Pervasive games in a mote-enabled virtual world using tuple space middleware. In: Proceedings of 5th ACM SIGCOMM Workshop on Network and System Support for Games, p. 29. ACM (2006)
83. Nain, G.: EnTiMid: Un modèle de composants pour intégrer des objets communicants dans des applications à base de services. Ph.D. thesis, Université Rennes 1 (2011)
84. Neuhaus, H., Compton, M.: The semantic sensor network ontology. In: AGILE Workshop on Challenges in Geospatial Data Harmonisation, Hannover, Germany, pp. 1–33 (2009)
85. Osello, A., et al.: Energy saving in existing buildings by an intelligent use of interoperable ICTs. Energy Effi. **6**(4), 707–723 (2013)
86. Palumbo, F., Barsocchi, P., Furfari, F., Ferro, E.: AAL middleware infrastructure for green bed activity monitoring. J. Sens. **2013** (2013)
87. Perera, C., Jayaraman, P.P., Zaslavsky, A., Georgakopoulos, D., Christen, P.: Mosden: an Internet of Things middleware for resource constrained mobile devices. In: 2014 47th Hawaii International Conference on System Sciences (HICSS), pp. 1053–1062. IEEE (2014)
88. Pérez, J.L., Carrera, D.: Performance characterization of the serviotic API: an IoT-as-a-service data management platform. In: 2015 IEEE First International Conference on Big Data Computing Service and Applications (BigDataService), pp. 62–71. IEEE (2015)
89. Pérez, J.L., Villalba, Á., Carrera, D., Larizgoitia, I., Trifa, V.: The compose API for the Internet of Things. In: Proceedings of the 23rd International Conference on World Wide Web, pp. 971–976. ACM (2014)
90. Pfisterer, D., et al.: SPITFIRE: toward a semantic web of things. IEEE Commun. Mag. **49**(11), 40–48 (2011)

91. Presser, M., Barnaghi, P.M., Eurich, M., Villalonga, C.: The SENSEI project: integrating the physical world with the digital world of the network of the future. IEEE Commun. Mag. **47**(4), 1–4 (2009)
92. Radhika, J., Malarvizhi, S.: Middleware approaches for wireless sensor networks: an overview. Int. J. Comput. Sci. Issues (IJCSI) **9**(3), 224–229 (2012)
93. Raychoudhury, V., Cao, J., Kumar, M., Zhang, D.: Middleware for pervasive computing: a survey. Pervasive Mob. Comput. **9**(2), 177–200 (2013)
94. Razzaque, M.A., Milojevic-Jevric, M., Palade, A., Clarke, S.: Middleware for Internet of Things: a survey. IEEE Internet of Things J. **3**(1), 70–95 (2016). https://doi.org/10.1109/jiot.2015.2498900
95. Riboni, D., Bettini, C.: OWL 2 modeling and reasoning with complex human activities. Pervasive Mob. Comput. **7**(3), 379–395 (2011). https://doi.org/10.1016/j.pmcj.2011.02.001
96. Roda, F., Musulin, E.: An ontology-based framework to support intelligent data analysis of sensor measurements. Expert Syst. Appl. **41**(17), 7914–7926 (2014)
97. Rodríguez, N.D., Cuéllar, M.P., Lilius, J., Calvo-Flores, M.D.: A fuzzy ontology for semantic modelling and recognition of human behaviour. Knowl.-Based Syst. **66**, 46–60 (2014)
98. Rodríguez, N.D., Cuéllar, M.P., Lilius, J., Calvo-Flores, M.D.: A survey on ontologies for human behavior recognition. ACM Comput. Surv. (CSUR) **46**(4), 43 (2014)
99. Rodríguez-Molina, J., Martínez, J.F., Castillejo, P., de Diego, R.: SMArc: a proposal for a smart, semantic middleware architecture focused on Smart City energy management. Int. J. Distrib. Sens. Netw. **2013** (2013)
100. Rueda, C., Bermudez, L., Fredericks, J.: The MMI ontology registry and repository: a portal for marine metadata interoperability. In: MTS/IEEE Biloxi-Marine Technology for Our Future: Global and Local Challenges, OCEANS 2009, pp. 1–6. IEEE (2009)
101. Schlenoff, C., Hong, T., Liu, C., Eastman, R., Foufou, S.: A literature review of sensor ontologies for manufacturing applications. In: 2013 IEEE International Symposium on Robotic and Sensors Environments (ROSE), pp. 96–101. IEEE (2013)
102. Scott, H.: Energy ontologies: wind, biomass, and fossil transportation. Humanities **5**(2), 37 (2016)
103. Seeger, C., Van Laerhoven, K., Buchmann, A.: MyHealthAssistant: an event-driven middleware for multiple medical applications on a smartphone-mediated body sensor network. IEEE J. Biomed. Health Informat. **19**(2), 752–760 (2015)
104. Seydoux, N., Drira, K., Hernandez, N., Monteil, T.: IoT-O, a core-domain IoT ontology to represent connected devices networks. In: Blomqvist, E., Ciancarini, P., Poggi, F., Vitali, F. (eds.) EKAW 2016. LNCS (LNAI), vol. 10024, pp. 561–576. Springer, Cham (2016). https://doi.org/10.1007/978-3-319-49004-5_36
105. Sixsmith, A., et al.: SOPRANO – an ambient assisted living system for supporting older people at home. In: Mokhtari, M., Khalil, I., Bauchet, J., Zhang, D., Nugent, C. (eds.) ICOST 2009. LNCS, vol. 5597, pp. 233–236. Springer, Heidelberg (2009). https://doi.org/10.1007/978-3-642-02868-7_30
106. Song, Z., Cárdenas, A.A., Masuoka, R.: Semantic middleware for the Internet of Things. In: Internet of Things (IOT), pp. 1–8. IEEE (2010)
107. Souza, A.M., Amazonas, J.R.: A novel smart home application using an Internet of Things middleware. In: Proceedings of 2013 European Conference on Smart Objects, Systems and Technologies (SmartSysTech), pp. 1–7. VDE (2013)

108. Spanakis, E.G., et al.: Diabetes management using modern information and communication technologies and new care models. Interact. J. Med. Res. **1**(2) (2012)
109. Su, X., Zhang, H., Riekki, J., Keränen, A., Nurminen, J.K., Du, L.: Connecting iot sensors to knowledge-based systems by transforming SenML to RDF. Procedia Comput. Sci. **32**, 215–222 (2014)
110. Triantafyllidis, A.K., Koutkias, V.G., Chouvarda, I., Maglaveras, N.: A pervasive health system integrating patient monitoring, status logging, and social sharing. IEEE J. Biomed. Health Informat. **17**(1), 30–37 (2013)
111. Tsiatsis, V., et al.: The SENSEI real world internet architecture (2010)
112. Villari, M., Celesti, A., Fazio, M., Puliafito, A.: AllJoyn lambda: an architecture for the management of smart environments in IoT. In: 2014 International Conference on Smart Computing Workshops (SMARTCOMP Workshops), pp. 9–14. IEEE (2014)
113. Villaverde, B.C., de Paz Alberola, R., Jara, A.J., Fedor, S., Das, S.K., Pesch, D.: Service discovery protocols for constrained machine-to-machine communications. IEEE Commun. Surv. Tutor. **16**(1), 41–60 (2014)
114. Waluyo, A.B., Ying, S., Pek, I., Wu, J.K.: Middleware for wireless medical body area network. In: Biomedical Circuits and Systems Conference, BIOCAS 2007, pp. 183–186. IEEE (2007)
115. Warriach, E.U., Kaldeli, E., Lazovik, A., Aiello, M.: An interplatform service-oriented middleware for the smart home. Int. J. Smart Home **7**(1), 115–141 (2013)
116. Witt, K.J., et al.: Enabling sensor webs by utilizing SWAMO for autonomous operations. In: 8th NASA Earth Science Technology Conference, pp. 263–270 (2008)
117. Wolf, P., et al.: openAAL - the open source middleware for ambient-assisted living (AAL) (2010)
118. Ye, J., Stevenson, G., Dobson, S.: KCAR: a knowledge-driven approach for concurrent activity recognition. Pervasive Mob. Comput. **19**, 47–70 (2015)
119. Zgheib, R.: SeMoM: a semantic middleware for IoT healthcare applications. Ph.D. thesis, Université de Toulouse, Université Toulouse III-Paul Sabatier (2017)
120. Zhu, N., et al.: Bridging e-health and the Internet of Things: the sphere project. IEEE Intell. Syst. **30**(4), 39–46 (2015)

The Role of Drones in Ambient Assisted Living Systems for the Elderly

Radosveta Sokullu, Abdullah Balcı, and Eren Demir(✉)

Department of Electrical and Electronics Engineering,
Ege University, Izmir, Turkey
radosveta.sokullu@ege.edu.tr, erendemir33@gmail.com

Abstract. Following years of restricted military applications, recently unmanned aerial vehicles (UAV) also known as drones have become the new disruptive force in many industrial and everyday life applications. Very obvious usage areas are transportation and parcel delivery. However, recent research reveals that there are a number of ways that drones can be employed to help elderly people sustain a better independent lifestyle.

This paper introduces some of the most recent and interesting applications that drones can find in creating ambient assisted living environments for the elderly. Advantages and disadvantages, possible healthcare models and challenges are discussed. Even though these are some very interesting and original applications there are a lot of challenges involved in accepting drones as "flying assistants" to extend the independent living environment of the elderly.

Keywords: Ambient assisted living systems · Unmanned aerial vehicles
Elderly · Drones · Daily activities monitoring

1 Introduction

Extending lifespan and increased aging population in many countries around the world present a considerable challenge for healthcare services and systems. The two main options – personal care at home or in care in a nursing facility – are very human labor demanding and place a huge financial burden both for the elderly and their relatives, and the healthcare system. Recent advances in networking, computing and sensor technologies have helped address these issues in an efficient and cost-effective way while extending the independent life of the elderly. In the past two decades numerous research projects have focused on various aspects of ambient assisted living systems. (AALS) – from sensor networks to context aware data services – trying to provide end-to-end solutions. Today there are many IoT based applications which ensure continuous and often real-time monitoring of the occupant and his surrounding environment, providing assessment and triggering assistance when necessary. AALS is a growing area of research where new enabling technologies help add new features and solve new challenges. Unmanned aerial vehicles, commonly known as drones, are one such technology. For years they have been indispensable for many military applications, but recently they have claimed their place in our everyday lives as well. From weather probing and gaming, to photography and transportation, drones have quickly become

I. Ganchev et al. (Eds.): Enhanced Living Environments, LNCS 11369, pp. 295–321, 2019.
https://doi.org/10.1007/978-3-030-10752-9_12

the new disruptive force in our society. Could they also add something new to AALS? How will the conservative elderly accept these flying mini robots? There are numerous questions that can come to one's mind.

In this chapter we first introduce the drones – their structure, features, general capabilities and limitations. Then we discuss the main characteristics of AALS, technologies and protocols. The third section presents an overview of existing drone based applications for ambient assisted living followed by a critical analysis and evaluation of drone related technologies and their relationship with ambient assisted living for the elderly.

2 Unmanned Aerial Vehicles – Structure and Main Features

2.1 Structure and Functionality of Unmanned Aerial Vehicles

Unmanned Aerial Vehicles (UAV), simply known as "drones" can be defined as small size vehicles capable of flying by utilizing air currents and driving forces, capable of autonomous flight, capable of carrying loads and can be controlled remotely. In general, an UAV flight system consists of five basic components as seen in Fig. 1. The first basic component is the set of sensors such as a barometer, a pitot tube, a current/voltage sensor, an IMU (inertia measurement unit), distance, temperature and magnetometer sensors. The barometer sensor provides altitude information by sensing pressure, while the pilot tube is generally incorporated in fixed wing aircrafts and is useful in measuring air velocity. This information is further used for flying at stall speed. Stall speed is the minimum speed the aircraft must fly without losing its altitude. The IMU sensor provides three or six axis gyro stabilization information to the flight controller and it is one of the most important and essential parts of an UAV flight control system. Distance sensor measures the distance between UAV and surrounding obstacles, thus providing information to avoid collision with other objects. Localization and navigation is very important for an UAV. Therefore, in most cases UAVs use magneto sensor and GPS satellites for navigation and localization. However, in closed places like inside buildings and sometimes in very rugged terrain, it is impossible or very difficult for an UAV to navigate because of non-existing or weak GPS signal. Thus, in some application scenarios more robust location system design might be required. One of the most important parameters affecting the wing lifting power of airplanes is pressure and temperature. Therefore, the temperature sensor provides the flight controller with the necessary information for the lift force account.

The second main component is the autopilot which interprets the information from all the other components, keeps the aircraft in balance and allows it to fly. For the motors to reach the desired speed it sends commands to the electronic speed controller (ESC). In addition, the autopilot receives commands from the remote controller and according to the information received it controls the servos and other motors. The third component is the communication unit which is also divided into three sub-components; remote controller, telemetric module and video transmitter. The Remote Controller (RC) unit is capable of transmitting control commands to the UAV. The communication link of the RC unit uses 433 MHz, 2.4 GHz or 5.8 GHz. Each frequency can be

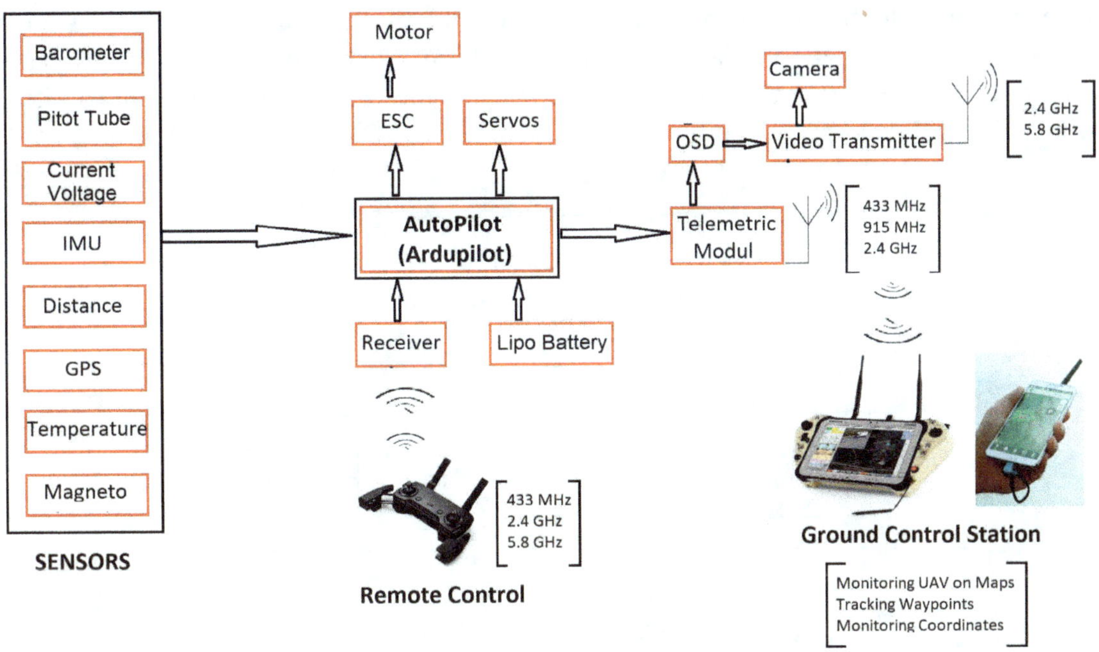

Fig. 1. Basic components of an UAV

used to meet different application requirements. UAVs can fly autonomously or with pilot (human) remote control navigation. In order to ensure safety, UAVs are obliged to be continuously in the RC coverage area, a rule regulated by law. The telemetric module sends the information from the sensors to the ground control station for evaluation. Also, if desired, sensor information can be superimposed on the camera image via the OSD (on screen display) module and sent to the GCS (ground control station) via the video transmitter. The fourth component is the GCS which displays real time data for the UAVs location and performance. It is also used to montitor live stream data generated by the UAV camera. The fifth and last main component is the battery. Lithium polymer (LiPo) is used almost entirely in batteries for UAVs, offering high capacity with low weight and high discharge rates. However, it has some disadvantages such as higher cost and ongoing safety issues.

2.2 Classification of UAVs

UAVs are categorized either based on their flight capabilities or on their structure. The categorization is given in Fig. 2. As far as flight capabilities are considered there are three main UAVs which are HALE, MALE and VTOL. HALE (high altitude long endurance) can fly over 9000 m and has long flight endurance whereas MALE (medium altitude long endurance) can fly up to 9000 m. VTOL (vertical take-off and landing) has the ability of vertical take-off and landing. In addition, after rising up to a specific altitude above sea level, VTOL can move to horizontal flight by the action of the propeller. Considering the configuration, the UAVs can be divided in three categories "fixed-wing", "multi-rotor" and "flap wing". Fixed wing UAVs have greater range and endurance when compared to multi-rotor ones, however multi-rotor UAV have the ability to hover and are easier to use. On the flip side, multi-rotor UAVs have greater drain on the battery. Flap wing UAVs are known to experience difficulties in the autopilot design because the wings have to support the control of movement in pitch, yaw and roll direction.

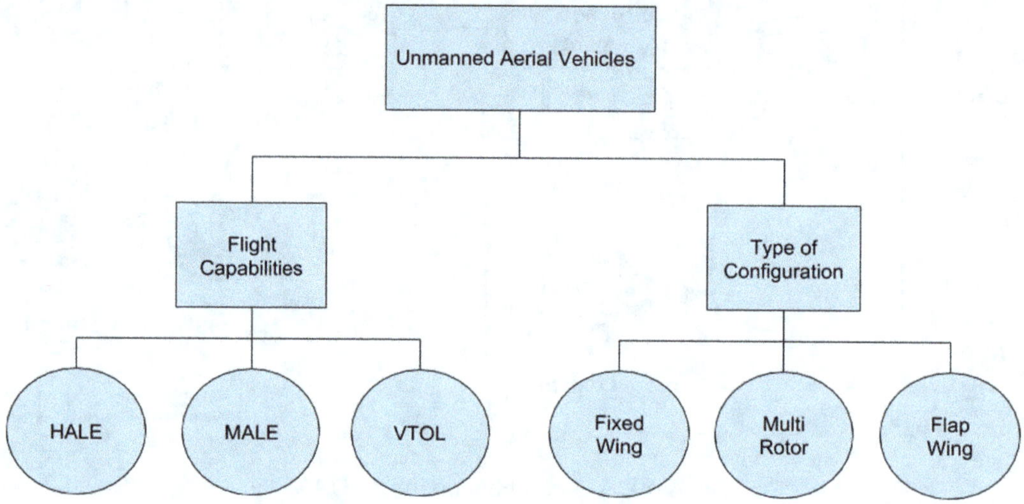

Fig. 2. Unmanned aerial vehicle categorization

In the literature there are a lot of examples related to the applications of UAV and general usage fields can be summarized as: civil transport and transportation, scientific monitoring, geological and ocean surveys, atmospheric research and weather forecasting, surveillance and monitoring (hurricane, volcanic, oil spills, earthquakes, landslides, coast protection, pipelines, water resources, water pollution), international border patrol and drug traffic control, emergency situations (search and rescue, firefighting, disaster operation management, post-disaster site scanning) control of high voltage lines, aerial photogrammetry, detection and analysis of archaeological sites, Earth mapping and 3D city/terrain modeling. Adding to this long list of applications we have also found that very recently drones are finding their place in applications that allow the elderly to live longer full, active lives – both physically and mentally.

3 Ambient Assisted Living – Technological and System Architecture Issues

3.1 Technologies for AALS

Assisted living technologies have become a very popular research area in the recent years because of providing more helpful and life enhancing approaches to the challenges in daily life of the elderly. As a rule, each assisted technology is specialized according to the application it addresses to perform a specific task. For instance, wearable technology such as eyeglasses, [1], or watches aim to improve the quality of life for people interested in fitness and physical exercises. In a similar way, ambient assisted living technologies address the challenges of an aging population.

A very in depth review is presented in [2], where the evolution of AAL technologies is divided into three categories; first, second and third generation technologies. First generation technologies are usually concentrated on emergency response mechanisms. Solutions consist of an alarm system which can be wearable detection sensors like pressure sensor, gyroscope, etc. to detect mainly falls and other life threatening emergency situations. Thanks to such systems and the notifications they send, the uneasiness of families and caregivers about the security and health of their elderly is greatly reduced. However, the wearable devices can be difficult to accept and cause high stress level for the patient himself. Because the older generation in general is not at ease with AAL, they may take off the wearable devices or damage them. In such cases, the alarm may not be triggered even if the patient is stuck in a difficult situation. The second-generation technologies differ from first-generation in terms of the functionalities. The automated systems, which involve home sensors, automatic response to emergencies, aim to reduce the negative effects of first-generation technology by giving less responsibility to the elderly. For instance, if there is a water leakage or flood in the house, the sensors may detect the hazards and automatically trigger the alarm. The third-generation technologies are the integration of first and second-generation technologies which not only monitor the home, but also monitor the physical activities of the person and possibly his environment. In general they are integrated systems which consist of the home automated system and wearable devices and provide continuous monitoring of the vital signs and activities of the elderly patient, reporting the situation to families and caregivers. Actuators play an important role in this technology to improve the quality of life. Actuators can be medical devices such as smart pillbox, or controlling mechanism such as cooker control. Such technologies highly increase the independence of the elderly patient.

AALS rely greatly on IoT-based technologies that support the connection between different devices over the Internet to enable monitoring and remote assisting. IoT has emerged as the new paradigm describing the world of connected physical or virtual things, devices, or machines equipped with sensors and actuators.

3.2 IoT-Based AAL Architecture

IoT based architectures are generally designed to ensure the connection between the sensing devices and end-user via gateways. Major standardization institutes, such as 3GPP and IEEE, focus on a general architecture based on comprising a three tier IoT structure: sensing layer, network layer, and application layer as shown in Fig. 3 [3]. The lowest layer, comprising different sensor units is responsible for the collection of the data from the environment. All data is transmitted through the network via specific gateways to the application layer/server. However, the evaluation of the data is only done at the application layer where the application server makes a decision and extracts the required information from the collected data.

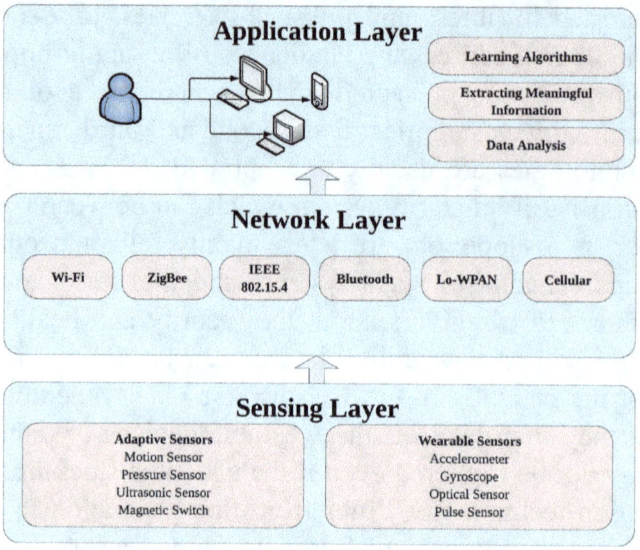

Fig. 3. IoT-based AAL architecture

Sensing Layer

Sensing equipment is responsible for gathering data about the environment and its inhabitants. This layer plays a big role in the system and constitutes the lower layer of the architecture. Because it is the immediate connection with the environment, lot of attention should be paid to the accuracy of sensors. Further, the sensors should be aggregated to generate more reliable data. In [4], the sensors for the AAL are divided into two main groups: ambient sensors used in smart environments and wearable and mobile sensors. Ambient sensors are generally used for monitoring the environment in order to track the activity of elderly people which are located in a predefined area. Because the ambient sensors are located in the home area, their main advantage is that they do not affect the mobility and comfort of elderly people. Without being exhaustive a list of such sensors is given in Tables 1 and 2.

Wearable and mobile sensors monitor the vital signs of elderly people which are generally incorporated in another electronic equipment such as mobile phones, smart watches, etc. or attached on human body. This type of sensors is used in Body Area Networks (BAN). While most of the smart phones include an accelerometer, gyroscope sensors, there are also some specific models which are even equipped with pulse sensors to measure the hearth rate. Instead of sticking or attaching the sensors to the human body, researchers concentrate on optical sensors to measure the blood pressure [5], heart rate [6], etc. Such an approach will provide a more comfortable sensor platform than most of today's wearable sensors.

Table 1. Ambient sensors

Sensor	Measurement
Infrared motion sensor	Motion
Radio frequency identification	Object information
Pressure	Pressure on chair, bed, tiles
Magnetic switches	Door opening/closing
Ultrasonic	Motion/distance
Camera	Activity
Microphone	Activity

Table 2. Wearable and mobile sensors

Sensor	Measurement
Accelerometer	Movements
Gyroscope	Motion
Optical sensors	Blood pressure
Electrocardiography	Cardiac activity
Electroencephalography	Brain activity
Pulse sensor	Heart rate
Thermal	Body temperature

Network Layer

The network layer is responsible for the communication functions and provides a connection between the device with attached sensor(s) and the gateway or center. Different wireless communication technologies can be used to enable the connection between machines, such as Wireless Sensor Networks (WSN), Machine-to-Machine Communication (M2M), Device-to-Device Communication (D2D), Drone-Assisted Communication, etc. The standardization institutes focus on wireless communication architectures for new emerging communication technologies. 3GPP and ETSI have already proposed an architecture for M2M communication over LTE Network which is in line with the AAL architecture. Besides the cellular network, Wi-Fi, ZigBee, IEEE 802.15.4, Bluetooth, Lo-WPAN, Sigfox are other wireless communication techniques that can enable the communication between machines and are expected to be integrated with M2M, D2D or Drone-Assisted Communication. In [7], the authors used ZigBee and IEEE 802.15.4 protocols in their smart home assistant which monitors the activity of elderly people suffering from dementia. An intelligent communication architecture for AAL is presented [8]. In order to monitor the house and control the objects (lamp, water, air conditioner) to detect hazards (high blood pressure, falls, etc.) the authors utilize more than one wireless communication technologies - wireless sensor network, wireless ad-hoc network and wireless mesh network. The purpose of wireless communication technologies is efficiently collecting, exchanging, and transmitting the collected environment data. In case when the sensing unit is wearable and mobile in AAL, the communication technologies should be harmless for the elderly people.

Application Layer

The application layer is the highest layer in the stack which is responsible for functions related to software based data processes like aggregation, analysis and generating meaningful information from the incoming sensor data. In the smart home applications, it is very important to be able to define and/or predict the activity of the elderly person by using the data coming from more than one sensor. The prediction of the activity is based on sophisticated learning algorithms which represents an emerging research area in smart home applications [9, 10].

The application layer is also responsible for the delivery of services to the end users and providing the necessary user interfaces. Existing projects focus on several categories of AAL applications; checking and reminding daily needs, continuous vital sign monitoring, and emergency detection and notification. Regarding the interfaces it is important that they are both functional and simple in order to be accepted by elderly users which in general have less technological skills than the general user.

4 AAL Applications Using Drones

As an important area of research, AALS applications have been discussed and evaluated in many comprehensive review papers. A very recent work in this area is [11] where the authors investigate approaches for developing AALS and identify current practices and directions for future research. Ambient assisted living is defined as the provision of sustainable care for the growing number of elderly in their homes or selected living environments, personalized care based on their profile and surrounding context, which will allow them to extend their independent existence. Having this definition in mind, four major aspects of AAL systems can be defined:

1. Health monitoring aspect.
2. Safety related aspect.
3. Daily activities and routines aspect.
4. Social connectedness aspect.

Historically the health monitoring aspect was the first to be considered and today there are elaborate systems and solutions spanning from monitoring of vital signs and chronic diseases to active telemedicine solutions like remote interaction with patients and assess of health records. What can drones contribute in this aspect? Some interesting projects are considered in Subsect. 4.1.

Safety of the elderly, whether living alone or in a nursing facility has always been a prime concern. Reduced mobility together with increased instability is a common reason for fatal falls and traumas. On the other hand, different emergencies like wandering away and getting lost are also related to the personal safety of the elderly. Fall detection has been a long term research topic and a number of possible response actions especially for elderly living alone have been proposed. [12–14] Can drone technology add something new to these systems? Several very innovative solutions are discussed in Subsect. 4.2.

With increased age people tend to become less active and more detached, even following simple routine daily activities can become a burden. Scientists from the medical and the engineering community have joined efforts to enhance the living environments in a way to help and motivate the elderly to continue an active daily life. This is much easier in nursing facilities, where more options exist and patients are more easily motivation for physical activities. For people living alone at home even routine physical exercises can become a considerable issue. Can robots or drones become the new era pets for the elderly that will help motivate them for physical activities? Some very intriguing proposals are covered in Subsect. 4.3.

As several major reviews have concluded, many of the existing AAL project and system solution address these first three aspects. However, the last one, social inclusion and contentedness, is most often overlooked. A major reason stems from the fact that the aging population in general is much less accustomed to the new emerging technologies and the acceptance rate at this late stage can be very low. Being usually physically restricted, as most elderly usually are, naturally but unfortunately unnoticeably leads to social isolation, which in its turn further reduces the motivation for physical activities and starts a vicious downward cycle of exclusion. Will drone technology and applications be more easily acceptable for the elderly to help them keep both physical and social inclusiveness? Some proposed solutions are discussed in Subsect. 4.4.

From here on this section is organized as follows: Subsects. 4.1–4.4 discuss the details of the UAV based AAL applications based on the characteristics defined in Subsect. 4.1. Subsect. 4.5 focuses on the challenges and possible evaluation criteria for these types of applications.

4.1 Drone Aided Health Monitoring Systems

According to an extensive study from 2004 and its update in 2012 in the USA [15] the cost of chronic diseases is an overwhelming component for overall healthcare expenses. In the US alone, 117 million people had one or more chronic disease in 2012, which included heart disease, diabetes, arthritis and obesity. A detailed study of medical costs for treating chronic diseases can be found in [16]. Table 3 below gives an idea about the annual cost chronic diseases incur.

Table 3. Annual medical cost for different number of chronic conditions

Number of chronic diseases	Annual medical cost (in USD)
No chronic diseases	1117
1 Chronic disease	2915
2 Chronic diseases	4731
3 Chronic diseases	6751
4 Chronic diseases	9162
5 Chronic diseases	15964

Chronic disease patients are required to visit medical facilities on a regular basis for routine checkups and medicine replenish. Different community solutions and pilot programs addressing the elderly combining healthcare with homecare delivery have been initiated. However, the price of these services even at a limited scale is overwhelming, especially for remote and rural areas. Lack of transportation is a major reason for failure of regular medication intake. Furthermore, according to the American Association of Retired Persons, 89% of the people above 50 want to receive healthcare in their homes due to difficulties in visiting medical centers. In their work [17], the authors propose to use drones in order to overcome such problems in rural areas and for elderly living in remote areas, providing a very interesting AAL solution.

Drones can be used to deliver routine test kits, medication refills and even pick up standard blood and urine tests. Such an application will immensely reduce travel time and workloads of caregiver and medical personnel. Drones are more competitive when time-sensitive tasks and goods are considered and are also independent of the ground roads and terrain. However, while such a solution will definitely contribute to extending the AAL systems in providing sustainable care for the elderly in their selected living environments, it is not as simple as it looks. The authors propose and detail the concept of drone-aided aerial healthcare delivery and pickup service for chronic disease and elderly people in remote/rural areas. The main architecture of the system is given in Fig. 4 below.

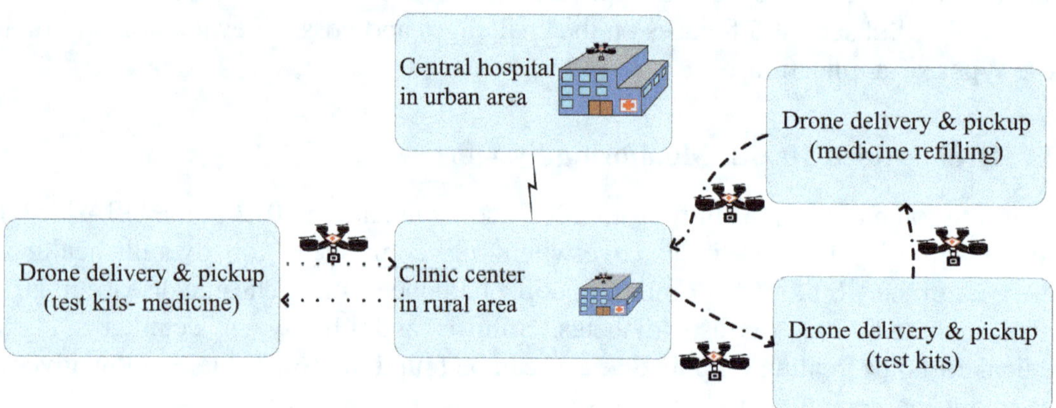

Fig. 4. Concept of drone-aided healthcare delivery and pickup service in rural area

The authors of [17] define and investigate two planning models that can allow the concept to be practically realized: a strategic model and an operational model. The strategic model allows deciding on the optimal location of drone centers and how many centers would be required for a given area, with a specific population and geographical terrain limitations. The algorithm proposed ensures that drones can reach all people regardless of demand levels and number of chronic diseases. The operational model on the other hand determines the optimal number of drones for each center as well as the optimal drone flight schedule for each center. The schedules are defined taking into consideration real life limitations like specific demands of the patients in terms of flying times and restrictions as well as the cost-benefit ratio to help provide an economically viable healthcare solution. The proposed decision making process and the factors taken into consideration by the authors are given in Fig. 5 below.

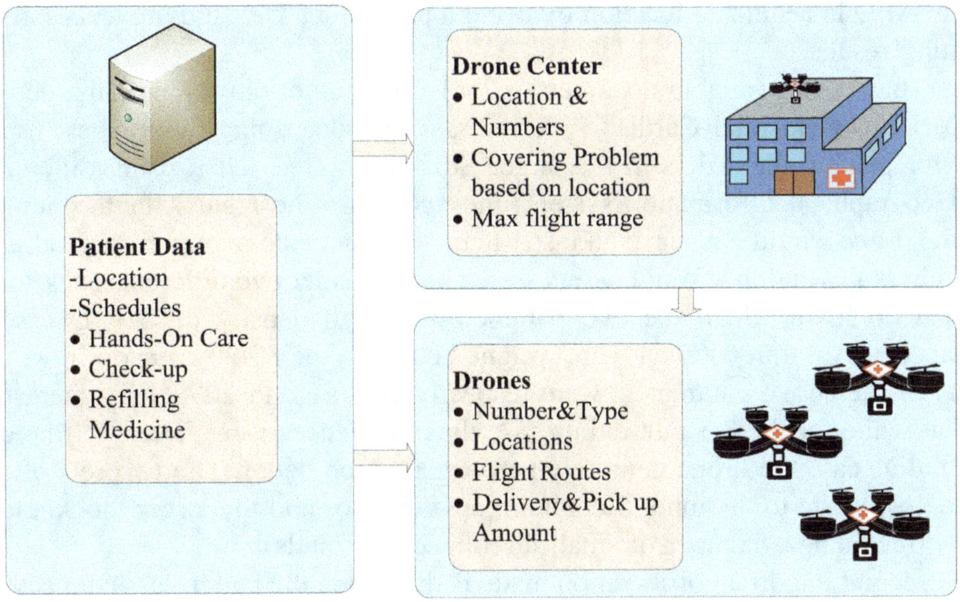

Fig. 5. Decision-making process

Based on collected data, including patient schedules for medical center care, regular check-up schedules, medicine refills, residency information etc. patients can be divided in two main categories: one which needs in-person hands-on care and one which only needs regular testing and medication replenish. The models and the provided solution algorithms address exclusively the second group of people. The authors carry out an illustrational cost-benefit analysis which can be used as a decision process for the stake holders. The suggested approach can be further extended to include variable flying times taking into consideration the battery consumption of the drones.

A major health problem that might lead to death especially in elderly people is cardiac arrest. An interesting niche application addressing distribution and delivery of AEDs (Automated External Defibrillators) which incorporates drones is discussed in the thesis work of Lennartsson [18]. When a cardiac arrest happens outside of a hospital the survival rate is very low, because the person has to be shocked with a defibrillator within minutes of the attack. The survival rate is said to be 74% if the patient is shocked within 3 min of the arrest [19] and is reduced to 50% after 5 min [20]. As a rule, defibrillators are carried in all ambulances and recently, in Sweden, there are AEDs placed in some public areas. However, as the study in [18] points out the average time for an ambulance to reach the patient in Stockholm is around 13 min. Even worse, there are many islands, where ambulances have difficulty to reach. In such situations, the authors propose the use of drones. Their extensive study investigates the records to determine the spots where cardiac arrest occurrences in Stockholm are difficult to reach by ambulances and evaluate whether drones can be used to arrive before the EMS system. The drone used in the tests is Deficopter, a drone carrying an AED [21] that can travel at a speed of 70 km/h within a radius of 10 km. When an emergency call arrives, the Deficopter is programed with the location information and sent out. The on-board camera allows the emergency personnel to spot the scene and drop the AED in a suitable location by using a parachute. The study reveals some very interesting results.

First, based on available document records, the authors investigate the density of OHCD (Out of Hospital Cardiac Arrest) cases and determine the 10 best (optimal) places for placing the AEDs in the larger Stockholm area. Then using different GIS data (Geographical Information system) they compare the results for the number of cases the drone would have arrived faster than an ambulance in an 8.5 min radius area, in a 5 min radius and in a 3 min radius area. They consider two different scenarios – the so called 50/50 in which the two parameters – high density of OHCD cases and ambulance arrival time interval – are weighed equally; the 80/20 scenario in which the weights of the above parameters were respectively 80% and 20%. It is interesting to note that while for the 8.5 min radius case the ambulances were faster, for the critical 3 min radius case the drone definitely performed much better. The two sets of graphs given below relate to the inner Stockholm area (Fig. 6) and the larger Stockholm area (Fig. 7) (including a number of small disconnected islands).

The second important observation made is that when the larger, less connected area is considered the drones definitely outperform the ambulances for the 5 min and the 3 min intervals. Despite the possibility of errors arising from the ArcGIS tools and the tuning of the parameters mentioned above these data show that drones can fit quite well in very specific niche AALS applications which other applications cannot cover. The idea of creating a network of AED centers, to cover different neighborhoods in and around large cities and maybe remote rural areas is yet another step towards making the immediate home and residential neighborhoods more convenient and safe for the elderly, thus in a sense extending the AAL concept.

Similar use of drones for delivery of defibrillators in the Netherlands is described in [22].

A step further in this line of work is the research presented in [23] which reviews the current status of innovative drone delivery with a particular emphasis on healthcare. It proposes two new models associated with the design of a drone healthcare delivery network which will facilitate timely, efficient and more economical drone healthcare delivery to potentially save lives and in the long run extend supportive living environments even further. The authors have compiled a comparative summary with data about the payload the drone can carry, its flying range and speed which is given below in Table 4.

In their work they consider the following scenario: emergency medical supplies need to be delivered to an outlying area that is not completely served by good roads but is too far for drone delivery alone. Such a case requires a tandem solution. For the first leg of the solution land based transportation is used to deliver the supplies/medications from a warehouse to the so called "drone nest", which is in sufficient proximity to the area/person in need. For the second leg usage of drones is suggested from the drone nest to the required precise location/person. For this general scenario two models are proposed and investigated: the first one has the objective to minimize the total weighted delivery time per drone nest; the second model aims to minimize the weighted time to

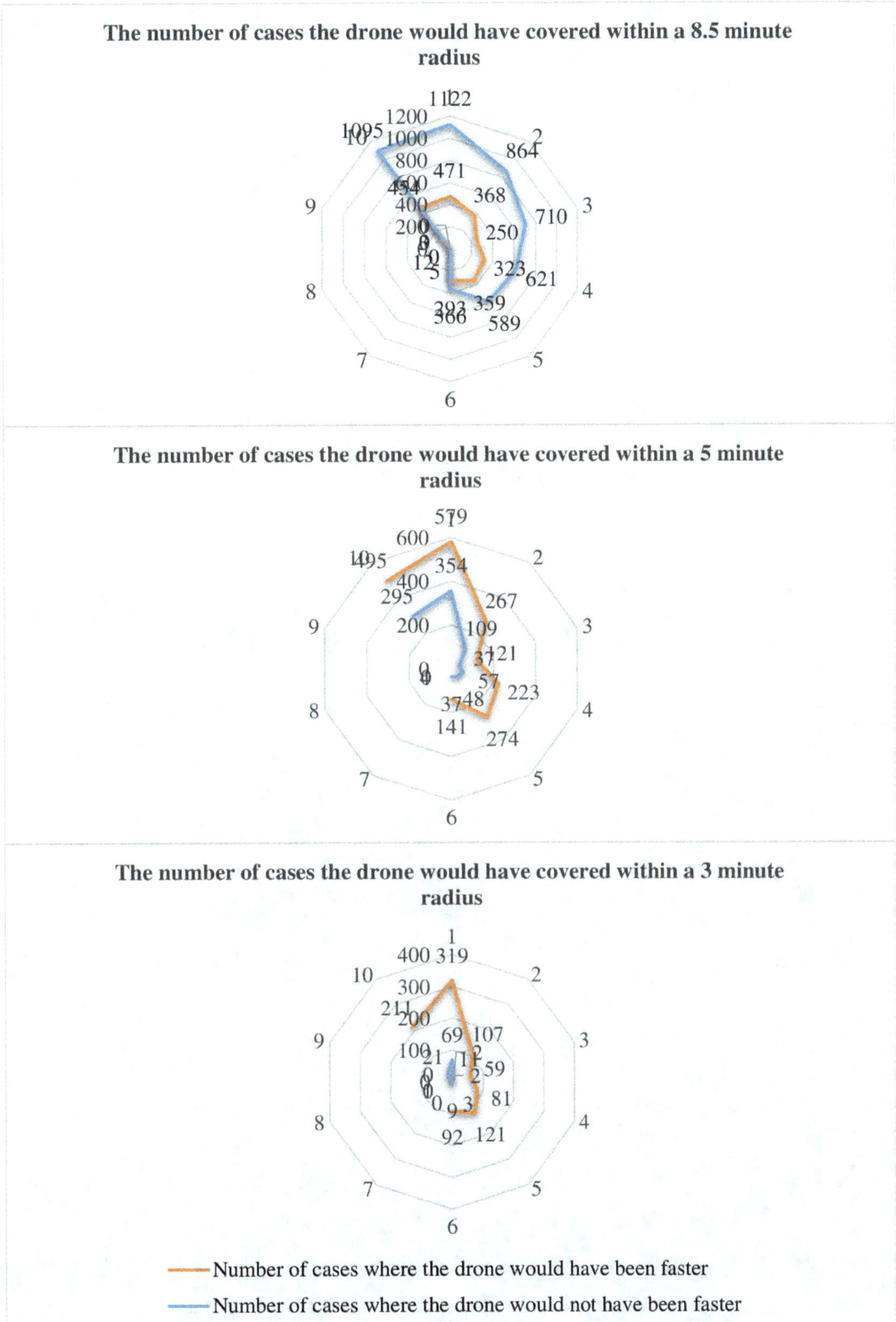

Fig. 6. The number of cases covered by drone/ambulance within 8.5, 5 and 3 min radius for inner Stockholm area

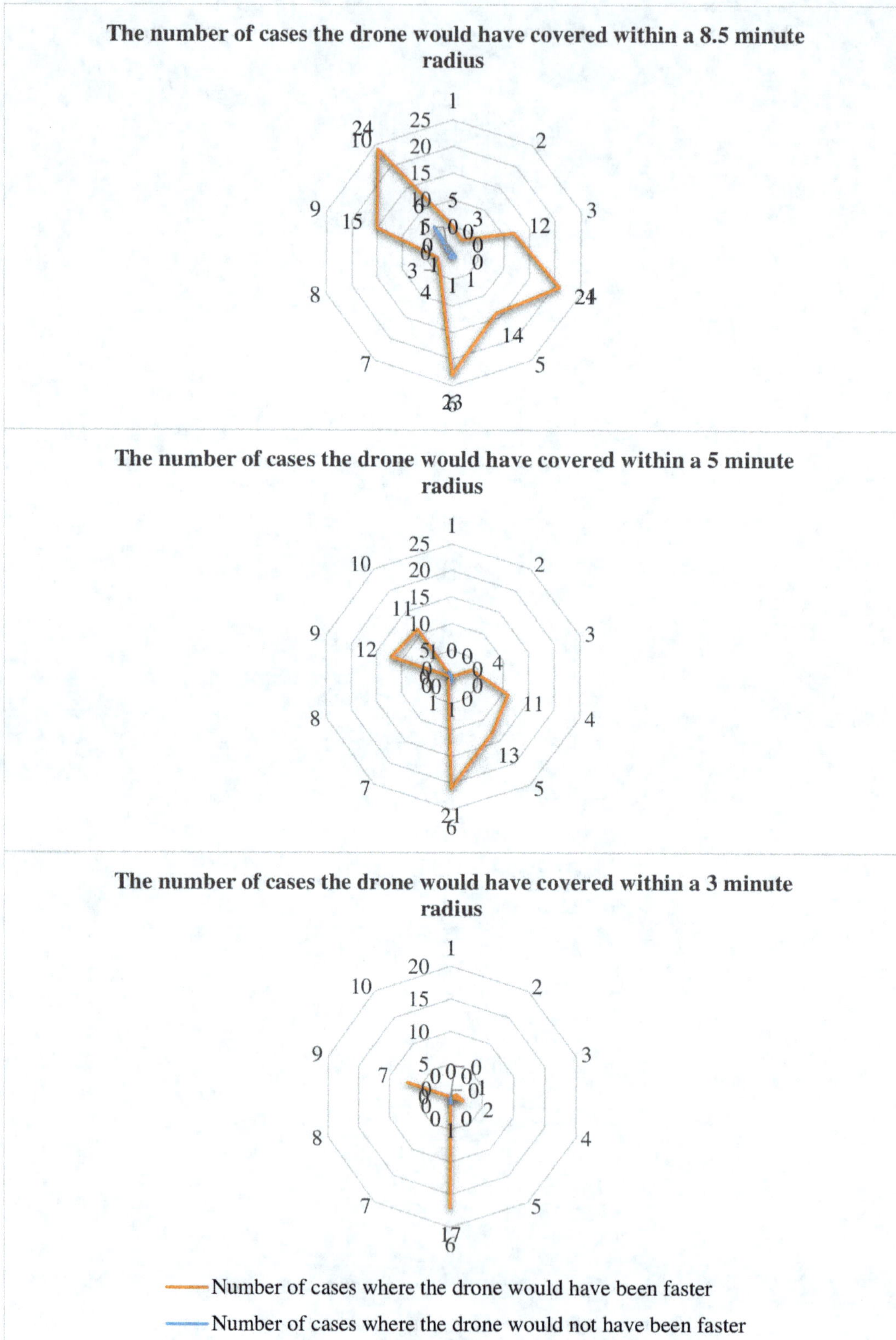

Fig. 7. The number of cases covered by drone/ambulance within 8.5, 5 and 3 min radius for larger Stockholm area

Table 4. Summary of drone specifications

Drone model/company	Payload	Flying range	Max speed
Matternet	2 kg	10 km	40 km/h
DHL parcel	2 kg	12 km	>40 km/h
Zipline	1.35 kg	72 km	144 km/h
Flirtey	2 kg	32 km	-
Delft University	4 kg	12 km	96 km/h

deliver to all demand points in a given area. Optimization functions are determined for the two models and the results of the simulations are given in terms of the "investment over delivery distance" tradeoff or similarly "investment over delivery time" tradeoff. The models use a budget constraint while providing location decisions for warehouses and drone nests that enable timely delivery. Since time is of essential importance in an emergency, faster response would prevent medical trauma and potentially save lives. The authors believe that such models will be especially useful not only in developed countries where road congestion or bad weather conditions can prevent servicing the "last mile" to the patient but also in developing countries i.e. African countries, where a large percentage of the population is not served by all year round operable roads.

4.2 Drone Aided Safety Related Applications

A common safety hazard for the elderly, especially people in early stages of dementia, is getting lost or wandering off. Some very interesting IoT and drone based solutions in this respect in recent years can be found in [24, 25].

The first work presents a detailed review of the subject of hazardous wandering and the existing technological solutions on wandering in the context of AAL for the elderly. An elaborate definition of wandering and a classification of wandering models are given followed by the examination of existing solutions for managing wandering. Different approaches for managing wandering range from event-monitoring-based wandering discovery, trajectory-tracking-based wandering detection to location combined with Geofence-based prevention of wandering-related adverse results. Building up on the definition, categorization, and the state of the art, the authors discuss major research challenges and future directions in detecting wandering locomotion in different settings. A detailed definition of wandering is cited from [26], Mapping the maze of terms and definitions in dementia-related wandering.

In this consequential work, the definition of wandering is given as follows: "A syndrome of dementia-related locomotion behavior having a frequent, repetitive, temporally disordered, and/or spatially disoriented nature that is manifested in lapping, random, and/or pacing patterns, some of which are associated with eloping, eloping attempts, or getting lost unless accompanied".

Wandering is so very difficult to define because it can take so many different forms: sometimes it is expressed in pacing back and forth between two points which do not have to be necessarily very close to each other; sometimes it is in the form of "lapping", as moving in a circle, visiting points in a sequential or random manner without repetitions. Such behavior, which in general is not necessarily dangerous, can become problematic in the case of the elderly; it may even lead to injuries and quite serious negative consequences. So far research in this area has focused mainly on wandering evaluation and wandering detection. In principle, the evaluation process involves recognition and testing of wandering movements. The main objective is to determine patterns and characteristics related to wandering based on an offline analysis of trajectory data collected from sensors, in most cases predominantly indoors. Wandering detection on the other hand aims for the development of assistive systems to provide safety assurance for patients with dementia considering both indoor and outdoor environments. In [24], the authors group the existing solutions in 3 major categories. The first one relates to systems that provide event based wandering discovery [27–31]. The second is called "trajectory-tracking-based wandering discovery" [32–39]; while the third category summarizes works on location-based prevention of wandering related adverse events [40–62]. A major research challenge is posed by the fact that wandering can appear in a very great variety of forms and the data collected so far is insufficient for comprehensive modelling. Studying the correlation between wandering and its related factors is a very crucial for in-depth analysis and mandates the use of elaborate statistical data mining methods. However, the authors believe that a possible solution lies not in designing isolated assistive systems but in enhancing human computer interaction in AALS for training and guiding such patients in order to reduce possible health risks and hazardous situations.

An interesting drone based application has been proposed that can help in cases of wandering dementia patients [25]. A team from Toronto University describes 3 different experiments involving the use of UAV for the purpose of locating a wandering person with dementia. The exact experiments are performed on test subjects simulating individual lost patients with dementia (PwD) employing drones together with Search and Rescue (SAR) operational methods for their rescue. Specific algorithms to determine the drones' paths are proposed and tested. Performance metrics include the time needed to detect the lost person and the complete duration of each mission. Furthermore the authors provide a differential longitude and latitude analysis from an initial parting point (IPP) and for that calculate the time to find the test subject and the battery life of the drone.

The first experiment is carried out in the area around the City of Hamilton, Ontario. Three attempts are made with different pilots and different drones (DGI Mavic Drone, Aeryon Labs Ranger Drone and a drone designed by IMR systems). The first attempt with DGI Mavic (743 g, 36 km/h, 5000 m above sea level, Field of View 78°) and the second attempt (Aeryon Labs Ranger Drone) use camera feed displayed on a mobile phone and are unsuccessful due to the poor picture quality on the mobile device. The third attempt (IMR Systems Drone) finds the person in 6:02 min. The second experiment is conducted in an open urban park with a drone DJI Phantom 4 Pro (1388 g, 72 km/h, 6000 m above sea level, Field of View 84°). The problem with this experiment is that regulations in Canada pose limitations on the areas that drones can be flown. Parks and recreation areas are restricted areas. So the experiment is carried out in a similar close location and the test subject is found in less than 10 min. The final experiment is carried out in the same area as the second one and uses the same drone DJI Phantom 4 Pro this time controlled through the DJI Go 4 app (v4.1.5) on an iPhone 5 s to make use of the software's features and to record the flight data. Its main focus is determining the differential latitude from the IPP and its relation to the time for discovering the target.

These experiments bring light to several very important issues related to the use of drone for tracking and locating wandering elderly people in outdoor areas. First of all, the authors are optimistic that the suggested approach allows locating the missing person within the first 10 min which is considered as the lower limit for safety independent of the terrain. Second, the authors point out the many major hurdles that have to be overcome before such operations can be considered of practical value. The first one is that in order to use drones for these purposes models based on underlying algorithms of wandering that can be technically implemented to automate the search process are required. Another important issue is that drones can help locate the person but monitoring battery usage as well as longitude and latitude is crucial for success. And last but not least, a major problem exists with the specific regulations and restrictions for flying drones in different countries which have to be clarified before drone-based search and localization can become a practically feasible option.

4.3 Drone Aided Daily Activities and Routines

Even though drones are more often associated with outdoor activities there is some interesting research on using UAV in indoor locations.

The first application is a UAV for indoor patient care, called Healthbuddy, which proposes a customized quadcopter design to provide assistive healthcare at home [63]. Its main goal is to facilitate independent living for the elderly in their living quarters. The application can help people suffering from long hours of isolation, both elderly, or cancer patients or patients with depression. Healthbuddy is designed to navigate around the house at regular intervals trying to detect the person/patient using image, sonar and voice recognition (VR) strategies. The drone can avoid collisions with walls and different objects in real-time. Once the drone locates and recognizes the person/patient it starts a wireless communication with a server and receives further instructions based on queries. Health based queries are designed to require simple yes/no responses; VR strategies are used to classify the speech responses extracted from surrounding noise; using the collected information the server provides patient analysis; and finally the Healthbuddy system as a whole determines what is the most appropriate line of action in the given situation.

The functional block diagram of Healthbuddy is given in Fig. 8 below.

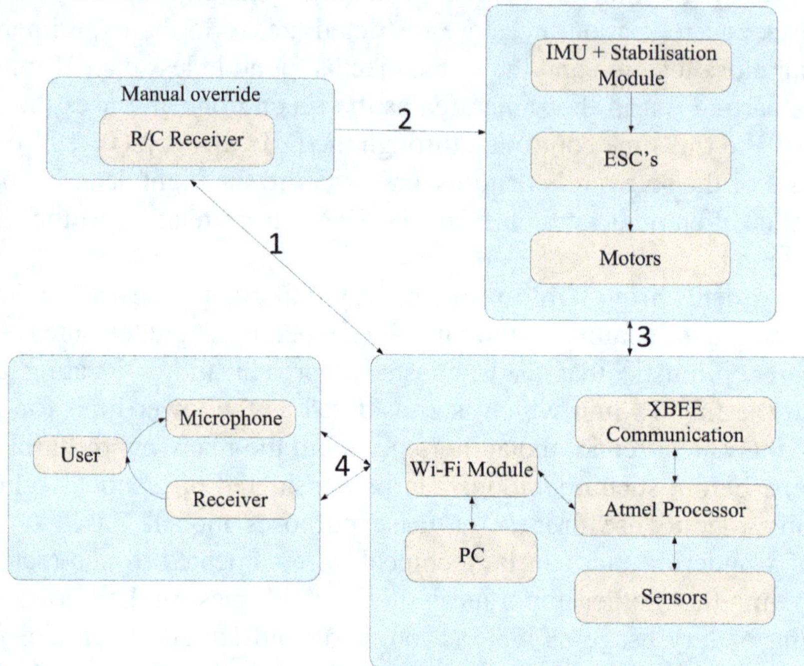

Fig. 8. The block diagram of Healthbuddy

The main hardware components comprise the AeroQuad Kit (Arduino Mega 2560) gyroscope, 3-axis accelerometer, magnetometer, barometer sensor and an ultrasonic sensor. Communication components include a VR Shield (EasyVR Shield 2.0), a speaker and an amplifier, power source (Lipo Battery Pack 5000 mAh); the wireless communication network components are ZigBee modules (the XBee Pro 60 mW), the XBee Explorer Dongle, and the ITEAD XBee Shield. Since the work is still in its development stage there aren't final published results but efforts are being put in combining different algorithmic solutions from literature. The authors believe that with time, the promising solutions existing separately in literature could be combined to form a unique platform to serve the objectives of their drone based AAL project.

A more evolved work on indoor drone application is presented in "QuadAALper – The Ambient Assisted Living Quadcopter", as the PhD thesis of Ricardo Miguel Gradim Nascimento from the University of Porto [64].

The work presents the design of a drone that can autonomously navigate inside the house and recognize a person lying on the floor. The authors propose an original method for flying the drone indoors without GPS information. Their method is based on QR code detection using a smartphone mounted on top of the drone. The QR codes, 20 × 20 are placed on the ceiling. The drone is a Arducopter, controlled by an open source controller Pixhawk. The mobile phone used in the project is a HTC One M8, equipped with a 2.5 GHz processor and a Duo Rear Camera, with a 2600 mAh battery.

The developers make full use of all the sensors coming with the mobile phone (gyroscope, accelerometer, proximity, compass and barometer) and add external sonar sensor and four Infra-Red sensors. The main algorithms use the OpenCV and Zxing libraries. From communication point of view, the two major protocols used are the NMEA and the MAVLink protocol. The NMEA protocol [65] is a combined electrical and data specification for communication between electronic devices like sonars, autopilot, GPS receivers and other types of instruments. In general, programs providing real time localization work with data in the NMEA format. The Pixhawk, the drone control unit used in the project also accepts NMEA data. The MAVLink (MAVLink Micro Air Vehicle Communication Protocol) [66] protocol enables communication between the mounted Android smartphone and the drone control module (Pixhawk) for mission planning, for receiving live telemetric data and for monitoring the Pixhawk status.

Tests have been carried out which prove that the suggested method is quite accurate and allows the drone to correctly capture and decode the QR code at angles of 45% and 30%, in different light environments (bright, medium, dark) and for different mobility of the drone. Main advantage of the proposed method is its simplicity as compared to other SLAM (Simultaneous Localization and Mapping) algorithms. Furthermore the authors add person recognition algorithms and are successful in detecting and recognizing a person lying on the floor. Even though this work is very elaborate, detailed and much more advanced in terms of practical realization than other similar attempts, there is still a lot to be done before a commercial drone can become the Flying Home Buddy of the elderly.

4.4 Drones for Better Social Inclusion

Many people can argue that computer games and virtually reality are one of major reason for social isolation among the younger generation. Obviously there is also the other camp which points out the positive effects of this modern pastime as well as its potential for enhancing both visual and motor skills. One group of researchers from Singapore has put these opinions to a test, not with children or adolescents, but with elderly citizens in a nursing facility, with ages ranging from 56 to 92 years [67].

They carried out an intervention project using Nintendo Wii to explore the long-term physiological effects of video games on the elderly. The intervention was a 6 weeks long program, carried out with two groups of people: one playing computer games the other playing conventional games for the same period every day. They measured loneliness (using UCLA Loneliness Scale), self-esteem (using Rosenberg Self-esteem Scale), affect (using Brandburn Affect Balance Scale). Amazingly, on all 3 metrics the Nintendo Wii group scored better; significantly higher on self-esteem and affect and significantly lower on loneliness as compared to the control group. Other literature on this subject can be found in [68–70].

This and some other similar studies inspired a group from the Polytechnic Institute of Leiria, Portugal together with a group from Ecuador, (Universidad de las Fuerzas Armadas Espe) to develop a drone based VR application for the elderly [71, 72].

Their work makes use of different wireless technologies, wearable and inertia measurement unit (IMU) sensors to generate a body area network that scans arm movement and sends information through Bluetooth Low Energy (BLE) to control a virtual UAV (Unmanned Aerial Vehicle) remotely. The developed system consists of a 3D simulator using VR glasses for immersive visualization and Raspberry Pi devices with Sense HAT board for hand controls. As a result, it emulates the control of a drone in a simulated environment. The general architecture of the system is given in the Fig. 9 below.

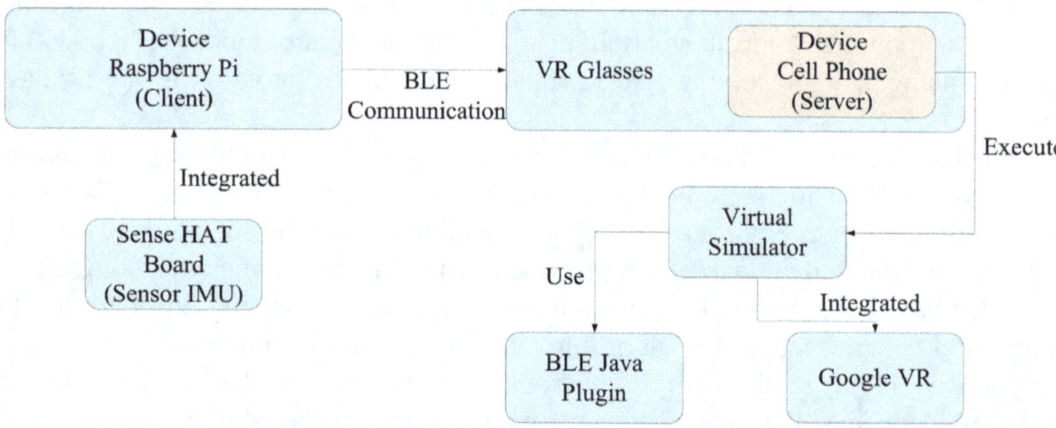

Fig. 9. General architecture of drone-based VR application

For practically implementing this system with elderly residents the researchers developed 2 visualization modes and 2 difficulty modes. The visualization modes determine the perspective in which the user looks at the environments. One possible perspective is to look as a third person – i.e. the user can both see and control the drone. The second perspective is that of first person – i.e. the user sees the environment through the eyes of the drone. Two separate difficulty levels are designed – easy, where only 4 movements are allowed and difficult, where the user has to make 6 different movements with both hands to control the drone. The application helps the elderly preserve and/or develop better cognitive skills (eye-hand coordination) and improve mental and physical state. The researchers performed tests with a group of elderly in a nursing facility and observed that their skill level increased when they used the system for a period of time, progressing from easy to difficult level. The proposed system is still a first prototype and further improvements can be made to increase the involvement of the players. More and longer tests are also required but the first results are really optimistic. Well it might not be surprising that there are quite some things in common between the children and the elderly. As Shakespeare put is centuries ago in his speech "Al the world's a stage" – "…one man in his time plays many parts, …Last scene of all, that ends this strange eventful history, is second childishness and mere oblivion."

4.5 Challenges and Discussion

The development of new technologies, new materials and technical solutions allows increasing the quality and versatility of the AALs for the elderly. Each new technology brings new possibilities for more elaborate and unobtrusive ways to protect the elderly and allow them to continue their fulfilling, dignified and independent living. In this chapter we introduced a new technology, the Unmanned Aerial Vehicles (UAV), or simply "the drones" and discussed its possible application in AALS. In the last decade UAVs have drawn a lot of interest from the academic and industrial sectors specifically because of their possibilities in the area of military applications. In the last several years however, a number of niche applications have been developed which open the way for using UAVs in different AALS. Thus the chapter focused on classifying and describing these very recent developments.

Different aspects of AALS like the health monitoring, the safety, the daily routines support and the social connectedness aspect were examined and applications and projects from literature were summarized. All of discussed applications are in their initial development stage, they are quite innovative, address very specific and intriguing cases and evaluating them is not a simple task. What can be done at this early stage is to point out the main challenges they present in terms of technical requirements and suggest some plausible evaluation criteria for the exploitation phase.

Considering the technical requirements UAV based systems for AAL applications have several very important features in common. They should definitely be designed for failure, should possess high degree of dynamism and adaptability to different specific conditions, should allow for ease of deployment and most of all should be able to ensure a desired level of privacy and confidentiality. Last but not least they should provide simple and easy-to-understand user interfaces since most of the elderly have lower levels of technical skills and acceptance of new technologies.

The most important evaluation angle of such systems is how well they are accepted by the targeted population group. All of the drone based projects discussed in this chapter address a specific niche application and provide an interesting non-traditional solution. Since most of the projects are either in their initial state or first prototype it is very difficult to evaluate the effect they will have on the elderly. That is why, instead of directly evaluating them we would like to consider some important criteria that the evaluation process should include. Naturally these criteria are user oriented i.e. subjective and their determination requires a minimum period over which the given system has been tested in practice. As mentioned before the projects discussed in this chapter are in their very initial stage so the evaluation criteria summarized below should be understood more in the sense of setting a roadmap for researchers working in this field than as a direct evaluation of the presented applications.

One of the most comprehensive assessments related to AALS is suggested in [73]. Based on that, the major main evaluation parameters are summarized below (Table 5).

Table 5. Main evaluation parameters

Evaluation criteria	Definition
Usability	The extent to which a technological product can be used by the specified user group to achieve the specified goal in an effective way
Acceptability	The degree of primary users predisposition to carry out activities using the intended system/device
Efficacy	The capability of the users to effectively complete tasks and achieve goal using the specific tool or system
Utility	The degree to which users believe that using a particular system would enhance their performance
Obtrusiveness	The degree of device caused encumbrance as perceived by users on themselves or in their environment

These criteria provide an exhaustive evaluation of a given system/technology and will be very useful if applied to todays and future AAL systems. However, the task is not as simple as it looks. Only the first criteria (usability) can partially be evaluated in an objective way, while all the others are related to the subjective experience of the user. This means that a proposed solution has to be put into practice and endure a specific evaluation period before reliable results can be obtained.

Another evaluation approach can be created considering the ideas proposed in [11]. The authors' baseline is that user's acceptance of personal space modifications depends on the user's needs and lifestyle preferences. They classified the developments in AALS into three groups: ambient-intelligent space (AmI-S), physical space (PS), and virtual space (VS)—integrated together to support independent life. Currently, there is a lot of interest for more detailed investigations on the linkage between AALS and user's lifestyles. Thus the discussed drone based systems can be evaluated in terms of their contribution to this so called "lifestyle change model".

At the current state of life we can only evaluate the proposed systems as singular, niche applications which if proven fiscally viable can pave the road to enhancing the AALS even more. Drones can fill in gaps where other technologies cannot (delivery functions), can extend scope of existing applications (localization and rescue of wandering PwD), or can enrich in content existing systems (virtual reality and gaming) and make them more appealing and easily acceptable for the elderly.

However, on the flip side, the drone technology is still not mature and feasible enough to be easily deployed on an everyday scale. There are a number of challenges and hurdles to be overcome. Roughly they can be divided into two groups: regulational and ethic challenges.

Many of the described applications are based on technologically mature solutions and promise to draw even more interest in the future. However, there are several major regulation challenges related to them:

- There is a definite lack of clear nationwide and international regulations related to how, when and where drones be flown and this is quite an important challenge. At the same time more research is required looking into existing (even though scatted and quite limited) regulations and how they have to be altered.

- Regulations in many countries do not allow for a drone above certain size and weight to be flown just by anybody; solutions require the creation and support of major organizational structures behind. It also mandates defining specific protocols regarding the planning of the flight and areas restricted for flying.
- As drones become more sophisticated and powerful questions of their proper management become even more important not only within the single countries but also internationally. Thus regulations have to be created and implemented at a much larger scale.

The second major aspect is the ethical aspect. The concepts of personal space and immediate environment are gaining completely new meanings and it has becomes even more difficult and elusive to define the borders of what is "good" and what is "bad". Since this chapter is focused more on the technological aspect details on the ethical aspect are given. A very good material on this subject can be found in [74].

5 Conclusion

Unmanned Aerial Vehicles (UAVs) simply known as "drones" have been a hot research issue for the last decade, mainly due to their attractive usage possibilities in the military and network communication areas. However, very recently, several groups of researchers from all different parts of the world have turned their attention to a new application area for this emerging technology – the ambient assisted living systems especially targeting the elderly. Quickly increasing percentage of the aging population is placing higher and more extensive demands on our society; meeting the goals with traditional methods places an extensive burden both in terms of human resources and financial structures. Thus, there is a large stream of scientific research focused on how to use emerging technologies to ease this burden and make life better, easier, more secure and fulfilling for the elderly. Many solutions have been offered so far but still there are niche applications which can have better solutions. Some of these very recent applications, which offer innovative AALS solutions based on the use of drones have been summarized and discussed in this chapter. Without trying to be exhaustive, the chapter covers major issues on the structure and principle of operation of drones, and provides information on recently published results from projects that utilize drones to improve the life, security, environment and connectedness of the elderly. Finally the authors discuss some major challenges and provide guidelines for user perspective evaluation of such systems in the future.

References

1. Glass Company Homepage. https://www.x.company/glass. Accessed 31 Aug 2018
2. Blackman, S., et al.: Ambient assisted living technologies for aging well: a scoping review. J. Intell. Syst. **25**(1), 55–64 (2015)
3. Wan, J., Gu, X., Chen, L., Wang, J.: Internet of Things for ambient assisted living: challenges and future opportunities. In: 2017 International Conference on Cyber-Enabled Distributed Computing and Knowledge Discovery, Nanjing, pp. 354–357 (2017)

4. Rashidi, P., Mihailidis, A.: A survey on ambient-assisted living tools for older adults. IEEE J. Biomed. Health Inform. **17**(3), 579–590 (2013)
5. McCombie, D.B., Shaltis, P.A., Reisner, A.T., Asada, H.H.: Adaptive hydrostatic blood pressure calibration: development of wearable, autonomous pulse wave velocity blood pressure monitor. In: Conference Proceedings of IEEE Engineering in Medicine and Biology Society, pp. 370–373 (2007)
6. Hasdemir, İ., Ertaş, G.: Experimental analysis of optical sensors in detecting heart beat. In: 2017 Medical Technologies National Congress (TIPTEKNO), Trabzon, pp. 1–4 (2017)
7. Demir, E., Köseoğlu, E., Sokullu, R., Şeker, B.: Smart home assistant for ambient assisted living of elderly people with dementia. In: International Workshop on IoT, M2M and Healthcare, Lund, pp. 609–614 (2017)
8. Lloret, J., Canovas, A., Sendra, S., Parra, L.: A smart communication architecture for ambient assisted living. IEEE Commun. Mag. **53**(1), 26–33 (2015)
9. Skocir, P., Krivic, P., Tomeljak, M., Kusek, M., Jezic, G.: Activity detection in smart home environment. In: 20th International Conference on Knowledge and Intelligent Information and Engineering System, pp. 672–681 (2016)
10. Fuxreiter, T., Mayer, C., Hanke, S., Gira, M., Sili, M., Kropf, J.: A modular platform for event recognition in smart homes. In: 12th IEEE International Conference on e-Health Networking, Applications and Services, pp. 1–6 (2010)
11. Al-Shaqi, R., Mourshed, M., Rezgui, Y.: Progress in ambient assisted systems for independent living by the elderly. Springerplus **5**(624), 1–20 (2016)
12. Rakhman, A.Z., Kurnianingsih, Nugroho, L.E., Widyawan: u-FASt: ubiquitous fall detection and alert system for elderly people in smart home environment. In: Makassar International Conference on Electrical Engineering and Informatics, pp. 136–140 (2014)
13. Kong, X., Meng, L., Tomiyama, H.: Fall detection for elderly persons using a depth camera. In: International Conference on Advanced Mechatronic Systems, pp. 269–273 (2017)
14. Bhati, N.: mHealth based ubiquitous fall detection for elderly people. In: 8th International Conference on Computing, Communication and Networking Technologies, pp. 1–7 (2017)
15. Epping-Jordan, J., Pruitt, S., Bengoa, R., Wagner, E.: Improving the quality of health care for chronic conditions. Qual. Saf. Health Care **13**(4), 299–305 (2004). Ward, B.W.: Multiple chronic conditions among us adults: A 2012 update (2014)
16. Gerteis, J., et al.: Multiple chronic conditions chartbook. Agency for Healthcare Research and Quality (2014)
17. Kim, S.J., Lim, G.J., Cho, J., Cote, M.J.: Drone-aided healthcare services for patients with chronic diseases in rural areas. J. Intell. Robot. Syst. **88**, 163–180 (2017)
18. Lennartsson, J.: Strategic placement of ambulance drones for delivering defibrillators to out of hospital cardiac arrest victims. Stockholm, KTH Royal Institute of Technology (2015)
19. Valenzuela, T.D., Roe, D.J., Nichol, G., Clark, L.L., Spaite, D.W., Hardman, R.G.: Outcomes of rapid defibrillation by security officers after cardiac arrest in casinos. New Engl. J. Med. **343**(17), 1206–1209 (2000)
20. Hjärtstartarregistret. https://www.hjartstartarregistret.se/#/faktasida/1. Accessed 31 Aug 2018
21. The Verge. Health from above: a drone to deliver defibrillators to heart attack victims. http://www.theverge.com/2013/8/24/4654514/definetz-height-tech-defibrillator-carrying-drone-in-germany. Accessed 31 Aug 2018
22. Prigg, M.: The ambulance drone that could save your life. http://www.dailymail.co.uk/sciencetech/article-2811851/The-ambulance-drone-save-life-Flying-defibrillator-reach-speeds-60mph.html. Accessed 31 Aug 2018
23. Scott, J.E., Scott, C.H.: Drone delivery models for healthcare. In: Proceedings of the 50th Hawaii International Conference on System Sciences, pp. 3297–3304 (2017)

24. Lin, Q., Zhang, D., Chen, L., Ni, H., Zhou, X.: Managing elders' wandering behaviour using sensors-based solutions: a survey. Int. J. Gerontol. **8**, 49–55 (2014)
25. Hanna, D., Ferworn, A., Lukaczyn, M., Abhari, A., Lum, J.: Using UAVs in locating wandering patients with dementia. In: IEEE/ION Position, Location and Navigation Symposium (2018)
26. Algase, D.L., Moore, D.H., Vandeweerd, C.: Mapping the maze of terms and definitions in dementia-related wandering. Aging Mental Health **11**(6), 686–689 (2007)
27. Doughtyt, K., Williams, G., King, P.J., et al.: DIANA - a telecare system for supporting dementia sufferers in the community. In: Proceedings EMBC, pp. 1980–1983 (1998)
28. Ota, K., Ota, Y., Otsu, M., et al.: Elderly-care motion sensor using UWB-IR. In: IEEE Sensors Applications Symposium (SAS 2011), pp. 159–162 (2011)
29. Masuda, Y., Yoshimura, T., Nakajima, K., et al.: Unconstrained monitoring of prevention of wandering the elderly. In: Proceedings of the 24th Annual Conference and the Annual Fall Meeting of the Biomedical Engineering Society EMBS/BMES Conference (EMBS/BMES 2002), pp. 1906–1907 (2002)
30. Jit, B., Zhang, D.Q., Qiao, G.P., et al.: A system for activity monitoring and patient tracking in a smart hospital. In: Proceedings of the 4th International Conference on Smart Homes and Health Telematics (ICOST 2006), pp. 196–203 (2006)
31. Rowe, M., Lane, S., Phipps, C.: CareWatch: a home monitoring system for use in homes of persons with cognitive impairment. Top Geriatr. Rehabil. **23**, 3–8 (2007)
32. Martino-Saltzman, D., Blasch, B.B., Morris, R.D., et al.: Travel behavior of nursing home residents perceived as wanderers and nonwanderers. Gerontologist **31**, 666–672 (1991)
33. Algase, D.L., Beattie, E.R., Leitsch, S.A., et al.: Biomechanical activity devices to index wandering behaviour in dementia. Am. J. Alzheimers Dis. Other Demen. **18**, 85–92 (2003)
34. Kearns, W.D., Nams, V., Fozard, J.: Tortuosity in movement paths is related to cognitive impairment. Wireless fractal estimation in assisted living facility residents. Methods Inf. Med. **49**, 592–598 (2010)
35. Kearns, W.D., Algase, D., Moore, D.H., et al.: Ultra wideband radio: a novel method for measuring wandering in persons with dementia. Gerontechnology **7**, 48–57 (2008)
36. Kearns, W.D., Fozard, J.L.: Evaluation of wandering by residents in an assisted living facility (ALF) using ultra-wide band radio RTLS. J. Nutr. Health Aging **13**, S54 (2009)
37. Kearns, W.D., Fozard, J.L., Nams, V.O., et al.: Wireless telesurveillance system for detecting dementia. Gerontechnology **10**, 90–102 (2011)
38. Kearns, W.D., Fozard, J.L., Becker, M., et al.: Path tortuosity in everyday movements of elderly persons increases fall prediction beyond knowledge of fall history, medication use, and standardized gait and balance assessments. J. Am. Med. Dir. Assoc. **13**(7), 665.e7–665.e13 (2012)
39. Nams, V.O., Bourgeois, M.: Fractal analysis measures habitat use at different spatial scales: an example with American marten. Can. J. Zool. **82**, 1738–1747 (2004)
40. Vuong, N.K., Chan, S., Lau, C.T., et al.: A predictive location-aware algorithm for dementia care. In: Proceedings of the 15th IEEE International Symposium on Consumer Electronics (ISCE 2011), pp. 339–342 (2011)
41. Sposaro, F., Danielson, J., Tyson, G.: iWander: an android application for dementia patients. In: Proceedings of the 32nd Annual International Conference of the IEEE Engineering in Medicine and Biology Society (EMBS 2010), pp. 3875–3878 (2010)
42. Wan, J., Byrne, C., O'Hare, G.M.P., et al.: Orange alerts: lessons from an outdoor case study. In: Proceedings of the 5th International ICST Conference on Pervasive Computing Technologies for Healthcare (Pervasive Health 2011), pp. 446–451 (2011)

43. Wan, J., Byrne, C., O'Hare, G.M.P., O'Grady, M.J.: OutCare: supporting dementia patients in outdoor scenarios. In: Setchi, R., Jordanov, I., Howlett, R.J., Jain, L.C. (eds.) KES 2010. LNCS (LNAI), vol. 6279, pp. 365–374. Springer, Heidelberg (2010). https://doi.org/10.1007/978-3-642-15384-6_39
44. Hoey, J., Yang, X., Quintana, E., et al.: LaCasa: location and context-aware safety assistant. In: Proceedings of the 6th International ICST Conference on Pervasive Computing Technologies for Healthcare (Pervasive Health 2012), pp. 171–174 (2012)
45. Hoey, J., Yang, X., Favela, J.: Decision theoretic, context aware safety assistance for persons who wander. In: Proceedings of the 7th International Workshop on Ubiquitous Health and Wellness (2012)
46. Rodriguez, M., Navarro, R., Favela, J., et al.: An ontological representation model to tailor ambient assisted interventions for wandering. In: AAAI Fall Symposium: Artificial Intelligence for Gerontechnology, AAAI Technical Report, vol. FS-12-01, pp. 32-37. AAAI (2012)
47. Ogawa, H., Yonezawa, Y., Maki, H., et al.: A mobile phone-based safety support system for wandering elderly persons. In: Proceedings of the 26th Annual International Conference of the IEEE Engineering in Medicine and Biology Society, pp. 3316–3317 (2004)
48. Matsuoka, S., Ogawa, H., Maki, H., et al.: 2011. A new safety support system for wandering elderly persons. In: Proceedings of the 33th Annual International Conference of the IEEE Engineering in Medicine and Biology Society, pp. 5232–5235 (2011)
49. Miskelly, F.: Electronic tracking of patients with dementia and wandering using mobile phone technology. Age Ageing **34**, 497–499 (2015)
50. Shimizu, K., Kawamura, K., Yamamoto, K.: Location system for dementia wandering. In: Proceedings of the 22nd Annual International Conference of the IEEE Engineering in Medicine and Biology Society (EMBS 2000), pp. 1556–1559 (2000)
51. Lin, C.C., Chiu, M.J., Hsiao, C.C., et al.: Wireless health care service system for elderly with dementia. IEEE Trans. Inf Technol. Biomed. **10**, 696–704 (2006)
52. Calvo-Palomino, R., de las Heras-Quirós, P., Santos-Cadenas, J.A., Román-López, R., Izquierdo-Cortázar, D.: Outdoors monitoring of elderly people assisted by compass, GPS and mobile social network. In: Omatu, S., et al. (eds.) IWANN 2009. LNCS, vol. 5518, pp. 808–811. Springer, Heidelberg (2009). https://doi.org/10.1007/978-3-642-02481-8_122
53. Mulvenna, M., Sävenstedt, S., Meiland, F., et al.: Designing and evaluating a cognitive prosthetic for people with mild dementia. In: Proceedings of the 2010 IEEE Energy Conversion Congress and Exposition (ECCE 2010), pp. 11–18 (2010)
54. Lin Q., Zhang D.Q., Huang X.D., et al.: Detecting wandering behavior based on GPS traces for elders with dementia. In: Proceedings of the 12th International Conference on Control, Automation, Robotics and Vision (ICARCV 2012), pp. 672–677 (2012)
55. Wherify Wireless. http://www.mightygps.com/wherify.htm. Accessed 31 Aug 2018
56. Blackburn, P.: Freedom to wander. Nurs. Times **84**(49), 54–55 (1988)
57. Miskelly, F.: A novel system of electronic tagging in patients with dementia and wandering. Age Ageing **33**, 304–306 (2004)
58. Omnilink. http://www.omnilink.com. Accessed 31 Aug 2018
59. Vivago WristCare. https://www.vivago.com/. Accessed 31 Aug 2018
60. Wong, G.: GPS shoe to track Alzheimer's patients. http://edition.cnn.com/2009/HEALTH/06/10/gps.shoes. Accessed 31 Aug 2018
61. Lifelinefl400. http://www.tunstall.co.uk/solutions/lifeline-vi. Accessed 31 Aug 2018
62. TRiLOC. http://www.iloctech.com/. Accessed 31 Aug 2018
63. Todd, C., et al.: A proposed UAV for indoor patient care. Technol. Health Care: Off. J. Eur. Soc. Eng. Med. (2015)

64. Nascimento, R.M.G.: QuadAALper - The Ambient Assisted Living Quadcopter, Porto (2015)
65. NMEA Data. http://www.gpsinformation.org/dale/nmea.htm. Accessed 31 Aug 2018
66. MAVLink Micro Air Vehicle Communication Protocol - QGroundControl GCS. http://qgroundcontrol.org/mavlink/start. Accessed 31 Aug 2018
67. Jung, Y., Li, W., Gladys, C., Lee, K.M.: Games for a better life: effects of playing Wii games on the well-being of seniors in a long-term care facility. In: Proceedings of the Sixth Australasian Conference on Interactive Entertainment, pp. 1–6 (2009)
68. Ijsselsteijn, W., Nap, H.H., de Kort, Y., Poels, K.: Digital game design for elderly users. In: The Proceeding of Future Play, Toronto, pp. 17–22 (2007)
69. Cota, T.T., Ishitani, L.: Motivation and benefits of digital games for the elderly: a systematic literature review. Revista Brasileira de Computação Aplicada **7**(1), 2–16 (2014)
70. De Schutter, B., Brown, J.A.: Digital games as a source of enjoyment in later life. Games Cult. **11**(1–2), 28–52 (2016)
71. Crespo, A.B.: Development a virtual reality model simulation in order to control a drone using a wearable device in a 3D environment, Leiria (2017)
72. Crespo, A.B., Idrovo, G.G., Rogrigues, N., Pereira, A.: Development of a virtual reality model simulation to control a drone by using wearable devices in a 3D environment. In: 1st International Conference on Technology and Innovation in Sports, Health and Wellbeing (2016)
73. Cavallo, F., Aquilano, M., Arvati, M.: An ambient assisted living approach in designing domiciliary services combined with innovative technologies for patients with Alzheimer's disease: a case study. Am. J. Alzheimer's Dis. Other Dementias **30**(1), 69–77 (2015)
74. Novitzky, P.: Ethics of ambient assisted living technologies for persons with dementia, Dublin (2016)

Author Index

Achkoski, Jugoslav 210
Al-Obeidat, Feras 53
Angelov, George Vasilev 226

Balcı, Abdullah 295
Bastide, Rémi 263
Belacel, Nabil 53
Benvenisti, Yael 96

Chiari, Lorenzo 96
Chorbev, Ivan 1
Conchon, Emmanuel 263

Danial-Saad, Alexandra 96
Davis-Owusu, Kadian 108
Demir, Eren 295
Díaz-Rodríguez, Natalia 19

Ekenel, Hazım Kemal 152
Elboim-Gabyzon, Michal 96

Feijs, Loe 108

Garcia, Nuno M. 1
Gieva, Elitsa Emilova 226
Goleva, Rossitza 1, 210
Grönroos, Stefan 19

Hu, Jun 108

Karvinen, Petteri 19
Koceska, Natasa 80
Koceski, Saso 80
Krukowski, Artur 177

Lameski, Petre 1
Laufer, Shlomi 96
Lavendelis, Egons 152
Lilius, Johan 19

Mladenovski, Oliver 210
Marcenaro, Lucio 108

Nikolakov, Dimitar Petrov 226

Owusu, Evans 108

Petrovica, Sintija 152
Pombo, Nuno 1
Pudane, Mara 152

Regazzoni, Carlo 108
Ruskova, Ivelina Nikolaeva 226

Smileska, Cvetanka 80
Sokullu, Radosveta 295
Spasova, Maria Liubomirova 226
Spencer, Bruce 53

Trajkovik, Vladimir 1, 80

Vogiatzaki, Emmanouela 177

Zdravevski, Eftim 1
Zgheib, Rita 263

www.ingramcontent.com/pod-product-compliance
Lightning Source LLC
LaVergne TN
LVHW060056220926
848484LV00008BA/1958